The reign of King Baldwin IV of Jerusalem (1174–85) has traditionally been seen as a period of decline when, because of the king's illness, power came to be held by unsuitable men who made the wrong policy decisions. Notably, they ignored the advice of Raymond of Tripoli and attacked Saladin, who was prepared to keep peace with the Franks while uniting the Islamic Near East under his rule.

This book challenges that view, arguing that peace with Saladin was not a viable option for the Franks; that the young king, despite suffering from lepromatous leprosy (the most deadly form of the disease), was an excellent battle leader who strove with some success to frustrate Saladin's imperial ambitions; that Baldwin had to remain king in order to hold factions in check; but that the society over which he presided was, contrary to what is often said, vigorous and self-confident.

BERNARD HAMILTON is Emeritus Professor of Crusading History, University of Nottingham.

THE LEPER KING AND HIS HEIRS

Baldwin IV topples a Muslim opponent at the battle of Mont Gisard.

THE LEPER KING
AND HIS HEIRS

Baldwin IV and the Crusader Kingdom of Jerusalem

BERNARD HAMILTON

CAMBRIDGE
UNIVERSITY PRESS

PUBLISHED BY THE PRESS SYNDICATE OF THE UNIVERSITY OF CAMBRIDGE
The Pitt Building, Trumpington Street, Cambridge, United Kingdom

CAMBRIDGE UNIVERSITY PRESS
The Edinburgh Building, Cambridge CB2 2RU, UK   http://www.cup.cam.ac.uk
40 West 20th Street, New York, NY 10011–4211, USA   http://www.cup.org
10 Stamford Road, Oakleigh, Melbourne 3166, Australia
Ruiz de Alarcón 13, 28014 Madrid, Spain

First published 2000

Printed in the United Kingdom at the University Press, Cambridge

Typeset in Baskerville 11/12.5pt [CE]

A catalogue record for this book is available from the British Library

Library of Congress cataloguing in publication data
Hamilton, Bernard, 1932–
The leper king and his heirs: Baldwin IV and the Crusader Kingdom of
Jerusalem / Bernard Hamilton.
p.   cm.
Includes bibliographical references and index.
ISBN 0 521 64187 x
1. Baudouin IV, king of Jerusalem, 1160–1185.
2. Jerusalem – Kings and rulers – Biography.
3. Jerusalem – History – Latin Kingdom. 1099–1244.   I. Title.
D184.4.H36   2000
956.94′03′092 – dc21   99–38628 CIP
[B]

ISBN 0 521 64187 x hardback

For Jan and Sarah and Alice

Contents

Illustrations

Acknowledgements

This book has grown out of a lecture that I was invited to give to the University of Edinburgh in 1982 as part of the Antiquary Visiting Scholars Programme of the Denys Hay Seminar, so my thanks are in the first instance due to the sponsors and to Dr Gary Dickson who arranged the programme. I have subsequently benefited from discussing different aspects of this subject at the Crusades Seminars convened by Professor Jonathan Riley-Smith and Dr Jonathan Phillips at the Institute of Historical Research in London; at seminars of the University of Oxford Crusades Special Subject organised by Dr Paul Hyams and Dr Miri Rubin; at a public lecture in the University of Leicester, arranged by Professor Norman Housley; and at the International Medieval Congress at Leeds in 1995 with the encouragement of Dr A.V. Murray. The opportunity to read papers connected with this book at two international conferences of the Society for the Study of the Crusades and the Latin East (SSCLE) has been particularly valuable.

Indeed, membership of the SSCLE has aided my work on this book in all kinds of ways. I am indebted to the published work and helpful comments of a wide range of fellow members and I should particularly like to thank Professor Malcolm Barber, Dr Peter Edbury, Professor Jaroslav Folda, Dr Rudolph Hiestand, Professor Robert Huygens, Professor Ben Kedar, Professor Hans Mayer, Dr Denys Pringle, Professor Jean Richard and Professor Jonathan Riley-Smith. Four friends have to be thanked posthumously: Joshua Prawer, R.C. Smail, Ruth Morgan and Rosalind Hill, who to the very end of her long and active life was always happy to discuss with me the problems arising from my work.

I owe a special debt to my pupils who, between the inception of this work and my retirement in 1997, helped me to formulate my ideas more precisely. Any inaccuracies which remain in this text, despite the best endeavours of my friends and colleagues, are, of course, entirely my responsibility.

In writing this book I have made use chiefly of the following libraries, to the staff of which I should like to extend my thanks: the Library of the University of Nottingham; the British Library; the Libraries of the School of Oriental and African Studies, of the Warburg Institute and of the Institute of Historical Research in the University of London. My special thanks are due to the librarian and staff of the London Library without whose resources it would have been difficult to complete this work.

I am particularly grateful to Dr Piers Mitchell, an expert in the history of medicine and particularly in the history of leprosy, who has made time in an unusually busy life to write an article about the nature of Baldwin IV's illness, published as an appendix to this book. This study has benefited greatly from his evaluation of the medical evidence, which I am not competent to handle.

Finally, I should like to thank William Davies and the staff of the Cambridge University Press for their encouragement, courtesy and practical help.

King Baldwin IV of Jerusalem has, for many years, been part of my family life. My children spent their adolescence to the sounds of early drafts of this work being torn up. To them, and to my wife, who has shared her marriage for the past seventeen years with the court of crusader Jerusalem, this book is affectionately dedicated.

Abbreviations

AOL	*Archives de l'Orient Latin.*
AS	Abu Shama, *The Book of the Two Gardens.*
Baha al-Din	Baha al-Din, *Anecdotes et beaux traits de la vie de Sultan Youssof,* RHC Or, III, pp. 3–370.
BEC	Bibliothèque de l'Ecole des Chartes.
BEFAR	Bibliothèque des Ecoles françaises d'Athènes et de Rome.
BHCTH	*Bulletin historique et philologique du Comité des Travaux historiques et scientifiques.*
BJRL	*Bulletin of the John Rylands Library.*
Bresc-Bautier	G. Bresc-Bautier (ed.), *Le Cartulaire du Chapître du Saint-Sépulcre de Jérusalem* (Paris, 1984).
CCCM	Corpus Christianorum Continuatio Mediaevalis.
CGOH	J. Delaville Le Roulx (ed.), *Cartulaire général de l'Ordre des Hospitaliers de Saint Jean de Jérusalem (1100–1310),* 4 vols. (Paris, 1894–1906).
CS	P.W. Edbury (ed.), *Crusade and Settlement* (Cardiff, 1985).
CSCO	Corpus Scriptorum Christianorum Orientalium.
CSHB	Corpus Scriptorum Historiae Byzantinae.
Delaborde	H.-F. Delaborde (ed.), *Chartes de la Terre Sainte provenant de l'abbaye de Notre Dame de Josaphat.* BEFAR, 19 (Paris, 1880)
DOP	*Dumbarton Oaks Papers.*
DRHC	Documents relatifs à l'histoire des Croisades publiés par l'Académie des Inscriptions et Belles-Lettres.
EHR	*English Historical Review.*
Eracles	*L'Estoire d'Eracles empereur et la conqueste de la terre d'Outremer.*

Ernoul	*La Chronique d'Ernoul* ed. L. de Mas Latrie (Paris, 1871).
HH	B.Z. Kedar (ed.), *The Horns of Hattin* (Jerusalem, 1992).
IA	Ibn al-Athir, *Kamil al-Tawarikh* (extract with French tr., RHC Or I, pp. 189–744).
Ibn Jubayr	Ibn Jubayr, *The Travels of Ibn Jubayr*, tr. R.J.C. Broadhurst (London, 1952).
Imperiale di Sant'Angelo	C. Imperiale di Sant'Angelo (ed.), *Codice diplomatico della Repubblica di Genova*, 3 vols., Fonti per la storia d'Italia (Rome, 1936–42).
JMH	*Journal of Medieval History.*
Kamal ad-Din	Kamal ad-Din, *History of Aleppo* (French tr. by E. Blochet, ROL 3–6 (1895–8)).
Kohler	Ch. Kohler (ed.), 'Chartes de l'abbaye de Notre Dame de la vallée de Josaphat en Terre Sainte (1108–1291). Analyses et extraits', ROL 7 (1900), pp. 108–222.
Lignages	*Les Lignages d'Outremer*, RHC Lois II, pp. 441–74.
Livre au roi	*Le Livre au roi*, ed. M. Greilsammer, DRHC 17 (Paris, 1995).
Mansi	G.D. Mansi (ed.), *Sacrorum Conciliorum . . . nova et amplissima collectio*, 31 vols. (Florence and Venice, 1759–98).
al-Maqrizi	al-Maqrizi, *A History of the Ayyubid Sultans of Egypt*, tr. R.J.C. Broadhurst (Boston, 1980).
de Marsy	A. de Marsy (ed.), 'Fragment d'un cartulaire de l'Ordre de Saint-Lazare en Terre Sainte, AOL IIB, pp. 121–57.
MGH	*Monumenta Germaniae Historica.*
MGH SS	*MGH Scriptores.*
Montjoie	B.Z. Kedar, J. Riley-Smith and R. Hiestand (eds.), *Montjoie. Studies in Crusade History in Honour of Hans Eberhard Meyer* (Aldershot, 1997).
MS	Michael the Syrian, *Chronicle* (ed. with a French tr., RHC Arm I, pp. 311–409).
Müller	G. Müller (ed.), *Documenti sulle relazioni delle città toscane coll'Oriente cristiano e coi Turchi fino all'anno 1531*, Documenti degli archivi Toscani 3 (Florence, 1879).

Outremer	B.Z. Kedar, H.-E. Mayer and R.C. Smail (eds.), *Outremer. Studies in the History of the Crusading Kingdom of Jerusalem Presented to Joshua Prawer* (Jerusalem, 1982).
P.L.	J.P. Migne (ed.), *Patrologia Cursus Completus. Series Latina*, 221 vols. (Paris, 1844–64).
QF	*Quellen und Forschungen aus italienischen Archiven und Bibliotheken.*
RHC	*Recueil des Historiens des Croisades*
RHC Arm	*RHC Documents Arméniens.*
RHC Grecs	*RHC Historiens Grecs.*
RHC Occ	*RHC Historiens Occidentaux.*
RHC Or	*RHC Historiens Orientaux.*
RHDFE	*Revue historique de droit français et étranger.*
ROL	*Revue de l'Orient Latin.*
RRH	R. Röhricht, *Regesta Regni Hierosolymitani (MXCVII–MCCXCI)*, 2 vols. (Innsbruck, 1893–1904).
RS	Rolls Series.
Salloch	M. Salloch (ed.), *Die lateinische Forsetzung Wilhelms von Tyrus* (Leipzig, 1934)
SCH	*Studies in Church History.*
Setton, *Crusades*	K.M. Setton (gen. ed.), *History of the Crusades*, 6 vols. (Philadelphia and Madison, 1958–91).
Strehlke	E. Strehlke (ed.), *Tabulae Ordinis Teutonici* (Berlin, 1869).
Tafel-Thomas	G.L.F. Tafel and G.M. Thomas (eds.), *Urkunden . . . der Republik Venedig*, Fontes rerum Austriacarum, section III, 12–14 (Vienna, 1856–7).
TRHS	*Transactions of the Royal Historical Society.*
WT	William of Tyre, *Chronicon*, ed. R.B.C. Huygens. Identification des dates par H.-E. Mayer et G. Rösch, CCCM 63, 63A (Turnholt, 1986).
ZDPV	*Zeitschrift des deutschen Palästina-Vereins.*

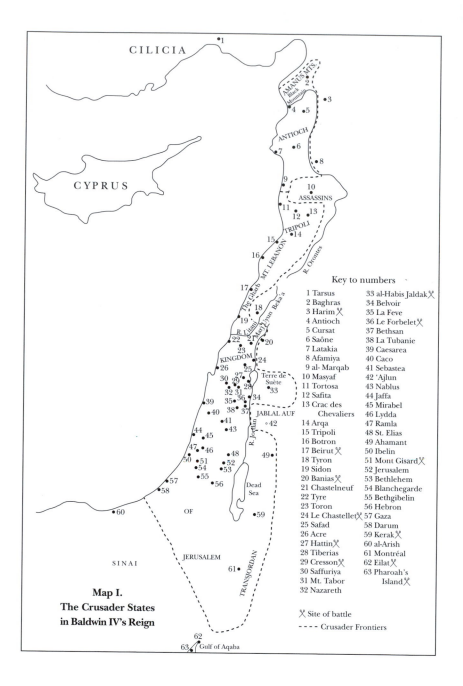

Key to numbers

1 Tarsus	33 al-Habis Jaldak ✗
2 Baghras	34 Belvoir
3 Harim ✗	35 La Feve
4 Antioch	36 Le Forbelet ✗
5 Cursat	37 Bethsan
6 Saône	38 La Tubanie
7 Latakia	39 Caesarea
8 Afamiya	40 Caco
9 al- Marqab	41 Sebastea
10 Masyaf	42 'Ajlun
11 Tortosa	43 Nablus
12 Safita	44 Jaffa
13 Crac des	45 Mirabel
Chevaliers	46 Lydda
14 Arqa	47 Ramla
15 Tripoli	48 St. Elias
16 Botron	49 Ahamant
17 Beirut ✗	50 Ibelin
18 Tyron	51 Mont Gisard ✗
19 Sidon	52 Jerusalem
20 Banias ✗	53 Bethlehem
21 Chastelneuf	54 Blanchegarde
22 Tyre	55 Bethgibelin
23 Toron	56 Hebron
24 Le Chastellet ✗	57 Gaza
25 Safad	58 Darum
26 Acre	59 Kerak ✗
27 Hattin ✗	60 al-Arish
28 Tiberias	61 Montréal
29 Cresson ✗	62 Eilat ✗
30 Saffuriya	63 Pharoah's
31 Mt. Tabor	Island ✗
32 Nazareth	

✗ Site of battle
- - - - Crusader Frontiers

Map I.
The Crusader States
in Baldwin IV's Reign

xvi

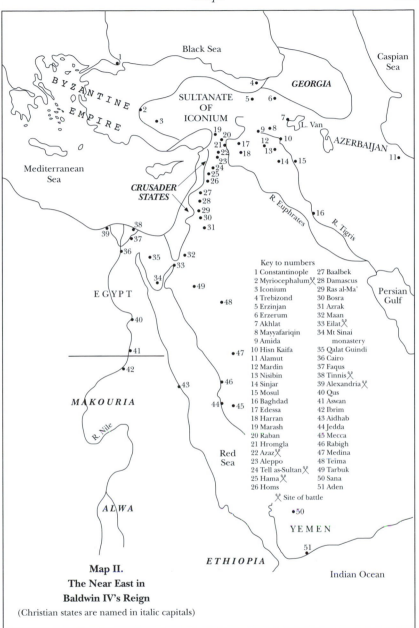

Black Sea

Caspian
Sea

BYZANTINE

EMPIRE

GEORGIA

SULTANATE
OF
ICONIUM

L. Van

AZERBAIJAN

Mediterranean
Sea

*CRUSADER
STATES*

R. Euphrates

R. Tigris

Persian
Gulf

E G Y P T

Red
Sea

Key to numbers

1 Constantinople
2 Myriocephalum
3 Iconium
4 Trebizond
5 Erzinjan
6 Erzerum
7 Akhlat
8 Mayyafariqin
9 Amida
10 Hisn Kaifa
11 Alamut
12 Mardin
13 Nisibin
14 Sinjar
15 Mosul
16 Baghdad
17 Edessa
18 Harran
19 Marash
20 Raban
21 Hromgla
22 Azaz
23 Aleppo
24 Tell as-Sultan
25 Hama
26 Homs

27 Baalbek
28 Damascus
29 Ras al-Ma'
30 Bosra
31 Azrak
32 Maan
33 Eilat
34 Mt Sinai
     monastery
35 Qalat Guindi
36 Cairo
37 Faqus
38 Tinnis
39 Alexandria
40 Qus
41 Aswan
42 Ibrim
43 Aidhab
44 Jedda
45 Mecca
46 Rabigh
47 Medina
48 Teïma
49 Tarbuk
50 Sana
51 Aden

Site of battle

M A K O U R I A

R. Nile

A L W A

50

Y E M E N

51

E T H I O P I A

Indian Ocean

Map II.
The Near East in
Baldwin IV's Reign

(Christian states are named in italic capitals)

Genealogy I. Baldwin IV's Kindred

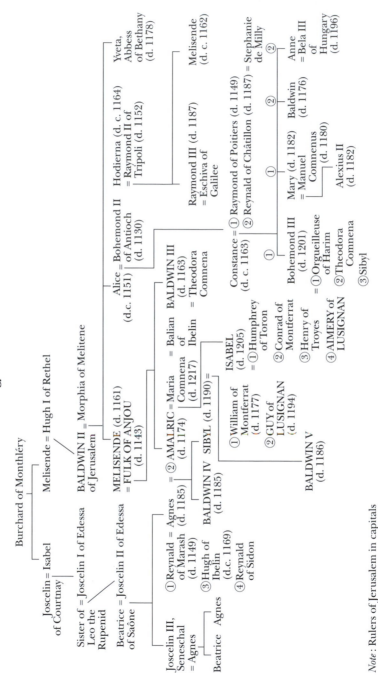

Note : Rulers of Jerusalem in capitals

Genealogy II. The Capetians and the Courtenays

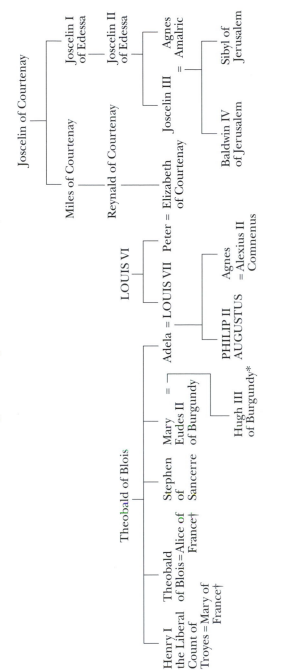

* Betrothed to Sibyl of Jerusalem
† The daughters of Louis VII and Eleanor of Aquitaine

Note: Kings of France in capitals

Genealogy III. Baldwin IV and the Angevins

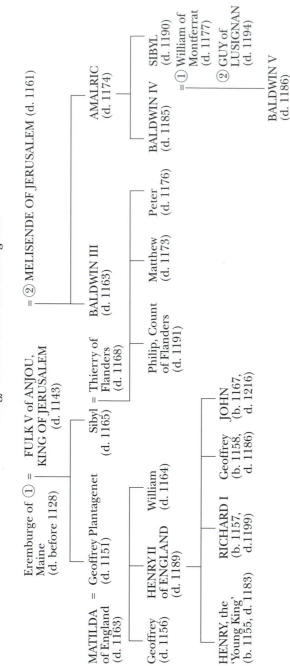

Note : Rulers of England and of Jerusalem in capitals

Genealogy IV. The House of Montferrat

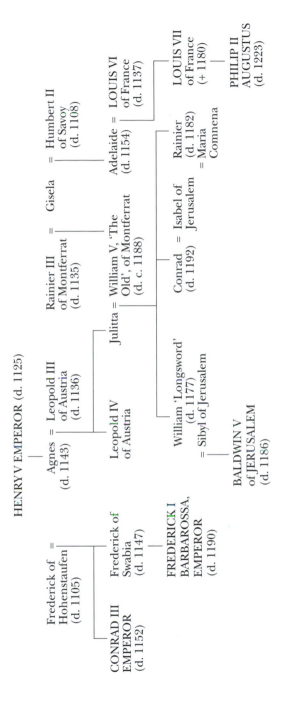

Genealogy V. The Boulogne Claimant

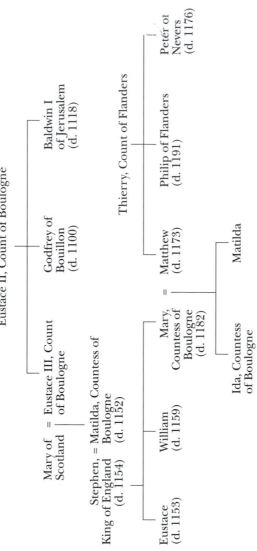

Eustace II, Count of Boulogne

Mary of = Eustace III, Count   Godfrey of   Baldwin I
Scotland   of Boulogne   Bouillon   of Jerusalem
                            (d. 1100)   (d. 1118)

Stephen, = Matilda, Countess of
King of England   Boulogne
(d. 1154)   (d. 1152)

Thierry, Count of Flanders

Eustace   William   Mary,   =   Matthew   Philip of Flanders   Peter ot
(d. 1153)   (d. 1159)   Countess of   (d. 1173)   (d. 1191)   Nevers
                     Boulogne   (d. 1176)
                     (d. 1182)

Ida, Countess   Matilda
of Boulogne

Genealogy VI. Manuel Comnenus and the Royal Family of Jerusalem

ALEXIUS I COMNENUS
(d. 1118)

JOHN II (d. 1143)

Isaac

ANDRONICUS I
(d. 1185)

Alexius, Protosebastus
(d. 1182)

Andronicus
(d. 1142)

John, Protovestiarius
(d. 1176)

Theodora = Bohemond III
(d. after 1180)   of Antioch
                  (d. 1201)

Bertha of ① = MANUEL I = ② Mary of
Salzbach   (d. 1180)   Antioch
                               (d. 1182)

ALEXIUS II
(d. 1183)
= Agnes of
France

Amalric of ① = Maria = ② Balian of
Jerusalem   Comnena   Ibelin
(d. 1174)   (d. 1217)   (d. c. 1194)

Isabel I of
Jerusalem
(d. 1205)

Rainier of = Maria
Montferrat   (d. 1182)
(d. 1182)

Glossary

Aman   A safe-conduct issued by a Muslim ruler.

Atabeg   In the Seljuk Empire the governor of a province for a prince who was a minor. The title was also assumed by the rulers of some states following the break-up of the Seljuk Empire in the twelfth century.

Cathena   The word means chain and refers to the chain placed across the entrance to the harbours in the Crusader States in the twelfth century to exclude enemy shipping. By association it came to mean the port authority acting on behalf of the crown.

Diwan   In Muslim societies a department of the central government.

Fidais   Members of the Order of Assassins (the Nizarite Ismailis), noted for their religious dedication, who were trained to carry out assassinations at the command of their superiors.

Haj   The pilgrimage to Mecca, incumbent once in a lifetime on all Muslims with the means to perform it.

Iqta   A grant by Muslim rulers of revenue from and sometimes also jurisdiction over estates, in return for service (often in return for military service).

Jihad   The holy war against unbelievers enjoined on Muslims.

Mamluks   The professional warriors who formed part of the

Islamic armies in the twelfth century, and who were recruited from white slaves, normally of Turkish or Caucasian origin.

Maphrian   In the Syrian Orthodox (Jacobite) Church the bishop who ranks second in dignity after the Patriarch.

Qadi   An Islamic judge.

Rais   In the Crusader Kingdom the non-Frankish headman of a village community.

Suq   The covered market of a Near Eastern city: a bazaar.

Ulema   The collective term for men learned in religious disciplines, including law, in an Islamic state.

Wadi   A river-bed that is dry except in the rainy season.

Prologue

On 15 May 1174 Nur ad-Din, the greatest ruler of western Islam, died at Damascus leaving an eleven-year-old heir, and his dominions were torn by faction as his kinsmen and generals fought for control. Two months later, on 11 July, King Amalric of Jerusalem died of dysentery at the age of thirty-eight. He was succeeded by his thirteen-year-old son, who was crowned king as Baldwin IV four days later. Although Baldwin suffered from leprosy, he remained king until his death in 1185, during which time Saladin, ruler of Egypt, made himself master of all Nur ad-Din's former territories until he ruled an empire stretching from the frontier of Libya to northern Iraq. It was like a giant Islamic nutcracker pivoted round the Latin Kingdom of Jerusalem. In 1187 Saladin sprang the mechanism: he invaded Galilee, defeated the Franks at Hattin on 4 July and the first Crusader Kingdom came to an end.

The classic description of the internal history of the Latin Kingdom 1174–87 is that of Sir Steven Runciman:

Now two definite parties arose, the one composed of the native barons and the Hospitallers, following the leadership of Count Raymond [of Tripoli], seeking an understanding with their foreign neighbours, and unwilling to embark on risky adventures; the other composed of newcomers from the West and the Templars. This party was aggressive and militantly Christian; and it found its leaders in 1175 when at last Reynald of Châtillon was released from his Moslem prison, together with Joscelin of Edessa, a Count without a county whom fate had turned into an adventurer.[1]

This colourful story gathers momentum as the leper king's reign continues and fresh actors line up on either side. On the 'good' side, that of Raymond of Tripoli, are the historian, William archbishop of Tyre, chancellor of the Kingdom, and the Ibelin brothers, Baldwin, who aspired to marry the leper king's sister and heiress, Sibyl, and

---

[1] S. Runciman, *A History of the Crusades*, 3 vols. (Cambridge, 1951–5), II, p. 405.

his brother Balian, who did marry King Amalric's widow, the Byzantine princess Maria Comnena, and thereby become the stepfather of the leper king's half-sister Isabel. On the 'bad' side the cast is led by Agnes of Courtenay, King Amalric's first wife, whose marriage had been annulled in 1163, but who was the leper king's mother and became very powerful during his reign. She is held responsible for two decisions that had a baneful effect on the future of the kingdom: first, she persuaded her daughter Sibyl, the heir to the throne, to reject the suit of Baldwin of Ibelin and to marry a handsome but useless young man from France, Guy of Lusignan; secondly, she used her influence to secure the appointment of her former lover, Heraclius, who lived in open concubinage and was poorly educated, as patriarch of Jerusalem in preference to the learned and godly William of Tyre. This group was joined in 1185 by the new, hot-headed master of the Temple, Gerard of Ridefort, an avowed enemy of the count of Tripoli. In 1186 this party seized power and excluded their more able rivals from government. The kingdom was therefore singularly ill-equipped to meet Saladin's attack in 1187 because all the wrong people were in positions of authority. Furthermore, had Raymond of Tripoli and his friends been in office the attack would never have taken place because they knew how to keep peace with Saladin.

The first two volumes of Sir Steven's *History of the Crusades* were published while I was an undergraduate. I read them with avidity, and although I now disagree with his account of the leper king's reign, I still think that his *History* is one of the great literary works of English historical writing, which has inspired an interest in and enthusiasm for the crusades in a whole generation. Any book dealing with so long a span of history is bound to be in part a work of synthesis, and in his account of the events leading up to Hattin Sir Steven accepted what was then the most recent modern account, that of Marshall Baldwin, *Raymond III of Tripolis and the Fall of Jerusalem*, which appeared to be borne out by the contemporary chronicle sources. Sir Steven was, of course, aware when he was writing that American scholars were planning a multi-volume history of the Crusades: 'It may seem unwise for one British pen to compete with the massed typewriters of the United States' he commented in the preface to his first volume.[2] That work, the

---

[2] *Ibid.*, I, p. xii.

Pennsylvania *History of the Crusades*, began to appear in 1958, and the last chapter in the first volume was entitled 'The decline and fall of Jerusalem, 1174–1189'. It was written by Baldwin, and told exactly the same story as that found in Runciman, and this congruence of opinion in the two standard modern histories made it appear that there was unanimity among scholars about the events of the leper king's reign.[3]

Baldwin did not make up the 'two-party' account of the fall of Jerusalem. Thomas Archer and Charles Kingsford, in their contribution to a series called *The Story of the Nations* in 1894, noted how by the end of Baldwin IV's reign: 'it would seem that there were two parties in the state; on the one side the native nobles, on the other the aliens'.[4] Indeed, the evidence on which this theory is based is found in the two principal narrative sources for the years 1174–87, both composed in the Holy Land, the *Chronicle* of William of Tyre, and the *Chronicle* of Ernoul. I shall consider in Chapter 1 the problems which those texts present.

The traditional interpretation of the history of the Crusader States in the period 1174–87 is convincing only if the view of Saladin that has been traditional in the English-speaking world ever since Sir Walter Scott published *The Talisman* in 1825 is accepted as true. This represents the sultan as a man of honour, who could always be relied upon to keep his word. Scott did not invent that view, but merely repeated what the sultan's official biographers had said about him. This view of Saladin appeared to validate the opinion of Baldwin; that Raymond of Tripoli and his supporters had been right in supposing that Saladin would honour the truces that he made with them, and that however great his power became, he would be willing to live at peace with his Christian neighbours even though they had turned Jerusalem, the third holy city of Islam, into an exclusively Christian city.

The first reappraisal of Saladin was made by Andrew Ehrenkreutz in 1972. He did not adduce much new evidence, but he brought a new critical approach to his subject, treating the contemporary lives of Saladin just as any western scholar would treat the contemporary lives of a saint, for example those of Saint Louis. I found his book

---

[3] M.W. Baldwin, 'The decline and fall of Jerusalem, 1174–1189', in Setton, *Crusades*, I, pp. 590–621.

[4] T.A. Archer and C.L. Kingsford, *The Crusades. The Story of the Latin Kingdom of Jerusalem* (London, 1894), p. 268.

refreshing, though I thought that he was overreacting to the work of
his predecessors and was reluctant to concede any good qualities to
Saladin.[5] Then in 1982 Malcolm Lyons and David Jackson published
Saladin. The Politics of the Holy War. This work is based on a wide
range of new archival material and provides a serious reappraisal of
Saladin and of his relations with the Franks.

Other studies made during the past twenty-five years of particular
aspects of the history of the Latin Kingdom in the years leading up
to Hattin have also shown that the traditional interpretation is
inadequate. In 1973 Jonathan Riley-Smith drew attention to the fact
that the constitutional issues involved in the appointment of a regent
for Baldwin V and of a successor to him in 1186 were far more
complex than the conventional interpretation allowed.[6] In 1978 I
published a paper on Reynald of Châtillon, in which I argued that
he was far from being a maverick robber baron, a view that modern
scholars have derived from the *Chronicle* of Ernoul, but was considered a serious military threat by Islamic contemporaries.[7] When
Joshua Prawer's *festschrift* appeared in 1983 it contained two revision-
ist essays about Baldwin IV's reign and its aftermath. R.C. Smail,
one of the most judicious of the older generation of English
crusading historians, in 'The predicaments of Guy of Lusignan',
examined sympathetically Guy's reasons for fighting the battle of
Hattin; whereas on the evidence of the accounts given in the Old
French *Continuations* of William of Tyre, this is usually dismissed as a
rash and irresponsible decision by the king and Gerard of Ridefort,
who disregarded the wise advice of Raymond of Tripoli that they
should not fight. The other essay, by Benjamin Kedar, was about the
Patriarch Heraclius. He has had an almost uniformly hostile press
since the twelfth century because of the stories in Ernoul about his
liaison with Pascha dei Rivieri, a merchant's wife known as
'Madame la Patriarchesse', and about his alleged avarice at the fall
of Jerusalem, when he left the city with the treasures of the Church,
which he refused to spend on ransoming poor Christian captives.
While not attempting to deny the patriarch's weaknesses, Kedar
wrote also of his strengths, notably his excellent education, equal to

[5] A.S. Ehrenkreutz, *Saladin* (Albany, 1972).
[6] J. Riley-Smith, *The Feudal Nobility and the Kingdom of Jerusalem, 1174–1277* (London, 1973),
pp. 106–12.
[7] B. Hamilton, 'The elephant of Christ: Reynald of Châtillon', SCH, 15 (Oxford, 1978),
pp. 97–108.

that of William of Tyre, and showed that he was not an unworthy head of the Catholic establishment in the kingdom, even though he may have been a worldly one.[8] In 1993 Peter Edbury published an article in which he argued that the traditional division into two factions of the powerful men in the Latin Kingdom during the years leading up to Hattin cannot be sustained.[9]

As these examples show, many scholars share the view that a re-examination of Baldwin IV's reign and the events leading up to Saladin's victory at Hattin is necessary. The most recent survey of the period, Pierre Aubé's *Baudouin IV de Jérusalem. Le roi lépreux*, published in 1981, runs to 500 pages, but is merely a retelling of the traditional account based on William of Tyre and Ernoul. Mark Pegg wrote an interesting article in which he examined what their readiness to have a leper as king tells us about the way in which the Franks of the East perceived their own society and the king's place within it.[10] Pegg is primarily concerned with the social implications of Baldwin's illness, but in any case Baldwin's reign needs more sustained exploration than the best article can provide. I have written this book in an attempt to meet that need.

I have tried to examine more fully Baldwin IV's own role in the events of his reign. Earlier writers have portrayed him as a brave warrior, but also as a man who, because of his poor health, had little power but was manipulated by court factions. My own conclusion, which the reader must judge, is that the leper king had a more dynamic role in the affairs of the Latin East.

[8] R.C. Smail, 'The predicaments of Guy of Lusignan, 1183–87', in *Outremer*, pp. 159–76 and B.Z. Kedar, 'The Patriarch Eraclius', in *Outremer*, pp. 177–204.

[9] P.W. Edbury, 'Propaganda and faction in the Kingdom of Jerusalem: the background to Hattin', in M. Shatzmiller (ed.), *Crusaders and Muslims in Twelfth-century Syria* (Leiden, 1993), pp. 173–89.

[10] M.G. Pegg, 'Le corps et l'autorité: la lèpre et Baudouin IV', *Annales. Économies, Sociétés, Civilisations* 45(2) (1990), pp. 265–87.

CHAPTER I

The sources for Baldwin IV's reign[1]

LATIN AND OLD FRENCH SOURCES

Narrative accounts

Two independent accounts of Baldwin IV's reign were written in the Latin East, William of Tyre's *Chronicle* and the *Chronicle* attributed to Ernoul. William was born in Jerusalem in c.1130, but as a young man went to western Europe where he was trained in the schools of France and Lombardy. After he returned to the Latin East in 1165 King Amalric commissioned him to write a history of the Crusader Kingdom.[2] This is divided into twenty-three books and covers the period from the origins of the First Crusade to the year 1184. Book XXIII is incomplete, consisting only of a separate preface and a single chapter.[3] Although the precise date of William's death is disputed, it occurred before 21 October 1186. William is justly considered one of the finest historians of the central Middle Ages and was uniquely well placed to be knowledgeable about public affairs in Baldwin IV's reign. King Amalric had appointed him tutor to Prince Baldwin in 1170, and then in 1175, during Baldwin IV's minority and while Raymond of Tripoli was regent, William was appointed archbishop of Tyre (a position second only to that of patriarch of Jerusalem in the Catholic hierarchy), and chancellor of

---

[1] I have not given references to those works mentioned in this chapter that can be readily identified in the bibliography.

[2] R. Hiestand, 'Zum Leben und zur Laufbahn Wilhelms von Tyrus', *Deutsches Archiv* 34 (1978), pp. 345–80; P.W. Edbury and J.G. Rowe, *William of Tyre. Historian of the Latin East* (Cambridge, 1988); H.-E. Mayer, *Die Kanzlei der lateinischen Könige von Jerusalem*, 2 vols., MGH Schriften, 40 (Hanover, 1996), I, pp. 167–253.

[3] Robert Huygens argued that William did complete Book XXIII, but that the remainder of the text has been lost, 'La tradition manuscrite de Guillaume de Tyr', *Studi Medievali* 5 (1964), pp. 281–373 at p. 314.

the kingdom, which meant that he had charge of the royal archive and writing office. But scholars have been reluctant to accept that because William was an important political figure he was unlikely to have been impartial in his reporting of events, for although his work as chancellor gave him an excellent opportunity to be well informed about matters of state, he was also constrained, as any political figure is, by the need to be discreet. He is too good an historian to falsify evidence, but he is guilty on occasion of suppressing the truth. Sometimes he appears to have done this for reasons of political necessity. His account of Philip of Flanders's negotiations with the crown in 1177, for example, is so guarded that it is difficult to make out what really happened, although it is clear from hints that William gives that he knew much more than he wrote.[4] But at other points in his narrative he uses silence as a weapon with which to attack those of whom he disapproved, by consigning their deeds to oblivion. This is particularly evident in his treatment of Reynald of Châtillon, who is seldom mentioned by William, but who occupies a central place in Muslim accounts of Saladin's wars with the Franks of Jerusalem. William also sometimes gives accurate information in a misleading way. This is a political skill, and his account of the leper king's reign has to be used as a political source; it is written by the chancellor of the kingdom, not by an impartial and detached observer. Robert Huygens has produced an exemplary edition of William's *Chronicle* which is a pleasure to read.

The other account of Baldwin IV's reign written in the Latin Kingdom is the work edited by Louis de Mas-Latrie as *La Chronique d'Ernoul et de Bernard le Trésorier*. In four manuscripts of this text the author is named as Ernoul. The relevant passage records how on 1 May 1187 Balian of Ibelin came to the castle of La Fève and found it deserted: 'Dont fist descendre i sien varlet qui avoit a non Ernous. Ce fu cil qui cest conte fist metre en escript.'[5] Nothing more is known for certain about him, although Mas-Latrie thought it possible that he was Arnaix de Gibelet, an Ibelin supporter in Cyprus in the early 1230s, an identification which Ruth Morgan found persuasive, but which is of necessity speculative.[6] In its present form the work contains an account of the history of the Kingdom of

---

[4] WT, XXI, 13–18, pp. 979–87 and 24, pp. 994–6.
[5] Ernoul, p. 149; M.R. Morgan, *The Chronicle of Ernoul and the Continuations of William of Tyre* (Oxford, 1973), p. 41.
[6] Morgan, *Chronicle*, pp. 44–6.

Jerusalem from 1099 until 1228, which becomes more detailed during the reign of Baldwin IV. Some manuscripts contain additional material covering the years 1228–32, and Ruth Morgan argued convincingly that Bernard the Treasurer, who is named in the colophons of two of them, was the compiler of that recension.[7]

If Ernoul was a page in 1187 he cannot have been more than about fifteen years old, and although this means that he was an eyewitness of events immediately preceding and following Hattin, he must have relied on verbal reports when writing about Baldwin IV's reign as he had only been a child at the time. It is not easy to determine how much he wrote himself of the chronicle which bears his name. It begins with the words:

Oiés et entendés comment la tiere de Jherusalem et la Sainte Crois fut conquise de Sarrasins sour Chrestiiens. Mais ançois que je vous die, vous noumerai les rois et les segneurs ki furent puis le tans Godefroi, qui le conquist sour Sarrasins, il et li Chrestiien ki avoec lui estoient.[8]

In view of this statement of intent it is reasonable to suppose that Ernoul's account extended to the end of the Third Crusade in 1192. He may himself have added material about the later history of the kingdom, or that may have been the work of later editors of his text. All the surviving manuscripts of this chronicle date from the second half of the thirteenth century or later, and it seems highly probable that in all of them some changes have been made to the original work.

It is a very different kind of text from William of Tyre's *Chronicle*. Much of the historical material is cast in an anecdotal form and is interspersed with long digressions about the topography of the Crusader States, which is often enlivened by stories drawn from the Old and New Testaments and occasionally from Josephus, together with some comments on the fauna of the region, largely derived from St Isidore.[9] Despite its loose structure, it is an important historical source. The material about Baldwin IV's reign is based on evidence supplied by eyewitnesses who had a different perspective from William of Tyre. The section of the work that covers the period

[7] *Ibid.*, pp. 46–58; see section II, parts A and C of J. Folda, 'Manuscripts of the *History of Outremer* by William of Tyre: a handlist', *Scriptorium* 27 (1973), pp. 90–5 at p. 93.

[8] Ernoul, pp. 4–5; Ruth Morgan argued convincingly that the preface published by Mas-Latrie on pp. 1–4 of his edition and attributed by him to Bernard the Treasurer was not part of the Chronicle at all, *Chronicle*, pp. 57–8.

[9] *Ibid.*, pp. 117–37.

1184–7 has a unique importance as the only sustained narrative account of the history of the Latin Kingdom in those critical years after William of Tyre's *Chronicle* ended. Nevertheless, Ernoul's *Chronicle* is a work of polemic, and the author's express purpose, as the opening words of his text show, is to place the blame for the loss of the kingdom on the people who were in power in 1187, almost all of whom were dead when his account was written. His chief informants were presumably his patron, Balian of Ibelin, and Balian's wife, King Amalric's widow, Maria Comnena. From the beginning of Amalric's reign, where an account is given of his divorce from Agnes of Courtenay, to the end of the Third Crusade in 1192, the work is, as Ruth Morgan pointed out, 'the story from the Ibelin point of view, answering by implication all those who saw the Ibelins as the villains and not the heroes [of the events leading up to Saladin's conquest]'.[10] This source certainly needs to be used with great caution, yet it has not always been handled in that way. I suspect that part of the reason for this is that the *Chronicle* has great charm both because of the language in which it is written and because of the vivid stories and imaginary conversations with which it is filled, which make it seem more like a twelfth-century romance than a conventional history. Historians have sometimes used it in preference to other, better sources, even sometimes in preference to William of Tyre, and have reached some strange conclusions as a result of this.

There is an Old French translation of William of Tyre known as *L'estoire de Eracles empereur et la conqueste de la terre d'Outremer*, a title taken from the opening words of William's *Chronicle*. This text is usually referred to simply as the *Eracles*. In the *Recueil* edition of William of Tyre the *Eracles* is printed as a kind of running footnote to the Latin text, but the best existing edition of it is that made by Paulin Paris in 1879–80. In 1987, under the auspices of the Institute of Advanced Studies of the Hebrew University of Jerusalem, a group of scholars, of whom I was one, investigated the relationship between William of Tyre and the *Eracles*, which contains many variant readings and additions to William's text. Robert Huygens made the important observation that the *Eracles* does not seem to be based on any of the known manuscripts of William of Tyre. It appears from internal information to have been written by a western

[10] *Ibid.*, p. 136; cf. pp. 112–14.

clerk, almost certainly of noble birth, who had visited the Holy
Land, and wrote at some time between 1205 and c.1234. John Pryor,
who wrote the official report of the 1987 seminar, concluded: 'The
text of the *Eracles* is useful to historians. It does contain important
information independent of that provided by William of Tyre . . . It
is not simply a translation of William of Tyre and is worthy of study
in its own right.'[11] This accurately reflects my own view.

Although some manuscripts of the *Eracles* contain only the
translation of William of Tyre's *Chronicle*, there are no fewer than
sixty which include continuations of it. All the continuations extend
to 1232, and in twenty-six manuscripts further continuations have
been added extending into the second half of the thirteenth century,
but these are not relevant to the present study.[12] The continuations
which cover the period 1184–1232 begin with Book XXIII of
William of Tyre's *Chronicle*, omitting the special preface but translating chapter 1. They then continue with an adaptation of the text
of the *Chronicle* of Ernoul for the years 1184–1232, but omitting the
earlier part of his work. The surviving manuscripts fall into three
main families. By far the largest number, represented by manuscripts
c and *g* in the *Recueil* edition, are, despite some variations, broadly in
agreement with the text of the Ernoul manuscripts; but important
differences are found in the Colbert-Fontainebleau *Continuation*,
while the text of MS Lyon 828 stands apart from the rest.[13] Ruth
Morgan argued that the *Chronicle* of Ernoul had only been preserved
in an abridged form, the work of later compilers, and considered
that Lyons 828 most closely represented Ernoul's original text for
the period 1184–97, albeit in an abbreviated form.[14]

---

[11] J.H. Pryor, 'The *Eracles* and William of Tyre: an interim report', in HH, pp. 270–93 at
p. 293.

[12] Sections III, IV, V of Folda 'Manuscripts of the *History of Outremer*', pp. 93–5. Related to the
Chronicle of Ernoul and to the Old French *Continuations* of William of Tyre is the *Estoires
d'Outremer et de la naissance Salehadin*, of which Margaret Jubb has recently produced a critical
edition. This is an historical account of the Crusader States from 1099 to 1230, which
contains long fictional interpolations, notably of the romances known as *La fille du comte de
Ponthieu* and *L'Ordre de chevalerie*. It is still unclear whether Samuel de Broë, seigneur de Citry
et de la Guette's *Histoire de la conqueste du royaume de Jérusalem sur les chrestiens par Saladin* (Paris,
1679) is based on a lost manuscript of the *Estoires d'Outremer*, or whether it is a seventeenth-
century reworking of the *Estoires*, of no interest to the historian of the Latin Kingdom. I
have not found material in either of these works relevant to the present study.

[13] Morgan, *Chronicle*, pp. 9–11; P.W. Edbury, 'The Lyons *Eracles* and the Old French
Continuations of William of Tyre', in *Montjoie*, pp. 139–53 at pp. 139–40.

[14] Morgan, *Chronicle*, pp. 98–116; see also her introduction to her edition of the Lyons text:
M.R. Morgan (ed.), *La continuation de Guillaume de Tyr (1184–1197)*, DRHC 14 (Paris, 1982),
pp. 7–16.

This view was challenged in 1982 by John Gillingham, who argued that Ernoul's contribution to the chronicle that bears his name ended in 1187 and that later materials were 'reworkings of an anecdotal text compiled in the 1220s'.[15] More recently Peter Edbury has suggested that the 'original version from which all the texts [of the continuations of the *Eracles*] covering the years 1184–97 are ultimately derived was basically similar to the *Chronique d'Ernoul*. With the appearance of the French translation of William of Tyre, the *Chronique* was trimmed and adapted and pasted on to the end.' In his view, therefore, it follows that while due consideration must be given to the variant readings in the Lyons text of the *Eracles*, that version is not automatically to be preferred to others.[16] This argument, which I find persuasive, means that significant variants in all the branches of the continuation have to be given serious attention. Fortunately, for the period between late 1184 and the eve of the battle of Hattin in 1187 with which the present study is concerned, there is broad general agreement between all three families of the manuscripts of this text.

There is a good deal of information in contemporary western chronicles about the Crusader States. Even in Germany, which did not have very strong ties of affinity or trade with the Latin East, some writers became interested in the affairs of the Crusader Kingdom, notably Arnold of Lübeck, whose interest was aroused by the Jerusalem pilgrimage of Henry the Lion, duke of Saxony, in 1172.[17] Many of these western writers included reports about events in the Latin East in their histories, based on information they received from returning pilgrims, from ambassadors from the Crusader Kingdom visiting the West, and from letters sent to the West, particularly by the military orders, some of which they transcribed.

The Anglo-Norman historians were particularly well informed about events in the Holy Land because of the close links that united the Angevin dynasty and the kings of Jerusalem.[18] A very important, though brief, source is the *Libellus de Expugnatione Terrae Sanctae per Saladinum*, an account written by a knight from the Angevin Empire

[15] J. Gillingham, 'Roger of Howden on Crusade', in D.O. Morgan (ed.), *Medieval Historical Writing in the Christian and Islamic Worlds* (London, 1982), pp. 60–75 at pp. 72–3, n. 33.

[16] Edbury, 'The Lyons *Eracles*', pp. 152–3.

[17] E. Joranson, 'The Palestine pilgrimage of Henry the Lion', in J.L. Cate and E.N. Anderson (eds.), *Medieval and Historiographical Essays in Honour of J.W. Thompson* (Chicago, 1938), pp. 146–225; K. Jordan, tr. P.S. Falla, *Henry the Lion. A Biography* (Oxford, 1986), pp. 150–4.

[18] See Genealogy No. III.

who was present in the Holy Land during Saladin's invasion and was wounded in the defence of Jerusalem in October 1187. This work opens with the death of Baldwin V and gives an account of the election of Guy of Lusignan and the events leading up to Hattin.

A good deal of information about the Crusader States is contained in the writings of Roger of Howden. There is now a general consensus that he wrote the *Gesta Regis Henrici Secundi* as events occurred, and redrafted parts of it in his *Chronica* after his return from the Third Crusade on which he had accompanied Richard I.[19] Other Anglo-Norman writers are primarily concerned with the part taken by Richard I in that crusade. The *Itinerarium Regis Ricardi* is a composite work. H.-E. Mayer edited the first recension (which consists of part of Book I in the final version) and argued that it had been written between 1 August 1191 and 2 September 1192 by an English Templar chaplain in Tyre. Helen Nicholson, who has recently made an English translation of the whole text, accepts Mayer's date, but has argued persuasively that there is not enough evidence to prove that the first author was a Templar, though he was almost certainly an English crusader. She has demonstrated that he compiled this work partly from oral traditions, partly from a written source about the German crusade and partly from his own observation.[20] In c.1217–22 a longer version of this text was produced by Richard de Templo, prior of the Augustinian house of the Holy Trinity, London 1222–1248/50. He used the earlier text, but added to it a Latin translation of the *Estoire de la guerre sainte*, composed by the Norman minstrel Ambroise who had accompanied Richard I on crusade. Richard de Templo also incorporated material drawn from Ralph de Diceto and Roger of Howden, and Helen Nicholson has argued that he had been on the Third Crusade himself and that that is why he sometimes amends and edits his sources.[21]

Related to this group of Angevin sources is a Latin *Continuation* of William of Tyre's *Chronicle*, preserved in a single manuscript in the British Library, Reg. 14, C.X. It covers the period from the accession

[19] Gillingham, 'Roger of Howden'; D.M. Stenton, 'Roger of Howden and Benedict', EHR 68 (1953), pp. 574–82.

[20] H.J. Nicholson, *Chronicle of the Third Crusade. A Translation of the 'Itinerarium Peregrinorum et Gesta Regis Ricardi'* (Aldershot, 1997), pp. 7–10; H. Möhring, 'Eine Chronik aus der Zeit des dritten Kreuzzugs: das sogennante *Itinerarium Peregrinorum* 1', *Innsbrucker Historische Studien* 5 (1982), pp. 149–67.

[21] Nicholson points out that there is no evidence that Richard de Templo was a former Templar, *Chronicle*, pp. 110–15.

of Baldwin V in 1185 to Richard I's retreat from Beit Nuba in January 1192, the point at which the crusade in effect abandoned any attempt to recapture Jerusalem. Marianne Salloch, who edited it, argued that it was composed in c.1220, and this view has gained general acceptance, whereas her contention that the *Itinerarium Regis Ricardi* drew on an earlier draft of the *Continuation* made in c.1204 has not.[22] As Helen Nicholson says: 'It does not seem very likely that a writer could have taken the tidy account of the "Continuation" and deconstructed it to form the dramatic early chapters of the *Itinerarium*.'[23] The author of the Latin *Continuation* has clearly drawn on the *Itinerarium*, and also on Roger of Howden and William of Newburgh, but his work contains information that is independent of them, particularly in his account of the events leading up to Hattin.

This group of historical writings is particularly important for a study of the Latin East because these accounts are written from a Lusignan point of view. The Lusignans were a Poitevin family and vassals of Richard I of England, who favoured the claims of Guy of Lusignan against those of Conrad of Montferrat for the crown of Jerusalem while he was on crusade. The information which these sources give about the events leading up to Saladin's invasion (the part which is important to the present study) was almost certainly derived, directly or indirectly, from Guy and Aimery of Lusignan and their Poitevin supporters in the Crusader Kingdom who talked of these matters to the crusaders who accompanied Richard I.

Records

Although no royal or princely archive from any of the four Crusader States has survived, a considerable body of charter evidence from the Latin East is known. This was calendared by Reinhold Röhricht at the turn of the century and additional documents have since come to light.[24] Hans Mayer has recently published a monumental work on the Royal Chancery of the Latin Kingdom, and in an appendix has edited some hitherto unpublished records.[25] The most important single group of non-royal documents drawn up in the Crusader

---

[22] M. Salloch (ed.), *Die lateinische Fortsetzung Wilhelms von Tyrus* (Leipzig, 1934), pp. 5–46.

[23] Nicholson, *Chronicle*, p. 4.

[24] R. Röhricht, *Regesta Regni Hierosolymitani (MXCVII–MCCXCI)*, 2 vols. (Innsbruck, 1893–1904).

[25] Mayer, *Die Kanzlei*, II, pp. 887–925.

States in this period relates to the Order of St John, which has the best-preserved twelfth-century archive from the Latin East. This is now in the Library of Valetta, and most of the twelfth-century material relating to the Order was published by Delaville Le Roulx.[26] The cartulary of the Holy Sepulchre, now in the Vatican Library, contains almost 200 documents, the greater part of which date from the twelfth century, and has been edited twice, first by Eugène de Rozière in 1849 and more recently by Geneviève Bresc-Bautier. A quite large group of charters relating to the monastery of Our Lady of Josaphat at Jerusalem, the archive of the Teutonic Order, and a substantial fragment of the cartulary of St Lazarus, the Jerusalem mother-house of the Order of that name, have also survived.[27] Twelfth-century documents from the other religious houses of the Latin East are limited in number and will be noted as they arise. The majority of documents come from the Kingdom of Jerusalem; those relating to Tripoli and Antioch are comparatively sparse. The greatest loss, of course, is the archive of the Knights Templar from which only a few stray charters relating to the Latin East are known.

An important body of documentary evidence comes from those Italian communes which had colonies in the Latin East and handled the trade of the Crusader States. The most important collections for the twelfth century are those of Venice, Genoa and Pisa.[28]

Papal registers do not survive for the years with which this book is concerned, although a collection of Alexander III's privileges was preserved by the church of Rheims;[29] but a large number of papal letters and diplomas relating to the Holy Land do exist and Rudolph Hiestand has edited those issued for the churches there, and also the

---

[26] Many of the twelfth-century documents that do not relate to the Order of St John were published by S. Paoli, *Codice diplomatico del sacro militare ordine gerosolimitano, oggi di Malta*, 2 vols. (Lucca, 1733–7).

[27] H.-F. Delaborde (ed.), *Chartes de la Terre sainte provenant de l'abbaye de Notre-Dame de Josaphat*, BEFAR 19 (Paris, 1880); Ch. Kohler (ed.), 'Chartes de l'abbaye de Notre-Dame de la vallée de Josaphat en Terre Sainte (1108–1291). Analyses et extraits', ROL 7 (1900), pp. 108–222; E. Strehlke (ed.), *Tabulae Ordinis Teutonici* (Berlin, 1869); A. de Marsy (ed.), 'Fragment d'un cartulaire de l'Ordre de Saint-Lazare en Terre Sainte', AOL IIB, pp. 121–57.

[28] G.L.F. Tafel and G.M. Thomas (eds.), *Urkunden zur älteren Handels- und Staatsgeschichte der Republik Venedig mit besonderer Beziehung auf Byzanz und die Levante*, Fontes rerum Austriacarum, section III, vols. 12–14 (Vienna, 1856–7); C. Imperiale di Sant'Angelo (ed.), *Codice diplomatico della Repubblica di Genova*, 3 vols. Fonti per la storia d'Italia (Rome, 1936–42); G. Müller (ed.), *Documenti sulle relazioni delle città toscane coll'Oriente cristiano e coi Turchi fino all'anno 1531*, Documenti degli archivi toscani, 3 (Florence, 1879).

[29] Alexander III, Pope, *Epistolae et Privilegia*, P.L. 200.

papal privileges for the Knights Templar and the Knights of St John.[30]

Legal treatises

A collection of legal treatises dating from the mid- to late-thirteenth century contains, if carefully used, a good deal of material about the twelfth-century Kingdom of Jerusalem, since it records legal precedents and sometimes even royal ordinances from that period, of which there is no other evidence. These treatises were published in the *Recueil* series in 1841–3, and Jonathan Riley-Smith, and more recently Peter Edbury, have done much to elucidate the context in which they were written, which explains the selective way in which the authors recorded the twelfth-century traditions that had been transmitted to them orally.[31] The treatise known as *Le Livre au roi* is particularly important for this study. It was drawn up for King Aimery of Lusignan before 1205 and claims to give an account of the laws of the Kingdom of Jerusalem before the battle of Hattin. Miriam Greilsammer has recently produced a new edition. The greatest of all the thirteenth-century treatises is John of Ibelin's *Livre des Assises*. Chapters 260–72 in the *Recueil* edition are based on materials relating to the Kingdom of Jerusalem before the battle of Hattin and give information about the organisation of the Latin Church in the kingdom, the distribution of lordships, with details of the knight-service each owed to the crown, the distribution of feudal and burgess courts throughout the kingdom, the services of sergeants owed to the crown by the Latin Church and the cities of the kingdom, together with a list of the knight-service owed by crown vassals in the royal demesne, which is of particular interest because the vassals are named. Peter Edbury has produced a new edition of this material, using Paris: BN: MS Fr 19025, written at Acre in c.1280, as his base text. He recognises that parts of this material have been revised in the thirteenth century, but on internal evidence has argued convincingly that the original source was drawn up in the

---

[30] R. Hiestand (ed.), *Vorarbeiten zum Oriens pontificius*: I, *Papsturkunden für Templer und Johanniter*; II, *Papsturkunden für Templer und Johanniter. Neue Folge*; III. *Papsturkunden für Kirchen im Heiligen Lande*, Abhundlungen der Akademie der Wissenschaften in Göttingen. Philologisch-historische Klasse, Dritte Folge, vols. 77, 135 and 136 (Göttingen, 1972, 1984 and 1985).

[31] Riley-Smith, *Feudal Nobility*; P.W. Edbury, *John of Ibelin and the Kingdom of Jerusalem* (Woodbridge, 1997).

years 1183–6.[32] The laws of the principality of Antioch are known in an early thirteenth-century Armenian translation, which was edited with a French translation by Léonce Alishan in 1876.[33]

Miscellaneous sources

In the late thirteenth century a set of pedigrees of noble families who traced their descent from the old nobility of the Latin Kingdom was composed in Cyprus. This is known as *Les Lignages d'Outremer* and exists in a shorter and a longer version, both of which were edited by Beugnot in the *Recueil* series. This genealogical information is of very uneven quality for the twelfth century, but sometimes helps to supply deficiencies in contemporary records.

Thousands of western pilgrims visited Jerusalem in the reign of Baldwin IV, but only a few of them wrote accounts of their travels and the information that they gave is idiosyncratic. The majority of the Latin texts were edited by Tobler and Molinier, and English translations have been made of some of them, and also of some additional sources, by John Wilkinson.[34]

The corpus of Frankish inscriptions from the Crusader Kingdom has been published by de Sandoli.[35]

ARABIC SOURCES

Islamic

It is a widely held opinion that Islamic historians in the Middle Ages were not aware of the crusading ideology of the Franks in the Latin East.[36] Francesco Gabrieli wrote:

---

[32] Edbury, *John of Ibelin*, pp. 105–26.

[33] L.M. Alishan (ed. and tr.), *Les Assises d'Antioche reproduites en français* (Venice, 1876).

[34] T. Tobler and A. Molinier (eds.), *Itinera Hierosolymitana*, 2 vols., Publications de la Société de l'Orient Latin, sér. géographique 1 and 2 (Geneva, 1879–80); Latin texts with an Italian translation by S. de Sandoli, *Itinera Hierosolymitana Crucesignatorum (saec. XII–XIII)*, 4 vols. (Jerusalem, 1978–84); J. Wilkinson, with Joyce Hill and W.F. Ryan, *Jerusalem Pilgrimage, 1099–1185*, Hakluyt Society, 2nd ser., 167 (London, 1988); three twelfth-century texts have been newly edited: R.B.C. Huygens, *Peregrinationes Tres: Saewulf, Johannes Wirziburgensis, Theodoricus*, CCCM 139 (Turnholt, 1994).

[35] S. de Sandoli (ed.), *Corpus Inscriptionum Crucesignatorum Terrae Sanctae* (Jerusalem, 1974).

[36] Though weight must be given to the view of P.M. Holt: 'There was, however, a growing recognition [among Muslims in the twelfth century] that the Crusaders, above all in their occupation of the holy city of Jerusalem, were different from other invaders of Dar al-Islam,

The cause of this mistake on the part of Islam in the evaluation of an historical phenomenon of which it was first the victim, then the bitter adversary and finally the victor, can be found in our opinion in the indifference, caused by a sense of superiority and contempt, which the Muslims always showed, except on a few occasions, for the western world, its history and culture, throughout the Middle Ages.[37]

This seems borne out by the attitude of contemporary Muslim writers towards the Crusader States. They took very little interest in the Franks' internal affairs, although occasionally their comments are of crucial importance. In the present study Islamic evidence is chiefly valuable for the information which it gives about the growth of Saladin's power and his policies towards the Franks.

There are two lives of Saladin written by contemporaries. Baha al-Din Ibn Shaddad (1145–1234) entered the sultan's service as a *qadi* in 1188, but was thereafter in close contact with him and his court until Saladin died in 1193. His *Life* was published, with a French translation, in the *Recueil* series, and an English translation was made from the French translation for the Palestine Pilgrims Texts Society in 1897.[38] Imad ad-Din al-Isfahani (1125–1201) entered Saladin's service in 1174 and became his secretary. He wrote a history of Saladin's conquest of the Crusader States, covering the period 1187–93, which has been translated into French by Henri Massé.[39]

Abu Shama (1203–67) is the author of *The Book of Two Gardens*, an account of the dynasties of Nur ad-Din and Saladin. In his treatment of Saladin he made careful use of contemporary sources, including a lost history of Saladin written by Yahya Ibn Abi Tayy (d.1232), a Shi'ite scholar of Aleppo.[40]

All these works are concerned with idealising Saladin, but the most important sources of information about his reign are the letters written by his administrator al-Fadil, for these, unlike the histories, were not written with hindsight, but reflect conditions at the time

---

even from the Byzantines, with whom they were at first confused': *The Eastern Mediterranean Lands in the Period of the Crusades* (Warminster, 1977), pp. ix, xii, n. 9.

[37] F. Gabrieli, 'The Arabic historiography of the Crusades', in B. Lewis and P.M. Holt (eds.), *Historians of the Middle East* (London, 1962), pp. 98–107 at p. 98.

[38] The translation was made by C.W. Wilson, and revised from the Arabic text by C.R. Conder, Beha ed-Din, *The Life of Saladin* (London, 1897).

[39] Imad ad-Din al-Isfahani, *La conquête de la Syrie et de la Palestine par Saladin*, tr. H. Massé, DRHC 10 (Paris, 1972).

[40] M. Hilmy M. Ahmad, 'Some notes on Arabic historiography during the Zengid and Ayyubid periods (521/1127–648/1250)', in Lewis and Holt, *Historians*, pp. 90–4; C. Cahen, *La Syrie du nord à l'époque des croisades et la principauté franque d'Antioche* (Paris, 1940), pp. 55–7.

they were composed. Although many of them are cited by other historians, such as Abu Shama, they usually only give extracts. Sir Hamilton Gibb drew attention in 1958 to the need for al-Fadil's correspondence to be collected and edited,[41] but it was not until the appearance of Malcolm Lyons's and David Jackson's *Saladin. The Politics of the Holy War* in 1982 that this advice was taken seriously. They had worked through the archives of Europe and the Near East, and had found not merely a large body of the unpublished writings of al-Fadil, but also new manuscripts of the well-known chronicles of Saladin's reign containing important variants. Their work has made possible a serious reappraisal of Saladin and his relations with the Franks, and frequent reference will be made to their discoveries in this study.

Saladin was shown in perspective, not placed at the centre of Islamic affairs, in the *Kamil at-Tawarikh*, or *The Perfect History*, of Ibn al-Athir (1160–1233), one of the greatest medieval historians, whose work covers the history of the Islamic world to 1231. Although he lived in Mosul, and was to that extent remote from events in Syria and Egypt, his *History* is important because he was a critic of Saladin. Extracts relating to the crusades are published in the *Recueil* edition with a French translation.[42]

Kamal ad-Din (1192–1262) was a citizen of Aleppo and wrote a history of that town which extends to 1243 and contains much valuable information about Syria in the time of Saladin. Taqi ad-Din al-Maqrizi (1364–1442) was an antiquarian, who used the work of earlier writers in compiling his history of Egypt, and is valuable because some of the works he used are known to us only in his citations.[43]

The other Islamic source which has proved very useful in writing this study is *The Travels* of Ibn Jubayr (1145–1217), the secretary of the Muslim governor of Granada, who made the *haj* in 1183–5 and returned by way of the Latin Kingdom.[44]

---

[41] 'A desideratum is a corpus of extant documents of al-Qadi al-Fadil': H.A.R. Gibb, 'The rise of Saladin, 1169–1189', in Setton, *Crusades*, I, pp. 563–89 at p. 563, n.

[42] Ahmad, 'Some notes on Arabic historiography', pp. 88–90; Cahen, *La Syrie*, pp. 58–60.

[43] Cahen, *La Syrie*, pp. 62–3; Sami Dahan, 'The origin and development of the local histories of Syria', in Lewis and Holt, *Historians*, pp. 111–13; Gabrieli claims that al-Maqrizi's *Kitab as-suluk*, 'which is almost entirely compiled from other writers. . . is indispensable in our present state of knowledge [for the study of Ayyubid history]', *Arab Historians of the Crusades*, tr. E.J. Costello (London, 1969), p. xxxiv.

[44] *The Travels of Ibn Jubayr*, tr. R.J.C. Broadhurst (London, 1952).

Christian

The History of the Patriarchs of the Egyptian Church is a Coptic work, written in Arabic, and the account of the reign of Mark III (1167–89) contains some useful information about Saladin's relations with the Franks on the eve of Hattin. An English translation of this text has been made by Antoine Khater and O.H.E. Khs-Burmester.

Three Maronite historians who wrote in Arabic long after the Crusader States had fallen, nevertheless provide some good material for a study of the Lebanon in the twelfth century, as Kamal Salibi has shown. Jibra'il Ibn al-Qila'i (d.1516), Maronite Bishop of Cyprus, was not a historian, but his theological writings and letters contain a good deal of material relating to the crusading era based on sources that are no longer extant. Istifan al-Duwayli, Maronite patriarch 1670–1704, was a historian, and has been described by Salibi as 'perhaps the richest source for the religious and political history of the Maronites in the later Middle Ages'. Finally, Tannus Ash-Shidyaq (c.1794–1861), despite his late date, is a particularly good source for the genealogies of the great families and the territorial divisions of the Lebanon in the Middle Ages.[45]

SYRIAC SOURCES

A particularly important source for the history of North Syria in the second half of the twelfth century is the *Chronicle* of Michael the Syrian, Jacobite patriarch of Antioch (1166–99), who was friendly to the Franks. Michael wrote in Syriac, and his text has been edited with a French translation by Jean Chabot. Gregory Abul'Faraj, more commonly known as Bar Hebraeus (1226–86), who was Maphrian of the Jacobite Church from 1264, wrote an *Ecclesiastical History* of his Church, as well as a world history, *The Chronography*. The latter depends very heavily on Michael the Syrian for twelfth-century information, although it can sometimes be used to elucidate Michael's text. Ernest Wallis-Budge edited the Syriac text of *The Chronography* with an English translation, and the *Ecclesiastical History* was edited with a Latin translation by Joannes Abbeloos and Thomas Lamy in 1872–7. More independent of Michael the Syrian is the anonymous Syriac history known as *The Chronicle of 1234*, which

---

[45] K.S. Salibi, *Maronite Historians of Mediaeval Lebanon* (Beirut, 1959).

Chabot edited in 1926 and Albert Abouna translated into English in 1974.

ARMENIAN SOURCES

Works written in Greater Armenia, which contain a little information about the Latin States before 1187, such as Guiragos of Kantzag's *History of Armenia* and Vartan the Great's *Universal History*, both dating from the thirteenth century, are published in the *Recueil* edition of Armenian sources with French translations, but arguably the most important source is the chronicle attributed to Smbat the Constable (1208–76), the brother of King Hethum I of Cilicia. An abbreviated version of this text was found in the library of Ejmiacin, and extracts of this were used in the *Recueil* edition, but a full text exists in MS 1308 of the Mekhitarist Library in Venice. Fr Leonce Alishan, who cited parts of this text in his own works, did not attribute it to Smbat, but referred to it as *The Royal Annals*, which led scholars to suppose that this was an independent text. Fr Akelian published an edition of the Venice manuscript in 1956, and Gérard Dédéyan has since produced an annotated French translation of that part of it which is independent of earlier historians, beginning with Manuel Comnenus's entry into Antioch in 1159 and ending in 1272.[46]

BYZANTINE SOURCES

On the whole, Byzantine historians have little to say about events in the Latin Kingdom, because these were of peripheral interest to them, except when emperors campaigned there, or when western crusades travelled through Byzantine territory. John Cinnamus (c.1144–c.1203), secretary to the Emperor Manuel, was in the best position to be well informed about diplomatic relations between the empire and the Crusader States, but his *Epitome*, written in 1180–3, only covers the period 1118–76, and is therefore only helpful for the opening part of this study. There is no more recent edition than that made by Meineke in 1836.[47] Eustathius of Thessalonica (d.1195), in his account of the sack of that city in 1185, gives important

---

[46] G. Dédéyan (tr.), *La Chronique attribuée au Connétable Smbat*, DRHC 13 (Paris, 1980), pp. 9–36.
[47] English translation, C.M. Brand, *The Deeds of John and Manuel Comnenus* (New York, 1976).

information about deteriorating Latin–Byzantine relations after the death of Manuel in 1180. The text was edited by Stilpo Kyriakidis in 1961 and has recently been reprinted with a parallel English translation by J.R. Melville Jones. Nicetas Choniates (c.1150–1213) wrote a history which covers the period from 1118–1206, but which is very hostile to the West because it was completed after the sack of Constantinople by the Fourth Crusade: there is a good modern edition of this work by Jan-Louis van Dieten and an English translation by Harry Magoulias.

The Life of Leontios Patriarch of Jerusalem is relevant to this study, because Leontios visited the Holy Land during Baldwin IV's reign. The *Life* was written by his disciple, Theodosius Goudelis, soon after 1203, and a new edition with parallel English translation was published by Dimitris Tsougarakis in 1993. John Phocas, a Byzantine pilgrim who visited the Holy Places in 1185, is a unique source for the position of the Orthodox community living under Latin rule in the last years of the First Kingdom. The only manuscript of his work was published by Leo Allatius (d.1669), and recently a new English translation has been made by John Wilkinson.[48]

Official exchanges between Byzantine emperors and patriarchs and the Crusader States have been calendared by Franz Dölger and Venance Grümel.[49]

HEBREW SOURCES

The *Itinerary* of Rabbi Benjamin of Tudela in Navarre, who visited the Latin Kingdom of Jerusalem during the third quarter of the twelfth century, contains useful information about political conditions in the Near East and is easily accessible because Adler published the Hebrew text with an English translation.[50] A wealth of material, inaccessible to most crusading historians for linguistic reasons, was opened up by Joshua Prawer in *The History of the Jews in the Latin Kingdom of Jerusalem*.

---

[48] Wilkinson, *Jerusalem Pilgrimage*, pp. 315–36.
[49] F. Dölger (ed.), *Regesten der Kaiserurkunden des östromischen Reiches*, 5 vols. (Munich and Berlin, 1924–65), II, *1025–1204*; V. Grumel (ed.), *Les Regestes des actes du Patriarcat de Constantinople*, I. *Les actes des Patriarches*, III, *1043–1206* (Paris, 1947).
[50] Adler's translation was republished, without the Hebrew text but with a new introduction and notes by M.A. Signer, *The Itinerary of Benjamin of Tudela* (Malibu, 1987).

NON-LITERARY SOURCES

The Frankish settlement of the Crusader States in the twelfth century has left an impressive range of material remains. Ronnie Ellenblum has published an important study of Frankish rural settlement in the Crusader Kingdom, while an excellent survey of the secular buildings in the Latin Kingdom of Jerusalem has been recently produced by Denys Pringle, who is also writing a magisterial work on the churches of the kingdom, of which the first two volumes have been published.[51] The northern states are less well served: there is no detailed survey of the ecclesiastical buildings there, although the castles of Antioch-Tripoli have been described by Paul Deschamps in the third volume of his corpus, while Robert Edwards has produced a definitive work on the fortifications of Cilician Armenia in the crusading period.[52]

Jaroslav Folda has written a masterly study of *The Art of the Crusaders in the Holy Land, 1098–1187*, which includes work produced in Tripoli and Antioch. There are excellent studies of the coinage of the Latin Kingdom by John Porteous, Michael Bates and D.M. Metcalf, and an important monograph on the use of seals in the Crusader Kingdom by H.-E. Mayer.[53] The evidence about weapons is very fully covered in David Nicolle's monumental work, *The Arms and Armour of the Crusading Era, 1050–1350*.

[51] R. Ellenblum, *Frankish Rural Settlement in the Latin Kingdom of Jerusalem* (Cambridge, 1998); D. Pringle, *Secular Buildings in the Crusader Kingdom of Jerusalem. An Archaeological Gazetteer* (Cambridge, 1997); *The Churches of the Crusader Kingdom of Jerusalem. A Corpus*, 2 vols. (Cambridge, 1993 and 1998).

[52] P. Deschamps, *Les châteaux des croisés en Terre Sainte*, III, *La défense du comté de Tripoli et de la principauté d'Antioche* (Paris, 1973); R.W. Edwards, *The Fortifications of Armenian Cilicia*, Dumbarton Oaks Studies 23 (Washington D.C., 1987).

[53] J. Porteous, 'Crusader coinage with Greek or Latin inscriptions', in Setton, *Crusades*, VI, pp. 354–420; M.L. Bates and D.M. Metcalf, 'Crusader coinage with Arabic inscriptions', in Setton, *Crusades*, VI, pp. 420–82; D.M. Metcalf, *Coinage of the Crusades and the Latin East in the Ashmolean Museum, Oxford* (London, 1983); H.-E. Mayer, *Das Siegelwesen in den Kreuzfahrerstaaten*, Bayerische Akademie der Wissenschaften, Phil.-hist. Klasse, Abhandlungen, n.s. 83 (Munich, 1978).

CHAPTER 2

Baldwin's childhood

The future Baldwin IV was born in the early summer of 1161 to Amalric, count of Jaffa, and his wife, Agnes of Courtenay.[1] Amalric's elder brother, King Baldwin III, stood godfather to his nephew who was named after him, and the story was later told that when a member of the court asked what christening present he intended to give the child he laughingly replied, 'The Kingdom of Jerusalem.'[2] It must have seemed a frivolous remark at the time, for Baldwin was only thirty-one and had recently married a young and beautiful wife, so that the likelihood of his nephew's inheriting the throne appeared remote. Yet less than two years later Baldwin died childless. His death had important consequences for his little nephew, for not only did his father become king, but his parents' marriage was dissolved.

Amalric was Baldwin III's only brother and therefore the undisputed heir apparent, yet when the members of the High Court met with the senior clergy to consider the succession, they refused to recognise him as king unless he repudiated his wife. Their spokesman was the patriarch of Jerusalem, Amalric of Nesle, who objected that the couple were related within the prohibited degrees. In fact they were related in the fourth degree, having a common great-great-grandfather, Burchard of Monthléry.[3] In the twelfth century impediments of consanguinity were reckoned to extend to the sixth or even the seventh degrees,[4] but it was extremely unusual for an objection of this kind to be made to a well-established marriage and this suggests that the canonical objection masked some

---

[1] Baldwin was 'vix annorum tredecim' when his father died in July 1174. He must therefore have been born in the early summer of 1161: WT, XXI, 2, p. 962.
[2] *Ibid.*, XVIII, 29, p. 854.
[3] *Ibid.*, XIX, 4, p. 869; see Genealogy I.
[4] A. Esmein, *Le mariage dans le droit canonique*, 2 vols. (Paris, 1891), I, pp. 344–56.

more deep-seated animosity towards Agnes on the part of the baronage.[5]

By 1163 Amalric and Agnes had been married for six years[6] and had two children, Baldwin and his elder sister Sibyl.[7] There certainly could have been no objection to Agnes becoming queen on grounds of her birth. Her father, Joscelin II of Courtenay, count of Edessa, was the second cousin of Queen Melisende of Jerusalem and of her sisters, Alice, princess of Antioch and Hodierna, countess of Tripoli, so that Agnes was related to all the ruling families in the Frankish East. In addition she could claim kinship with the Capetians, for the heiress of the senior branch of the Courtenay family had recently married Peter of France, the youngest brother of Louis VII, who had taken his wife's title.[8]

Agnes was a widow when she married Amalric. Her first husband, Reynald, lord of Marash, had been killed at the battle of Inab in 1149. She cannot have been more than fifteen at that time, and there were no children of the marriage.[9] Marash was conquered by the Turks a few months later, so Agnes lost her dower-rights there[10] and in 1150 her father was captured by Nur ad-Din who blinded him and held him prisoner at Aleppo until his death in 1159.[11] Agnes's mother, Beatrice, sold the remaining castles of Edessa, which she was unable to defend, to the Byzantine Emperor Manuel I Comnenus in return for an annual pension to be paid for life to her and to her children.[12] She then retired with her son Joscelin and with Agnes to her own estates at Saône in the principality of Antioch, where Agnes remained until 1157 when she married Amalric.[13]

---

[5] J. Dauvillier comments on Alexander III's legislation, 'L'autorité ecclésiastique ne devra prononcer la nullité des mariages contractés au troisième et au quatrième degré que si la parenté est notoire et publique': *Le mariage dans le droit classique de l'église depuis le Décret de Gratien (1140) jusqu'à la mort de Clément V (1314)* (Paris, 1933), p. 148.

[6] Robert of Torigni, *Chronicon*, ed. R. Howlett, RS 82(iv) (London, 1889), p. 194.

[7] Sibyl was the elder child, and was therefore born between her parents' marriage in 1157 and Baldwin's birth in 1161: WT, XXI, 2, p. 962.

[8] See Genealogy II.

[9] Agnes was born in the period 1134–7, B. Hamilton, 'The titular nobility of the Latin East: the case of Agnes of Courtenay', in CS, pp. 197–203 at p. 202, n. 6; WT, XVII, 9, p. 772.

[10] R. Grousset, *Histoire des Croisades et du royaume franque de Jérusalem*, 3 vols. (Paris, 1934–6), II, pp. 288–9; Alishan, *Assises d'Antioche*, c. 6, pp. 18–20.

[11] L. Elisséeff, *Nur ad-Din, un grand prince musulman de Syrie au temps des croisades (511–569H/1118–1174)*, 3 vols. (Damascus, 1967), II, pp. 453–4.

[12] WT, XVII, 16, p. 781.

[13] Beatrice's first husband had been William, lord of Saône, WT, XIV, 3, p. 635; C. Cahen, 'Notes sur les siegneurs de Saône et de Zerdana', *Syria* 12 (1931), pp. 154–9; P. Deschamps, 'Le château de Saône et ses premiers seigneurs', *Syria* 16 (1935), pp. 73–88. MS, XVII, 12,

Two stories are told about the circumstances of that marriage. William of Tyre relates that Amalric of Nesle's predecessor, the Patriarch Fulcher, objected that the couple were related within the prohibited degrees but that his advice was ignored, whereas a late thirteenth-century source, the *Lignages d'Outremer*, tells how Agnes was betrothed to Hugh of Ibelin, lord of Ramla, but that when she came to Jaffa to marry him, Amalric married her himself, and this led the patriarch to protest that the marriage was uncanonical.[14] Yet neither of these factors would have invalidated the marriage in the view of twelfth-century canon lawyers and have led the High Court to demand an annulment in 1163.[15]

Hans Mayer has argued that Agnes had been married to Hugh of Ibelin in 1157, not simply betrothed to him, and that her marriage to Amalric was therefore bigamous. Although this would satisfactorily explain the strength of baronial opposition to the marriage, I do not find the evidence which Mayer adduces convincing. The marriage was opposed by the Patriarch Fulcher and had it been bigamous Agnes and Amalric would have been excommunicated and no later attempt to disguise this fact by claiming that the marriage had to be annulled because of consanguinity would have been possible.[16]

Some scholars have argued that the High Court objected to Agnes's becoming queen on moral grounds. It is true that the *Chronicle* of Ernoul credits her with being the mistress of both the Patriarch Heraclius and Aimery of Lusignan, but these liaisons, if they happened at all, were still in the future in 1163 when neither man had come to the East.[17] Ernoul is very hostile to Agnes, probably because his information about her was derived from her rival, Maria Comnena, King Amalric's second wife.[18] It is certainly unlikely that Agnes would have been able to make an advantageous marriage immediately after her annulment, as she did, if her reputation had been publicly defamed.

III, p. 297, says Beatrice and her children accompanied Baldwin III to Jerusalem in 1150, but this need imply only that they left Tell Bashir under his protection. Beatrice is never mentioned as present in the Kingdom of Jerusalem, while Agnes and Joscelin are not recorded as living there until after Agnes's marriage in 1157; Hamilton, 'Titular nobility', p. 197.

14 WT, XIX, 4, p. 869; *Lignages*, c. ii, RHC Lois II, p. 442.
15 Dauvillier, *Le mariage*, p. 31. 'Alexandre III fit triompher la coutume de l'Eglise romaine, qu'à lui seul l'*interdictum Ecclesiae* ne constituait pas un empêchement dirimant': *ibid.*, p. 195.
16 H.-E. Mayer, 'The beginnings of King Amalric of Jerusalem', in HH, pp. 121–35.
17 Ernoul, pp. 59 and 82; see below pp. 96–8.
18 See p. 9 above.

Mayer has demonstrated that the opinion advanced by some scholars, that the High Court feared that Agnes, if she became queen, would use her powers of patronage to favour the numerous noble but landless exiles who had come to Jerusalem from her father's county of Edessa, rests on insufficient evidence.[19] Nevertheless, it remains true that the members of the High Court in 1163 were hostile to the Courtenays of Edessa because they had rank but no land, and felt threatened by the prospect of the influence and patronage which Agnes would exercise if she were allowed to become queen.

Amalric had no option, if he wanted the crown, but to defer to the wishes of the High Court. His marriage was duly annulled on grounds of consanguinity in the presence of Alexander III's legate to the Holy Land, the Cardinal of SS. Giovanni e Paolo, but the king asked the pope for a dispensation to legitimise his children and to exonerate Agnes from any moral censure.[20] This was granted, presumably because the couple had proved to the satisfaction of the court that they had contracted the marriage in good faith.[21] Agnes received no settlement, but she retained the title of countess, which she had held as Amalric's wife and which she used for the rest of her life.[22] Soon after this, she married Hugh of Ibelin to whom she may once have been betrothed.[23]

Baldwin cannot have known his mother during his childhood. He was less than two years old when his parents separated and thereafter he would only have seen Agnes on public occasions as the wife of Hugh of Ibelin. He probably saw very little of his sister either, for Amalric sent Sibyl to live in the convent of Bethany near Jerusalem of which his aunt Yveta was abbess.[24] When Baldwin was

---

[19] Hamilton, 'Titular nobility', pp. 197–203; J. Richard, *Le royaume latin de Jérusalem* (Paris, 1953), p. 77; Mayer, 'Beginnings', pp. 123–5.

[20] Morgan, *Continuation*, c. 3, p. 20; WT, XIX, 4, p. 869. Because of his contention that Agnes and Amalric had been bigamously married, Mayer argued that the legitimacy of their children remained open to dispute despite Alexander III's ruling, 'Die Legitimität Balduins IV von Jerusalem und das Testament der Agnes von Courtenay', *Historisches Jahrbuch* 108 (1988), pp. 63–89.

[21] That was certainly later practice, *Decretales Gregorii IX*, Book IV, title xvii, ch. ii, ed. E. Friedberg, *Corpus Iuris Canonici*, 2 vols. (Leipzig, 1882), I, p. 710.

[22] Jaffa and Ascalon was the only county in the Kingdom of Jerusalem. The title countess therefore conferred a certain distinction, and until 1176 when her daughter Sibyl became the new countess of Jaffa and Ascalon, Agnes was the only countess in the kingdom. RRH, nos. 410a, 433, 472 and 654.

[23] WT, XIX, 4, p. 870; *Lignages*, c. 1, RHC Lois II, p. 422; Ernoul, p. 17.

[24] WT, XXI, 2, p. 962.

six his father married again. Amalric's new wife was a Byzantine princess, Maria Comnena, great-niece of the Emperor Manuel.[25] There is no evidence that the relationship between the queen and her young stepson was ever more than formal: certainly Baldwin showed little affection for her in later life. Maria subsequently proved to be a very ambitious woman and this may account for the coolness between her and Baldwin who, as the legitimised son of Amalric's first marriage, would always have taken precedence over her own children.[26]

Amalric recognised that his heir needed a good education and when Baldwin was nine he appointed as his tutor William, archdeacon of Tyre, one of the most learned men in the kingdom.[27] William was not quite forty at the time. He had been born in Jerusalem but had spent twenty years in western Europe studying under some of the greatest teachers there, and in 1170 he had just successfully accomplished a mission to Constantinople on the king's behalf.[28] The prince went to live in the household of this cultivated, cosmopolitan churchman, but the archdeacon soon diagnosed illness in his young ward:

While he was staying with me . . . it happened that, as he was playing with some boys of noble birth who were with him and they were pinching each other on the arms and hands with their nails, as children often do when playing together, the others cried out when they were hurt, whereas he bore it all with great patience, like one who is used to pain, although his friends did not spare him in any way. When this had happened several times, and I was told about it, I thought it was a consequence of his patient disposition, not of his insensitivity to pain, and calling him to me I began to ask him questions about it. And finally I came to realise that half of his right arm and hand was dead, so that he could not feel the pinchings at all, or even feel if he was bitten. Then I began to feel uncertain in my mind, recalling the words of the wise man who said: 'It is a certainty that a limb which is without feeling is not conducive to health and that a sick man who does not feel himself to be so incurs great danger.'[29] His father was told, and after the doctors had been consulted, careful attempts were made to help him with poultices, ointments and even charms, but all in vain. For

---

[25] *Ibid.*, XX, 1, p. 913; Ernoul, p. 18.

[26] B. Hamilton, 'Women in the Crusader States: the queens of Jerusalem 1100–90', in D. Baker (ed.), *Medieval Women* (Oxford, 1978), pp. 161–74.

[27] WT, XXI, 1, p. 961.

[28] *Ibid.*, XIX, 12, pp. 879–81 and XX, 4, pp. 915–17; Hiestand, 'Zum Leben . . . Wilhelms von Tyrus', *Deutsches Archiv* 34 (1978), pp. 345–7; R.B.C. Huygens, 'Guillaume de Tyr étudiant. Un chapître (XIX, 12) de son *Histoire* retrouvé', *Latomus* 21 (1962), pp. 811–29.

[29] Huygens notes that this is probably a translation of Hippocrates, *Aphorisms*, 2, 6.

with the passage of time we came to understand more clearly that this marked the beginning of a more serious and totally incurable disease. It grieves me greatly to say this, but when he became an adolescent he was seen to be suffering from leprosy to a dangerous degree.[30]

When the first symptoms of Baldwin's illness appeared, his father employed Arab doctors to treat him, among whom was a Christian, Abu Sulayman Dawud.[31] He also engaged Abul'Khair, Abu Sulayman's brother, to teach the boy to ride.[32] This was an essential accomplishment for any Frankish nobleman, but Baldwin, who was effectively one-handed, needed to learn special skills if he intended to fight, because he would have to control his mount in battle with his knees alone. The training he received was clearly first-rate because he remained an excellent rider until he became too ill to mount.

Piers Mitchell has examined in the Appendix below, the evidence about the type of leprosy from which Baldwin suffered. He points out that there would have been no visible symptoms of leprosy during Baldwin's childhood, so that no positive diagnosis could have been made then.

A misdiagnosis of the disease would have been unforgivable due to the dire social consequences, so clearly his doctors would have held back from making any diagnosis until they were convinced that this was correct. However, any physician would have known that leprosy was a possible cause for the loss of sensation.[33]

In the twelfth century leprosy was believed to be contagious and was considered incurable except by divine intervention. The consequences of being diagnosed a leper would have been daunting even for a king's son. Although Shulamith Shahar has convincingly argued that lepers received more generous treatment in the Latin Kingdom of Jerusalem than in western Christendom, her evidence for this comes almost entirely from the thirteenth century.[34] In the twelfth century both societies seem to have reacted in an ambivalent way to the illness. On the one hand, because most people were

---

[30] WT, XXI, 1, pp. 961–2.
[31] See Appendix; E. Kohlberg and B.Z. Kedar, 'A Melkite physician in Frankish Jerusalem and Ayyubid Damascus: Muwaffaq al-Din Ya'qub b. Siqlab', *Asian and African Studies* 22 (1988), pp. 113–26 at pp. 114–15.
[32] C. Cahen, 'Indigènes et croisés', *Syria* 15 (1934), pp. 351–60.
[33] See p. 250 below.
[34] S. Shahar, 'Des lépreux pas comme les autres: l'Ordre de Saint-Lazare dans le royaume latin de Jérusalem', *Revue Historique* 267 (1982), pp. 19–41.

frightened of catching the disease, lepers were segregated from the rest of the community. On the other hand, charitable individuals endowed hospitals for them which were served by volunteers such as 'the French nobleman Ralph, who had been a lord and the leader of 700 men, who abandoned all his possessions, and served the lepers who lived in a certain house outside the city of Jerusalem'.[35]

By the 1140s, and perhaps earlier, the Order of St Lazarus was founded in the Kingdom of Jerusalem for the care of lepers. This was a military Order with hospitaller functions. It was composed of knights and sergeants who had contracted leprosy, and who, as professed members of the Order, continued to fight as long as they were well enough to do so. They had charge also of some of the leper hospitals of the kingdom, and by the 1170s their headquarters was situated outside St Stephen's Gate at Jerusalem. The master of the Order in the twelfth century had to be a leper, but knights and sergeants who were not suffering from the disease might also be professed as brethren.[36]

The *Livre au roi*, a treatise about the laws of the kingdom drawn up for King Aimery (1198–1205), and believed to have been based on the laws in force before 1187, stated that if a vassal, either a knight or a sergeant, contracted leprosy, he must enter the Order of St Lazarus. He should arrange for a substitute to perform his military duties, but he would continue to hold his fief for the rest of his life and to receive the surplus revenues from it. Special provisions were made for the wives of such men, but they do not concern us here.[37] If Baldwin had been diagnosed as a leper in his childhood, then he would, presumably, have been required to enter the Order when he came of age.

But even though no diagnosis of Baldwin's illness was made, King Amalric must have been told of the possibility that this was incipient leprosy. He was already concerned about the problems of the succession. The fate of his immediate predecessors must have made him aware of the possibility that he too might die unexpectedly. His father, King Fulk, had been killed while coursing a hare, when his

---

[35] B.Z. Kedar, 'Gerard of Nazareth: a neglected twelfth-century writer in the Latin East. A contribution to the intellectual and monastic history of the Crusader States', DOP 37 (1983), p. 72.

[36] Shahar, 'Des lépreux pas comme les autres'; M. Barber, 'The Order of Saint Lazarus and the Crusades', *Catholic Historical Review* 80 (1994), pp. 439–56.

[37] *Livre au roi*, c. 42, pp. 256–62.

horse threw him, his saddle-girth broke and the heavy wooden saddle fractured his skull;[38] while his brother, Baldwin III, had died after a brief illness at the age of thirty-three.[39] It was perhaps the memory of his brother's death which led Amalric, when he too reached the age of thirty-three in 1169, to empower Archbishop Frederick of Tyre to arrange a marriage for the king's only daughter, Princess Sibyl, while visiting the West on a diplomatic mission.[40] Baldwin was at that time eight years old; the age of majority in the Latin Kingdom was fifteen,[41] so that if the king were suddenly to die there would be a long minority. Amalric had no close male kin who could take over the work of government in the event of his death, so the obvious solution to this problem was to marry his daughter to an older man of suitable rank and experience who would act as regent should the need arise. Sibyl was about eleven at this time, the age known in canon law as 'pubertati proximi', when it was considered normal to arrange marriages.[42]

Amalric's choice of a son-in-law was Count Stephen of Sancerre, a member of the house of Blois. He was extremely well connected: his sister, Adela, had married Louis VII of France, two of his brothers were married to the daughters of Louis VII by his first wife, Eleanor of Aquitaine, and Stephen was also related in his own right to the English royal house.[43] He responded favourably to Amalric's proposals and came to Jerusalem in 1171, accompanied by Hugh III, duke of Burgundy, who brought gifts from Louis VII.[44]

The first symptoms of Prince Baldwin's illness may have appeared by that time and it may have been necessary for Amalric to consider the possibility that Baldwin might not become king. In that case Sibyl and her husband would be the heirs to the throne. Mayer has drawn attention to a piece of evidence which suggests that this was indeed the case; in 1170 one of Amalric's vassals, Henry the Buffalo, died leaving three daughters and no sons, but the High Court delayed making a decision about the inheritance of his fief for almost a year until Stephen of Sancerre could be consulted. Stephen was not noted as a lawyer, and yet his decision was accepted and passed

---

[38] WT, XV, 27, p. 710.
[39] *Ibid.*, XVIII, 34, p. 860.   [40] *Ibid.*, XX, 25, p. 947.
[41] John of Ibelin, *Livre des Assises*, c.169, RHC Lois I, p. 260.
[42] '. . .*pubertati proximi*, c'est à dire quand la jeune fille était dans sa onzième année et près de sa douzième année': Dauvillier, *Le mariage*, p. 47.
[43] See Genealogy II.   [44] WT, XX, 25, p. 947.

into the law of the kingdom: that in such cases the fief should be divided equally between all the daughters, but that the eldest should do homage to the king for the entire fief.[45] It is difficult to explain why his opinion should have carried such weight unless the High Court regarded him as a possible future king.

Yet, for reasons which are not known, Stephen refused to marry Sibyl and returned to France. His change of heart is unlikely to have been caused by his discovering some scandal about her, since she was still a child and was living under the strict supervision of her great-aunt in the convent of Bethany. It is possible that negotiations broke down because the situation in the Latin Kingdom had changed since Stephen had accepted the terms offered to him in the king's name by the archbishop of Tyre: before Stephen reached Jerusalem Amalric, realising that no military help would be forthcoming from the West, had made a state visit to Constantinople in 1171 and had recognised the Byzantine emperor, Manuel I Comnenus, as his overlord in return for his protection.[46] Western princes from the time of the First Crusade had found great difficulty in accepting Byzantine claims to their allegiance, and it may have been for this reason that Stephen declined to marry Sibyl, because as a possible future regent or king he would not accept Byzantine suzerainty. This is conjectural, but the consequence of Stephen's refusal was that Sibyl was still unmarried at the time of her father's death. Amalric had had no other son; Queen Maria had borne him two daughters, one of whom had died in infancy, while the other, Isabel, was only about two years old in 1174.[47]

King Amalric's death was as unexpected as that of his father and brother. In June 1174 he led his army against Banias, but accepted

[45] Philip of Novara, *Le Livre de forme de plait*, cc. 71–2, RHC Lois I, pp. 542–3, records the change in the law. Stephen of Sancerre's role is related in P.W. Edbury (ed.), 'The disputed regency in the Kingdom of Jerusalem 1264/6 and 1268', Camden Miscellany, 4th ser., 22 (1979), pp. 1–47 at pp. 31 and 34 (a new edition of the text commonly called 'Documents relatifs à la successibilité au trône et à la régence'); H.-E. Mayer, 'Die Seigneurie de Joscelin und der Deutsche Orden', in J. Fleckenstein and M. Hellmann (eds.), *Die geistlichen Ritterorden Europas, Vorträge und Forschungen* 26 (1980), pp. 141–216 at p. 183, n. 29.

[46] WT, XX, 22–4, pp. 940–6. See below, Chapter 4, p. 66.

[47] H.-E. Mayer (ed.), *Das Itinerarium peregrinorum. Ein zeitgenössische englische Chronik zum dritten Kreuzzug in ursprünglicher Gestalt*, MGH Schriften 18 (Stuttgart, 1962), pp. 336–7; Queen Maria deposed to the papal legate in 1190 that her daughter Isabel had been eight years old when she married Humphrey of Toron in October 1180. She must therefore have been born between November 1171 and September 1172. *Itinerarium Peregrinorum et Gesta Regis Ricardi*, Book I, ch. 63, ed. W. Stubbs, RS 38(1) (London, 1864), pp. 119–22; Morgan, *Continuation*, c. 104, p. 106.

the favourable peace terms offered by the government of Damascus. Before he struck camp the king complained that he was feeling unwell, and when he reached Tiberias he began to suffer from dysentery. As he returned slowly to Jerusalem his health grew steadily worse, and he died there on 11 July at the age of thirty-eight.[48]

William of Tyre reports that an assembly was held, attended by the lay and ecclesiastical leaders of the kingdom, at which it was unanimously decided that Baldwin should be crowned.[49] This seems to have been a meeting of the *curia regis*, the High Court, which consisted of the tenants-in-chief of the crown, to which leading churchmen had also been invited. It was a peculiarity of the Latin Kingdom that only two bishops sat in the High Court,[50] but in matters relating to the succession the concurrence of the higher clergy was essential, because the rite of coronation was in their hands. There is some reason to doubt whether the election of Baldwin as king was as smooth as William of Tyre implies. Malcolm Lyons and David Jackson have called attention to a letter written by Saladin to his nephew Farrukh-Shah three days after Amalric's death, in which he states that he had heard from an informant in Darum that the Franks had not yet agreed on a successor.[51] There is every reason to suppose that this report is true. William of Tyre wrote his account of the election during the new reign, when personal affection for the king and loyalty to the kingdom would have inclined him to keep silent about any doubts which had been voiced concerning Baldwin's capacity to rule. Nevertheless, such doubts must have been aired, and Saladin would have learned about the prolonged meeting of the High Court from his excellent system of informers in the Latin Kingdom.

William of Tyre does not list those who attended the assembly of 1174, but most of the powerful men in the kingdom must have been present, otherwise, as the events of 1186 were to show, the election would have proved divisive.[52] During a royal vacancy the seneschal, Miles of Plancy, would have presided.[53] He was a royal kinsman,

---

[48] WT, XX, 31, p. 957. Cf. W.B. Stevenson, 'William of Tyre's Chronology', in *The Crusaders in the East* (Cambridge, 1907), pp. 361–71.

[49] WT, XXI, 2, p. 962.

[50] The archbishop of Nazareth and the bishop of Lydda.

[51] Citing MS of al-Fadil, B.M. Add. MSS 25757.146. M.C. Lyons and D.E.P. Jackson, *Saladin. The Politics of the Holy War* (Cambridge, 1982), p. 75.

[52] See below pp. 217–21.

[53] John of Ibelin, *Livre*, c. 256, RHC Lois I, p. 408.

probably related to Amalric through the Monthlérys, the family of Baldwin II's mother.[54] He had come to the East in Amalric's reign and been appointed seneschal in 1167, and shortly before the king's death had become lord of the great fief of Montréal by marriage to its widowed heiress, Stephanie of Milly.[55]

Ten other noblemen occupied positions of major importance in the kingdom and were influential members of the High Court.[56] The constable, Humphrey II of Toron, was in charge of the army under the king, and lord of Toron and Chastelneuf.[57] He was the longest-serving member of the High Court, having made his début there in 1137, when he was described as 'newly knighted and very young', and had been constable for more than twenty years.[58] His second-in-command was the marshal of the kingdom, Gerard of Pugi, whom King Amalric had also appointed chamberlain towards the end of his reign.[59]

Reynald Grenier, lord of Sidon, had married Agnes of Courtenay after Hugh of Ibelin died in c.1169. It is generally said, on the authority of William of Tyre, that his father, Gerard of Sidon, objected to the match and secured an annulment by testifying before a church court that the couple were related within the prohibited degrees, but this assumption is not borne out by later sources, including William of Tyre's *Chronicle*, in which Agnes is referred to as Reynald of Sidon's wife. This seems to indicate that after Gerard of Sidon's death in c.1171 Reynald and Agnes had successfully appealed

[54] J. Richard, *The Latin Kingdom of Jerusalem*, tr. J. Shirley, 2 vols. (Amsterdam, 1979), vol. A, p. 152, n. 28; cf. A. Roserot, *Dictionnaire historique de la Champagne méridionale (Aube) des origines à 1790*, publié par J. Roserot de Melin, 4 vols. (Langres, 1945), II, pp. 1129–36.

[55] CGOH, no. 409 (as seneschal). WT, XXI, 4, p. 964, records the marriage. Miles did not style himself lord of Montréal on 24 February 1174, de Marsy, no. 28, AOL IIB, pp. 145–6, but did so on 18 April 1174, CGOH, no. 463. The marriage occurred therefore between those dates, and since marriages were not normally solemnised during Lent, probably took place on or after Easter Day, 24 March 1174. H.-E. Mayer, *Die Kreuzfahrerherrschaft Montréal (Šōbak). Jordanien im 12 Jahrhundert*, Abhandlungen des deutschen Palästinevereins 14 (Wiesbaden, 1990), pp. 229–37.

[56] The greatest of the crown vassals, Walter of St Omer, prince of Galilee, died shortly before the king: CGOH, no. 459 of 1174 records him as dead and was dated by Amalric's reign. M. Rheinheimer, *Das Kreuzfahrerfürstentum Galiläa* (Frankfurt am Main, 1990), p. 61.

[57] John of Ibelin, *Livre*, c. 257, RHC Lois I, pp. 409–11; S. Tibble, *Monarchy and Lordships in the Latin Kingdom of Jerusalem 1099–1291* (Oxford, 1989), pp. 13–23.

[58] WT, XIV, 26, p. 665; C. du Fresne Ducange, *Les Familles d'Outremer*, ed. E.G. Rey (Paris, 1869), pp. 619–20.

[59] He was marshal by 1171, WT, XX, 22, p. 942; by 1174 he had also become chamberlain, CGOH, no. 463. Ducange states that Gerald held both offices in 1169, citing as evidence the sixteenth-century Cypriot antiquary, Etienne de Lusignan, but no contemporary source corroborates this, *Familles*, pp. 626 and 631.

to the pope to have the annulment quashed.[60] However, Rudolph Hiestand has recently shown that William's account has been misunderstood. William records the marriage of Agnes and Reynald near the beginning of Book XIX in the context of Agnes and Amalric's divorce:

[After her marriage to Amalric had been annulled, Agnes] was joined in marriage to the noble and eminent Lord Hugh of Ibelin . . . and after he died, during King Amalric's lifetime, she gave herself with the same affection to Lord Reynald of Sidon, the son of Lord Gerard, with whom she is said to have had a relationship no less unlawful than with the Lord Amalric previously. For the Lord Gerard, his aforementioned father, asserted under oath that there was consanguinity between the two aforementioned people, as he had learned from his forefathers and as he knew for certain since he was related to both of them, whence a divorce took place as is related above.

Hiestand points out that the only divorce described in this passage is that between Agnes and Amalric and that they must therefore be 'the aforementioned people' against whom Gerard of Sidon had given evidence. In other words, Gerard was a key witness in the annulment of Amalric's marriage in 1163, but he did not object to his son's marriage to Agnes. Hiestand argues that it was William of Tyre, not Gerard of Sidon, who pointed out that the relationship between Agnes and Reynald was 'no less unlawful' than that between Agnes and Amalric, and that this was an inference made by William from Gerard's claim to be related to Agnes, since the corollary of this must have been that Reynald also was related to her. But William does not say that Reynald and Agnes's marriage was annulled, or even that Gerard spoke out publicly against it. Consequently, in 1174 Reynald of Sidon was the husband of Agnes and thus the stepfather of Prince Baldwin and Princess Sibyl.[61] He was reputed to have been a very ugly man, but both his Christian and Muslim contemporaries admired his intelligence.[62] Unlike most Frankish noblemen he had an excellent command of Arabic and was able to read Arabic literature for pleasure.[63]

Guy Grenier, lord of Caesarea, was a distant cousin of Reynald of Sidon. His father had been one of Amalric's closest advisers, but

---

[60] Hamilton, 'Queens of Jerusalem', pp. 163–4.
[61] WT, XIX, 4, p. 870; R. Hiestand, 'Die Herren von Sidon und die Thronfolgekrise des Jahres 1163 im Königreich Jerusalem', in *Montjoie*, pp. 77–90.
[62] This was remembered about him over a century later, *Lignages*, c. 18, RHC Lois II, p. 456.
[63] Baha al-Din, RHC Or III, pp. 121–2.

Guy had only recently succeeded to the lordship and had little experience in the work of government.[64]

Baldwin of Ibelin had held the fief of Mirabel since c.1156 and that of Ramla since the death of his elder brother Hugh in c.1169 and was therefore one of the longer-serving members of the High Court.[65] He was to prove himself a man of forceful character and he had an excellent reputation as a warrior.[66] His young brother Balian was also a royal vassal, and held the small fief of Ibelin from which the family took its name.[67]

Gormond, lord of Bethsan, had sat in the High Court for twenty years,[68] and his son Adam was married to the heiress of the fief of St George of Labaene.[69] Walter III Brisebarre had served in the Court since Baldwin III's reign and although in 1174 he only held the small fief of Blanchegarde he had formerly been lord of Beirut and was therefore used to having power and influence.[70] Finally there was John of Arsuf, one of King Amalric's most trusted advisers.[71] It is also possible that Amalric's widow, Maria Comnena, took part in this debate, just as Baldwin IV's mother was to do in the debate about the succession in 1183.[72]

If all the abbots as well as the bishops attended the assembly (and many of them would have been able to do so because they lived in or near Jerusalem), the clergy would have equalled their lay colleagues in number. At their head was Amalric of Nesle, who had been patriarch of Jerusalem for seventeen years. Whereas ten years earlier he had taken a leading part in the debates about the succession of King Amalric, he is not recorded as having played any significant

---

[64] J.L. Lamonte, 'The lords of Caesarea in the period of the Crusades', *Speculum* 22 (1947), pp. 145–61 at p. 146; WT, XIX, 17–19, pp. 886–9.

[65] W.H. Rudt de Collenberg, 'Les premiers Ibelins', *Le Moyen Age* 71 (1965), pp. 433–74; H.-E. Mayer, 'Carving up Crusaders: the early Ibelins and Ramlas', in *Outremer*, pp. 101–18; Tibble, *Monarchy and Lordships*, pp. 40–6; Edbury, *John of Ibelin*, pp. 5–9.

[66] One version of the Old French Continuation of William of Tyre describes Baldwin of Ibelin as 'le miaudre chevalier et le plus sage qui seit en vostre terre' [i.e. 'la terre de Gui de Lusignan'], Morgan, *Continuation*, c. 24, p. 37.

[67] It owed service of ten knights to the crown, John of Ibelin, *Livre*, c. XIII, ed. Edbury, *John of Ibelin*, p. 118; Tibble, *Monarchy and Lordships*, p. 46.

[68] He is first recorded as lord of Bethsan in 1153, CGOH, no. 219.

[69] *Lignages*, c. 16, RHC Lois II, p. 454.

[70] M. Nickerson, 'The seigneury of Beirut in the twelfth century and the Brisebarre family of Beirut-Blanchegarde', *Byzantion* 19 (1949), pp. 141–85 at pp. 166–7; B. Hamilton, 'Miles of Plancy and the fief of Beirut', in HH, pp. 136–46.

[71] He formed part of Amalric's suite on the state visit to Constantinople in 1171, WT, XX, 22, p. 942.

[72] See below p. 194.

role in determining the choice of a new king in 1174. King Amalric seems quite deliberately to have excluded him from any active role in government, presumably because of the humiliating conditions he had imposed on him at his accession, and by 1174 the patriarch was an elderly man and in any case lacked a forceful temperament.[73] William of Tyre was scornful of his abilities, dismissing him as 'reasonably well-educated, but bereft of intelligence and virtually useless'.[74]

The most dynamic member of the bench was Frederick, archbishop of Tyre, a nobleman from Lorraine who had been appointed bishop of Acre in c.1150 and translated to Tyre in 1164. He had been King Amalric's chief ecclesiastical adviser, and also had wide experience in secular affairs, having accompanied the king on many of his campaigns and having been sent by him on diplomatic missions.[75] Archbishop Ernesius of Caesarea was the nephew of a former patriarch of Jerusalem and had held major offices in the Church for more than thirty years. Like Frederick of Tyre he had experience in diplomacy and had taken a leading part in the negotiations that led to the marriage of Amalric and Maria Comnena.[76] Archbishop Letard II of Nazareth had an equally distinguished ecclesiastical career and, although he had taken no major part in secular affairs, had a wide theoretical knowledge of them, having sat in the High Court since 1158 because Nazareth was an ecclesiastical lordship.[77] He was therefore in a position to be better informed about constitutional issues than any of the other bishops. Bernard of Lydda was the only other bishop with a right to sit in the High Court, but he had only been appointed in 1168. Before that he had been abbot of the Mount Tabor monastery and he was the only Benedictine on the bench.[78] None of the other bishops or abbots showed any great capacity in secular affairs with the exception of Bishop Joscius of Acre. He was later to play a very active part in the life of the Church and kingdom, but when Amalric

[73] B. Hamilton, *The Latin Church in the Crusader States: the Secular Church* (London, 1980), pp. 76–9.

[74] WT, XXII, 4, p. 1012.

[75] H.-E. Mayer, 'Frederick of La Roche, bishop of Acre and archbishop of Tyre', *Tel Aviver Jahrbuch für deutsche Geschichte* 22 (1993), pp. 59–72; Hamilton, *Latin Church*, pp. 125–6.

[76] Hamilton, *Latin Church*, pp. 124–5; WT, XX, 1, p. 913.

[77] WT, XVIII, 22, p. 842. Nazareth owed service of six knights to the crown and Lydda that of ten knights, John of Ibelin, *Livre*, c. XIII, ed. Edbury, *John of Ibelin*, p. 119.

[78] Hamilton, *Latin Church*, p. 122.

died he had only been a bishop for two years and can have had little influence.[79]

William of Tyre does not say whether the masters of the military Orders were invited to attend, but their presence seems likely. They certainly played a very central part in the election of a king twelve years later, by which time they and the patriarch had joint custody of the regalia, and there is no suggestion in any source that that was an innovation.[80] In 1174 the masters were men of contrasting temperaments. Jobert, master of the Hospital, had been elected after the brief reign of Cast de Murols (1170–2), but Cast de Murols's predecessor, Gilbert d'Assailly, was still alive throughout Jobert's reign.[81] Gilbert had been forced to abdicate because he had involved the Order in huge debts as a result of the massive support which he had given to King Amalric during his Egyptian campaigns.[82] Jobert is best remembered for enacting that property should be set aside to provide white bread for the sick poor in the Hospital of Jerusalem. As Riley-Smith has rightly pointed out, there is no reason to suppose, as some scholars have done, that Jobert concentrated on the charitable activities of the Order and paid little attention to its military commitments,[83] but because of the example of Gilbert d'Assailly it is reasonable to infer that he was a moderate man, not given to advocating extreme or impetuous policies.

Odo of St Amand, master of the Temple, had had a distinguished career in the service of the crown before he entered religion. In Baldwin III's reign he had been successively marshal of the kingdom, viscount of Jerusalem and castellan of the citadel of Jerusalem.[84] King Amalric appointed him his butler, an honourable but largely ceremonial post, and had sent him to the Byzantine court as one of his ambassadors in 1165.[85] Soon after this Odo became a Templar and was elected master of the Order in 1171 when Philip of Nablus abdicated.[86] Although his rapid promotion suggests that the

---

[79] *Ibid.*, pp. 120–1. [80] Morgan (ed.), *Continuation de Guillaume de Tyr*, c. 18, p. 32.

[81] J. Riley-Smith, *The Knights of St John in Jerusalem and Cyprus 1050–1310* (London, 1967), pp. 61–3.

[82] WT, XX, 5, pp. 917–18; he died in 1183, Roger of Howden, *Gesta Regis Henrici Secundi*, RS 49(I), pp. 305–6.

[83] RRH, no. 547; Riley-Smith, *Knights*, pp. 63–4.

[84] Marshal in 1156, CGOH, no. 244; viscount and castellan of Jerusalem in 1160, Strehlke, no. 2, pp. 2–3.

[85] Bresc-Bautier, no. 135, p. 266; WT, XX, 1, p. 913.

[86] M.-L. Bulst-Thiele, *Sacrae Domus Militiae Templi Hierosolymitani Magistri. Untersuchungen zur Geschichte des Tempelordens 1118/19–1314* (Göttingen, 1974), pp. 87–105.

king may have influenced the election, Odo was not at all subser-
vient to Amalric when he was master.[87] William of Tyre, who almost
certainly held him responsible for his own brother's death, described
him as 'a man of naught, proud and arrogant, having the spirit of
fury in his nostrils. A man who neither feared God nor showed
respect for his fellow men.'[88] Yet Odo's actions show him to have
been a man of great personal courage who was totally committed to
the ideals of his Order and to the prosecution of a holy war against
the infidel.

These were the more important members of an assembly, which
may have numbered some forty or fifty people in all, who met to
consider the succession to King Amalric. Two of the greatest men in
the Latin East were not present: Bohemond III, prince of Antioch,
and Raymond III, count of Tripoli, but there was no tradition of
consulting the northern rulers about the election of a new king of
Jerusalem.

The assembly had to determine the succession, but this was not a
formality. Stephen Lay has recently argued that Baldwin's illness had
not been diagnosed as leprosy at the time of his father's death, that
the unmistakable symptoms only became apparent during his
adolescence after he had become king, and that therefore the
possibility of crowning a leper did not arise.[89] Piers Mitchell's
consideration of the evidence confirms that the outward signs of
leprosy would not have been visible in 1174, and that no formal
diagnosis would have been made, but that the doctors attending the
prince would have been aware that his illness might be leprosy.[90]
King Amalric must certainly have been told of this possibility, and
members of the court would soon have become aware of it too. It
was surely this that the assembly debated in 1174: Prince Baldwin
was a minor and in ill health, and although no positive diagnosis had
yet been made, the symptoms of his illness were compatible with
those of incipient leprosy. Should he in those circumstances be
anointed king?

It is important to remember that although primogeniture was

---

[87] WT, XX, 30, II, pp. 954–5; M. Barber, *The New Knighthood. A History of the Order of the Temple*
(Cambridge, 1994), pp. 100–5.
[88] WT, XXI, 28, p. 1002; AS, RHC Or IV, p. 202.
[89] S. Lay, 'A leper in purple: the coronation of Baldwin IV of Jerusalem', JMH 23 (1997),
pp. 317–34.
[90] See p. 250 below.

beginning to become the norm in most western European monarchies in the second half of the twelfth century, and had long been so in Capetian France (the western state with which the nobility of Jerusalem felt the closest ties), it was not the accepted practice in the Kingdom of Jerusalem. This was largely a matter of historical accident. Godfrey of Bouillon, the first ruler, had died childless and been succeeded by his younger brother, Baldwin I, count of Edessa, who was living in the East, rather than by his elder brother, Eustace III, count of Boulogne, who had returned to the West. When Baldwin I in his turn died childless in 1118 he was succeeded by his first cousin once-removed, Baldwin II of Le Bourg, who was living in the East, rather than by his own elder brother, Eustace III, who was not. Baldwin II had no son to succeed him when he died in 1131, so the crown passed to his eldest daughter, Melisende, jointly with her husband, Fulk of Anjou. When Fulk died in 1143 his elder son, Baldwin III, was associated in power with his mother, for Melisende was queen-regnant and it was not until Baldwin III forced her to abdicate in 1152 that he became sole ruler.[91] He died childless in 1163 and was succeeded by his younger brother, Amalric, but, as has been seen, Amalric's succession had not been automatic.

Nevertheless, the lay members of the assembly must also have been influenced in their choice of a king by the laws regarding the transmission of fiefs. It was beyond dispute that a fief should descend to the eldest legitimate son of the previous holder. Prince Baldwin fulfilled that condition: he was Amalric's only son, and although his parents' marriage had been annulled, his legitimacy had been validated by the pope. If the prince's health had been good his succession would not have been in any serious doubt; the problem arose because if his illness proved to be leprosy, it might be impossible for him to remain king. The laws of the kingdom enacted that if the holder of a fief became a leper he must enter the Order of St Lazarus, although he should continue to hold the fief for the rest of his life and should arrange for it to be served by another knight, though it is not clear how this rule would be applied in the case of the king himself.[92]

Yet if Baldwin were excluded from the succession on grounds of health, the only serious alternative candidate was his sister Sibyl,

---

[91] She is often, in my view wrongly, referred to as a regent for her son: Hamilton, 'Queens of Jerusalem', pp. 148–57.

[92] *Livre au roi*, c. 42, pp. 256–7.

who was aged about fifteen. There was a precedent for a queen-
regnant in Jerusalem, for King Amalric's mother, Melisende, had
been recognised as Baldwin II's heir. Moreover, the new legislation
about the partible inheritance of fiefs among all surviving daughters
in cases where there was no son, which had been enacted in
Amalric's reign, specifically excluded the kingdom and the four great
baronies. In those fiefs the older custom prevailed that the entire
inheritance should pass undivided to the eldest daughter.[93]

It was unthinkable to commit the government of the kingdom to a
young girl who had grown up in the sheltered atmosphere of the
convent of Bethany. It is true that Queen Melisende had exercised
sole power during her son's minority, but she was then a woman of
mature age who had already had twelve years of experience in
government as the wife of King Fulk and as co-ruler with him.[94] If
Sibyl were to become queen she would have to be married to an
older man, capable of shouldering the responsibilities of kingship;
but a suitable husband could not be found for her in the Latin East
because the elevation of one of the barons as king would necessarily
have caused resentment unless he had himself been a member of the
ruling house. Sibyl could not marry princes of the ruling houses of
Antioch or Tripoli because she was related to all of them within the
prohibited degrees: this ruled out, for example, Raymond III of
Tripoli and Baldwin, brother of Bohemond III of Antioch, both of
whom were single men, because the marriage of Sibyl's parents had
been annulled on the grounds of consanguinity and she was related
more closely to Raymond of Tripoli and Baldwin of Antioch than
her parents had been to each other. Moreover, it would have taken
time, perhaps quite a long time, to arrange a foreign marriage for
her.

The claims of Princess Isabel, the only surviving child of Amalric's
second marriage, could not have been seriously considered, for she
was only two years old and her succession would have led to a long
minority, which was not in the best interests of the kingdom.[95] If the
claims of all three of King Amalric's children were passed over, then
the choice of a new king would lie among his male cousins:
Bohemond III of Antioch, his younger half-brother, Baldwin, and

---

[93] John of Ibelin, *Livre*, c. 177; Philip of Novara, *Livre*, c. 71, RHC Lois I, pp. 280 and 542.
[94] H.-E. Mayer, 'Studies in the history of Queen Melisende of Jerusalem', DOP 26 (1972),
  pp. 93–183.
[95] See n. 47 above.

Raymond III of Tripoli. Because they all traced their descent from Baldwin II in the female line the law of the kingdom was unclear about which of them had the best claim; Bohemond and Baldwin's grandmother Alice had been Baldwin II's second daughter, whereas Raymond's mother, Hodierna, had been his third daughter and in the view of some lawyers this might give Bohemond and Baldwin a better claim. On the other hand, Raymond was one generation closer to the common ancestor from whom the claim derived, and in the view of other lawyers this would have given him the better claim.[96] Thus, whichever of them was chosen, it was likely to prove divisive. Moreover, there were practical considerations. It would be very difficult to rule both Antioch and Jerusalem, yet Bohemond III had no adult son to whom he could delegate the government of Antioch were he to become king of Jerusalem, while his younger brother Baldwin was in the service of the Byzantine Emperor Manuel, and might be considered too subject to imperial influence to be acceptable as a ruler in either Jerusalem or Antioch.[97] The county of Tripoli could have been ruled jointly with the Kingdom of Jerusalem, but Raymond III had spent nine years as a Muslim prisoner of war and had only recently been released. He was not well known to the members of the High Court who, as later events were to show, viewed him with a certain measure of reserve.[98]

It was, no doubt, considerations of this kind which led the assembly to elect Prince Baldwin as king. He had not been formally diagnosed as suffering from leprosy, and suspicions that he had the disease might prove to be unfounded. There was clearly some element of risk in this choice, but Baldwin's youth was in some measure a safeguard. He was only thirteen and would not be able to assume direct rule until he came of age at fifteen, so during his minority a suitable husband could be found for Sibyl among the nobility of western Europe. When the king came of age he would then have a brother-in-law who would be able to take power if Baldwin did prove to have leprosy and had to abdicate. In the meantime Jerusalem would have a constitutional head of state.

Once a decision had been reached the coronation could take place immediately because most of the leading men of the kingdom were already present in Jerusalem. Coronations were normally

---

[96] Edbury, 'The disputed regency', pp. 1–47.
[97] See below p. 112.
[98] Baldwin, *Raymond III*, pp. 14–15; see below p. 93.

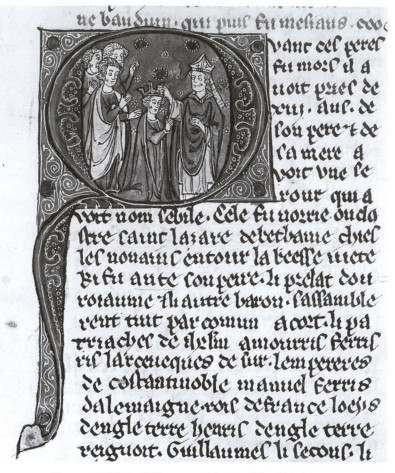

Figure 1 Baldwin IV is crowned by Amalric of Nesle.

performed on Sundays in the Middle Ages, but Baldwin IV's was held on a Monday, 15 July. This was an auspicious day, because it marked the seventy-fifth anniversary of the capture of Jerusalem by the First Crusade. Thus the thirteen-year-old Baldwin, suffering from incipient but undiagnosed leprosy, was anointed and crowned by the Patriarch Amalric of Nesle and enthroned in the Church of the Holy Sepulchre as the sixth Latin king of Jerusalem.[99]

[99] WT, XXI, 2, p. 962.

William of Tyre, who knew Baldwin well, gives a vivid picture of him as he was at the time he became king and before his health had begun to deteriorate:

He made good progress in his studies and as time passed he grew up full of hope and developed his natural abilities. He was a good-looking child for his age and more skilled than men who were older than himself in controlling horses and in riding them at a gallop. He had an excellent memory and he loved listening to stories. He was inclined to be thrifty, but he always remembered the good things that people had done for him, and the bad things as well. He was very like his father; not only did they look alike, but they were of similar build. They walked in the same kind of way and their speech patterns were similar. He had a quick understanding, but he had a stammer. Like his father he had a passion for hearing about history, and he paid attention to the good advice which he was given.[100]

This is a credible picture of a bright child, with a strong imagination and a determination to become a good rider despite his physical handicap.

[100] *Ibid.*, XXI, 1, p. 962.

CHAPTER 3

The kingdom

At the beginning of Baldwin IV's reign the Franks ruled the whole of the coastal territory of Syria and Palestine from the Amanus mountains to the Sinai desert. As Map I makes plain there were serious weaknesses in the Frankish defences at several points on the eastern frontier, and the implications of this will be examined in the next chapter.

The states of Antioch, Tripoli and Jerusalem were autonomous. The prince of Antioch was completely independent of the crown of Jerusalem, although his sovereignty was challenged by the Byzantine emperors who claimed suzerainty over the principality and sometimes succeeded in enforcing their demands.[1] Byzantine claims to overlordship of parts of the county of Tripoli were a dead letter by the 1170s, and although the counts were bound by ties of personal homage to the kings of Jerusalem, the king had no right to intervene in Tripoli's internal administration, while the count was not bound by treaties which the king made with foreign powers.[2] Nevertheless, it would be misleading to overemphasise the degree of separatism between the states; they had always been willing to assist each other when threatened by Muslim powers, and by Baldwin IV's reign, as a result of intermarriage, all three ruling houses were closely related, and this increased the likelihood of mutual intervention. Although there were important differences in some areas, the political, military and social structures of Tripoli and Antioch had a great deal in common with those of the Kingdom of Jerusalem.[3]

The central government in Jerusalem was carried out by the king

---

[1] 'La tiere de Triple ne d'Antioce n'est mie dou roiaume', Ernoul, p. 27; C. Cahen, *La Syrie du nord à l'époque des croisades et la principauté franque d'Antioche* (Paris, 1940); R.-J. Lilie, tr. J.C. Morris and J.E. Ridings, *Byzantium and the Crusader States 1096–1204* (Oxford, 1993).

[2] J. Richard, *Le comté de Tripoli sous la dynastie toulousaine (1102–87)* (Paris, 1945), pp. 26–30; John of Ibelin, *Livre des Assises*, c. x, ed. Edbury, *John of Ibelin*, pp. 113–14.

[3] Richard, *Tripoli*, pp. 9–92; Cahen, *La Syrie*, pp. 435–578.

with the help of great officers of state, very like those employed by the French crown at the time of the First Crusade. The fullest accounts of their duties are given by thirteenth-century jurists, but these agree in the main with the reports of their activities in twelfth-century sources. None of these posts was hereditary and so the appointments were an important part of crown patronage.[4] The chancellor, head of the king's writing office and keeper of the royal archive, was always a cleric, but the other officials were laymen.[5] The seneschal was the king's *alter ego*, who when necessary deputised for him in the work of civil government. He was also in charge of the treasury, known as the *Grant Secrète*, where records were kept of the boundaries of royal fiefs, and of the services and dues owed to the crown, together with records of the revenues paid to the crown by royal officials throughout the kingdom; and he was responsible for the garrisoning and provisioning of royal castles.[6] The constable was supreme commander of the army under the king and was responsible for keeping military records, for hiring and paying mercenary troops and for enforcing martial law during a campaign.[7] His deputy was the marshal.[8] The chamberlain had charge of the *camera*, which dealt with the expenses of the royal household, and was also responsible for arranging the performance of homage by the royal vassals.[9] The duties of the butler seem to have been purely ceremonial.[10] Yet although these officials had considerable powers, their offices did not develop during the twelfth century into large departments of state as did those of their counterparts in Angevin England and Capetian France. This was very probably because the almost constant state of war in the Frankish East made it esssential for kings to delegate authority to local lords and this inhibited the growth of centralised government.

[4] For example, Humphrey of Toron was appointed constable by Baldwin III, and Miles of Plancy was appointed seneschal by Amalric. There is no evidence that the High Court was consulted in either case, WT, XVII, 14, XXI, 4, pp. 779, 964.

[5] H.-E. Mayer, *Die Kanzlei der lateinischen Könige von Jerusalem*, 2 vols., MGH Schriften 40 (Hanover, 1996).

[6] John of Ibelin, *Livre*, c. 256, RHC Lois I, pp. 407–9.

[7] *Ibid.*, c. 257, pp. 409–11.

[8] *Livre au roi*, cc. 9–13, 15, pp. 157–73 and 176; John of Ibelin, *Livre*, cc. 257–8, RHC Lois I, pp. 409–14.

[9] John of Ibelin, *Livre*, c. 259, RHC Lois I, p. 414; L. de Mas-Latrie, 'Le fief de la Chamberlaine et les Chambellans de Jérusalem', BEC 43 (1882), pp. 647–52.

[10] J. Prawer, *The Latin Kingdom of Jerusalem. European Colonialism in the Middle Ages* (London, 1972), p. 125.

The king was advised by the High Court, composed of the tenants-in-chief of the crown, which had a triple function. It was a judicial body that dealt with all civil and criminal cases relating to the king's vassals, apart from those reserved to the church courts. Much of this business was of a routine character, concerned with the conveyancing of property, and for that purpose the court was quorate if the king and three of its members were present.[11] The High Court was also the king's council, which normally debated all important issues of policy. Finally, it had the power to enact laws for the whole kingdom.[12]

The great crown vassals held their lands in military tenure. In 1174 there were some sixteen lay vassals and a few ecclesiastical tenants-in-chief,[13] but almost half the lordships were directly controlled by the crown.[14] The lords enjoyed considerable powers: each of them presided over a court composed of his own vassals, which had jurisdiction over all Frankish noblemen, while in each lordship there were one or more burgess courts, presided over by a viscount appointed by the lord, who was always a Frank and was assisted by twelve Frankish jurors. These courts dealt with cases relating to all Frankish commoners and with all important cases relating to the non-Frankish population.[15] No right of appeal lay to the king from any of these courts. The majority of sub-tenants both in the royal and seigneurial lands appear to have been simple knights, some of whom only held money fiefs, which conferred no jurisdiction, and consequently the royal vassals formed a small élite group of powerful men.[16]

---

[11] 'Partout la ou le seignor et trois de ces houmes ou plus est, si sont court.' *La clef des assises de la Haute Cour du royaume de Jérusalem et de Chypre*, c. lx, RHC Lois I, p. 584.

[12] These laws were later known as the *Lettres dou Sepulcre* and were said to have been written down and deposited in the shrine of the Holy Sepulchre, but lost in 1187 when Saladin conqered Jerusalem, Philip of Novara, *Le Livre de forme du plait*, c. 47, RHC Lois I, pp. 521–3. This seems unlikely. It is more probable that the assises of the twelfth century, like those of the thirteenth, were known only through the memory of the High Court, than that a tradition of written law had been abandoned at the end of the First Kingdom.

[13] When crown fiefs such as Gaza were held by the military Orders, the commander presumably had the right to sit in the High Court.

[14] The crown held Jerusalem and Judaea, the fiefs of Nablus, Beirut, Darum and Hebron, the double county of Jaffa and Ascalon and the cities of Acre and Tyre.

[15] Other courts existed with powers to deal with minor offences and with minor civil law cases involving non-Franks: Prawer, *Latin Kingdom*, pp. 151–8.

[16] Of the hundred people listed owing knight-service to the crown, sixteen owed service of two knights and fifty-eight the service of one knight only: John of Ibelin, *Livre*, c. XIV, ed. Edbury, *John of Ibelin*, pp. 120–2, and cf. pp. 141–54.

Although there were very few ecclesiastical lordships in the Crusader States this did not mean that the Church was unimportant there. Catholicism was the established religion of all three states, and the hierarchy was organised under two Latin patriarchs, one at Antioch with jurisdiction over the northern states, the other at Jerusalem as head of the Church in the kingdom. The patriarchate of Jerusalem was divided into four archbishoprics: Tyre, Caesarea, Nazareth and Petra.[17] Many of the great shrine churches were administered by Catholic religious communities, chiefly Austin canons and Benedictine monks and nuns. The most important of them, the Church of the Holy Sepulchre, was the cathedral of the Latin patriarch.[18]

These shrine churches occupied a central role in the life of the Crusader Kingdom. The crusade movement had been launched to free the Holy Places from infidel rule; the kings of Jerusalem and their vassals were perceived throughout the West primarily as guardians of those shrines; and every year huge numbers of pilgrims came from western Europe to pray in Jerusalem, and were able to worship at the sites hallowed by the life, death and resurrection of Christ in the familiar forms of the Latin liturgy. The accounts of their experiences which they spread on their return home made a profound impact on the West, and this was of considerable practical importance to the Latin Kingdom,[19] for it kept alive the commitment of western society to maintain Catholic rule in the Crusader States, and it also led to the generous endowment by western benefactors of the shrine churches in the Holy Land.[20]

The population of the Kingdom of Jerusalem in the second half of the twelfth century has been estimated at c.620,000, of whom c.140,000 were Franks.[21] Although there are not even any approximate statistics for the population of the northern states at this time, there is no reason to suppose that the proportion of Franks was very different there. The Frankish settlers had come from all parts of

---

[17] Hamilton, *The Latin Church in the Crusader States. The Secular Church* (London, 1980), pp. 1–187; Y. Katzir, 'The patriarch of Jerusalem, primate of the Latin Kingdom', in CS, pp. 169–75.

[18] B. Hamilton, 'Ideals of holiness: crusaders, contemplatives and mendicants', *International History Review* 17 (1995), pp. 693–712.

[19] B. Hamilton, 'The impact of Crusader Jerusalem on western Christendom', *Catholic Historical Review*, 80 (1994), pp. 695–713.

[20] E.g. G. Bresc-Bautier, 'Les possessions des églises de Terre-Sainte en Italie du sud', in *Roberto il Guiscardo e il suo tempo* (Rome, 1975), pp. 13–34.

[21] Perhaps a conservative estimate. J. Prawer, *Crusader Institutions* (Oxford, 1980), p. 380, n. 38; M. Benvenisti, *The Crusaders in the Holy Land* (Jerusalem, 1972), pp. 18 and 215.

Figure 2 The *Cenaculum* on Mount Sion, shrine of the Last Supper, built in Baldwin IV's reign.

western Europe and the one thing that they had in common was their membership of the Catholic Church, and a Frank was therefore defined in law as a Christian *de la ley de Rome*. Whatever their status in the West may have been, Franks who settled in the Crusader States were legally free men and women and those who were not noble were classed as burgesses. This name was applied to them irrespective of whether they lived in towns or villages.[22]

Most of the inhabitants of the Latin East were not Franks but Muslims or eastern-rite Christians. There were also substantial Jewish communities as well as some smaller groups, such as the Samaritans.[23] Despite the massacre of Jews and Muslims which had been perpetrated by the First Crusade at Jerusalem in 1099, once their rule had been established the Franks proved remarkably tolerant in their treatment of their non-Christian subjects. Muslims and Jews were required to pay a religious poll-tax, but there were no forced conversions and few attempts were made to proselytise the adherents of other faiths. Indeed, the Franks allowed complete religious freedom to all their subjects. Jewish synagogues and rabbinic schools existed in many of their towns;[24] while recent research by Benjamin Kedar and his pupils has shown that Muslim villagers in the Nablus area enjoyed full rights to practise their own religion in the traditional way, which may even have included permission to make the *haj*.[25] In some cities mosques were open for the use of visiting Muslim merchants.[26]

There were four main groups of eastern-rite Christians living in Frankish territory: Byzantine Orthodox, Armenians, Syrian Orthodox, sometimes called Jacobites, and Maronites. Byzantine Orthodox communities were found in most cities, while in the Kingdom of Jerusalem almost all the Christian peasantry were members of that Church.[27] The Franks treated the Byzantine Orthodox as members of the Catholic Church to which they belonged themselves. Although no attempt was made to interfere with their traditional forms of worship and no pressure was put on them to conform to western doctrinal and disciplinary norms, the Orthodox were placed under the authority of Latin bishops and thus implicitly were forced

22 Prawer, *Crusader Institutions*, pp. 102–42.
23 J. Prawer, *The History of the Jews in the Latin Kingdom of Jerusalem* (Oxford, 1988).
24 Prawer, *Latin Kingdom*, pp. 233–51.
25 B.Z. Kedar, 'Some new sources on Palestinian Muslims before and during the Crusades', in H.-E. Mayer (ed.) and E. Müller-Luckner (assistant ed.), *Die Kreuzfahrerstaaten als multi-kulturelle Gesellschaft. Einwandere und Minderheiten im 12 und 13 Jahrhundert*, Schriften des Historisches Kollegs, Kolloquien, 37 (Munich, 1997), pp. 129–40.
26 Ibn Jubayr, pp. 318–19 and 321.
27 Although some Byzantine Orthodox used Greek as their liturgical language, many of them worshipped in Syriac, and for that reason twelfth-century writers often refer to them as Syrians.

to recognise the papal primacy,[28] but in areas where there were large Orthodox congregations co-adjutor Orthodox bishops were appointed to assist the Latin bishops in their pastoral work,[29] and the Orthodox kept all their monasteries. Nevertheless, they resented the fact that, unlike other eastern Christian churches, they did not enjoy ecclesiastical autonomy, and this was exacerbated by the policies of the Byzantine emperors, who appointed titular Orthodox patriarchs in exile at Constantinople and, when political circumstances permitted, sought to restore these prelates to power and to subvert the Catholic establishment.[30]

The other eastern-rite Churches were granted virtual autonomy by the Franks under their respective religious leaders. They were freed from the payment of the religious poll-tax to which they had been subject under Muslim rule and they retained their own churches, monasteries and endowments and were not made subject to the Catholic hierarchy.[31] All three groups were important to the Frankish rulers in different ways.

Armenian communities were found in most of the Frankish cities. The head of the Armenian Church, the Catholicus, lived in Muslim territory at Hromgla, and ruled over a huge diaspora in the Muslim world and also in the Byzantine Empire.[32] Unlike the other eastern-rite Christians the Armenians had preserved a landowning nobility throughout the centuries of Arab power, and so the Frankish nobility were able to treat with them on terms of social equality and to intermarry freely with them. Moreover, the independent Armenian state in Cilicia was a potential Frankish ally.[33] The Jacobites, or Syrian Orthodox, were found chiefly in the principality of Antioch,

---

[28] They continued to recite the Nicene Creed in the traditional way without the addition of the *Filioque*, to celebrate the Eucharist with leavened bread and to have married priests. There is no evidence that they were ever required to make any *explicit* profession of obedience to the Holy See before 1187. Hamilton, *Latin Church*, pp. 163–5.

[29] *Ibid.*, pp. 179–84.

[30] *Ibid.*, pp. 173–81.

[31] John of Ibelin lists the archbishops of the Jacobites and Armenians among the suffragans of the Latin patriarch of Jerusalem, *Livre*, c. II, ed. Edbury, *John of Ibelin*, p. 110. This presumably represents an updating of the source after the Armenian Church and the Jacobite Patriarch had entered into union with Rome in 1198 and 1236 respectively.

[32] The Catholicus Gregory III bought Hromgla from Beatrice of Edessa in c.1150, A.A. Bournoutian, 'Cilician Armenia', in G. Hovannisian (ed.), *The Armenian People from Ancient to Modern Times*, 2 vols. (London, 1997), I, pp. 278–9.

[33] B. Hamilton, 'The Armenian Church and the papacy at the time of the Crusades', *Eastern Churches Review* 10 (1978), pp. 61–87 at pp. 61–8.

although there were groups of them in other parts of the Frankish East including Jerusalem. The Jacobite patriarch normally lived in Muslim territory, but Frankish rulers were anxious to obtain his goodwill because of his contacts in the Muslim lands of northern Syria and also because his Church was in full communion with the Coptic Church of Egypt.[34] The Maronites and their patriarch lived mostly in Frankish territory in the Lebanon mountains. They were good fighting men and had an important role in the defence of Frankish border territory.[35]

Frankish lords owned more than 90 per cent of the land in the Crusader States and employed officials, some of whom were Franks and some native Christians, to superintend the collection of their dues and to enforce justice among their tenants.[36] Villages were normally inhabited by people of a single faith. Some new villages were estabished that were inhabited exclusively by Franks, but Ronnie Ellenblum has shown that in the Kingdom of Jerusalem Franks quite often settled in villages inhabited by eastern Christians, but avoided Muslim and Jewish villages.[37] In the latter, the Frankish landlords did not interfere with the peasants' way of life. Each village was under the authority of a *rais*, or headman, who was normally a substantial landholder in his own community. He was invested by the Frankish lord but was allowed to administer his village with minimum interference.[38]

The Frankish lords treated most of the non-Frankish peasants as serfs: they were bound to the land, but they enjoyed the usufruct of their holdings and security of tenure. They were required to pay a proportion of their produce to their Frankish landlords: normally this was assessed at between a quarter and a third of the grain crops and between a quarter and a half of the produce of vineyards, olive plantations and orchards. By the mid-twelfth century it was quite common for part or all of these dues to be commuted for money

---

[34] Hamilton, *Latin Church*, pp. 188–99.

[35] *Ibid.*, pp. 207–8.

[36] On the archaeological evidence for rural settlement in the Crusader Kingdom, see D. Pringle, *Secular Buildings in the Crusader Kingdom of Jerusalem. An Archeological Gazetteer* (Cambridge, 1997), pp. 11–13.

[37] R. Ellenblum, *Frankish Rural Settlement in the Kingdom of Jerusalem* (Cambridge, 1998).

[38] For a detailed general account of Frankish rural administration see J. Riley-Smith, *The Feudal Nobility and the Kingdom of Jerusalem, 1174–1272* (London, 1973), pp. 40–61; for a case study of the lordship of Tyre see Prawer, *Crusader Institutions*, pp. 143–200.

payments. But the peasants were not normally required to perform labour services for their lords, because the Franks did not introduce the manorial system in the Latin East and it was exceptional for a lord to have any demesne land.[39] Peasants had sometimes to supply corvées of labour for public works and this obligation must have proved very burdensome, for example when new Frankish castles were being built.[40]

Cities and castles were the centre of Frankish life. No independent communes developed in the Crusader States before 1187, but all towns were part of a royal or seigneurial lordship, and were governed by viscounts on behalf of the lord.[41] The Franks made Jerusalem an entirely Christian city: no Muslims, and very few Jews, were allowed to live there, although eastern Christians were encouraged to do so.[42] Even so, it remained rather sparsely inhabited in the twelfth century. In the other cities of the kingdom eastern Christians made up an important part of the population, and there were also Jewish communities in some of them.[43] The Franks had initially considered Muslims a security risk and had killed them or, more commonly, expelled them from the cities which they captured, but by the 1170s small numbers of Muslims were to be found in many cities. Large communities existed only in a very few, notably Tyre and some of the cities in the northern states.[44]

The coastal cities had been captured chiefly with the help of the Italian maritime communes, Venice, Genoa and Pisa, and in return the rulers of Antioch, Tripoli and Jerusalem had negotiated treaties guaranteeing to the communes privileges in one or more ports of the host state.[45] The Italian power was normally granted a quarter in

---

[39] Some Frankish lords owned vines or sugar plantations which were worked by their tenants, but the labour required seldom amounted to more than one day's service a week.

[40] E.g. the description of the fortification of Blanchegarde in 1142: 'vocatis artificibus simul et populo universo necessariis ministrante edificant solidis fundamentis et lapidibus quadris oppidum cum turribus quattuor congrue altitudinis': WT, XV, 25, p. 708.

[41] Prawer, *Crusader Institutions*, pp. 49–54.

[42] J. Prawer, 'The Latin settlement of Jerusalem', in *ibid.*, pp. 85–101.

[43] Jews were allowed to settle everywhere freely except in Jerusalem where Benjamin of Tudela found only four Jewish dyers in c.1170, Prawer, *Jews in the Latin Kingdom*, pp. 46–63. A variant reading of Benjamin of Tudela, accepted by Adler, numbered the Jews of Jerusalem at that time at 200: *Itinerary*, ed. and tr. M.N. Adler, p. 22.

[44] B.Z. Kedar, 'The subjected Muslims in the Frankish Levant', in J.M. Powell (ed.), *Muslims under Latin Rule, 1100–1300* (Princeton, NJ, 1990), pp. 135–74 at pp. 143–8; Muslims had not been completely excluded from Acre, Benvenisti, *Crusaders*, p. 82.

[45] G. Airaldi and B.Z. Kedar (eds.), *I communi italiani nel regno crociato di Gerusalemme* (Genoa, 1986).

each of the designated ports, to be governed by officials appointed by and responsible to the mother city, together with partial or total exemption from the payment of tariffs on all or some of their imports and exports.[46] Although at first Italians tended to stay in the Crusader States only for brief periods in order to conduct specific business deals, by the middle of the twelfth century some families had begun to settle there permanently, thus helping to restore the population of these cities to adequate levels. As the Italians established permanent colonies in Syria and Palestine their privileges produced many problems of interpretation and later rulers tried to restrict the immunities of the communes with varying degrees of success.[47] Yet despite such friction, the Italian communes had a vital role in the survival of the Crusader States. Their fleets kept the lines of communication with the West open, bringing out each year large numbers of pilgrims, soldiers and settlers, all of whom were needed to strengthen Frankish rule in the conquered territories. Moreover, the Italians had commercial skills which the Franks lacked, but which were needed to develop the economic wealth of the states, which lay chiefly in trade.

Good farming land, although it existed in the Latin East, was not abundant, although the Frankish states were able to produce enough food to supply their own needs except in times of prolonged drought.[48] Their most important export was cane sugar, for which there was a huge market in the West. Large plantations were developed wherever enough water was available for refining, notably at Jericho in the Jordan valley and around Sidon and Acre on the coastal plain. But the principal trade was in luxury goods of high intrinsic value, such as Damascus steel, Arab goldsmiths' work and jewellery, incense, Persian carpets and ceramics, Chinese silks, and spices and medicinal drugs from the East Indies. This trade was conducted with merchants from Damascus and Aleppo, who were willing to have commercial dealings with the Franks because they controlled all the Syrian outlets of Mediterranean trade. The ports of the Crusader States in the twelfth century thus came to occupy a

[46] Prawer, *Crusader Institutions*, pp. 217–49.
[47] *Ibid.*, pp. 226–9.
[48] J. Richard, 'Agricultural conditions in the Crusader States. A. Agriculture in Latin Syria', in Setton, *Crusades*, V, pp. 253–66.

key position in the Mediterranean economy and this generated the financial resources that these states needed for survival.[49]

Despite their amicable commercial relations with neighbouring Muslim powers, the Franks were seldom free from the threat of attack by them. Most important cities were walled, and stone towers were built in some substantial villages to shelter the population from Muslim raiding parties.[50] Many castles were built throughout the Crusader States that served a dual purpose; they were centres of Frankish administration and government, but they were also centres of defence, capable of resisting a siege by an invading army until a relief force could be mustered.[51] Provided that these castles were adequately garrisoned it was impossible for an invader to make any substantial conquests, since he would inevitably become involved in a series of lengthy sieges. But it was not always possible for the Franks to remain shut up in their fortresses in the face of an invasion, because a large enemy army could jeopardise the economic well-being of the kingdom by laying waste the countryside. Yet in order to muster a large enough field army to repel such invasions, Frankish rulers were forced to reduce castle and city garrisons to dangerously low levels. That is why they were often reluctant to fight pitched battles, even when the host had been assembled, because if the battle were lost the undermanned fortresses would be unable to offer much resistance.

The backbone of the Frankish field army consisted of the knight-service owed to the crown by the royal vassals. According to a list dating from the reign of Baldwin V (1185–6) preserved by the thirteenth-century jurist John of Ibelin, the king of Jerusalem was owed service of between 670 and 677 knights.[52] In addition, 5,025 sergeants were owed to the crown by the burgesses of the cities and by the Latin Church.[53] R.C. Smail has argued convincingly that

---

[49] For a brief survey of the commerce of the Latin East, see Prawer, *Latin Kingdom*, pp. 382–415.

[50] Benvenisti, *Crusaders*, pp. 273–6.

[51] P. Deschamps, in *La défense du royaume de Jérusalem* (vol. II of *Les châteaux des croisés en Terre Sainte* (Paris, 1939)), argued that castles in the Frankish East were built in conformity with an overall strategy of defence, but this view has received little support from later writers. See specially the critique of R.C. Smail, *Crusading Warfare 1097–1193*, 2nd edn. (Cambridge, 1995), pp. 204–44; H. Kennedy, *Crusader Castles* (Cambridge, 1994); Pringle, *Secular Buildings*.

[52] John of Ibelin, *Livre*, c. XIII, ed. Edbury, *John of Ibelin*, pp. 118–20. The figures that John gives can be differently computed, Smail, *Crusading Warfare*, pp. 89–90; Edbury, *John of Ibelin*, p. 133.

[53] John of Ibelin, *Livre*, c. XV, ed. Edbury, *John of Ibelin*, pp. 124–6.

these sergeants were infantrymen who could normally only be deployed for defensive purposes, since they lacked the mobility essential for raids into enemy territory.[54]

The prince of Antioch had commanded the service of 700 knights in the first quarter of the twelfth century,[55] but although there are no comparable figures for Baldwin IV's reign that number must have been considerably reduced because the principality had lost a great deal of territory. The prince was not under any obligation to supply knights to the crown, but normally sent a contingent of troops to the help of the southern kingdom in an emergency if his own military commitments permitted this. The count of Tripoli commanded the service of some 300 knights and owed service of 100 to the King of Jerusalem.[56]

It is self-evident that armies of this size were never large enough to defend territories as extensive as those which the Franks ruled. As Edbury has pointed out, the crown vassals almost certainly maintained more fighting men than those knights whose service they owed to the king,[57] and the crown certainly recruited additional troops from the local population, both Frankish and indigenous, as well as from western soldiers who had come to seek their fortunes in the Latin East. In times of crisis the king might issue the *arrière ban* and summon all able-bodied Franks to the defence of the kingdom, but that was a desperate and not very effective measure since most of the men who responded would have had no adequate military training.[58]

Because the realm was under continual threat of attack by Muslim powers, Jerusalem differed from western monarchies in that knight-service was not limited to a forty-day period, but the king might in theory call on his vassals to serve for the entire year. But knight-service was only given freely for defensive campaigns and if the king wanted his vassals to serve outside the realm, for example in Egypt, he had to pay them.[59] Visiting western princes were often willing to

---

[54] Smail, *Crusading Warfare*, p. 91.

[55] Walter the Chancellor, *Bella Antiochena*, ed. H. Hagenmeyer (Innsbruck, 1896), II, 5, p. 88.

[56] John of Ibelin, *Livre*, c. X, ed. Edbury, *John of Ibelin*, p. 114; Richard, *Tripoli*, p. 33, n. 1.

[57] Edbury, *John of Ibelin*, p. 131.

[58] See p. 134 below.

[59] John of Ibelin, *Livre*, c. 217, RHC Lois I, p. 346. H.-E. Mayer, 'Le service militaire des vassaux à l'étranger et le financement des campagnes en Syrie du nord et en Egypte au XIIe siècle', *Mélanges sur l'histoire du royaume latin de Jérusalem*, Mémoires de l'Académie des Inscriptions et Belles-Lettres, n.s., 5 (Paris, 1984), pp. 93–161.

place their retinues at the disposal of the crown for a particular campaign, but such sources of help were unpredictable and that is why all the rulers of the Frankish East welcomed the formation of the military Orders.

The Knights Templar and the Knights of St John (or Knights Hospitaller) were members of international religious Orders which considered the defence of the Holy Land their chief priority. In addition, the Order of St John was committed to charitable work, and the hospital that it ran in Jerusalem had more than 750 beds and was the biggest in Christendom.[60] By 1174 both Orders had come to play a major part in the defence of the Latin East. The Templars held the Amanus march to the north-west of Antioch, and the lordship of Tortosa and the castle of Safita (Chastel Blanc) in the county of Tripoli.[61] The Knights of St John also held a great marcher lordship in that county centred on Crac des Chevaliers, and in 1168 Bohemond III of Antioch granted them the march of Afamiya. Both grants included lands which the Muslims had conquered but which it was hoped the Order would regain, and when making these donations the secular rulers renounced all rights of lordship to the Knights, who thus came to enjoy virtually sovereign powers in those areas.[62] In the Kingdom of Jerusalem by 1174 the Templars held the castles of Gaza, Safad, Ahamant and La Fève, and the Hospitallers those of Bethgibelin and Belvoir.[63] The evidence suggests that by Baldwin IV's reign the Orders could jointly supply almost as many knights to the host as the royal vassals.[64]

The knights and sergeants of the military Orders were the most professionally trained and ideologically committed contingents in the Frankish armies and were respected and feared by their Muslim

---

[60] John of Würzburg estimates the number at 2,000 beds: *Description of the Holy Land*, tr. in J. Wilkinson, *Jerusalem Pilgrimage, 1099–1185*, Hakluyt Society, 2nd ser., 167 (London, 1988), pp. 266–7. That is probably an exaggeration, but the hospital was able to admit 750 casualties at once after the battle of Mont Gisard: R. Röhricht (ed.), *Beiträge zur Geschichte der Kreuzzüge*, 2 vols. (Berlin, 1874–8), II, p. 128, no. 45.

[61] J. Riley-Smith, 'The Templars and the Teutonic Knights in Cilician Armenia', in T.S.R. Boase (ed.), *The Cilician Kingdom of Armenia* (Edinburgh, 1978), pp. 92–117 at pp. 92–7; J. Riley-Smith, 'The Templars and the castle of Tortosa in Syria: an unknown document concerning the acquisition of the fortress', EHR 84 (1969), pp. 278–88.

[62] J. Riley-Smith, *The Knights of St John in Jerusalem and Cyprus (1050–1310)* (London, 1967), pp. 55–6 and 66.

[63] *Ibid.*, pp. 52 and 69; M. Barber, *The New Knighthood. A History of the Order of the Temple* (Cambridge, 1994), pp. 73 and 86–7.

[64] Prawer, *Latin Kingdom*, p. 261.

opponents. Moreover, the Orders were financially independent. They owned property in the Latin East and throughout western Europe from which they drew the income to support and train their brethren and to build and maintain an impressive range of fortresses (and, in the case of the Order of St John, of hospitals also) in the Latin East.

Despite their long coastline the Syrian Franks never developed a navy of their own. The only Muslim power in the Levant during the twelfth century that had a navy was Fatimid Egypt, but once the Franks had captured Ascalon in 1153 it became impractical for the Fatimid fleet to stay at sea long enough to raid the Syrian coast because it could no longer take new supplies of fresh water aboard. The Fatimid navy began to decline and when Baldwin IV became king the Franks had not been threatened from the sea for some twenty years and had no incentive to build up a fleet of their own.[65]

By 1174 the Franks had been settled in the Levant for three-quarters of a century and had adapted to local conditions. Many of them lived in stone-built houses and could afford to dress in fabrics such as silk and cotton, which were prohibitively expensive in the West. They made regular use of the public baths which existed in all the main cities and they ate the more varied and exotic foods which the land supplied, although there were limits to their adaptability – they were, for example, unwilling to eat rice.[66] These evidences of a more prosperous and self-indulgent lifestyle surprised and sometimes shocked newcomers from the West,[67] but such changes were super-ficial. Some intermarriage had taken place between them and the indigenous population. Franks were forbidden by law to marry, or indeed to have any kind of sexual relations with Muslims, unless they were first willing to accept Christian baptism,[68] but they could marry freely with eastern-rite Christians and such unions were reasonably common: Baldwin IV had Armenian great-grandmothers on both sides of his family.[69] Even so, the Franks remained fundamentally

[65] J.H. Pryor, *Geography, Technology and War. Studies in the History of the Maritime Mediterranean, 649–1571* (Cambridge, 1988), pp. 112–25, specially p. 116.

[66] Prawer, *Latin Kingdom*, p. 363.

[67] The most impassioned denunciation of the effeminate luxury of the Syrian Franks was made a generation later than this by James of Vitry, bishop of Acre, R.B.C. Huygens (ed.), *Lettres de Jacques de Vitry (1160/70–1240), évêque de Saint-Jean d'Acre* (Leiden, 1960), pp. 79–97.

[68] Canons XII–XV of the Council of Nablus of 1120, Mansi, XXI, col. 264.

[69] On his father's side Baldwin was descended from Morphia of Melitene, wife of Baldwin II, on his mother's side from the unnamed Rupenid princess, sister of Leo I, who married Joscelin I of Edessa. See Genealogy I.

distinct from their native subjects. They were Catholic in religion, French in speech,[70] and western in culture. They even dressed in a western way, for although some of their clothes might be made from eastern fabrics, they were normally cut in contemporary western styles.[71] Moreover, all power in central and regional government was vested in their hands. Intermarriage between Franks and native Christians did not modify this situation in any material way, since the children of mixed marriages followed their fathers' religion and thus inherited their legal status.

But it should be stressed that the barrier between the Franks and their native subjects was a religious and not an ethnic one, for Franks were defined in law not as people of western European origin, but as Christians 'of the law of Rome'. This was an important distinction, because it meant that a member of any native community, Muslim or eastern Christian, could enjoy full legal rights as a Frankish citizen if he was received into the Catholic Church. There is evidence that such conversions did take place,[72] but they were uncommon, because conversion entailed not merely a change of religion but also a break with an entire cultural tradition.

Most of the indigenous population who did not change their faith were relegated to the position of second-class citizens, for they were barred from all real exercise of power and from many of the legal privileges that the Franks enjoyed. The Muslims and Jews living under Frankish rule, although comparatively well treated, did not consider their situation idyllic. Since Islam makes no distinction in the community of the faithful between 'church' and state, Christian lordship was itself a cause of religious tension for the Muslims, a fact that their Christian rulers failed to appreciate. Ibn Jubayr, who visited these communities in 1184, expressed the orthodox Muslim view: 'There can be no excuse in the eyes of God for a Muslim to stay in any infidel country, save when passing through it, while the way lies clear to Muslim lands.'[73] As Prawer has shown, the Jews were alienated because, with rare exceptions, they were forbidden to live in the Holy City, even though they were allowed to visit it and to

---

[70] French was the official language in all three states, though other western ethnic groups, notably the Italians, kept their own languages. Prawer has drawn attention to the paucity of Arabic loan-words in western sources from the Latin East, *Latin Kingdom*, pp. 521–2.
[71] J. Prawer, *The World of the Crusaders* (Jerusalem, 1972), p. 87.
[72] Riley-Smith, *Feudal Nobility*, pp. 10–11.
[73] Ibn Jubayr, pp. 321–2.

pray at the Western Wall. They therefore welcomed Saladin as a new Cyrus when, after 1187, he allowed them to return to the old Jewish quarter of the city.[74]

Many even of the eastern Christians regarded the Franks as alien. The problem here was mainly one of language, for many eastern Christians were Arabic speakers who shared a common cultural tradition with their Muslim neighbours. Most Frankish nobles did not speak Arabic well,[75] and because of this some native Christians found Muslim rulers more approachable despite the differences in religion.[76]

Such was the kingdom which Baldwin IV was called to rule in 1174. Yet it should be emphasised that although strong devolutionary tendencies were at work in the state the powers of the crown were by no means negligible. The king was, of course, undisputed commander-in-chief of the army. Moreover, the vast extent of the royal demesne in some measure acted as a counterpoise to the power of the magnates. The crown also possessed alternative sources of income: minting was a royal monopoly in twelfth-century Jerusalem,[77] and in addition the king received taxes paid by Beduin tribesmen as well as the religious taxes of his non-Christian subjects.[78] Customs and harbour dues formed a particularly important part of the royal revenues,[79] for despite the immunities granted to Italian merchants they did not then normally travel to the interior. Consequently Muslim merchants had to come to Frankish ports to trade with them, and Muslims had no commercial privileges and had to pay full tariffs on all imports and exports.[80] Since every port in the kingdom, irrespective of who held the lordship of the city in

[74] Prawer, *Jews in the Latin Kingdom*, pp. 64–71.
[75] E.g. Baha al-Din remarks that Reynald of Sidon 'knew Arabic, and was able to speak it', RHC Or III, pp. 121–2. Conversely, Huygens points out that there is no proof that William of Tyre knew Arabic, WT, p. 2.
[76] C. Cahen, 'Indigènes et croisés', *Syria* 15 (1934), pp. 351–60.
[77] Prawer, *Latin Kingdom*, p. 81. This monopoly was sometimes flouted, D.M. Metcalf, *Coinage of the Crusades and the Latin East in the Ashmolean Museum, Oxford* (London, 1983), pp. 24–5.
[78] Prawer, *Crusader Institutions*, p. 214; *Latin Kingdom*, pp. 49–50.
[79] Among the reasons for which a king might confiscate the fief of a tenant-in-chief without judgment of peers was this: 'se aucun home lige ou terrier ou baron dou reaume faiseit faire port en sa terre, de naves et de vaisseaus et chemin en paienime por amender sa terre et amermer les droitures dou roi': *Livre au roi*, c. 16, pp. 180–1. On the revenues of ports in the Crusader Kingdom, Riley-Smith, *Feudal Nobility*, pp. 62–80.
[80] J. Riley-Smith, 'Government in Latin Syria and the commercial privileges of foreign merchants', in D. Baker (ed.), *Relations between East and West in the Middle Ages* (Edinburgh, 1973), pp. 109–32.

which it was situated, was directly under the control of the king, commercial dealings were an important source of income to the crown.[81] The royal officials who staffed the port authority, known as the *cathena*, had high professional standards. Ibn Jubayr, who visited Acre in the reign of Baldwin IV, was clearly impressed by the 'Christian clerks of the customs with their ebony inkstands ornamented with gold', who were fluent Arabic speakers and were efficient and polite as well.[82]

The kings of twelfth-century Jerusalem also possessed considerable powers of church patronage.[83] By contrast, their powers over their lay vassals, although not insignificant, were more restricted. According to the *Livre au roi* there were certain offences for which a king might dispossess a vassal without judgment of the High Court.[84] Moreover, in theory the *Assise sur la ligèce* enacted in Amalric's reign greatly increased royal power by requiring all rear-vassals in the lordships to do homage to the king.[85] It is difficult to know how often this law was invoked. It was framed to allow rear vassals who were dispossessed of their fiefs by their lords without judgment of peers to appeal to the king for justice. In theory this meant that all rear vassals had a right to attend the High Court, but there is no evidence that they ever normally exercised it. Although this law was used in the thirteenth century to restrict the power of the crown, its initial consequence was to strengthen royal authority, at least in theory. In other ways the king's powers over his vassals were very limited. Except in unusual circumstances the crown did not exercise rights of wardship for minor heirs: the child's mother or nearest kinsman would normally administer the fief until he came of age.[86] Nor could the king require a widowed heiress to remarry until a year and a day had elapsed after the death of her husband, and he was then obliged

---

[81] Knights were granted *fiefs en besant*, money fiefs, from the crown revenues in the maritime cities: Prawer, *Crusader Institutions*, pp. 31–4.

[82] Ibn Jubayr, pp. 317–18.

[83] Hamilton, *Latin Church*, pp. 52–85 and 113–36.

[84] *Livre au roi*, c. 16, pp. 177–84.

[85] John of Ibelin, *Livre*, cc. 140 and 198–202, RHC Lois I, pp. 214–15 and 318–24; James of Ibelin, *Livre*, cc. 3 and 10–11, RHC Lois I, pp. 455 and 457–8; Geoffrey Le Tort, *Livre*, c. 11, RHC Lois I, p. 438; Philip of Novara, *Livre*, cc. 50–1, RHC Lois I, pp. 525–7. For some interpretations of the Assise see J. Richard, 'Pairie d'Orient latin: les quatres baronnies des royaumes de Jérusalem et de Chypre', RHDFE, sér. 4, 28 (1950), pp. 67–88; Riley-Smith, *Feudal Nobility*, pp. 34–7; Prawer, *Crusader Institutions*, pp. 36–45; G.A. Loud, 'The Assise sur la ligèce and Ralph of Tiberias', in CS, pp. 404–12.

[86] Riley-Smith, *Feudal Nobility*, p. 38.

to offer her the choice of three suitors, none of whom might be disparaging in rank to her or to her former husband.[87] This provision considerably limited the king's patronage.

A successful king needed to work harmoniously with a relatively small group of powerful men, some forty in number, consisting of the other members of the royal family, the great officers of state, the principal crown vassals, the leaders of the Catholic hierarchy, the masters of the military Orders and the representatives of the Italian communes. Although the High Court of Jerusalem was in theory the chief advisory body in the kingdom, it was not a suitable forum for discussing major issues because many of the most influential men had no seat in it. The custom therefore grew up of the king's summoning a more representative assembly to consider major questions of policy. William of Tyre uses the term *curia generalis* to describe such meetings and it has been adopted in this book. Such assemblies might be attended by whatever advisers the king chose to call. They normally included all important members of the High Court, the great officers of state, the patriarch of Jerusalem and some of the Catholic bishops and abbots, the masters of the military Orders, and in certain circumstances representatives of the Frankish burgesses.[88]

Yet although this machinery for broadly based discussion existed and was used, much of the responsibility for successful government rested with the king. Some of the more important men in the kingdom, for example the masters of the military Orders, were not his subjects, and a king needed, in more than common measure, gifts of tact, firmness and sound judgment of character to hold in check the sectional interests represented at those gatherings and to inspire their members with unity of purpose. Although the *curia generalis* was the most representative policy-making body in the kingdom, it consisted only of Frankish members. The king had also to provide for the interests of his non-Catholic subjects, and this traditionally had been done by treating with the heads of their religious communities.[89] This was an important royal function and one that was entirely personal to the monarch.

[87] Philip of Novara, *Livre*, c. 86, RHC Lois I, pp. 558–9.
[88] This is implied by William of Tyre in his account of the *curia generalis* of 1183. The text that he gives of the decree about taxation states that it has been enacted 'de communi omnium principum tam ecclesiasticorum quam secularium, et de assensu universe plebis regni Ierosolimorum': WT, XXII, 24, p. 1044.
[89] Hamilton, *Latin Church*, pp. 188–211.

In the summer of 1174 the international situation of the Latin Kingdom was particularly critical. It was unfortunate that this should have coincided with a royal minority when the king was unable to act as a unifying force in the government. There was no precedent to which the king's advisers could look for guidance, because the only other royal minority, that of Baldwin III in 1143, had occurred when his mother, Melisende, had already been co-ruler with King Fulk so that there was no break in the conduct of government. Nobody could provide the same degree of continuity in 1174.

CHAPTER 4

The international status of the kingdom

When Amalric became king in 1163 the Crusader States were menaced by the power of Nur ad-Din, ruler of Damascus and Aleppo, whose brother, Qutb ad-Din Mawdud, ruled northern Iraq from Mosul. Nur ad-Din and Amalric fought each other for control of the weak and faction-torn Fatimid caliphate of Cairo, and early in 1169 Nur ad-Din's general Shirkuh was victorious. When Shirkuh died two months later his nephew Saladin became effective ruler of Egypt although in theory he was only the vizir of the Fatimid caliph, and Amalric's attempt in the autumn of 1169 to dislodge him from power with the support of the Byzantine navy was a fiasco.[1] The situation of the Crusader States then became extremely hazardous because they were surrounded by a single and hostile Islamic power.

Amalric and his advisers did not consider that trying to live at peace with Nur ad-Din was an option. His dedication to the *jihad* was not in doubt, for he had commissioned a pulpit which he intended to place in the al-Aqsa mosque when he recaptured Jerusalem.[2] In any case, Frankish experience during the previous seventy years led Amalric to reject as unrealistic the possibility of peaceful coexistence. Strong Muslim powers had consistently been hostile to the Franks and during that time Edessa had been lost, Antioch shorn of half its territory, the eastern marches of Tripoli had been overrun and the defences of the Kingdom of Jerusalem seriously weakened. Unless they attempted to exploit Muslim weaknesses the Syrian Franks would be surrounded by a unified Muslim

[1] WT, XX, 13–17, pp. 926–34; H. Ahrweiler, *Byzance et la mer* (Paris, 1966), pp. 263–7; R.-J. Lilie, *Byzantium and the Crusader States, 1096–1204*, tr. J.E. Ridings (Oxford, 1993), pp. 200–2.
[2] N. Elisséeff, 'Les monuments de Nur ad-Din', *Bulletin d'études orientales de l'Institut français de Damas* 13 (1949–51), pp. 5–43.

63

state whose ruler would then use his combined resources to wage the holy war against them. Yet if the Franks were to adopt an aggressive policy they needed allies.

Their natural allies were the Catholic powers of western Europe to whom they were linked by ties of kinship, faith and culture, and in 1169 Amalric sent an embassy led by the archbishop of Tyre to ask the chief rulers of the West for help, but it proved fruitless.[3] This was a consequence of the complex political situation in western Europe. Since 1159 there had been a papal schism. Alexander III (1159–81) was recognised as lawful pope in the Latin East[4] and in almost all the rest of western Christendom except the Empire. Frederick I Barbarossa acknowledged the rival candidate, Victor IV (1159–64), and after his death secured the appointment of a succession of antipopes. Frederick wished to make imperial power a reality in Italy and to enthrone his antipope in Rome, but he was opposed by a group of Lombard communes, which supported Alexander III and were subsidised by the king of Sicily and the Byzantine emperor, both of whom feared the growth of western imperial power in Italy. This struggle was unresolved at the time of Amalric's death, and while it lasted no new crusade would be preached.[5]

The realisation that he would receive no help from the West drove Amalric to look for allies elsewhere, and the only realistic alternative was the Byzantine Empire, the greatest Christian power in the eastern Mediterranean. Recent scholarship has emphasised how considerable Byzantine economic resources were in the twelfth century and how expertly they were harnessed by the central government. The emperor, Manuel I Comnenus, strove hard and successfully to restore the image of Byzantium as a great world power. The empire in his reign certainly looked very strong: it comprised the fertile coastlands of Asia Minor, Cyprus, Crete and the Greek islands, Greece, Thrace and Bulgaria, while for the first time in centuries the western Balkans also acknowledged Byzantine overlordship. Manuel had built up a powerful navy once more and his large, well-equipped and professionally trained armies

---

[3] WT, XX, 12, p. 926 and 25 p. 947; R.C. Smail, 'Latin Syria and the West, 1149–1187', *TRHS*, 5th ser., 19 (1969), pp. 1–20 at pp. 13–14.

[4] B. Hamilton, *The Latin Church in the Crusader States. The Secular Church* (London, 1980), p. 76.

[5] M. Pacaut, *Alexandre III. Etude sur la conception du pouvoir pontifical dans sa pensée et dans son œuvre* (Paris, 1956).

campaigned in Hungary, South Italy, Syria and Egypt, while his ambassadors were sent to most of the courts of the known world.[6]

Foreign ambassadors who visited his court were impressed, as Manuel intended they should be, by his wealth. Constantinople was itself a great diplomatic asset. It was the largest city in the Christian world, and the only city of the ancient Roman Empire which had survived into the twelfth century without ever having been sacked. It was a treasure-house of antique sculpture; it had fine stone buildings, well-paved main streets, and many churches adorned with costly mosaics. Its harbour, the Golden Horn, was one of the great centres of Mediterranean trade, situated at the confluence of the Aegean and Black Seas, and visitors were impressed by the volume and variety of its commerce and by the amount of money that the emperor received in customs dues.[7]

Manuel made astute use of the amenities of his capital and of the antique ceremonial of the imperial court to impress ambassadors. The liturgy in the Cathedral of the Holy Wisdom was the most splendid in Christendom; lavish public displays were provided for official visitors in the Hippodrome; the emperor took great care to furnish the rooms in which he gave audience with objects of intrinsic value and aesthetic merit; and he was willing to spend large sums of money, with apparent indifference to cost, on the entertainment of his guests.[8] Ambassadors sent to Constantinople came away impressed by the magnificence of the capital and the lavish display of imperial wealth.

Manuel had campaigned in Syria in 1159 and had shown then that he was willing to accept the existence of the Crusader States provided that their rulers would acknowledge him as their overlord. This marked a radical change from the policies of his predecessors, who had wished to impose direct imperial rule in Antioch.[9] Manuel strengthened his ties with the Latin East in 1161 by taking as his second wife Mary, the sister of Bohemond III of Antioch.[10]

Baldwin III of Jerusalem had been prepared to co-operate with Manuel, but at first Amalric was not. The reasons for this were

[6] P. Magdalino, *The Empire of Manuel I Komnenos, 1143–1180* (Cambridge, 1994).

[7] Benjamin of Tudela, who was widely travelled in the Islamic as well as the Christian world, is a gauge of the impression which the commercial wealth of Constantinople made on visitors during Manuel's reign: *Itinerary*, ed. and tr. M.N. Adler (London, 1907), pp. 11–14.

[8] Magdalino, 'Ceremonial', in *Manuel I*, pp. 237–48.

[9] Lilie, *Byzantium*, pp. 175–84.

[10] WT, XVIII, 31, p. 857; Cinnamus, *Epitome*, IV, 17, V, 4, ed. Meineke, pp. 178–80 and 211.

partly cultural, and his attitude towards the Byzantines was shared by many of his subjects. Twelfth-century Byzantium was rather like eighteenth-century China: both empires were heirs of a very ancient tradition, and both had rulers who regarded themselves as the only divinely constituted secular authority on earth. While willing to treat foreign visitors with consideration, both empires regarded all other peoples as barbarians. The Byzantines saw little to admire either in the chivalric code by which the Frankish nobility lived or in their dedication to the holy war against Islam. Not unnaturally this Byzantine sense of innate superiority was greatly resented by the Frankish nobility in the Crusader States.[11]

When the Franks suffered a major defeat at the hands of Nur ad-Din in 1164, whereas Bohemond III of Antioch turned to Manuel for help and did homage to him for his principality, Amalric appealed to Louis VII of France to come to the East to save the Franks there from 'that emperor whom we greatly fear', adding that otherwise it would be necessary to surrender Antioch either to the Turks or to the Greeks.[12] His views gradually changed when no western aid came, and in 1167 he formed closer links with Byzantium by marrying Manuel's great-niece, Maria Comnena.[13] But it was not until after the failure of his second appeal to the West in 1169 that he resolved, in consultation with his advisers, to make a firm commitment to Byzantium. In 1171 he paid a state visit to Constantinople, which was unprecedented, for no earlier king of Jerusalem had ever left the Latin East. He was received with great cordiality and discussed the problems of his kingdom with the emperor, and there seems no reason to doubt the Byzantine assertion that he acknowledged Manuel as his overlord.[14]

Manuel did not impose any onerous conditions on the Franks, but

---

[11] The tone of twelfth-century Byzantine sentiments about the West is perhaps best exemplified by Anna Comnena. Although the *Alexiad* was a history of her father's reign, she was still writing it when she died in Manuel's reign. She represented the conservative views of the Byzantine aristocracy of the mid-twelfth century. Anna Comnena, *Alexiad*, ed. with French tr., B. Leib, 3 vols. (Paris, 1937–45).

[12] *Regum et Principum Epistolae*, no. IX, ed. J. Bongars, 2 vols. in 1 (Hanover, 1611), I, p. 1176.

[13] Cinnamus, *Epitome*, V, 13, ed. Meineke, pp. 237–8; WT, XX, 1, p. 913; B. Hamilton, 'Women in the Crusader States: the queens of Jerusalem 1100–1190', *Medieval Women* (Oxford, 1978), pp. 161–74 at p. 161.

[14] WT, XX, 22–4, pp. 940–6; J.L. Lamonte, 'To what extent was the Byzantine emperor the suzerain of the Latin Crusading States?', *Byzantion*, 7 (1932), pp. 253–64; Lilie, *Byzantium* pp. 204–9; S. Runciman, 'The visit of King Amalric I to Constantinople in 1171', in *Outremer*, pp. 153–8.

he did reassert his traditional role as protector of the Holy Places and of the Orthodox community in the Holy Land.[15] He paid for the restoration of various Orthodox monasteries in the Judaean desert and also commissioned artists to redecorate the shrines of the Holy Sepulchre and the Holy Nativity with elaborate mosaics.[16] This was excellent publicity, since all pilgrims, of whatever rite, visited those churches and at Bethlehem they saw a painting of the emperor hanging in the sanctuary of the Latin cathedral in recognition of his work as a benefactor.[17]

Perhaps as an outward sign of their commitment to the emperor, the rulers of Jerusalem on formal occasions adopted Byzantine court dress.[18] Although there was no Byzantine military presence in the Latin East, Byzantine protection was undoubtedly very valuable: Nur ad-Din had certainly been deterred from attacking Antioch after his victory at Harim in 1164 because he feared Byzantine reprisals, and it seems likely that he did not attempt to exploit the weak points in the defences of Tripoli and Jerusalem after 1171 for the same reason. But this, of course, is only evident in retrospect, and the Byzantine protectorate did not inhibit Amalric from seeking other allies in addition.

There was little prospect of finding them in the Near East. The Franks had no ideological objections to forming alliances with Muslim rulers and had done so since the early years of their settlement. In Amalric's reign the nearest independent Muslim power to the Crusader States was that of Kilij-Arslan II (1156–92), Seljuk sultan of Iconium. He too was hostile to the growth of Nur ad-Din's empire and, indeed, in 1157 'had proposed to the Christian princes of Cilicia, Antioch and Jerusalem a coalition against Nur ad-Din'.[19] When Manuel campaigned in Syria in 1159, Nur ad-Din,

---

[15] The Fatimid caliphs had recognised this before the First Crusade. E.g. the Holy Sepulchre was rebuilt in 1048 under the patronage of Constantine IX: B.C. Corbo, *Il Santo Sepolcro a Gerusalemme*, 3 vols. (Jerusalem, 1981–2), I, pp. 139–81, II, pl. 4 and 5.

[16] Hamilton, *Latin Church*, pp. 164, 166–8 and 184; A. Jotischky, 'Manuel Comnenus and the reunion of the Churches. The evidence of the Conciliar mosaics in the Church of the Nativity in Bethlehem', *Levant* 26 (1994), pp. 207–23; J. Folda, *The Art of the Crusaders in the Holy Land, 1098–1187* (Cambridge 1995), pp. 347–78, 404–9; D. Pringle, *The Churches of the Crusader Kingdom of Jerusalem. An Archaeological Gazetteer* (Cambridge, 1997), I, pp. 137–56.

[17] John Phocas, in J. Wilkinson, *Jerusalem Pilgrimage, 1099–1185*, Hakluyt Society, 2nd ser., 167 (London, 1988), p. 333.

[18] H.-E. Mayer, 'Das Pontifikale von Tyrus und die Krönung der lateinischen Könige von Jerusalem', *DOP* 21 (1967), pp. 171–216 at pp. 174–82.

[19] C. Cahen, *Pre-Ottoman Turkey. A General Survey of the Material and Spiritual Culture and History, c.1071–1330*, tr. J. Jones-Williams (London, 1968), p. 100.

who did not want to fight the Byzantines, made peace with him and agreed to aid the emperor against the sultan of Iconium. Faced by imperial attacks from the west and those of Nur ad-Din from the east, Kilij-Arslan went to Constantinople in 1162 to sue for peace, and that peace was kept as long as Nur ad-Din lived. Thus the Franks could not look to Kilij-Arslan for help against Nur ad-Din, and he concentrated on imposing his authority on the independent Turkish emirs in Anatolia, notably the Danishmendids and the Mangujakids of Erzinjan.[20]

Other Muslim powers were either too weak or too distant to be of any help to the Franks. The Artuqid Turks, who ruled in eastern Anatolia at Hisn Kaifa and Amida, and at Mardin and Mayyafariqin, acknowledged Nur ad-Din as their overlord,[21] while the lesser Turkish rulers, who had become independent after the collapse of the power of the Seljuk sultans in the western lands, such as the Saltakids of Erzerum and the Shah Arman at Akhlat, were too remote and too weak to challenge the power of the Zengids even had they wished to do so.[22] To the east of the Zengid lands was Iraq, where the Caliph al-Muqtafi (1136–60) had thrown off Seljuk control, and where he and his successors exercised temporal power for the first time in two centuries.[23] Although the caliphs were not always in agreement with the Zengid princes, they could clearly never ally with the infidel Franks against Sunnite rulers. The greatest power in the eastern lands of the caliphate was Shams ad-Din Eldiguz (1137–75), whose power-base was in Azerbaijan but whose lands extended as far south as Isfahan, and who, through his marriage to the widow of the Seljuk Sultan Toghril II, became the stepfather and protector of the Sultan Mu'izz ad-Din Arslan (1161–76). Yet although he might have had the strength to challenge the Zengids, his energies were concentrated on holding in check the growing power of the Khwarazm shahs to the east and the kings of Georgia to the north.[24] There were thus no potential Muslim allies to whom the Franks might turn for support against Nur ad-Din.

There were independent Christian kings in Nubia, but the rulers

[20] Magdalino, *Manuel I*, pp. 76–8; Cahen, *Pre-Ottoman Turkey*, pp. 96–103.
[21] Cahen, *Pre-Ottoman Turkey*, p. 102; Elisséeff, *Nur ad-Din*, II, pp. 678–81.
[22] Cahen, *Pre-Ottoman Turkey*, pp. 106–7.
[23] C.E. Bosworth, 'The political and dynastic history of the Iranian world (A.D. 1000–1217)', in *The Cambridge History of Iran*, V, ed. J.A. Boyle, *The Saljuq and Mongol Periods* (Cambridge, 1968), pp. 1–202 at pp. 127–8 and 167–8.
[24] *Ibid.*, pp. 169–70 and 176–9.

of the Crusader States had no contact with them. There were two kingdoms: Makouria, with its capital at Dongola, comprised the region from Aswan to Abu Hamed, just north of the fifth cataract, and the kingdom of Alwa lay to the south of that. The kings of Makouria could have been useful allies to the Franks in any attack they made on Egypt.[25] When Saladin seized power the Makourians invaded and sacked Aswan, and an army had to be sent against them, led by Saladin's brother, Turan-Shah, which retook Aswan and carried the war into Nubia. A Muslim garrison was stationed briefly at Qasr Ibrim in Nubian territory, but was soon withdrawn, and there was peace between the two states for the rest of Saladin's reign.[26] Thus two Christian powers, Makouria and the Latin Kingdom, both hostile to Saladin, were unable to take concerted action because they knew very little about each other. The Nubian churches in the Middle Ages were under the authority of the Coptic patriarch of Alexandria, and communications between the two kingdoms would have had to be conducted through Nubian pilgrims to Jerusalem, but the Latin kings paid comparatively little attention to the Coptic Church before the reign of Baldwin IV.[27]

The nearest Christian power was the Armenian state of Cilicia. This had come into being when in 1132 the Armenian lords who ruled the Taurus mountains had seized the coastal plain and its cities from the Franks of Antioch who had held them since the First Crusade.[28] To protect themselves from further Armenian encroachment the rulers of Antioch created a marcher lordship in the Amanus mountains, which separate the plain of Antioch from Cilicia, and entrusted it to the newly founded Order of Knights Templar in c.1136.[29] The Templars built a network of castles to guard the passes: Port Bonnet, Baghras, La Roche de Roissel (perhaps Calan Kalesi), Trapesak, La Roche Guillaume, Sari Seki and perhaps the Pillar of Jonah.[30]

---

[25] W.Y. Adams, *Nubia* (London, 1977), pp. 459–71.
[26] M.C. Lyons and D.E.P. Jackson, *Saladin. The Politics of the Holy War* (Cambridge, 1982), pp. 60–1.
[27] Hamilton, *Latin Church*, pp. 190, 194, 196 and 208–9.
[28] A brief account of Cilicia in this period, S. Der Nersessian, 'The Kingdom of Cilician Armenia', in Setton, *Crusades*, II, pp. 630–45; more detailed information in F. Tournebize, *Histoire politique et religieuse de l'Arménie depuis les origines des Arméniens jusqu'à la mort de leur dernier roi à l'an 1393* (Paris, 1910), pp. 175–84.
[29] J. Riley-Smith, 'The Templars and the Teutonic Knights in Cilician Armenia', in T.S.R. Boase (ed.), *The Cilician Kingdom of Armenia* (Edinburgh, 1978), pp. 92–117 at pp. 92–5.
[30] R.W. Edwards, *The Fortifications of Armenian Cilicia*, Dumbarton Oaks Studies 23 (Washington,

Matters were further complicated because the Byzantines claimed that Cilicia was a province of their empire, but in 1159 an amicable settlement was made between Emperor Manuel, the Armenian Prince Thoros II (1145–68), and the Frankish leaders, who for some years thereafter co-operated in trying to stem the growth of Nur ad-Din's power. The Byzantines resumed direct control over the coastal plain of Cilicia and appointed a governor in Tarsus, but allowed Thoros to rule the rest of his lands as an imperial vassal.[31] When Thoros died in 1168 the situation changed very rapidly as a result of dynastic intrigue. He left a minor heir, Rupen II, and Thoros's brother Mleh, who had been living in exile at the court of Nur ad-Din, staged a successful *coup* with the *atabeg*'s help. Rupen II was deposed and murdered, and Mleh drove the Byzantine garrisons from Cilicia and handed the governor, Constantine Coloman, over to Nur ad-Din in return for the cession of Marash.[32] In 1172 he captured the Amanus march and the Templar castles there.[33] Manuel did not intervene because he was heavily involved in securing the succession of a pro-Byzantine king in Hungary, which was crucial to his Balkan ambitions.[34] Although King Amalric led an attack on coastal Cilicia in 1173, he could not follow up his initial success because Nur ad-Din invaded Transjordan and Amalric had to hurry back to relieve Kerak, to which Nur ad-Din had laid siege.[35] So long as Mleh remained in power the Franks of Antioch would get no help from Cilicia.

It was, no doubt, this paucity of allies which led Amalric to respond favourably to a mission from the master of the Syrian Assassins. The Assassins were Nizarite Ismailis, a Shi'ite group who owed obedience to a grand master who lived in the castle of Alamut in north-eastern Persia, and whom they regarded as the Imam, the

D.C., 1987), pp. 99–102, 204–6, 215–16 and 253; A.W. Lawrence, 'The castle of Baghras' and Riley-Smith, 'The Templars', both in Boase (ed.), *Cilician Kingdom*, pp. 34–83 and 92–5, respectively.

[31] Der Nersessian, 'Cilician Armenia', pp. 640–1; Magdalino, *Manuel I*, p. 67; Lilie, *Byzantium*, pp. 176–83.

[32] Der Nersessian, 'Cilician Armenia', pp. 642–3; Grousset, *Histoire des Croisades et du royayme franque de Jérusalem*, 3 vols. (Paris, 1934–6), II, pp. 566–9; C. Cahen, *La Syrie du nord à l'époque des croisades et la principauté franque d'Antioche* (Paris, 1940), pp. 413–14; Elisséeff, *Nur ad-Din*, II, pp. 655–6.

[33] WT, XX, 26, pp. 948–9; Riley-Smith, 'The Templars', p. 97.

[34] A.B. Urbansky, *Byzantium and the Danube Frontier* (New York, 1968), pp. 109–10 and 114–15; Magdalino, *Manuel I*, pp. 78–83.

[35] WT, XX, 26, pp. 948–50; Elisséeff, *Nur ad-Din*, II, pp. 681–4.

sole divinely appointed interpreter of the Islamic revelation in their own age. They sought to make the Imam's authority recognised throughout the Islamic world and this entailed the subversion of the entire religious and secular establishment. Since they were few in number, they used assassination as their chief weapon, but they did not murder indiscriminately. Their victims were chosen with care and were usually political or religious leaders whose deaths might be expected to cause major disruption and thereby to favour the work of revolution. Their high success rate made them feared, and their enemies called them Assassins, a name derived from the word *hashish*, or hemp. Their leaders, it was claimed, controlled supplies of the drug and were thus able to coerce their followers into murdering victims whom those leaders designated. Since Assassins needed excellent co-ordination of hand and eye to carry out their missions successfully, and those are precisely the qualities that are impaired by drug addiction, such rumours would seem to have been unfounded.[36]

Most Nizarite Ismailis were not trained to kill. There was a religious diaspora throughout the Near East consisting of converts made by Nizarite preachers. Most people who lived in the Assassin lordships were peasants, but there were also some conventional soldiers who garrisoned the castles and formed a field army. The true Assassins were a highly trained specialist group, and their position was comparable in some ways to that of the SAS in the modern British armed services. These men were skilled in the use of weapons and carried out their murders in a spirit of religious dedication. They entered the service of Islamic princes and were often required to remain there for years, attaining positions of trust, before they were activated by their religious superiors to strike down their employers. Among their victims were the caliphs and viziers of Baghdad and Cairo.[37]

Between 1132 and 1141 the Assassins had gained control of a group of castles in the Nosairi mountains and had set up their headquarters there at Masyaf. Their master, appointed from Alamut, was known

[36] M.G.S. Hodgson, *The Order of Assassins. The Struggle of Early Nizari Isma'ilis against the Islamic World* (The Hague, 1955), pp. 1–120 and 133–7; F. Daftary, *The Isma'ilis: Their History and Doctrines* (Cambridge, 1990), pp. 324–57; B. Lewis, *The Assassins. A Radical Sect in Islam* (London, 1967), pp. 11–12.

[37] B. Lewis, 'The Isma'ilites and the Assassins', in Setton, *Crusades*, I, pp. 99–132 at pp. 109–19; Hodgson, *Order of Assassins*, p. 104 (the murder of the Abbasid Caliph Mustarshid).

as the *sheikh al-Jabal*, a title which the Franks correctly translated as
the Old Man of the Mountain.[38] Although they had no quarrel with
Christians in principle, the Assassins were involved in disputes with
the Templars who held the neighbouring fief of Tortosa. William of
Newburgh reports that the Old Man of the Mountain:

knew it was a useless act if his servants should perchance kill a Master of
the Temple, because they would soon appoint another one, who would
strive more fiercely to avenge the death of his predecessor.[39]

After a time, relations between them became more peaceful and
when a dispute arose over border territory the Assassins agreed to
pay the Templars 2,000 bezants a year for the contested lands.[40]

Rashid ad-Din Sinan became Syrian master in 1162. Two years
later he was ordered by Hassan II, grand master of Alamut, to
introduce radical religious changes among his followers. Hassan
proclaimed as Imam that the spiritual resurrection of believers had
taken place and that therefore the Muslim ritual law was abrogated.
As a loyal subordinate Sinan complied with his orders: mosques
were destroyed throughout his territories, public prayers were no
longer said, his followers feasted in the month of Ramadan, and they
broke Islamic food taboos by eating pork and drinking wine.[41] This
caused great scandal among orthodox Muslims, and Sunni vigilante
groups massacred some of Sinan's religious adherents who lived in
Nur ad-Din's territories.[42] This must have alarmed Sinan, for Nur
ad-Din was a devout Sunnite who might turn the power of his
empire against this nest of dissidents on his borders. Sinan could
expect no help from his superiors, because in 1166 a new grand
master, Muhammad II, came to power at Alamut and devoted his
time to theological speculation, abandoning the design of world
revolution that had motivated his predecessors. Under his leadership

---

[38] Lewis, *Assassins*, pp. 97–109; Hodgson, *Order of Assassins*, pp. 105–7; Daftary, *Isma'ilis*, pp. 357–60 and 374–80; C. Nowell, 'The Old Man of the Mountain', *Speculum* 22 (1947), pp. 497–519.

[39] William of Newburgh, *Historia Rerum Anglicarum*, IV, 24, ed. R. Howlett, R.S. 82(1) (1884), pp. 364–5.

[40] James of Vitry, writing in the early thirteenth century, says that 'tribute' was paid annually by the Assassins to the Templars of Tortosa in compensation for a small frontier district that the Assassins held but the Templars claimed: *Historia Orientalis*, I, 14 in James of Vitry, *Libri duo* (Douai, 1597), pp. 42–3. James, as bishop of Acre (1216–28), was in a position to see Templar records no longer extant.

[41] B. Lewis, 'Kamal al-Din's biography of Rašid al-Din Sinan', *Arabica* 13 (1966), pp. 225–59 at pp. 239–42; WT, XX, 29, pp. 953–4.

[42] E.g. the Shi'ites of el-Bab: Ibn Jubayr, pp. 259–60; Elisséeff, *Nur ad-Din*, II, pp. 687–8.

the Assassins of Persia became an inward-looking, quietist religious sect.[43] A similar way of life was not open to Sinan: threatened by powerful Sunnite neighbours, he stood in great need of allies.

This is the background to the story told by William of Tyre, that in the winter of 1173–4 Sinan sent an envoy to King Amalric claiming that he had become convinced of the truths of the Christian religion and offering the conversion of himself and his people to the Catholic faith. In return he asked to be freed from the annual payment of 2,000 bezants which he made to the Templars. The king, William relates, agreed to those terms and sent the ambassador home under royal safe conduct, but as he was entering Assassin territory he was ambushed by a party of Templars from Tortosa and killed by a one-eyed knight called Walter of Mesnil. The king sent to Sinan protesting his innocence, and his apologies were formally accepted. He also tried to punish Walter of Mesnil, but this brought him into conflict with the master of the Temple, Odo of St Amand, who claimed that Walter's case was reserved to the pope for judgment. The king nevertheless seized Walter and lodged him in the royal prison at Tyre, where he was still being held at the time of Amalric's death.[44]

It is impossible to know what Sinan envisaged when he negotiated with King Amalric about conversion to Christianity. Most modern historians have refused to believe William of Tyre's report,[45] and it seems likely that there was misunderstanding on the Christian side. The abandonment by the Syrian Nizarites of the outward practice of their faith was no doubt seen as evidence that they had rejected Islam. In any case, as is clear from the account of conversations that took place in 1251 between St Louis's envoy, Yves Le Breton, and the master of the Syrian Assassins, Christian observers were misled by the Nizarites' reverence for and interest in Jesus. They considered that this was evidence that they favoured Christianity, whereas the Nizarites regarded Jesus as the prophet of the fifth era in human history.[46]

---

[43] Hodgson, *Order of Assassins*, pp. 160–84; Daftary, *Isma'ilis*, pp. 391–6.

[44] WT, XX, 29–30, pp. 953–5.

[45] E.g. 'Assertion entièrement invraisemblable': Grousset, *Croisades*, II, p. 599; 'Needless to say that this story can be regarded as purely fictitious': Daftary, *Isma'ilis*, p. 398.

[46] John of Joinville, *Histoire de Saint Louis*, cc. 462–3, ed. N. de Wailly (Paris, 1868), pp. 164–5; Daftary, *Isma'ilis*, p. 169; J. Hauzinski, 'On alleged attempts at converting the Assassins to Christianity', *Folia Orientalia* 15 (1974), pp. 229–46.

But it may be conjectured that King Amalric was more interested in the political than the religious advantages of an alliance with the Assassins. Because they had a network of supporters scattered throughout Nur ad-Din's dominions they could have provided the court of Jerusalem with intelligence reports which the Franks could never have obtained themselves; while the Assassin agents, whose ability to murder Muslim leaders was a proven fact, could have caused chaos throughout western Islam if they had acted in conjunction with the Franks.

Yet despite these obvious advantages, the Templars tried to wreck the negotiations by murdering the Assassin ambassador, even though he had a royal safe conduct. The motive that William of Tyre ascribes to them – the loss of 2,000 bezants in revenue each year – is scarcely credible. The Temple by this time was a rich Order and 2,000 bezants was a paltry sum equivalent to the annual rents of four small villages.[47] Moreover, William relates that the king had agreed to indemnify the Order for this loss. Although the murder was carried out by the Templars of Tortosa, there was nothing maverick about their action. They had the full support of the master, Odo of St Amand, who was prepared to have a full-scale confrontation with the king in order to reserve judgment of this case to the pope. William of Tyre has clearly not written all that he knew about this incident, but is intent on showing the Templars in the worst possible light. The true reasons for their hostility to the alliance are not known, but it might be argued that because they were professional warriors who lived by a chivalric code of honour and were committed to fight to the death in the defence of their faith, they were not willing to work with Muslims whose chief skill lay in political assassination, and that they were prepared to antagonise the king to prevent this from happening.

The murder of the Assassin envoy did not end all hopes of an alliance between Sinan and the Latin Kingdom, but it did make co-operation between the two powers very difficult.[48] This highlights the problem which Amalric faced in his conduct of diplomacy, for

---

[47] J. Prawer, *The Latin Kingdom of Jerusalem. European Colonialism in the Middle Ages* (London, 1972), p. 378.

[48] William of Tyre emphasises this: 'rex tamen et apud Assissinorum magistrum, cuius tam sinistro casu legatus deperierat, de sua allegans innocentia, immunis apparuit': WT, XX, 30, p. 955.

negotiations could be wrecked by the opposition of some powerful group in the kingdom who were not subject to his authority. It is important to recognise that this was not a phenomenon that developed for the first time in Baldwin IV's reign as a consequence of the king's youth and ill-health, but was one that was inherent in the structure of the Latin Kingdom by the second half of the twelfth century.

By 1173 it also seemed possible that a new western crusade might be launched. In 1172 Henry II of England was reconciled to the Church at Avranches for his part in the murder of Thomas Becket. Part of the penance imposed on him then was that he should take the cross for three years and leave for the Holy Land before Easter 1173.[49] It is debatable whether Henry really intended to fulfil that obligation, but in any case he was unable to do so immediately for his eldest son, Henry 'the young king', led a revolt against him with the support of Louis VII of France, William I of Scotland and Count Philip of Flanders, and peace was not restored until September 1174, by which time Amalric was dead.[50]

A more hopeful prospect of western aid was provided by the young king of Sicily, William II, who had come of age in 1172. As his later policy was to show, he was concerned about the growth of Saladin's power, and particularly about his westward expansion into Libya.[51] Amalric may have learned of this from contacts in Sicily.[52] In 1173 he sent a new mission to the West, headed by Bernard, bishop of Lydda, and the sub-prior of the Holy Sepulchre. We only know of this from a letter of Alexander III, written on Christmas Day 1173 to the archbishop of Rheims, saying that he had given the envoys legatine powers to recruit help for the Crusader Kingdom in northern Europe.[53] It seems likely that this mission, like that of Frederick of Tyre in 1169, had been sent with letters from King Amalric to the principal rulers of the West, including the king of

---

[49] *Materials for the History of Thomas Becket, Archbishop of Canterbury*, eds. J.C. Robertson and J.B. Sheppard, 7 vols., RS 67 (London, 1875–85), VII, pp. 517–18; W.L. Warren, *Henry II* (London, 1973), pp. 530–1.

[50] Warren, *Henry II*, pp. 54–136.

[51] D. Abulafia, 'The Norman Kingdom of Africa and the Norman expedition to Majorca and the Muslim Mediterranean', *Anglo-Norman Studies* 7 (1984), pp. 26–49 at pp. 43–7; A.S. Ehrenkreutz, *Saladin* (Albany, 1972), pp. 109–10.

[52] The shrine churches of Jerusalem had priories in the Sicilian Kingdom: G. Bresc-Bautier, 'Les possessions des églises de Terre–Sainte en Italie du sud', in *Roberto il Guiscardo e il suo tempo* (Rome, 1975), pp. 13–34.

[53] *Non sine gravi dolore*, PL, 200, col. 928; Smail, 'Latin Syria', pp. 16–17.

Sicily, and that the envoys had called first at Palermo before visiting the papal court.[54] Whether as a result of this or of some other mission, a joint attack on Egypt was certainly planned by the Frankish army and the Sicilian navy for the summer of 1174.[55]

It might have been expected that while Amalric was searching for allies Nur ad-Din would have attempted to exploit the weaknesses of the Frankish frontier. Three areas were particularly vulnerable. The control of Antioch over the lands to the north of the river Orontes had been considerably weakened by Nur ad-Din's seizure of the key fortress of Harim in 1164.[56] Further south, one of the weakest points in Frankish defences was the hinterland of Beirut, where the Buhturid emirs in the Gharb retained a large measure of independence and when Nur ad-Din became ruler of Damascus he recognised the Buhturid Prince Zahr al-duala Karama as emir of the Gharb and in 1161 gave him a sizable *iqta*. However, when Karama died in c.1170 King Amalric's governor in Beirut dealt with that problem in a ruthless but effective way by inviting the emir's three eldest sons to a feast at which he murdered them. Their seven-year-old brother, Gamal al-Din Hajji, took refuge with Nur ad-Din and maintained his claim to the emirate, but the Muslims of the Gharb were effectively left without a leader until Saladin conquered Beirut in 1187.[57]

Frankish control over the hinterland of Sidon was permanently weakened when in 1167 Nur ad-Din's forces captured the great cave fortress of Tyron, central to the Frankish defence of southern Lebanon, together with another cave fortress situated somewhere on the borders of Tripoli and garrisoned by the Templars.[58] This weakness was exacerbated by the fact that many of the inhabitants of the Shuf mountains were Druzes, who were fiercely independent. Rabbi Benjamin of Tudela, who visited the area in King Amalric's reign, reported that:

---

[54] WT, XX, 12, p. 920.

[55] See below, pp. 86–8.

[56] Elisséeff, *Nur ad-Din*, II, pp. 590–5; WT, XIX, 9, pp. 874–5.

[57] K.S. Salibi, 'The Buhturids of the Gharb, medieval lords of Beirut and southern Lebanon', *Arabica* 8 (1961), pp. 74–89. Nejla M. Abu-Izzedin, citing as her source *The Arslan Genealogical Register*, claims that the Buhturids were Druzes, *The Druzes. A New Study of their History, Faith and Society* (Leiden, 1984), pp. 133–55. Contemporary Christian and Muslim sources do not support this view, but consider the Buhturids as Sunni Muslims.

[58] WT, XIX, 11, pp. 878–9; Elisséeff, *Nur ad-Din*, II, pp. 595–6 and 599–600.

Ten miles from Sidon a people dwell who are at war with the men of Sidon; they are called Druzes and are pagans of a lawless character. They inhabit the mountains and clefts of the rocks; they have no king or ruler, but dwell independent in these high places and their border extends to Mount Hermon.[59]

In 1164 Nur ad-Din had captured Banias (the ancient Caesarea Philippi) from the Franks. It was situated to the east of the Jordan at the foot of Mount Hermon and controlled the main road from Damascus to Upper Galilee.[60] Then in 1167 Nur ad-Din's troops destroyed the important castle of Chastel-Neuf to the west of the Jordan: they did not occupy the fief, but the castle was not rebuilt for more than a decade.[61] This opened the way to attacks from Damascus on the Frankish coastal areas by way of Marj Uyun, the area separating the Litani valley from the headwaters of the Jordan.

By contrast the situation in the lands to the east of the Sea of Galilee was very peaceful. Since 1108 the revenues of the lands of Sawad (which the Franks called *La terre de Suète*) had been divided between Jerusalem and Damascus.[62] This agreement suited both sides and despite recurrent wars remained in force until the end of the First Kingdom. It caused great surprise to Ibn Jubayr when he travelled that way in 1184:

The cultivation of the vale is divided between Franks and Muslims, and in it there is a boundary known as 'the Boundary of Dividing'. They apportion the crops equally and their animals are mingled together, yet no wrong takes place between them because of it.[63]

---

[59] Benjamin of Tudela, *Itinerary*, p. 118. His visit is variously dated, but there is agreement that it took place in the third quarter of the twelfth century.

[60] WT, XIX, 10, pp. 876–7; cf. RRH, nos. 407 and 411. R. Ellenblum, 'Who built Qalat al-Subayba ?', DOP 43 (1989), pp. 103–12, has shown conclusively that Subeibé, on the hill above Banias, was a thirteenth-century Ayyubid fortification. The lordship of Asebebe, mentioned by John of Ibelin, *Livre des Assises*, c. XIII, ed. Edbury, *John of Ibelin*, p. 119, cannot have taken its name from this castle. As Richard has suggested, Asebebe may have been the town of Hatzbaya: J. Richard, 'Les listes des seigneuries dans le Livre de Jean d'Ibelin, recherches sur l'Assebebé et Mimars', RHDFE, ser. 4, 32 (1954), pp. 565–72. Asebebe does not seem to have been in Frankish control in Baldwin IV's reign: Tibble, *Lordships*, pp. 19–20.

[61] Its destruction is recorded by IA, RHC Or I, p. 551. It had been rebuilt by 1179: WT, XXI, 26, p. 999; P. Deschamps, *La défense du royaume de Jérusalem* (vol. II of *Les châteaux des croisés en Terre Sainte* (Paris, 1939)) p. 130; Tibble, *Lordships*, p. 22.

[62] Ibn al-Qalanisi, *The Damascus Chronicle of the Crusades*, tr. H.A.R. Gibb, (London, 1932), p. 92; IA, RHC Or I, p. 269.

[63] Ibn Jubayr, p. 315.

This area was guarded on the southern side by the great Frankish cave fortress of al-Habis Jaldak.[64]

To the south of Sawad was the ancient territory of Jerash, known in the twelfth century as Jabal 'Auf, from a Beduin tribe, the Banu 'Auf, who lived there. In 1174 this was independent territory: the Franks had no control there, and it was remote from Damascus. Although potentially it was a weak spot in Frankish defences, it was one that the Muslims had not yet exploited.[65]

To the south of that was the lordship of Transjordan, defended by a string of castles that extended from Ahamant to the gulf of Aqaba.[66] Hitherto that area had had little strategic importance, and the castles seem to have been built as administrative centres to control the grain-producing areas on which the kingdom depended and as collecting centres for tolls levied on caravans travelling between Egypt and Damascus.[67] But when Nur ad-Din's lieutenant ruled in Egypt, Transjordan became of vital strategic importance because it controlled the land route between Cairo and Damascus. It is true that messengers, and indeed whole armies, could evade contact with the Franks by striking deep into the desert, for Muslims were expert in the use of camels, both for travel and as war-mounts, an art which the Franks never mastered, while Frankish cavalry could not venture far into the desert during much of the year because of the lack of fodder.[68] The fortresses deep in the Syrian desert, such as Ma'an, Azrak and Bosra, were all held by Muslims, so that an Islamic army travelling that way would meet with no obstruction. Nevertheless, it was a long and dangerous route for a large army to take because water supplies were far apart.[69]

---

[64] D. Nicolle, 'Ain al Habis. The cave de Sueth', *Archéologie mediévale* 18 (1988), pp. 113–40; Kennedy, *Crusader Castles* (Cambridge, 1994), pp. 52–4.

[65] C.N. Johns, 'Medieval 'Ajlun', *Quarterly of the Department of Antiquities in Palestine* 1 (1931), pp. 21–33.

[66] F. Cardini, M. Papi, G. Vannini, L. Marino and R. Berretti, 'Ricognizione agli impiante fortificati di epoca crociata in Transgiordania. Prima relazione', *Castellum* 27–8 (1987), pp. 5–38.

[67] The caravans to Egypt travelled from Damascus through Transjordan to Eilat, then north through the Sinai to Qalat Guindi. The *haj* route turned south near Montréal towards Ma'an.

[68] Abu Shama cites a letter from Imad ad-Din to the Caliph explaining that Prince Reynald's raid on the *haj* route in 1181–2 had been possible because 'the desert was crowned this year with abundant pasturage': RHC Or IV, p. 215.

[69] C.P. Grant, *The Syrian Desert. Caravans, Travel and Exploration* (London, 1937), pp. 33–45.

The lords of Transjordan had claimed jurisdiction over southern Sinai and when Fatimid power grew weak had extended their protection to the Mount Sinai monastery.[70] One of the few acts of Shirkuh during his brief vizierate in 1169 was to confirm the privileges of the Sinai community, thereby asserting Egyptian over-lordship once again.[71] In 1170 Saladin annexed the port of Eilat and perhaps also the fortress on Pharoah's island (the Ile de Graye), near the head of the gulf of Aqaba.[72] This looked like the beginning of an attempt to conquer Transjordan, but Saladin's chief concern seems to have been to enable pilgrims from Egypt making the *haj* to use the land route across the Sinai, because the alternative sea route from Aidhab to Jedda, so vividly described by Ibn Jubayr, was extremely hazardous.[73] The pilgrimage route was important to Saladin for political as well as for religious reasons, because as ruler of Egypt he had taken over the role of the Fatimid caliphs as protector of the holy cities of Arabia.

An important element in the defence of the Kingdom of Jerusalem were the Beduin. These pastoral nomads lived along the desert frontiers to the east and south of Frankish territory. Some were Christians, some were Muslims, but when they came to pasture their flocks in the kingdom they were all taken directly under royal protection and a detailed register was kept of them. Because they crossed the frontiers between Christian and Islamic territory freely, these transhumant herdsmen were able to give the kings of Jerusalem useful information about Islamic troop movements. On occasion

---

[70] 'Apriès si est Mons Synaï, en la tierre le seignor de Crac', Ernoul, 'Fragments relatifs à la Galilée', in H. Michelant and G. Raynaud (eds.), *Itinéraires à Jérusalem et descriptions de la Terre Sainte rédigés en français aux XIe, XIIe et XIIIe siècles*, Publications de la Société de l'Orient Latin, sér. géographique, 3 (Paris, 1882), pp. 53–76 at p. 63. In 1169 Philip of Nablus, master of the Temple, authenticated a relic of St Catherine of Alexandria and described how he had obtained it when he was lord of Transjordan (before 1166) when visiting the Sinai monastery as a pilgrim; B. de Broussillon, *La Maison de Craon, 1050–1480*, 2 vols. (Paris, 1893), I, p. 101, no. 138.

[71] S.M. Stern, *Fatimid Decrees. Original Documents from the Fatimid Chancery* (London, 1964), no. 10, pp. 80–4.

[72] IA, RHC Or I, p. 578; cf. al-Fadil's letter in RHC Or IV, pp. 174–5. Mayer argues that there is no evidence that the crusaders fortified Pharoah's Island, *Die Kreuzfahrerherrschaft Montréal (Sôbak). Jordanien im 12 Jahrhundert*, Abhandlungen des deutschen Palästinavereins 14 (Weisbaden, 1990), pp. 52–4; Kennedy, *Crusader Castles*, pp. 30 and 202, n. 17; but see the, admittedly inconclusive, evidence of a cross in a window of the castle there, B. Rothenberg, *God's Wilderness. Discoveries in Sinai* (London, 1961), pp. 86–92, pl. 44.

[73] Ibn Jubayr, pp. 63–70.

they could also be of more direct help by harrying the baggage trains of retreating Muslim armies.[74]

From 1169 to 1174 Saladin was intent on consolidating his own position in Egypt. In 1172 his forces drove off a Nubian attack on Upper Egypt and placed a garrison at Ibrim, just north of Abu Simbel.[75] In the following year troops under Sharaf al-Din Qaragush campaigned to the west, annexing Cyrenaica, and taking Tripoli from the Almohad caliph of Morocco who had held it for twelve years.[76] In February 1174 Saladin's brother, Turan-Shah, led an expedition to the Yemen. By 13 May he had taken Zalid, and he subsequently conquered Sana and the port of Aden.[77] This gave Saladin control of the Red Sea and with it the pilgrim traffic from Muslim Africa and also of the lucrative trade in oriental luxuries and spices, which came to Aden from across the Indian Ocean and which formed a vital element in the Egyptian economy.

In September 1171 Saladin restored Egypt to the spiritual obedience of the Abbasid caliph of Baghdad and when, three days after this edict had been published, the Fatimid caliph died, he did not allow a successor to be proclaimed. The Fatimid schism was at an end and Saladin had shown himself a loyal Sunnite.[78] He continued to show all outward signs of deference to Nur ad-Din,[79] but when in 1171 he was ordered by the *atabeg* to join forces with him in besieging the Frankish fortresses of Kerak and Montréal, although he did not technically disobey the summons, he retired to Egypt before a junction had been effected between their armies.[80] It was not altogether fanciful for Saladin's critics to conjecture that he would not co-operate with Nur ad-Din in attacking Transjordan because he wanted to preserve the Christian Kingdom of Jerusalem as a

---

[74] J. Prawer, 'Serfs, slaves and Bedouin', in *Crusader Institutions* (Oxford, 1980), p. 214; cf. CGOH, no. 550; see below p. 136.

[75] Lyons and Jackson, *Saladin*, pp. 60–1.

[76] Ehrenkreutz, *Saladin*, pp. 109–10.

[77] Elisséeff, *Nur ad-Din*, II, pp. 684–6; Ehrenkreutz, *Saladin*, pp. 110–12; Lyons and Jackson, *Saladin*, pp. 65–6.

[78] Elisséeff, *Nur ad-Din*, II, pp. 563–670; G. Schlumberger, *Campagnes du roi Amaury Ier en Égypte* (Paris, 1906).

[79] Until 1171 Saladin was vizier of the Fatimid caliph, thereafter he ruled as Nur ad-Din's lieutenant. Nur ad-Din was prayed for as ruler after the Abbasid caliph, and the coinage was minted in his name. Saladin only assumed sovereign power in 1175: Ehrenkreutz, *Saladin*, pp. 106 and 138.

[80] Elisséeff, *Nur ad-Din*, II, pp. 671–4 and 681–4; Ehrenkreutz, *Saladin*, pp. 100–1 and 105–6. Lyons and Jackson, *Saladin*, pp. 48–9 and 62–3, argue that Nur ad-Din was not seriously interested in a concerted attack on Transjordan in 1173.

buffer between himself and the *atabeg*. It was even rumoured that Nur ad-Din was considering the possibility of sending an expedition to Egypt to replace Saladin by a more loyal deputy.[81]

Despite these tensions between the *atabeg* and Saladin, Amalric could not afford to be complacent about the growth of Saladin's power, and when in the winter of 1173–4 he was approached by a dissident group of Egyptian Shi'ites he responded favourably to them, for a pro-Fatimid revolt would mesh particularly well with the campaign he was planning with William II of Sicily for a joint attack on Egypt. Some senior officials in the service of Saladin, together with some Egyptian scholars, were plotting to overthrow the sultan and restore the Fatimid caliphate, for Saladin had left the kinsmen of the last caliph alive, although he had deprived them of all political power.[82] Plans for a *coup* were made in an atmosphere of intrigue reminiscent of the plot of a modern spy story. Amalric tried to be ingenious and sent an official embassy to Saladin, one of whose members was instructed to make contact with the rebel leaders in Cairo. Saladin had a good spy network, and his agents in Jerusalem told him of the plan, so that he was able to counter it by using a double-agent. This man was a Coptic Christian who, on Saladin's orders, made contact with the Egyptian dissidents and professed sympathy with their cause. Saladin then attached him to the Frankish ambassador's staff as his official representative and the Copt arranged secret meetings between Amalric's agent and the Egyptian rebels at which he was himself present and about which he made regular reports to the sultan. Saladin took no action against the Franks, but as soon as the embassy left he arrested the conspirators and on 6 April 1174 they were executed. He also placed the male members of the Fatimid dynasty under stricter surveillance in their palace quarters, hoping in that way to deprive dissident Shi'ite groups of leadership.[83]

---

[81] Elisséeff, *Nur ad-Din*, II, pp. 692–3; Ehrenkreutz, *Saladin*, pp. 115–16; Lyons and Jackson, *Saladin*, pp. 65 and 68–9.

[82] al-Maqrizi, p. 47; Saladin, in a letter written by al-Fadil, complained that the Assassins were involved in this plot, but this assertion may simply have been intended to discredit the other participants: Lyons and Jackson, *Saladin*, p. 67; Lewis, *Assassins*, p. 114. Assassin involvement seems unlikely because they had been hostile to the Fatimids, whom they accused of usurping the prerogatives of Imam, which by right belonged to the Hidden Imams of Alamut. But Sinan was not an orthodox Nizarite Ismaili, so his involvement in a pro-Fatimid plot cannot be totally ruled out. IA, RHC Or I, p. 599; Ehrenkreutz, *Saladin*, pp. 95–6.

[83] al-Maqrizi, p. 47; IA, RHC Or I, pp. 599–602; Ehrenkreutz, *Saladin*, p. 114.

The collapse of the Shi'ite conspiracy did not in any way affect the planned Franco-Sicilian attack on Egypt, but news of this had reached the Emperor Manuel and he was not well pleased by it. Relations between Sicily and Byzantium had been stormy ever since the Normans had first settled in south Italy, but in 1158 Pope Hadrian IV had negotiated a thirty-years' truce between the two powers in order that they might present a united front to the threat posed by the Italian ambitions of Frederick Barbarossa.[84] Although that truce was still operative in 1174 it had recently been placed under a severe strain, for Manuel had betrothed his only daughter Maria to William II and had then humiliated the young king by refusing to allow her to marry him.[85] Fear of Barbarossa led William II to keep the peace with Manuel despite this provocation, but it was an uneasy peace, and there was no guarantee that it would prove durable should Frederick I cease to threaten Sicilian interests. Manuel therefore was not disposed to allow the king of Sicily to extend his influence to the eastern Mediterranean, and when news reached Constantinople of William II's plan to attack Egypt, Manuel warned Saladin about it.[86] It would not, of course, have been possible to conceal the marshalling of a large Sicilian war fleet, but without Manuel's warning the court of Cairo might well have been uncertain of its destination and therefore less well prepared to meet a seaborne invasion.

Nur ad-Din's unexpected death on 15 May 1174 removed pressure from the Franks on their Syrian frontiers. His heir was his eleven-year-old son, as-Salih, so struggles between Nur ad-Din's generals and kinsmen over the regency seemed inevitable. The emirs did homage to the young prince and Ibn al Muqaddam was appointed administrator of the Zengid dominions for as-Salih. Almost immediately, Nur ad-Din's nephew, Saif ad-Din of Mosul, took possession of all the Zengid lands to the east of the Euphrates.[87]

As soon as he heard of Nur ad-Din's death, Amalric mustered his army and led it against Banias in June 1174. The defences of the kingdom would have been strengthened by its recovery, but at the

---

[84] P. Lamma, *Comneni e Staufer. Ricerche sui rapporti fra Bisanzio et l'Occidente nel secolo XII*, 2 vols. (Rome, 1955–7), I, pp. 275–83; Magdalino, *Manuel I*, pp. 62–6.

[85] Magdalino, *Manuel I*, pp. 92–3; D. Matthew, *The Norman Kingdom of Sicily* (Cambridge, 1992), p. 271.

[86] Correspondence of al-Fadil, Brit. Mus. Add. 25757, cited in Lyons and Jackson, *Saladin*, p. 76.

[87] Elisséeff, *Nur ad-Din*, II, pp. 694–5.

end of fifteen days Ibn al-Muqaddam sued for peace, offering the Franks an indemnity together with the release of twenty Frankish knights if they would raise the siege, and Amalric accepted those terms, perhaps because he was feeling ill.[88] His own death on 11 July occurred at a critical time, just when Nur ad-Din's empire was disintegrating and when Sicilian intervention offered the Franks of Jerusalem some real possibility of replacing Saladin's government in Egypt by one more favourable to the Crusader States.

[88] *Ibid.*, p. 696; WT, XX, 31, p. 956.

CHAPTER 5

The king's minority

No regent was appointed for Baldwin IV even though he was a minor. This matter must have been considered by the High Court at the time of his election, and the decision which it reached may be reflected in a passage in the *Livre au roi*, a treatise on the laws of the kingdom drawn up for Aimery of Lusignan (1197–1205):

> The regency of the kingdom should be entrusted to the nearest relation, male or female, on the mother's side if the claim to the throne comes through the mother, or the nearest male relation on the father's side if the claim to the throne comes through him. And that is the law and true sense of the assise.[1]

This enactment excludes the mother of a child ruler from the regency if he inherits the throne from his father, and almost certainly reflects a decision made when Baldwin IV became king.[2] The ruling ran contrary to the custom of the kingdom in the case of lordships, where a mother normally had the right to administer the fief on behalf of a child heir.[3] In Baldwin IV's case that custom could not be applied because his parents' marriage had been annulled and his mother, Agnes of Courtenay, was not legally King Amalric's widow, while the dowager-queen, Maria Comnena, was not the young king's mother.

It would appear that the High Court did not reach any decision about who Baldwin's 'nearest male relation on the father's side' was, and the work of government automatically devolved on the seneschal, Miles of Plancy. John of Ibelin, writing some eighty years later about the customs of the kingdom, noted:

---

[1] 'Et deit remaindre le baillage de la terre en la main dou plus prochein parent ou parente que les anfans aient de par leur mere de par qui la reauté meut, ou as plus procheins parents des anfans de par leur pere, se li reaumes meut de par luy; et ce est dreit et raison par l'assise': *Livre au roi*, c. 5, p. 146.

[2] The other minors who ruled before the *Livre au roi* was drawn up, Baldwin III and Baldwin V, both inherited the throne through their mothers.

[3] John of Ibelin, *Livre des Assises*, c. 178, RHC Lois I, pp. 280–1.

If it come to pass that the king is absent from the kingdom and his representative is also absent, the seneschal, by virtue of his office, should hold the king's place save in matters relating to the army and to military campaigns.[4]

William of Tyre used the phrase 'procurante Milone de Planci regni negotia' to describe the seneschal's term of office, and some scholars have taken this to mean that Miles was appointed regent.[5] But it is clear from what William goes on to say that Miles was not a regent and, significantly, the Old French translator of William did not use the phrase 'le bail du roiaume', as he did when speaking of Raymond of Tripoli, but rendered this passage: 'Eu roiaume de Surie maintenoit toutes les besoignes Miles de Planci . . . et touz seus s'estoit fez sires del Roi et de sa cort.'[6]

Much of what is known about Miles of Plancy is derived from William of Tyre, who disliked him: 'He was totally lacking in caution. He was proud and arrogant. He talked a great deal to little purpose and had far too good an opinion of himself.'[7] This cannot be the whole truth. Miles may have owed his rapid promotion to the favour of King Amalric and that certainly made him enemies who envied his good fortune, but if he had failed to prove himself a capable administrator he would never have been left in sole charge of the government by the High Court.

He undoubtedly had considerable power. He was lord of Transjordan, chief finance minister of the crown, had charge of all the royal castles, and could preside over the judicial business of the High Court in the king's absence.[8] William of Tyre relates how:

In order . . . to lessen the envy of his fellows, Miles . . . suborned a certain man called Rohard, the castellan of the citadel of Jerusalem, a common soldier of little ability, and obeyed his [Rohard's] orders as though he were set over him. In fact the reverse was true. For one man held the title which sounded good but conferred no power, while the other, using this pretence, dealt with the business of the kingdom as seemed good to himself.[9]

Riley-Smith has suggested that William is here implying that Miles

---

[4] *Ibid.*, *Livre*, c. 256, RHC Lois I, p. 408.

[5] WT, XXI, 3, p. 963; M.W. Baldwin, *Raymond III of Tripolis and the Fall of Jerusalem* (Princeton, 1936), p. 25.

[6] *Eracles*, XXI, 2, ed. P. Paris, 2 vols., II, p. 365.

[7] WT, XXI, 4, p. 964.

[8] The king might even delegate to him pleas relating to the fiefs and persons of liege vassals, John of Ibelin, *Livre*, c. 256, RHC Lois I, pp. 407–9.

[9] WT, XXI, 4, pp. 964–5.

of Plancy arranged for Rohard to be formally appointed regent while he exercised all real power himself, but an alternative explanation is possible.[10]

Rohard the castellan was Rohard of Jaffa, and he and his brother Balian had both been in the service of Amalric while he was count of Jaffa.[11] When he became king he appointed Rohard castellan of Jerusalem and clearly held him in high regard.[12] He witnessed an important set of royal diplomas[13] in two of which he took precedence over all the other witnesses except the seneschal and the constable,[14] and he was chosen as a member of the distinguished suite which accompanied Amalric on his state visit to Constantinople in 1171.[15] Yet although Rohard was clearly a trusted servant of the crown, he was not a great lord and could not be suspected of aspiring to political power. It is therefore possible that Miles appointed him to be the personal guardian of Baldwin IV. If that was the case then Rohard would indeed have had, as William of Tyre reports, 'a title which sounded good but conferred no power'. Yet as the king's guardian he would have been able, in appearance at least, to give orders to the seneschal in the king's name. He would certainly have been in a position to give orders to William of Tyre, the king's tutor, and this might explain William's hostility towards him.[16]

Although Miles had almost complete control over civil government he had no military powers. The army was commanded by the constable, Humphrey II of Toron, while any major military activity also involved the co-operation of the masters of the military Orders. To succeed as acting head of state Miles needed to be able to work harmoniously with those three men. The first test of his capacity to do so occurred almost immediately after Baldwin IV's coronation. The plan that had been matured in Amalric's reign for a joint attack

---

[10] Riley-Smith, *The Feudal Nobility and the Kingdom of Jerusalem, 1174–1277* (London, 1973), p. 101.

[11] William of Tyre calls Balian of Jaffa 'Rohardi predicti fratrem': XXI, 4, p. 965.

[12] Rohard first appears as castellan in 1163, CGOH, no. 312.

[13] Bresc-Bautier, no. 135, p. 266 [1164]; CGOH, no. 344 [1165]; Kohler, no. 37, ROL 7 (1899), p. 146 [1168]; Delaborde, no. 36, pp. 83–4 [1168]; CGOH, no. 409 [1169]; de Marsy, no. 27, AOL IIB, pp. 144–5 [1171]; Bresc-Bautier, no. 156, p. 306 [1171]; de Marsy, no. 28, AOL IIB, pp. 145–6 [1174]; Kohler, no. 39, ROL 7 (1899), pp. 147–8 [1174]; CGOH, no. 463 [1174]; Strehlke, no. 7, p. 8 [1174].

[14] Bresc-Bautier, no. 156, p. 306; de Marsy, no. 28, AOL IIB, pp. 145–6.

[15] WT, XX, 22, p. 942.

[16] This may have created the precedent, followed when Baldwin V became sole king in 1185, of separating the office of personal guardian of the king from that of regent. See Chapter 10.

on Egypt by the land forces of Jerusalem and the Sicilian navy had not been countermanded, because there had not been time to inform the court of Palermo about Amalric's death before the Sicilian fleet set sail for Alexandria.[17] In the name of the new king Miles renewed the peace with Damascus which Amalric had negotiated shortly before his death.[18] Although Saladin wrote a formal letter to Baldwin IV condoling with him on the death of his father,[19] he nevertheless prepared for war, stationing his main army to the east of the Nile delta to repel the expected Frankish invasion.[20]

On 28 July the Sicilian fleet anchored off Alexandria.[21] Arab writers estimated the size of the Christian army at 30,000 men, 1,500 of whom were knights,[22] and although these figures are certainly exaggerated because the authors wished to enhance the valour of Islam in repelling so formidable a force, the Sicilian army was clearly substantial and constituted a real threat to the city. The Sicilians immediately established a land base and within a day of their arrival had driven the garrison inside the walls.[23] Saladin's troubles were compounded by a revolt in Upper Egypt, led by pro-Fatimid supporters, who were joined by Kanz al-Daula, the governor of Aswan.[24] Had the army of Jerusalem invaded at this point Saladin would have been in considerable difficulty, but the threat did not materialise. Saladin learned from his agents in the Holy Land that the Franks had not even mustered their army and so when the garrison of Alexandria sent him an urgent appeal for help he was able to march to their relief. The Sicilians had already suffered a setback, for the garrison had made a sortie and burnt their siege-engines, so when news of the sultan's approach reached them they decided to withdraw. On 2 August they sailed for Sicily: the siege had lasted exactly five days. Saladin's brother, al-Adil, put down the

---

[17] Amalric died on 11 July. The Sicilian fleet reached Alexandria on 28 July. An envoy from Jerusalem could not have reached Palermo with news of the king's death before the fleet set sail.

[18] MS, XX, i, III, p. 356.

[19] al-Qalqashandi cited by M.C. Lyons and D.E.P. Jackson, *Saladin. The Politics of the Holy War* (Cambridge, 1982), p. 75.

[20] al-Maqrizi, p. 49

[21] IA, RHC Or I, p. 611; William of Tyre dates it about the beginning of August, WT, XXI, 3, p. 963.

[22] al-Maqrizi, p. 49.

[23] Lyons and Jackson, *Saladin*, p. 76; Randall Rogers points out that 'Norman forces had much experience in siege warfare, albeit of a very different kind from that usually seen in crusader operations': *Latin Siege Warfare in the Twelfth Century* (Oxford, 1992), p. 86.

[24] AS, RHC Or IV, p. 167; IA, RHC Or I, pp. 611–14.

revolt in Upper Egypt and by early September the entire country had been restored to peace.[25] Baha al-Din, Saladin's secretary and biographer, describes the defeat of the Sicilians in 1174 as 'one of the greatest mercies ever granted by God to the Muslims'.[26] As he did not enter the sultan's service until many years later he was almost certainly recording Saladin's own opinion.

Miles of Plancy had failed in his first test of leadership. A campaign of this importance could not successfully be mounted by the feudal host of the kingdom alone without the support of the military Orders, but they could not be commanded to take part, only persuaded. Jobert, the master of the Hospital, may well have been reluctant to commit his Order once again to a course of action which had overstrained its resources six years before and left a legacy of debt which he was still striving to clear; while the portrait that William of Tyre gives of Odo of St Amand, master of the Temple, suggests that he was a man of imperious temper with little gift for conciliating opponents, and it does not seem likely that he would have found it easy to co-operate with the seneschal, who had similar character traits.[27] Because of their lack of co-operation, Humphrey of Toron made no attempt to muster the host.

The failure of the Franks to intervene in Egypt in 1174 was a major error of judgment, for if Saladin could have been overthrown at that stage and a weak government composed of pro-Fatimid elements restored there, then the chief threat to Frankish security would have been removed. Nur ad-Din's dominions were already fragmented; Egypt alone at this time posed a serious danger to the Franks, and Saladin emerged from this crisis with the reputation in Egypt of being the ruler who had saved the country from a humiliating defeat.

Dissatisfaction with Miles's rule became apparent immediately after these events, when Raymond III, count of Tripoli, came before the High Court and requested to be made regent.[28] He was about thirty-four years old and had succeeded to the county of Tripoli while still a child, when his father was assassinated in 1152.[29] He was virtually unknown in the Kingdom of Jerusalem at that time. He had been a prisoner of war at Aleppo since his capture at Harim in 1164

---

[25] al-Maqrizi, pp. 49–51; Lyons and Jackson, *Saladin*, pp. 76–81.
[26] Baha al-Din, RHC Or III, p. 57.
[27] See above p. 38.   [28] WT, XXI, 3, p. 964.
[29] Raymond was about twelve in 1152, WT, XVII, 19, p. 787; Baldwin, *Raymond III*, p. 7.

and had only been released a few months before Amalric's death.[30] His claim was supported by Humphrey of Toron, Reynald of Sidon, Baldwin of Ramla and his brother, Balian of Ibelin. William of Tyre relates that almost all the people (*populus*) favoured Raymond, as did the entire bench of bishops, though this may merely be a commonplace, intended to make clear William's own support for the count.

Humphrey of Toron may have supported Raymond because he found Miles difficult to work with, but what united Raymond's three other supporters was their relationship by marriage to the king's mother, Agnes of Courtenay. Reynald of Sidon was her husband, and Baldwin and Balian of Ibelin were her brothers-in-law through her earlier marriage to Hugh of Ibelin. Because her marriage to Amalric had been annulled, Agnes had no official position at court in the new reign. Yet as mother of the child king and of Princess Sibyl, the heir apparent, she was, potentially, very important. Her return to court depended entirely on the goodwill of the acting head of state, but obviously if she succeeded in asserting her position as the king's mother she would enjoy considerable powers of patronage, and her husband and brothers-in-law might expect some share in her power and influence.

Raymond claimed the regency for three reasons: because he was Baldwin IV's closest kinsman; because he was the richest and most powerful of his vassals; and because while he had been a prisoner of war he had ordered his own vassals in Tripoli to recognise King Amalric as regent of the county. Only the first reason had any force; the second was irrelevant and the third was an appeal to sentiment. He was, as the assise required, related to the king on his father's side,[31] but, as the royal genealogy makes plain, his claim to be Baldwin's closest kinsman was not self-evident, for Bohemond III of Antioch and his brother Baldwin had equally good claims.[32]

Miles of Plancy ruled that consideration of the count's request should be deferred until a plenary session of the High Court could be convened. Before this happened, he sent Balian of Jaffa, the brother of Rohard the castellan, to northern Europe with letters and

---

[30] WT, XX, 28, p. 952; Baldwin places Raymond's release between September 1173 and April 1174: *Raymond III*, p. 14, n. 23; he is first recorded as free in a document of 18 April 1174, CGOH, no. 463; J. Richard, *Le Comté de Tripoli sous la dynastie toulousaine (1102–87)* (Paris, 1945), pp. 30–8.

[31] 'allegans domini regis adhuc infra pubertatis annos degentis tutelam legitimam iure agnationis sibi debere': WT, XXI, 3, p. 963.

[32] See pp. 40–1 above and Genealogy I.

gifts from the king. This was a secret mission and Miles's enemies therefore began to spread rumours that he was seeking help from his friends and kinsmen in France in order to seize the throne himself.[33] This seems most improbable, since he had no claim to it. Nevertheless, the fact that the High Court was not informed of the reasons for this embassy implies that its mission was controversial and this suggests that it may have been related to the appointment of a regent. It is clear from William of Tyre's account that Miles did not want Raymond of Tripoli to become regent because that would curtail his own powers. One sure way of preventing this would have been to secure the appointment as regent of one of the royal kinsmen living in the West who had a better claim than Raymond. There were three potential candidates: Henry II of England, the son of King Amalric's half-brother, Geoffrey Plantagenet; and Philip, count of Flanders and his brother, Peter, bishop-elect of Cambrai, the sons of Amalric's half-sister, Sibyl, the wife of Count Thierry of Flanders.[34] Miles may well have hoped that one of these western princes might claim the regency and empower Miles to rule on his behalf until he came to the East. This is conjectural, but an embassy from Jerusalem was certainly in the West that autumn. *The Royal Chronicles of Cologne* report that in September 1174, as Frederick Barbarossa was approaching Alessandria:

envoys of the king of Jerusalem met him, carrying many gifts and a golden apple filled with musk, and letters from the same king in which he thanked the emperor saying that he would have been driven from his kingdom if the pagan kings were not restrained by fear of the emperor.[35]

The embassy may have reached Flanders that winter, for on Good Friday 1175 Count Philip took the cross, but by that time Miles was dead.[36]

William of Tyre relates that hostility to Miles was so widespread that 'certain men were suborned to make an attempt on his life'. Miles was warned about this but refused to take precautions and one evening in October he was murdered in the street at Acre.[37] A Genoese source, the continuation of the *Annals* of Caffaro written

---

[33] WT, XXI, 3–4, pp. 964–5.   [34] See Genealogy III.

[35] *Chronica Regia Coloniensis*, ed. G. Waitz, MGH Scriptorum rerum Germanicarum in usum scholarum (Hanover, 1880), p. 125.

[36] Continuator of Sigebert of Gembloux, *Chronographia*, ed. D.L.C. Bethmann, MGH SS, VI (Hanover, 1844), p. 415; Roger of Howden, *Gesta Henrici*, RS 49(1), p. 83.

[37] William places this in the same month as the death of Archbishop Frederick of Tyre which occurred on 30 October: WT, XXI, 4, p. 965.

c.1200 after all the main participants were dead, says that the assassination was carried out by the lords of Beirut.[38] This merits serious attention because of what is known independently about relations between this family and the seneschal.

Walter III Brisebarre succeeded his father as lord of Beirut in 1157.[39] It was an important fief, owing service of twenty-one knights to the crown, but by 1167 it had passed into royal control and Amalric granted it to Andronicus Comnenus.[40] A late thirteenth-century source, the *Lignages d'Outremer*, relates how this had come about. Walter and his brothers, Guy and Bernard, were taken captive by the Muslims, and their mother, only being able to raise part of the money for their ransom, offered herself as a hostage in their place until the outstanding sum had been paid.[41] The crown forbade anybody to lend the Brisebarre brothers money when they were released and they were therefore forced to exchange Beirut for the crown fief of Blanchegarde. Only then did the sovereign pay the outstanding ransom and their mother was freed, but died a month later. Errors of fact have crept into this account: this episode, for example, is dated to the reign of Aimery of Lusignan, whereas it should be placed between 1164, when Walter Brisebarre's mother was still alive, and 1167 when Beirut was a crown fief.[42] Moreover, as Mayer has argued, the *Lignages* are at fault in stating that Beirut was exchanged for Blanchegarde, because contemporary evidence shows that the exchange was made for a money fief.[43]

The reason for Amalric's sharp practice may be inferred. Walter had married Helena, the elder daughter of Philip of Milly, lord of Transjordan.[44] Late in 1165 Philip of Milly resigned his fief to enter

---

[38] *Regni Iherosolymitani Brevis Historia*, ed. L.T. Belgrano, *Annali Genovesi di Caffaro e de' suoi continuatori dal MXCIX al MCCXCIII*, Fonti per la Storia d'Italia, 5 vols. (Rome, 1890–1929), I, p. 135.

[39] CGOH, no. 258.

[40] John of Ibelin, *Livre*, c. XIV, ed. Edbury, *John of Ibelin*, p. 122; WT, XX, 2, p. 914.

[41] Walter, Guy and Bernard are attested in contemporary records CGOH, no. 258; de Marsy, no. 24, AOL IIB, p. 142; Strehlke, no. 11, p. 12; a fourth brother, Hugh, mentioned in the *Lignages*, c. 20, RHC Lois II, p. 458, is attested in no other source.

[42] Walter's mother, Maria, is last attested in 1164, de Marsy, no. 23, AOL IIB, p. 141; cf. M. Nickerson, 'The seigneury of Beirut in the twelfth century and the Brisebarre family of Beirut-Blanchegarde', *Byzantion* 19 (1949), pp. 141–85 at pp. 166–7.

[43] H.-E. Mayer, *De Kreuzfahrerherrschaft Montréal (Sobak). Jordanien im 12 Jahrhundert*. Abhandlungen des deutschen Palästinavereins 14 (Wiesbaden, 1990), pp. 229–35, citing RRH, no. 512.

[44] de Marsy, no. 24, AOL IIB, p. 142.

the Temple.[45] Before 1171 it was the custom of the kingdom that if a lord had no sons but more than one daughter the eldest daughter should inherit the whole fief.[46] The fief of Montréal would therefore have passed in its entirety to Philip's elder daughter Helena and her husband Walter III Brisebarre, and it would seem that Amalric forced Walter to surrender Beirut in order to prevent his holding two of the great fiefs of the kingdom simultaneously.[47]

Helena of Milly died in 1168 leaving Walter guardian of their only child, Beatrice.[48] If she died while a minor the fief would pass to her mother's closest kin, Helena's younger sister, Stephanie, the wife of Humphrey III of Toron. Humphrey III died in c.1173 and before Easter 1174 Stephanie married Miles of Plancy who styled himself lord of Montréal,[49] while in a document of 24 February 1174 Walter Brisebarre was described as lord of Blanchegarde.[50] This indicates that Walter Brisebarre's daughter Beatrice had died and that the fief had reverted to her aunt, Stephanie. King Amalric had presumably granted Blanchegarde to Walter as compensation for his loss of Transjordan, but it was a small fief, owing service of only eight knights to the crown.[51] Bernard of Brisebarre seems to have died soon after 1165,[52] but Guy was still living, and it is presumably to him and to Walter that the *Annals* of Caffaro refer when they speak of the 'lords of Beirut'.

Miles of Plancy could not be held responsible for the decline of the Brisebarre fortunes, but he was the beneficiary of this. Walter III and his brother Guy may therefore well have felt some resentment towards the seneschal because after Amalric's death he failed to restore Beirut to them, even though it had reverted to the crown when Andronicus Comnenus defected to Nur ad-Din's court in c.1168.[53] It is not clear whether the assassination of Miles of Plancy

---

[45] J. Delaville Le Roulx, 'Chartes de Terre Sainte', no. 2, ROL XI (1905–8), pp. 181–91 at pp. 183–5.

[46] Philip of Novara, *Livre*, c. 71, RHC Lois, I, p. 542.

[47] Philip of Milly had a son, Rainier, and two daughters, Helena and Stephania: de Marsy, no. 14, AOL IIB, pp. 133–4 [1155]. Rainier is mentioned in no source after 1161, Strehlke, no. 3, p. 4, and presumably died before his father became a Templar.

[48] de Marsy, no. 24, AOL IIB, p. 142.

[49] WT, XXI, 4, p. 964; CGOH, no. 463.

[50] de Marsy, no. 28, AOL IIB, pp. 145–6.

[51] John of Ibelin, *Livre*, c. XIV, ed. Edbury, *John of Ibelin*, p. 122.

[52] Last recorded that year, Kohler, ROL 7 (1899), no. 36, p. 145.

[53] WT, XX, 2, p. 914; C. Diehl, 'Les romanesques aventures d'Andronic Comnène', in *Figures byzantines*, 5th edn (Paris, 1918), pp. 107–33; R.-J. Lilie, *Byzantium and the Crusader States, 1096–1204*, tr. J.E. Ridings (Oxford, 1993), pp. 193–6.

was a simple act of private vendetta on the part of the Brisebarres or whether, as William of Tyre reports, they had been incited by some of the seneschal's more powerful enemies to carry out the killing.[54]

William of Tyre comments on Miles's death: 'Some said that this happened to him because of the loyalty which he faithfully displayed towards the lord king.'[55] This is a just assessment. Miles could have bought peace with the Brisebarres by granting away the king's lands, and it was praiseworthy in him that he did not do so, because the power of the crown depended in large measure on the resources of the royal demesne. Miles had integrity: his weakness was that he had an autocratic temperament and was unable to work harmoniously with the military leaders and the other barons. The friction that this caused undoubtedly harmed the kingdom.

Miles of Plancy's death left the kingdom without an effective ruler, so Raymond of Tripoli's claim to the regency was considered by a joint assembly of the High Court and the senior clergy held in Jerusalem at which the thirteen-year-old king presided since, in the absence of a seneschal, nobody could deputise for him. Some of those present clearly had reservations about Raymond's candidacy, for the debate lasted for two days.[56]

No doubt the meeting considered other candidates, but there was an additional factor which must have caused unease. Nur ad-Din had fixed Raymond's ransom at 80,000 bezants.[57] Part of this sum had been raised by the Knights of St John, but 60,000 bezants remained outstanding and the hostages whom Raymond had given as surety were being held in the citadel of Homs until the debt was cleared.[58] It might well have been thought imprudent to appoint as regent a man who was in debt to Nur ad-Din's heir, as-Salih, since that might make him vulnerable to Muslim pressures.

The discussions took place in an atmosphere of general anxiety about the security of the realm, because when Miles of Plancy was killed Saladin was marching through Transjordan at the head of the Egyptian army and on 28 October, at about the time the assembly

[54] For a more detailed account see B. Hamilton, 'Miles of Plancy and the fief of Beirut', in HH, pp. 136–46.

[55] WT, XXI, 4, p. 965.   [56] *Ibid.*, XXI, 5, p. 966.

[57] *Ibid.*, XX, 28, p. 952; MS, XX, 3, III, p. 365. Muslim writers place the ransom at 150,000 dinars: IA, RHC Or I, p. 619; AS, RHC Or IV, pp. 167–8; Kamal ad-Din, ROL 3 (1895), p. 563.

[58] CGOH, no. 467; WT, XXI, 8, p. 972.

met, he entered Damascus.[59] Clearly there was urgent need for a regent to be appointed and Raymond had the full support of Humphrey of Toron, which augured well for the defence needs of the kingdom. So he was invested as regent.

William of Tyre admired Raymond and the description which he gives of him is all the more convincing because it is not entirely flattering:

He was a slight-built, thin man. He was not very tall and he had a dark skin. He had straight hair of a medium colour and piercing eyes. He carried himself stiffly. He had an orderly mind, was cautious, but acted with vigour. He was more than averagely abstemious in his eating and drinking habits, and although he was liberal to strangers he was not so affable towards his own men.[60]

Raymond was also highly intelligent, a fact admitted even by his Muslim contemporaries.[61]

Raymond was a bachelor and very soon after he took office he married the greatest heiress in the kingdom, Eschiva II, princess of Galilee. She had four sons by her first marriage, Hugh, William, Ralph and Odo, but they were all still minors.[62] Her marriage to Raymond proved childless, but William of Tyre reports that it was a happy one and that the count was on excellent terms with his stepsons.[63] As prince of Galilee and count of Tripoli, Raymond became the greatest of the crown vassals, owing the service of 200 knights, and as prince of Galilee remained a member of the High Court of Jerusalem after he had ceased to be regent.[64]

The other great heiress, Stephanie of Milly, lady of Montréal, was not required to marry again when her year of formal mourning ended in 1175. This shows how limited a regent's authority was, for Stephanie had powerful supporters in her father-in-law, Humphrey of Toron, and in the master of the Temple, an Order of which her father had earlier been master, and Raymond could not afford to antagonise them by forcing her to marry. So despite its strategic importance, Transjordan remained without a lord.

Soon after he came to power Raymond appointed William of Tyre to the vacant office of chancellor and gave him the arch-

[59] 28 October 1174, Lyons and Jackson, *Saladin*, pp. 81–3.
[60] WT, XXI, 5, pp. 966–7.   [61] Baha al-Din, RHC Or III, p. 95.
[62] M. Rheinheimer, *Das Kreuzfahrerfürstentum Galiläa* (Frankfurt am Main, 1990), pp. 61–2.
[63] WT, XXI, 5, p. 967.
[64] John of Ibelin, *Livre*, cc. X, XIII, ed. Edbury, *John of Ibelin*, pp. 114–18.

deaconry of Nazareth to hold in plurality with that of Tyre so that he should enjoy an income commensurate with his dignity.[65] William's wide learning enabled the chancery of Jerusalem to correspond on terms of parity with those of western Europe, which were also staffed by men who, like himself, had been trained in the new learning of the western schools.

The post of seneschal was left vacant for almost two years. This meant that there could be no dispute about who exercised final authority in civil government, and that was important because Raymond's military duties necessarily took him away from the capital, sometimes for several consecutive months, while he also needed to spend some time in his own county of Tripoli.[66] Because there was no seneschal the king himself at such times presided at meetings of the High Court which dealt with legal business.[67] This must have been burdensome to a boy who was not yet fourteen and who was in poor health.

Agnes of Courtenay returned to court while Raymond of Tripoli was regent, probably as a condition imposed by Reynald of Sidon and the Ibelin brothers in return for their support. The dowager-queen Maria Comnena had retired to her fief of Nablus,[68] so Agnes became in fact the queen-mother of Jerusalem, although in name she was merely the countess of Sidon. She received a bad press in her lifetime and has been consistently criticised by later historians as an unscrupulous, self-seeking woman of doubtful moral character. She is often accused of exploiting the ill-health of her son in order to build up a faction of corrupt and inefficient favourites who monopolised power and excluded their more able rivals from office. This view rests on the evidence of two biased sources, William of Tyre's *Chronicle* and the *Chronicle* of Ernoul. William calls her 'a woman who was relentless in her acquisitiveness and truly hateful to God', but was not an impartial witness since he held her responsible for his defeat in the patriarchal election of 1180,[69] while Ernoul portrays her as a woman of loose morals. Agnes was obviously an attractive woman: there is no other reason why Amalric count of Jaffa, and Hugh of Ibelin

[65] WT, XXI, 5, p. 967; CGOH, no. 468.
[66] CGOH, no. 467 was issued by him at Tripoli in December 1174. He was absent on campaign from January to May 1175, see below pp. 98–9.
[67] E.g. the charter issued by the king at Nazareth in July 1175, CGOH, no. 480.
[68] WT, XXI, 17, p. 986.   [69] *Ibid.*, XXII, 10, p. 1019; see below pp. 162–3.

should have married her when she was virtually penniless and, in Hugh's case, when she was no longer young. She must also have had a forceful character, otherwise she would not have provoked so much resentment.

In 1174 she had to build a relationship with her adolescent son who can have had no conscious memories of his mother. Baldwin IV evidently became extremely fond of her and she would seem to have shown great kindness towards him in ways which would have earned her praise as a devoted mother from witnesses who were less hostile than William of Tyre and Ernoul. Thus when the king's illness became acute she accompanied him on campaign, and in his last years attended meetings of the High Court at which he was presiding.[70] Baldwin no doubt welcomed the presence of his attractive and capable mother who was genuinely concerned about his health and whom he could trust to take charge of his household efficiently. Given the circumstances of his childhood, his relationship with her must have been more like that between nephew and aunt than between son and mother.

Raymond of Tripoli was willing to share church patronage with Agnes while he was regent. When Frederick de la Roche, archbishop of Tyre, died on 30 October 1174, Raymond appointed William of Tyre to succeed him and he was consecrated on 8 June 1175.[71] When archbishop Ernesius of Caesarea died in 1175 he was succeeded by Heraclius, Archdeacon of Jerusalem.[72] Ernoul attributes his appointment to the patronage of Agnes of Courtenay and alleges that he had been her lover.[73] There is no reason to doubt that he owed his promotion to Agnes, though the allegation that he was her lover may have been malicious gossip. Yet even if it were true, Heraclius was not an unsuitable candidate for high church office at a time when clerical concubinage was still relatively common. Indeed, his career was very similar to that of William of Tyre. He had been born in Gévaudan[74] and trained in the schools of Bologna, where he became a *magister* and the friend of Stephen of Tournai.[75] In 1168 he

---

[70] WT., XXII, 26, p. 1049 and 30, p. 1058.   [71] *Ibid.*, XXI, 4, p. 965 and 8, pp. 973–4.

[72] *Ibid.*, XXI, 9, p. 974. This occurred after August 1175 at which time Heraclius was still archdeacon of Jerusalem: CGOH, no. 483.

[73] Ernoul, p. 82.

[74] M.R. Morgan (ed.), *La Continuation de Guillaume de Tyr (1184–97)*, DRHC, XIV (Paris, 1982), c. 39, p. 51.

[75] B.Z. Kedar, 'The Patriarch Eraclius', in *Outremer*, pp. 177–204. J. Desilve (ed.), *Lettres d'Etienne de Tournai*, no. 78 (Valenciennes and Paris, 1893), pp. 92–3.

came to Outremer and in the following year was made archdeacon of Jerusalem.[76]

In December 1174 the king ratified a donation made by Baldwin of Ibelin to Jobert, master of the Hospital, and this was witnessed by the regent, by Odo of St Amand, master of the Temple, by Berengar, seneschal of the Temple, by Humphrey II of Toron, constable of the Kingdom, by Balian of Ibelin, by Aimery of Lusignan and by Rohard of Jaffa.[77] The witness list is significant because Raymond was at that time planning a campaign and had done what Miles of Plancy had failed to do – summoned the masters of the military Orders, the constable of the kingdom and the chief crown vassals to discuss strategy. The presence of Rohard of Jaffa shows that Raymond had not attempted to exclude Miles of Plancy's supporters from power, and Rohard also remained castellan of Jerusalem.[78]

Aimery of Lusignan, who was present on this occasion, was to become very important later in Baldwin IV's reign. The Lusignans were a noble family from Poitou and vassals of Henry II of England. They had an excellent crusading record extending over four generations. Aimery's great-grandfather, Hugh VI, had come on the 1101 crusade and died at the battle of Ramla in 1102; his grandfather, Hugh VII, had accompanied Louis VII on the Second Crusade; while his father, Hugh VIII, had come on pilgrimage to the Holy Land in 1163, been captured by Nur ad-Din at the battle of Harim in the following year, and died in a Muslim prison.[79] Aimery, one of Hugh VIII's younger sons, came to Syria some years later and he too was captured in battle by the Muslims but was ransomed by King Amalric. Aimery was one day to become king of Jerusalem himself and the story of how in his youth King Aimery had been ransomed by King Amalric passed into the folklore of the Latin East, for people were struck by the similarity of their names.[80] Ernoul later credited Aimery with having been the lover of Agnes of Courtenay;

---

[76] Bresc-Bautier, nos. 147–8 and 150, pp. 288–91 and 292–6.

[77] CGOH, no. 468.

[78] Although he did not use the title in this document he was holding the office a year later while Raymond was still regent: Bresc-Bautier, no. 160, pp. 311–12.

[79] S. Painter, 'The lords of Lusignan in the eleventh and twelfth centuries', *Speculum* 32 (1957), pp. 27–47; WT, X, 18, XIX, 8, 9, pp. 476, 873, 875; letter of Aimery of Limoges to Louis VII, E. Martène and U. Durand (eds.), *Veterum Scriptorum et Monumentorum Amplissima Collectio*, 9 vols. (Paris, 1724–33), I, p. 870; W.H. Rudt de Collenberg, 'Les Lusignans de Chypre', *Epeteris* 10 (1979–80), p. 90; M. Maupilier, 'Les Lusignans du Bas-Poitou et l'Outremer' in P.J. Arrignon (ed.), *Les Lusignans d'Outremer* (Poitiers, 1995), pp. 190–4.

[80] Philip of Novara, *Le Livre de forme de plait*, c. 94, RHC Lois, I, pp. 569–70.

again, it is impossible to know with what truth.[81] What is certain is
that Aimery married Eschiva, the elder daughter of Baldwin of
Ibelin, and when he first came to Baldwin IV's court in December
1174 he did not do so as Agnes's protégé but as Baldwin of Ibelin's
son-in-law.[82]

Meanwhile, Saladin's power was growing as he was able to
profit from disputes about the custody of Nur ad-Din's heir, as-
Salih. The generals at Damascus who were ruling in his name
feared that Nur ad-Din's nephew, Saif ad-Din of Mosul, would
seek to take charge of as-Salih and of Nur ad-Din's lands. They
therefore sent as-Salih to Aleppo, which was governed by Nur
ad-Din's *mamluk* Gumushtekin, because it was strongly fortified.
But Gumushtekin, who himself wanted to be regent for as-Salih,
promptly made peace with Saif ad-Din.[83] This was seen as a
hostile act by the generals in Damascus who appealed to Saladin
for support. Leaving his brother al-Adil in charge of Egypt,
Saladin marched his army into Syria and took possession of
Damascus in the name of as-Salih;[84] but he wanted to gain
custody of the prince and to rule all of Nur ad-Din's former lands,
and so he went to war with Gumushtekin.

On 8 December 1174 Saladin captured Homs, but the garrison,
loyal to Gumushtekin, held out in the citadel. Leaving a force in the
town, Saladin took his main army to Aleppo, which he reached on
30 December.[85] The Franks were alarmed by his rapid progress.
Before the end of the year the army of the kingdom had assembled
under Raymond and Humphrey of Toron and, supported by the
Knights of St John under their master, Jobert, had marched to Arqa
in the county of Tripoli.[86] They remained there for about a month
until the beleaguered garrison in the citadel of Homs appealed to
them for help. Even then they refused to attack the city unless the
commander of the citadel would first release Frankish prisoners held
there, who included the hostages standing surety for the payment of
Raymond of Tripoli's ransom, and also Eustace of Sidon, the
brother of King Baldwin's stepfather, and understandably the com-

---

[81] Ernoul, p. 59.   [82] CGOH, no. 488.

[83] IA, RHC Or I, p. 615; Baha al-Din, RHC Or III, pp. 57–8.

[84] IA, RHC Or I, p. 616; Kamal ad-Din, ROL 3 (1895), pp. 557–60; al Maqrizi, p. 51; Baha al-Din, RHC Or III, pp. 58–9.

[85] Kamal ad-Din, ROL 3 (1895), pp. 561–3; IA, RHC Or I, p. 617.

[86] CGOH, no. 467; William of Tyre places the start of this campaign in January 1175, XXI, 7–8, pp. 971–3.

mander did not feel able to agree to this request.[87] Saladin was in a dilemma. He knew that a relief army from Mosul was preparing to march on Aleppo, but he could not afford to let the Franks capture Homs because that would impede his lines of communication with Damascus. Deciding that Homs was his priority, he marched to its relief. The Franks made no attempt to fight him, but withdrew to Crac des Chevaliers, and this enabled Saladin to capture the citadel of Homs on 17 March. He then opened negotiations with the Franks, who agreed to withdraw from the frontier if the hostages at Homs were released and if the ransoms were remitted for which they were standing security. Saladin readily agreed to those terms and the Frankish army withdrew to the coast, although it did not disband.[88] That left Saladin free to deal with the threat from Mosul without fear of Frankish intervention. He allied with Saif ad-Din's brother, the prince of Sinjar, thus forcing the ruler of Mosul to divide his forces. The main force attacked Sinjar, and only a small relief army came to Aleppo, and Saladin had little difficulty in defeating this Mosul contingent together with the forces of Gumushtekin when they marched against him on 13 April 1175.[89]

This victory left Saladin free to renew his attack on Aleppo, and he took two key fortresses, Kafartab and Maarat an-Numan. But his army had campaigned for nine consecutive months and wished to return home, so early in May he agreed to make peace provided that the Aleppans recognised the conquests he had already made. During his second attack on Aleppo he had abandoned all pretence of ruling in the name of as-Salih: the prince was no longer prayed for in the sultan's dominions and the coinage was not struck in his name.[90]

The Frankish army had remained at Tripoli until Saladin withdrew from Aleppo and only disbanded at the beginning of May. The combined forces of Jerusalem and Tripoli, together with the Knights of St John, had been kept in the field for five months, yet apart from the bloodless and fruitless demonstration against Homs they had achieved nothing. They had conducted a defensive campaign which had been pointless since their territories had not been threatened,

---

[87] IA, RHC Or I, p. 619.
[88] Baha al-Din, RHC Or III, pp. 59–60; al-Maqrizi, p. 52; Kamal ad-Din, ROL 3 (1895), p. 563; IA, RHC Or I, pp. 619–20; WT, XXI, 8, pp. 972–3.
[89] Kamal ad-Din, ROL 3 (1895), pp. 563–4.
[90] *Ibid.*, pp. 564–5; IA, RHC Or I, pp. 621–2.

but Saladin had considerably strengthened his position in north Syria as a result of Frankish non-intervention. William of Tyre expressed dissatisfaction with the treaty of Homs:

This was done against our interests, for our favour was extended to a man who ought to have been resisted with vigour lest, having become more powerful, he should behave with greater insolence towards us; and so he dared to place his hopes in us, although all the time he was increasing his power at our expense.[91]

Such fears were not groundless, for Saladin had written to the caliph justifying his campaign against the Zengid princes by claiming that he wished to unite western Islam under his leadership in order to attack the Franks and recover Jerusalem and the mosque of al-Aqsa.[92]

William of Tyre makes no mention at all of the full peace that Raymond concluded with Saladin in the summer of 1175. Nevertheless, Islamic sources are unanimous in affirming that such a peace was made, and that the initiative was taken by the Franks.[93] William gives the misleading impression that Raymond continued the war against Saladin, by describing two raids, one against Damascus and the other in the Beka'a valley, which he implies took place in 1175.[94] Although it is clear from other contemporary sources that both campaigns occurred in 1176 after Raymond's regency had come to an end, almost without exception historians of the crusades have attributed these events to 1175.[95] It is difficult to avoid the conclusion that William of Tyre was deliberately trying to obscure the issue, perhaps because he was embarrassed by Raymond III's conduct of foreign affairs.

It was almost certainly during the regency that it became evident that the king really was suffering from leprosy. William of Tyre says this happened 'as he began to approach the age of puberty' (*cum ad pubertatis annos cepit exsurgere*), which implies that it occurred before he came of age in 1176. No doubt could any longer be entertained: 'he was seen to be suffering to a dangerous degree from leprosy. It grew more serious each day, specially injuring his hands and feet and his face, so that his subjects were distressed whenever they looked at

[91] WT, XXI, 8, p. 973.   [92] AS, RHC Or IV, pp. 175–80.
[93] al-Maqrizi, p. 53; AS, RHC Or IV, pp. 181–2; IA, RHC Or I, p. 622.
[94] WT, XXI, 9, 10, pp. 974–5.
[95] E.g. J. Prawer, *Histoire du royaume latin de Jérusalem*, tr. G. Nahon, 2 vols. (Paris, 1969), I, p. 545.

him.'[96] As Piers Mitchell suggests, 'It is possible that puberty triggered Baldwin's downgrading to the lepromatous form of the disease in his teenage years.'[97] No attempt was made to segregate him either then or at any later stage of his life. This surprised Muslim observers: '[The Franks] were concerned to keep him in office, but they took no notice whatsoever of his leprosy', wrote Saladin's biographer, Imad ad-Din al Isfahani.[98]

Nevertheless, the king's illness made it imperative to find a husband for his sister Sibyl, who could act as regent and, in due course, succeed Baldwin as king. This matter was discussed by the High Court, and a marriage was arranged between Sibyl and William Longsword, the eldest son of William V, marquis of Montferrat in Piedmont.[99] He was first cousin both to Louis VII of France and to the Emperor Frederick, and the family was well respected in the Latin East because William V had taken part in the Second Crusade.[100] The decision to form this alliance may have been determined by events in Italy. The Montferrats were vassals and kinsmen of Frederick Barbarossa, by the spring of 1175 the emperor appeared to be winning his long struggle against Pope Alexander III and his allies, the Emperor Manuel, William II of Sicily and the Lombard League, for the League had opened negotiations with him.[101] Saladin too seems to have thought an imperial victory likely, and in 1173 had sent an embassy to Frederick.[102] Frederick had accompanied Conrad III on the Second Crusade, and his commitment to the Crusader Kingdom was beyond question. Raymond of Tripoli and his advisers may therefore have considered that by forming a marriage alliance with the Montferrats they would be placing the kingdom under the protection of the western emperor. Raymond may also have supposed that this would justify his chosen policy of *détente* with Saladin, since the sultan would be afraid of antagonising the most powerful ruler in western Europe, particularly one who controlled the Italian maritime cities that contributed significantly to the commercial prosperity of Egypt, by attacking the Franks in the Holy Land who were under his protection.

---

[96] WT, XXI, 1, p. 962.   [97] See p. 252 below.

[98] Imad ad-Din al-Isfahani, *La conquête de la Syrie et de la Palestine par Saladin*, tr. H. Massé, DRHC 10 (Paris, 1972), p. 18.

[99] WT, XXI, 12, pp. 977–8.   [100] See Genealogy No. IV.

[101] M. Pacaut, *Frederick Barbarossa*, tr. A.J. Pomerans (London, 1970), pp. 147–53.

[102] *Annales Colonienses Maximi*, ed. G.H. Pertz, MGH SS, XVII (Hanover, 1861), p. 786.

From Raymond's point of view, and it was one which no doubt other members of the High Court shared, such an arrangement would have had the advantage of making the Byzantine protectorate redundant. Raymond had a deep antipathy towards the emperor, which dated from 1160 when Manuel, having recently become a widower, had negotiated a marriage with Raymond's only sister, Melisende. It was assumed in Tripoli that a formal betrothal had taken place and in a charter of July 1161 Melisende styled herself 'future empress of Constantinople',[103] but Manuel's ambassadors sent an unfavourable report to him about Melisende and he therefore broke his engagement to her and later that year married her cousin, Mary of Antioch.[104] Melisende's prospects of making a suitable marriage were irreparably damaged, and she died soon afterwards.[105] Raymond took vengeance by equipping a pirate fleet which ravaged the coasts and islands of the Byzantine Empire,[106] and nothing in his later conduct suggests that he ever forgave this affront to his honour.

One immediate consequence of Raymond's policy of peace with Saladin and friendship with Barbarossa was that his government was unable to assist the Sicilians when they made a fresh attack on Egypt. In 1175 a fleet of forty galleys attacked the port of Tinnis, and Saladin, who had remained in Damascus having disbanded most of his troops, would have faced serious problems if the Franks had invaded Egypt at that point; but without the support of a Frankish land force the Sicilians did not pose a serious threat.[107] The chief long-term flaw in Raymond's policy was that Frederick had not yet won the war in Italy, it only seemed probable that he would do so. Yet by committing the Kingdom of Jerusalem to this alliance, Raymond deprived her of other potential allies, the Byzantines and the Sicilians, who were Barbarossa's enemies, and he also antagonised Pope Alexander. This was a high-risk strategy, and one which left Saladin free to make conquests in north Syria without hindrance from the Franks.

In the winter of 1175 Saif ad-Din of Mosul formed a new coalition against Saladin, consisting of his brother, Imad ad-Din of Sinjar, the Artukid prince of Mardin and the ruler of Hisn

[103] Strehlke, no. 3, p. 3.   [104] WT, XVIII, 31, pp. 856–7.
[105] *Lignages*, c. 7, RHC Lois II, p. 448.   [106] WT, XVIII, 33, pp. 858–9.
[107] al-Maqrizi, *al Muwa'iz [Description of Egypt]*, A.H. 571, in M. Amari, *Biblioteca Arabo-Sicula*, Italian tr., 2 vols. (Turin and Rome, 1880–9), I, p. 297.

Kaifa.[108] This forced Saladin to bring his army back to Syria from Egypt in the first quarter of 1176 and, because he was at peace with the Franks, his troops were able to march unopposed through Transjordan.[109] He met the prince of Mosul and his allies in battle at Tell al-Sultan, south of Aleppo, on 22 April 1176 and decisively defeated them.[110] He then marched on Aleppo.

The *atabeg* Gumushtekin made an alliance with Bohemond III of Antioch, who was not bound by the peace which Raymond of Tripoli had made. It was in his interest to support Aleppo as a buffer state between Antioch and Saladin and he was now able to do so, whereas when Saladin had attacked Aleppo in 1174 Bohemond had remained neutral because of the hostility of Prince Mleh of Cilicia on his northern frontier.[111] In 1175 a revolution in Cilicia had overthrown Mleh and brought his pro-Frankish nephew Rupen III to power.[112] Bohemond no longer feared an Armenian attack on his principality while he was away on campaign. He made it a condition of his support that Gumushtekin should release Frankish prisoners of war held in Aleppo, among whom were Joscelin III of Courtenay and Reynald of Châtillon, Bohemond III's stepfather, both of whom Nur ad-Din had steadfastly refused to set free.[113]

Joscelin, titular count of Edessa since 1159, was Agnes of Courtenay's brother and Baldwin IV's uncle. Baldwin III of Jerusalem, while he was administering Antioch during Bohemond III's minority, had appointed him regent of the important frontier fief of Harim.[114] From that base Joscelin carried out intensive raids on the territory of Aleppo in order to avenge his father's death, but in 1164 he was captured by Nur ad-Din and imprisoned at Aleppo.[115] Gumushtekin

---

[108] Kamal ad-Din, ROL 3 (1895), pp. 564–5.

[109] During Shaban (14 February–13 March 1176): al-Maqrizi, p. 53.

[110] Baha al-Din, RHC Or III, pp. 61–3; al-Maqrizi, p. 53.

[111] F. Tournebize, *Histoire . . . de l'Arménie* (Paris, 1910), pp. 181–2; S. Der Nersessian, 'The kingdom of Cilician Armenia', in Setton, *Crusades*, II, pp. 642–3; R. Grousset, *Histoire des Croisades et du royaume franque de Jérusalem*, 3 vols. (Paris, 1934–6), II, pp. 566–9; C. Cahen, *La Syrie du nord à l'époque des croisades et la principauté franque d'Antioch* (Paris, 1940), pp. 413–14; J. Riley-Smith, 'The Templars and Teutonic knights in Cilician Aarmenia', in T.S.R. Boase (ed.), *The Cicilian Kingdom of Armenia* (Edinburgh, 1978), pp. 92–117 at p. 97.

[112] MS, XX, 2, III, p. 361; Cahen, *La Syrie*, p. 417.

[113] Bar Hebraeus, *The Chronography*, ed. and tr. E.A. Wallis Budge, 2 vols. (Oxford, 1932), II, p. 307.

[114] Hamilton, 'The titular nobility of the Latin East: the case of Agnes of Courtenay', in CS, pp. 198 and 202, n. 18.

[115] The Armenian version of Michael the Syrian's *Chronicle* (with French tr.), RHC Arm I, p. 353; WT, XIX, 9, p. 875.

fixed his ransom at 50,000 dinars, a huge sum for a landless man, but a reasonable price for the uncle of the king of Jerusalem, and the sum was raised by his sister Agnes.[116] She cannot have met this vast demand from her own resources, but the ransom must have been paid by the royal treasury and Raymond of Tripoli must have agreed to this.

Prince Reynald was a controversial figure. He had been born in c.1125, a younger son of the lord of Donzy, and was given the lordship of Châtillon-sur-Loire, now Châtillon-Coligny. William of Tyre, who could not bear him, described him as 'almost a common soldier', but as Jean Richard has shown, his family were great lords in twelfth-century Burgundy and claimed descent from the Roman senatorial family of the Palladii. Reynald's grandfather, Geoffrey II count of Chalon, had been a first cousin of St Hugh of Cluny.[117] Reynald accompanied Louis VII on the Second Crusade and stayed in the East, where in 1153 he married Constance of Antioch, the widow of Raymond of Poitiers, and for the next eight years ruled the principality.[118] He obtained a not-unmerited reputation for violence. When the patriarch of Antioch, Aimery of Limoges, refused to place part of the wealth of the Church at his disposal, Reynald tortured him;[119] and when Manuel Comnenus failed to recompense him for the expenses he had incurred on the emperor's behalf, Reynald avenged himself by sacking the Byzantine island of Cyprus.[120] In 1159 Manuel campaigned in Syria and Reynald was forced to make a humiliating submission and to recognise the emperor as his overlord.[121] In 1161 he was captured by Nur ad-Din and imprisoned at Aleppo for fifteen years. During that time his wife died and his stepson Bohemond III became prince of Antioch.[122] Reynald thus became a landless man, but his prestige increased because his

---

[116] MS, XX, 3, III, pp. 365–6; WT, XXI, 10, p. 976.

[117] J. Richard, 'Aux origines d'un grand lignage: des Palladii à Renaud de Châtillon', in *Media in Francia. Recueil de Mélanges offerts à Karl Ferdinand Werner* (Paris, 1989), pp. 409–18. There is no more recent biography of Reynald than that of G. Schlumberger, *Renaud de Châtillon, Prince d'Antioche, Seigneur de la terre d'Outre-Jourdain*, 3rd edn (Paris, 1923).

[118] WT, XVII, 21, 26, pp. 790 and 795–6.

[119] *Ibid.*, XVIII, 1, pp. 809–10; B. Hamilton, 'The elephant of Christ: Reynald of Châtillon', SCH, 15 (1978), pp. 97–108 at p. 98, n. 9.

[120] WT, XVIII, 10, pp. 823–5; John Cinnamus, *Epitome rerum ab Iohanne et Alexio Comnenis gestarum*, IV, 17, ed. A. Meineke, CSHB (Bonn, 1836) pp. 178–80; Cahen, *La Syrie*, pp. 391–3.

[121] WT, XVIII, 23, pp. 844–5; John Cinnamus, *Epitome*, IV, 18, ed. Meineke, pp. 181–3.

[122] Hamilton, 'Elephant', p. 98, n. 13. Bohemond III came to power in 1163: Cahen, *La Syrie*, p. 407.

stepdaughter Mary married the Emperor Manuel and his own daughter Agnes married King Bela III of Hungary.[123] Because of these illustrious connections Gumushtekin fixed Reynald's ransom at the astronomical sum of 120,000 dinars and hostages must have been given to ensure its payment.[124]

Saladin campaigned in the area of Aleppo for almost three months. Having captured Buza'a and Manbij to the north-east, he then wheeled west to attack Azaz on 14 May. The Franks of Antioch marched to its relief under the command of Prince Reynald who thus returned to active service at the first possible opportunity, but his intervention was unavailing and after fierce fighting Azaz fell to Saladin on 22 June.[125] Yet although Saladin was waging a highly successful campaign, he suddenly made peace with the Aleppans on 29 July and was so anxious to end the war that he restored Azaz to them.[126] This change of policy seems to have been caused by a change of government in Jerusalem.

On 15 July 1176, the second anniversary of his coronation, Baldwin IV came of age and Raymond of Tripoli's regency ended. The peace treaty made by Raymond with Saladin in 1175 was not ratified by the king. Arab writers relate that in July 1176 King Baldwin led a raid into the lands around Damascus while the sultan was at Aleppo.[127] This change of policy may well have reflected the young king's own wishes, but it reflected also the appointment of a new chief minister. Joscelin of Courtenay, who together with Reynald of Châtillon had come to Jerusalem, was appointed to the vacant post of seneschal.[128] Baldwin was no doubt influenced by his mother in making this choice, but it was a sensible and indeed an obvious one. The king could trust Joscelin absolutely because he was

---

[123] Mary: John Cinnamus, *Epitome*, V, 4, ed. Meineke, pp. 210–11; WT, XVIII, 31, p. 857. Agnes: Nicetas Choniates, *Historia*, ed. van Dieten, I, p. 170; Alberic of Trois-Fontaines, *Chronica*, ed. P. Scheffer-Boichorst, MGH SS, XXIII (Hanover, 1874), p. 850; John Cinnamus, *Epitome*, VI, 11, ed. Meineke, p. 850.

[124] MS, XX, 3, III, pp. 365–6.

[125] WT, XXI, 10, p. 976, places Reynald's release in the second year of Baldwin IV (15 July, 1175–14 July 1176). Abu Shama places it during Saladin's siege of Aleppo (26 April 1176–29 July 1176): RHC Or IV, p. 183. As Reynald took part in the fighting at Azaz (14 May–22 June 1176) he must have been released before then; MS, XX, 3, III, p. 366; IA, RHC Or I, pp. 623–4.

[126] Kamal ad-Din, ROL 4 (1896), p. 146; Baha al-Din, RHC Or III, p. 63.

[127] Abu Shama places this raid between 10 July and 10 August 1176: RHC Or IV, p. 184; IA places it A.H. 572 (10 July 1176–29 June 1177). RHC Or I, p. 627; as does al-Maqrizi, p. 55.

[128] WT, XXI, 9, p. 974. They arrived before 1 September 1176, CGOH, nos. 495, 496 (dated by the 9th indiction. which ended on 31 August 1176).

his closest kinsman yet had no claim to the throne. He proved a very competent administrator and was completely loyal to his nephew's interests. In order to provide him with an income commensurate with his status, the king arranged his marriage to Agnes of Milly, the youngest daughter and co-heiress of Henry the Buffalo, who brought to Joscelin the fiefs of Montfort and Chastiau dou Roy in the territory of Acre.[129]

Count Raymond's regency had lasted for just over eighteen months. He had not abused his power, but rather had used it to restore unity and had worked in harmony with the military leaders, Humphrey II of Toron and the masters of the military Orders. He had used his powers of patronage with wisdom and discretion. He had not monopolised royal appointments, but had allowed Agnes of Courtenay some share in making them. Those which he had made himself were praiseworthy and he had also proved himself a faithful steward of the king's temporalities. He had arranged a suitable marriage for the heir to the throne, Princess Sibyl, and made no difficulty about handing over the government to the young king when he came of age. In all matters relating to internal policy Raymond had shown himself a capable, prudent and honourable man.

But his conduct of foreign affairs had been more open to criticism. He made peace with Saladin believing that this would be guaranteed by Frederick Barbarossa when he emerged victorious in Italy and became protector of the Latin Kingdom. But those benefits were hypothetical, because Frederick I had not yet achieved victory. In the meantime the chief beneficiary of Raymond's foreign policy was undoubtedly Saladin. When Raymond became regent considerable opportunities still existed to prevent Saladin from encircling the Frankish states, but Raymond made no use of them and by 1176 Frankish room for manoeuvre had been much diminished. If he was virtually excluded from power when the king came of age and did not receive the public recognition which he clearly thought he had a right to expect, the explanation is chiefly to be sought in his conduct of foreign affairs while he was regent.

The new government in Jerusalem left Saladin with no option but

---

[129] *Lignages*, c. 16, RHC Lois II, p. 454. R.L. Nicholson, *Joscelin III of Edessa and the Fall of the Crusader States (1134–1199)* (Leiden, 1973), p. 74, n. 174; H.-E. Mayer, 'Die Seigneurie de Joscelin und der Deutsche Orden', in J. Fleckenstein and M. Hellmann (eds.), *Die geistlichen Ritterorden Europas, Vorträge und Forschungen* 26 (1980), pp. 171–216 at p. 182, n. 28.

to make peace with Aleppo, but on his way back to Damascus he attacked Masyaf, the headquarters of the Syrian Assassins. They had been opposed to him since he first campaigned against Aleppo in 1174, probably because he had attacked some Isma'ili settlements on his march there.[130] While he was besieging the city in 1174 they had made an attempt on his life, which was unsuccessful because the emir of Abu Qubais recognised the *fidais* and gave the alarm before they reached the sultan.[131] A second attempt had been made during the 1176 campaign, and this was particularly alarming because the assassins involved were members of the corps of *mamluks* belonging to Saladin's uncle Shirkuh, the most trusted troops in his army, and their attempt only failed because he was wearing armour beneath his robes.

Saladin's war against the Assassins can only have lasted about a week and would seem to have been inconclusive.[132] Observers in the Islamic world were puzzled by this. Some said that it was because Saladin's army had been in the field for a long time and wished to return home, while others said that the Assassins had threatened to kill Saladin's maternal uncle, the governor of Hama, who persuaded his nephew to withdraw. But Ibn abi Tayy attributed the Sultan's abandonment of the campaign to Frankish intervention.[133] It was certainly in the Franks' interests to prevent Saladin from conquering Assassin territory, which would have laid Tripoli and Antioch open to attack. The king and his advisers may also have hoped by their intervention to reactivate negotiations with the Assassins, which had been allowed to lapse after Amalric's death; for Raymond of Tripoli was the only secular Frankish leader who had cause to be hostile to them because they had murdered his father in 1152,[134] and although the Assassins and the Franks both fought against Saladin in 1175 as allies of Aleppo, they had no direct dealings with each other.

On 1 August 1176 Baldwin IV led the army of the kingdom to the Beka'a valley, where he was joined by Raymond III and the army of Tripoli. They raided this fertile area with impunity and defeated an attack by the garrison of Damascus led by Saladin's nephew Shams

---

[130] B. Lewis, *The Assassins. A Radical Sect in Islam* (London, 1967), p. 114.
[131] B. Lewis, 'Saladin and the Assassins', *Bulletin of SOAS* 15 (1953), pp. 225–59 at p. 239; IA, RHC Or I, pp. 618–19.
[132] Lyons and Jackson, *Saladin*, pp. 108–9.
[133] Cited by AS, RHC Or IV, pp. 183–4; IA, RHC Or I, p. 626.
[134] WT, XVII, 19, pp. 786–7.

al-Daula Turan-Shah.[135] This probably led Saladin to abandon the siege of Masyaf. If the Franks wanted to fight a war, it was not good sense to tie his army up in a long series of sieges in the Jabal Bahra.[136] But Baldwin's intervention did not lead to a renewal of negotiations with the Assassins, because soon after his return to Damascus Saladin made peace with them. The thirteenth-century historian of Aleppo, Kamal ad-Din, reported that a member of Saladin's staff had told him how after Saladin had returned to Damascus the Assassins made a further attempt on his life and, although that too was unsuccessful, the sultan realised that such attempts would be repeated and that on some future occasion one of them would succeed and therefore sent to Sinan to negotiate peace.[137] The Assassins did not threaten Saladin again and sixteen years later he insisted that they should be included in the treaty that he made with Richard I at the end of the Third Crusade.[138] The Assassins seem to have remained neutral in the war between the Franks and Saladin. No Franks are reported to have been killed by them until Conrad of Montferrat was murdered in 1192,[139] and Saladin did not use their territory as a base from which to attack the Franks in north Syria.

These two brief campaigns in the summer of 1176 had given Baldwin IV his first experience of war. Although William of Tyre refers to him as commander of the army, which was technically true, the king must have relied on the experience of his vassals, particularly that of the constable, Humphrey of Toron. Nothing is directly known about the king's own reaction to his illness, except that he was obviously resolved to fight the disease. He could easily have become an invalid and delegated at least the military duties of his office, but he never attempted to do so until he became too ill to ride. He led his armies in person and took part in fighting even though he was effectively one-handed, using the skills which his Arab riding-master had taught him. His physical courage and sheer willpower command respect and admiration.

---

[135] IA, RHC Or I, p. 627; AS, RHC Or IV, pp. 183–4. This raid is misdated by William of Tyre, XXI, 10, pp. 975–6; see above p. 100.

[136] Lyons and Jackson, *Saladin*, pp. 109–10.

[137] B. Lewis, 'Kamal ad-Din's biography of Rašid al-Din Sinan', *Arabica* 13 (1966), pp. 225–59 at p. 236.

[138] AS, RHC Or V, p. 77.   [139] On Conrad's murder see Lewis, *Assassins*, pp. 117–18.

CHAPTER 6

Western aid. William of Montferrat and Philip of Flanders

William Longsword of Montferrat reached the Holy Land at the beginning of October 1176 escorted by a Genoese fleet.[1] Giuseppe Ligato is probably right in arguing that no specific promises had been made to him during the marriage negotiations about his future constitutional position in the Latin Kingdom, although almost certainly the assumption must have been that he would become king either when Baldwin died, or when he became too ill to rule:[2] for Baldwin could not marry and beget a legitimate heir because it was believed that leprosy could be sexually transmitted.[3] William of Tyre reports that William's marriage was 'unwelcome to and openly opposed by certain of those men by whose advice he had been summoned [to Jerusalem]'.[4] Although he does not give any reason for this reaction, it probably reflected the changing fortunes of Frederick Barbarossa, since the Montferrat marriage had been arranged in order to secure his protection for the Crusader States. On 29 May 1176 the emperor had been decisively defeated by the forces of the Lombard League at Legnano, and his protection then came to appear more of a liability than a benefit, since not only was he in no position to intervene in the Latin East, but he was also still

---

[1] William promised to help the Genoese recover their property in the Latin Kingdom: Imperiale di Sant'Angelo, II, pp. 234–6, no. 165; cf. H.-E. Mayer and M.-L. Favreau, 'Das Diplom Balduins I für Genua und Genuas goldene Inschrift in der Grabeskirche', QF 55–6 (1976), pp. 22–95; B.Z. Kedar, 'Genoa's golden inscription in the Church of the Holy Sepulchre: a case for the defence', in G. Airaldi and B.Z. Kedar (eds.), *I comuni italiani nel regno crociato di Gerusalemme* (Genoa, 1986), pp. 319–35; W. Haberstumpf, 'Guglielmo Lungaspada di Monferrato, conte di Ascalona e di Giaffa (1176–1177)', *Studi Piemontesi* 18 (1989), pp. 601–8.
[2] G. Ligato, 'Guglielmo Lungaspada di Monferrato e le istituzioni politiche dell'Oriente latino', in L. Balletto (ed.), *Dai feudi Monferrini e dal Piemonte ai nuovi mondi oltre gli oceani* (Alessandria, 1993), pp. 153–88.
[3] See Piers Mitchell, Appendix below, p. 255.
[4] WT, XXI, 12, p. 978.

at war with the pope and the king of Sicily, whose aid the Franks of Jerusalem needed.[5] This may explain why some members of the High Court of Jerusalem were opposed to the marriage.

Nevertheless, William was so well connected that to have broken his marriage contract would have antagonised too many influential people in the West on whose goodwill the Crusader Kingdom depended, including the republic of Genoa, and perhaps King Louis VII of France.[6] Moreover, Sibyl's marriage prospects might have been irretrievably damaged had she not married William, because she had already been rejected as a bride by Stephen of Sancerre.[7] William's marriage to Sibyl was therefore finally solemnised in November 1176, six weeks after his arrival, and he was invested with the double county of Jaffa and Ascalon, which had formerly been the appanage of King Amalric.[8] This marked the beginning of the process whereby the royal demesne, so extensive at the start of Baldwin IV's reign, was divided among members of the royal family.

Sicard of Cremona relates that Baldwin offered to abdicate in William's favour, but that William would not agree to this, but, he adds, William held the whole kingdom in his care.[9] It is indeed possible that Baldwin did wish to abdicate now that he knew he was suffering from leprosy and had a brother-in-law to whom he could responsibly hand over power; but if he made such an offer, then William declined it, being aware that a substantial group of nobles were opposed to him. There is no evidence that William 'held the whole kingdom in his care', except in the sense that, as the king's male next-of-kin, he may have been expected to deputise for him if he became too ill to rule.

William of Tyre describes William of Montferrat in this way:

He was reasonably tall and was a good-looking young man with reddish-gold hair. He was brave, but quick-tempered and liable to over-react. He was very generous and completely frank, totally lacking in any kind of pretence. He ate to excess and was a very heavy drinker, but this did not impair his judgment. It was said that he had been trained in the art of war from his earliest youth.[10]

---

[5] P. Lamma, *Comneni e Staufer. Ricerche sui rapporti fra Bisanzio et l'Occidente nel secolo XII*, 2 vols. (Rome, 1955–7), II, pp. 260–2.

[6] See Genealogy IV.   [7] See pp. 30–1 above.

[8] WT, XXI, 12, p. 978.

[9] 'sed in custodia regnum tenuit universum', Sicard of Cremona, *Cronicon*, ed. O. Holder-Egger, MGH SS, XXXI, (Hanover, 1903), p. 173.

[10] WT, XXI, 12, p. 978.

In other words he had the virtues which were admired at the time in the nobility, courage, liberality and proficiency in arms, but lacked the qualities of moderation and tact needed in a king of Jerusalem.

Saladin meanwhile was unable to consolidate his Syrian conquests. There had been a severe drought throughout the region in 1176 and the spring harvest had been negligible. Consequently he could not station his Egyptian army in Damascus through the winter in a time of famine, nor could he tax his Syrian conquests to pay back the money supplied by Egypt to finance his Syrian campaigns.[11] This led to unrest in Egypt, and he therefore returned there with his army on 10 September 1176, leaving Turan-Shah as his viceroy in Syria with only a few troops at his disposal.[12]

Baldwin and his advisers were, from the start of his personal rule, planning a full-scale attack on Egypt, the hub of Saladin's power. One of the king's first acts was to renew the grant of land in Egypt which his father had made to the Knights of St John, and to promise their master, Jobert, an additional 30,000 bezants of revenue in the territory of Bilbeis.[13] For this he needed naval support and he therefore turned once more to Byzantium for help, seeking to revive the protectorate arranged by King Amalric in 1171. The embassy to Constantinople was led by Prince Reynald. This is known from the dedicatory letter to Aimery of Limoges, Latin patriarch of Antioch, with which Hugh Eteriano prefaced his *De Processione Sancti Spiritus*. Hugh was living in Constantinople and was the adviser to the Emperor Manuel on western Church affairs, and he states that he was sending a copy to Aimery 'per manum gloriosissimi principis Rainaldi'.[14] Hugh was resident in Constantinople from c.1165, so Reynald's visit cannot have taken place before his capture by Nur ad-Din in 1161, and the only time after his release when it could have occurred was during the winter of 1176–7 (for his presence in the Crusader Kingdom is securely attested from the late spring of 1177 until his death), and this agrees with Dondaine's dating of Eteriano's treatise.[15] Despite his earlier turbulent relations with Manuel,

---

[11] MS, XX, 3, III, p. 367; M.C. Lyons and D.E.P. Jackson, *Saladin. The Politics of the Holy War* (Cambridge, 1982), p. 111.

[12] Baha al-Din, RHC Or III, p. 63; al-Maqrizi, p. 55.

[13] CGOH, no. 496, issued before 1 September 1176.

[14] E. Martène and U. Durand (eds.), *Thesaurus Novus Anecdotorum*, 5 vols. (Paris, 1717), I, p. 479.

[15] Röhricht noted the significance of this passage but dated Reynald's visit 1170, RRH, no. 482, I, p. 127. That is not possible because he was a prisoner at Aleppo at that time. Reynald is not mentioned in any source relating to the Crusader States between the high

Reynald was an obvious choice as ambassador: he was a kinsman of Baldwin IV and, as stepfather of Mary of Antioch, a member of Manuel's affinity. His long imprisonment by the Muslims and the recent death of his only son, Baldwin, in the emperor's service may have softened any resentment which Manuel may still have felt towards him for his ravaging of Cyprus twenty years before.[16] It is probable that the emperor paid Reynald's enormous ransom of 120,000 gold dinars. It is unlikely that either Bohemond III or Baldwin IV had the resources to do so, whereas Manuel would have been under a certain moral pressure to pay the ransom of his wife's stepfather, particularly as it had been fixed so high because of Reynald's imperial connections.

William of Tyre describes the outcome of Reynald's embassy as a renewal 'on almost identical terms between the . . . emperor and the lord Baldwin who is now king' of 'the agreements which had formerly been entered upon between the lord emperor and the lord king Amalric'.[17] The agreements covered two main areas. The first was a joint attack on Egypt by the Byzantine navy and the Frankish army. Manuel's willingness to contemplate a new expedition of this kind after the fiasco of 1169 is surprising, but his interest in Egypt was independent of his commitment to the Franks of Jerusalem because he was concerned to prevent the Sicilians from seizing the Nile delta. William II's attacks on Alexandria in 1174 and Tinnis in 1175 had shown that Palermo was seriously interested in gaining control of the Egyptian ports. It was clear that Barbarossa was about to make peace with his enemies in Italy and this would leave the Kingdom of Sicily free to resume its traditional anti-Byzantine policy. If it controlled the Egyptian ports it would be more powerful than ever, and would also be in a position to harm Byzantine trade by offering attractive terms there to Italian merchants, while at the same time depriving the Byzantines of their western naval allies.

Paul Magdalino has made the important observation that Cinnamus's *History* of Manuel's reign breaks off in the middle of a sentence reporting how, when Manuel launched his attack on Iconium in

---

summer of 1176 (CGOH, no. 495, written before 1 September 1176), and spring 1177 (see n. 42 below). This accords with the view of A. Dondaine that the treatise of Hugh Eteriano was completed 'en 1176 (ou bien au début de 1177)', 'Hugues Ethérien et Léon Toscan', *Archives d'histoire doctrinale et littéraire du Moyen Age* 19 (1952), pp. 67–134 at p. 102.

[16] See n. 30 below.
[17] WT, XXI, 15, p. 982.

1176, he also 'sent a fleet of 150 ships against Egypt . . . but having insufficient troops for the expedition to Egypt. . .': at this point the manuscript ends. This expedition never took place, but Magdalino suggests that it may have been planned in the course of discussions with the envoys from Jerusalem in 1176 and then postponed until the following year.[18] It does not seem likely that Prince Reynald could have reached Constantinople early enough in 1176 to influence the assembly of this fleet, but it is quite possible that Manuel had intended to launch a pre-emptive strike against Egypt in 1176 without Frankish help. Moreover, when these plans were made, Raymond of Tripoli was regent and the Franks were still at peace with Saladin. Although Manuel could not proceed with the attack on Egypt after the defeat of his field army at Myriocephalum, he would have welcomed the Frankish proposals for a joint attack in the following year, since the fleet was already prepared and the Franks would supply the troops.

The price which Manuel demanded for his help was the same as that which he had required of King Amalric in 1171 – the establishment of a Byzantine protectorate in the Crusader States. For this to be effective the emperor needed permanent representatives at Jerusalem and Antioch. The Orthodox patriarch Athanasius, who had fulfilled that role at Antioch, had been killed in an earthquake in 1170,[19] while Amalric's queen, Maria Comnena, who with her household had represented Byzantine interests in Jerusalem, had retired from public life in Baldwin IV's reign. As there was no possibility of arranging a new Byzantine marriage alliance with the royal family of Jerusalem because Baldwin IV could not marry and his sister was married already, Manuel proposed to restore an Orthodox patriarch there.

While western sources say nothing about this (from their point of view) shameful condition of the treaty, *The Life of Leontios, Patriarch of Jerusalem* provides clear evidence about it. This is a reliable source: Leontius died in 1185, his biographer, Theodosius Goudelis, knew him well and wrote the *Life* soon after 1203.[20] Leontius had been

[18] P. Magdalino, *The Empire of Manuel I Komnenos, 1143–1180* (Cambridge, 1994), p. 97, citing John Cinnamus, *Epitome rerum ab Iohanne et Alexio Comnenis gestarum*, ed. A. Meineke, CHSB (Bonn, 1836), p. 300.

[19] Cinnamus, *Epitome*, ed. Meineke, V, 13, pp. 237–8; MS, XVIII, 11, III, p. 326; B. Hamilton, *The Latin Church in the Crusader States. The Secular Church* (London, 1980), pp. 175–7.

[20] *The Life of Leontios Patriarch of Jerusalem*, ed. and tr. D. Tsougarakis (Leiden, 1993), pp. 11–27.

abbot of Patmos and was appointed patriarch of Jerusalem by the emperor at some time after April 1176.[21] Since the crusader conquest the Orthodox patriarchs of Jerusalem had lived in Constantinople attached to the Cathedral of the Holy Wisdom. But Theodosius tells us that 'Since he was appointed archpriest of Sion . . . [Leontios] was being reminded by the ruler to go there.'[22] The patriarch spent the winter of 1176–7 at Patmos and in the spring went to Cyprus, where he examined property belonging to the patriarchal see, while waiting to come to Acre. Although the *Life* does not date these events, Richard Rose has correctly placed his arrival in the Holy Land in the summer of 1177 because the account which the *Life* goes on to give of his activities there is consonant with political events in the years 1177–8, but with those of no other time between the election of Leontius and the death of the Emperor Manuel in 1180.[23] Although Leontius's biographer describes the journey as a pilgrimage to Jerusalem, that is clearly nonsense.[24] The Orthodox patriarch could not enter the kingdom without royal licence unless he came incognito, which Leontius did not do. An official visit was a serious matter, for in the view of the Frankish government there was only one patriarch of Jerusalem, Amalric of Nesle, who had authority over Orthodox as well as Catholic Christians.[25] Baldwin IV must therefore have agreed to Leontius's coming, and the only reason he can have had for doing so was that Manuel had made his protection of the Latin Kingdom against Saladin conditional on the restoration of the Orthodox patriarch.

In the case of Antioch, Manuel arranged a marriage for Prince Bohemond III and his own great-niece Theodora, who is thought to have been the daughter of the Protovestiarius John and thus the sister of Maria, dowager-queen of Jerusalem.[26] This almost certainly happened during the negotiations of 1176–7. Bohemond was free to marry, as his first wife, Orgueilleuse of Harim, had died in c.1175.[27]

---

[21] *Ibid.*, c. 66, n. 2, pp. 195–6.

[22] *Ibid.*, c. 67, pp. 110–11.

[23] *Ibid.*, pp. 196–7, n. 2; R.B. Rose, 'The *Vita* of Saint Leontios and its account of his visit to Palestine during the Crusader period', *Proche-Orient Chrétien* 35 (1985), pp. 238–57.

[24] Tsougarakis writes: 'There is no doubt that this journey had little or nothing to do with the completion of a personal pilgrimage, a journey he had begun when he followed his first master about forty-five years before': *Life*, p. 196.

[25] Hamilton, *Latin Church*, pp. 179–87.

[26] C.M. Brand, *Byzantium Confronts the West, 1180–1204* (Cambridge, Mass., 1968), p. 22.

[27] Orgueilleuse of Harim is last mentioned in March 1175, CGOH, no. 475; cf. *Lignages*, c. 5, RHC Lois II, p. 446 (where Theodora is wrongly named Irene).

Theodora and her household represented Byzantine interests at the court of Antioch and it is clear from the speed with which Bohemond repudiated her as soon as Manuel was dead that this marriage had not been of his choosing.[28]

Manuel was particularly receptive to Frankish requests for help in the winter of 1176–7 because his armies had been defeated by the Seljuk sultan of Iconium at Myriocephalum on 17 September.[29] Prince Reynald's only son, Baldwin, had been among those killed in the emperor's service.[30] In military terms the defeat was not particularly serious. Kilij-Arslan made no attempt to follow up his victory beyond demanding that the new frontier fortresses that Manuel had built should be dismantled. Cahen argues persuasively that the sultan was more concerned to unify his newly conquered dominions than to become involved in a prolonged war with his Christian neighbour.[31] Moreover, the capacity of the Byzantine army was not seriously affected by its losses on this occasion.[32] But the defeat did seriously damage the international prestige of the empire, and it occurred at a particularly sensitive time, when the war between Frederick Barbarossa and Pope Alexander III and his allies was coming to an end. Despite his support for Alexander III and the Lombard League, Manuel was not invited to take part in the negotiations which began in the autumn of 1176 and culminated at the Peace of Venice in the following July.[33] The end of the Italian wars would mean the end of peace on Manuel's western frontiers, once potentially hostile powers such as Sicily and Venice were no longer preoccupied by the threat of Hohenstaufen dominance, and he would also face the hostility of Barbarossa.[34] In those circumstances the fact that he, rather than the Emperor Frederick, was recognised as protector of the Crusader States would be of great diplomatic advantage to him in his dealings with the papacy and the other western powers.

[28] See pp. 164–5, below.

[29] M. Angold, *The Byzantine Empire, 1025–1204. A Political History*, 2nd edn (London, 1997), pp. 222–5; Magdalino, *Manuel I*, pp. 98–9.

[30] Nicetas Choniates, *Historia*, ed. J.A. Van Dieten, Corpus Fontium Historiae Byzantinae 11, 2 vols. (Berlin, 1975), I, p. 181; cf. the note to this passage in RHC Grecs II, p. 406.

[31] C. Cahen, *Pre-Ottoman Turkey. A General Survey of the Material and Spiritual Culture and History c.1071–1330*, tr. J. Jones-Williams (London, 1968), pp. 104–5.

[32] Angold, *Byzantine Empire*, pp. 223–5; R.-J. Lilie, *Byzantium and the Crusader States, 1096–1204*, tr. J.E. Ridings (Oxford, 1993), pp. 214–15.

[33] Lamma, *Comneni e Staufer*, II, pp. 283–92.

[34] See p. 82 above.

Saladin was aware that the Franks were planning to attack Egypt, but supposed that this would take place in conjunction with an attack by the Sicilian fleet, though William II could not, of course, intervene until the peace negotiations with Frederick Barbarossa had been satisfactorily concluded. Saladin spent much of the winter of 1176–7 putting Egypt in readiness to resist an invasion. He supervised the completion of the new defence works at Damietta, Alexandria and Tinnis, and started to fortify his capital, which entailed enclosing the cities of Cairo and Fustat within a single wall and building a massive citadel. Much of the labour for these projects was supplied by Frankish prisoners of war.[35] The sultan also began to construct a fleet to protect the Egyptian coast and sent an embassy to Genoa to negotiate the import of shipbuilding materials.[36] The Franks of Jerusalem were already causing Saladin problems. His letters were full of complaints about the difficulties of communication between Cairo and Damascus and eastern Islam, which had culminated in the arrest by the Frankish garrison of Kerak of the envoys of Hisn Kaifa and Mardin who were travelling to Cairo to ratify the truce made in 1176. As a preliminary to the Egyptian campaign, the government of Jerusalem sought to negotiate a truce with Turan Shah at Damascus, in order to avoid the problem which had beset Amalric, of being distracted by attacks from the north while the main army of the kingdom was in Egypt. Saladin was equally glad that he would not have to fight on two fronts simultaneously and told his brother that he did not object to his making such a truce provided that its terms did not preclude him from sending troops to Egypt. Saladin became aware that an attack was imminent when in 1177 no Christian ships came to the Egyptian ports with the spring sailing. This presumably indicates that the Italian republics that traded with Constantinople and the Franks of Jerusalem had been informed by them of the planned attack. Saladin therefore moved his army to Faqus, to the west of the delta, at the end of June in readiness to repel a Frankish invasion.[37]

---

[35] Saladin informed the caliph that the Lord of Sicily had a fleet in readiness to help the Franks of Jerusalem. Lyons and Jackson, *Saladin*, p. 113, citing al-Fadil, B.M. Add. MSS 25757:108. Ibn Jubayr (p. 43) found work still in progress on the citadel when he visited Cairo in 1183.

[36] A.S. Ehrenkreutz, 'The place of Saladin in the naval history of the Mediterranean Sea', *Journal of the American Oriental Society* 75 (1955), pp. 100–16; Lyons and Jackson, *Saladin*, p. 114.

[37] Lyons and Jackson, *Saladin*, pp. 115–17.

Prince Reynald returned to Jerusalem in the spring of 1177 having carried out his mission with outstanding success and also having discharged his ransom.[38] Baldwin IV consented to Reynald's marriage to Stephanie of Milly, widow of Miles of Plancy and in her own right lady of Montréal. The exact date of the wedding is not known, but it took place during the lifetime of William of Montferrat.[39] The king augmented Reynald's power by granting him the lordship of Hebron, which had previously formed part of the royal demesne.[40] This fief owed service of twenty knights to the crown and, combined with the service of forty knights owed by the lordship of Montréal and Kerak, this made Reynald the fourth greatest vassal in the kingdom.[41]

Prince Reynald and William of Montferrat between them thus came to control the southern defences of the kingdom, which also formed Saladin's Achilles' heel – the lines of communication linking his two capitals, Cairo and Damascus. The two men appear to have co-operated well and, although they were only colleagues for a very brief time, agreed a common policy. In 1177 Count Rodrigo Alvarez of Sarria in Leon came to the Crusader Kingdom. He had been professed in the Spanish military Order of Santiago, but had been licensed by Pope Alexander III in 1175 to found a new military Order of stricter observance, which was later to be known as the Order of Mountjoy. Reynald and William could see the potential value of this new Order to help them to defend their long eastern and southern frontiers against Saladin. With Baldwin IV's consent, they therefore gave Rodrigo 'a great extent of land with the farms which were situated there'.[42] This seemed a sensible policy. The Order was still small, but the Templars had been a very small and poor Order at first and yet had come to make a major contribution to the defence of the kingdom. Count Rodrigo had the support of

---

[38] William of Tyre states that the ransom was paid, but does not specify by whom: WT, XXI, 10, p. 976.

[39] *Ibid.*, XXI, 12, p. 978; Baldwin IV confirmed a grant made to Count Rodrigo by William of Montferrat and Reynald of Châtillon 'du consentement d'Estiennette sa femme': J. Delaville Le Roulx (ed.), 'Inventaire de pièces de Terre Sainte de l'Ordre de l'Hôpital', ROL 3 (1895), pp. 36–106 at p. 61, no. 119. Reynald and Stephanie must therefore have married before William's death in June 1177.

[40] H.-E. Mayer, *Die Kreuzfahrerherrschaft Montréal (Šōbak). Jordanien im 12 Jahrhundert*, (Abhandlungen des deutschen Palästinavereins 14 (Wiesbaden, 1990), p. 149, n. 29; H.-E. Mayer, 'Die Herrschaftsbildung in Hebron', ZDPV 101 (1985), pp. 64–81.

[41] John of Ibelin, *Livre des Assises*, c. XIII, ed. Edbury, *John of Ibelin*, p. 118.

[42] Delaville Le Roulx, 'Inventaire', p. 61, no. 119.

the pope and of Alfonso II of Aragon and there was every reason to think that his Order would prosper.[43]

But when everything in the Latin Kingdom seemed to be going reasonably well, William of Montferrat fell sick at Ascalon. His illness lasted for two months and the king came to visit him, but he too fell gravely ill. In June William died, leaving his wife pregnant. His body was taken to Jerusalem and buried in the vestibule of the Hospital of St John.[44] When news of his death reached Italy it was inevitably suspected that he had been poisoned,[45] but it seems likely that he had contracted some illness to which he had no immunity, while his intemperate eating habits, about which William of Tyre comments, may have weakened his resistance. His death could scarcely have happened at a less opportune time, for it created problems about the regency when the king was seriously ill and the kingdom on the verge of a major war.

Baldwin nominated Prince Reynald as his executive regent. He was his kinsman and an experienced military commander, and because he had just negotiated the treaty with Manuel he could be relied on to work in harmony with the Byzantine high command in the forthcoming attack on Egypt. This appointment met with general approval even from Reynald's critics. William of Tyre described him as 'a man of proven loyalty and unusual steadfastness of character'.[46] Yet the appointment was divisive because the king had not chosen Raymond of Tripoli and was, implicitly at least, criticising the way he had conducted affairs during Baldwin's minority.

The peace conference at Venice lasted from May to July 1177; Frederick Barbarossa was reconciled to Alexander III, negotiated a truce with the Lombard League and on 21 July confirmed a fifteen-year truce with William II in which, for the first time, the emperor acknowledged the sovereign status of the Kingdom of Sicily.[47] These events made Manuel all the more anxious to press ahead with his attack on Egypt in order to prescind Sicilian intervention there.

---

[43] A. Forey, 'The Order of Mountjoy', *Speculum* 46 (1971), pp. 250–66. Alexander III confirmed the possessions of the Order in 1180, J. Delaville Le Roulx, 'L'Ordre de Montjoye', ROL I (1893), pp. 42–57 at pp. 51–4.

[44] WT, XXI, 12, p. 978.

[45] Continuator of Sigebert of Gembloux, *Chronographia*, ed. D.L.C. Bethmann, MGH SS, VI (Hanover, 1844), p. 415.

[46] WT, XXI, 13, pp. 979–80.

[47] Lamma, *Comneni e Staufer*, II, pp. 283–92; P. Munz, *Frederick Barbarossa* (London, 1969), pp. 328–32.

Then on 1 August 1177 Count Philip of Flanders reached Acre with a sizable army. He had taken the cross on Good Friday 1175, when he learned of King Amalric's death and the accession of the thirteen-year-old Baldwin IV, and he considered staying in the Holy Land for a long time.[48] He wrote to St Hildegard, Abbess of Bingen, a woman of great learning and sanctity, who was believed by her contemporaries to have the gift of spiritual discernment:

I humbly ask . . . that you ask God what I ought to do . . . so that the Christian cause may benefit in these days and the extreme savagery of the Saracens may be brought low, and whether it would be useful for me to stay in the Holy Land or to return.

St Hildegard's reply was guarded: 'if the time shall come when the infidels seek to destroy the fountain of faith, then fight them as hard as, with God's help, you may be able to do'.[49]

Philip was concerned about Jerusalem for a variety of reasons. His parents had set him an example of zeal for the Holy Places: his father, Thierry of Flanders, had been on crusade four times, while his mother had separated from her husband in order to remain in the convent of Bethany, where she had died in 1165.[50] In addition, Philip was first cousin to Baldwin IV and one of the few people with a constitutional claim to the regency during his minority.[51] Although he was unable to set out in 1175 because there was a rebellion in Flanders,[52] once peace had been restored he could plan to leave for an indefinite period because he had a deputy there, his brother Peter, who was married to the heiress of Nevers. But when Peter died in 1176 leaving only an infant daughter, Philip no longer had a close kinsman to defend his extensive family lands during his absence, and could only go to the East for a limited time.[53] Indeed, it says much for his commitment to the crusading cause that he still went ahead with his preparations for the Jerusalem journey.

---

[48] WT, XXI, 13, p. 979; Roger of Howden, *Gesta Regis Henrici Secundi*, RS 49(i), p. 83; Continuator of Sigebert of Gembloux, *Chronographia*, MGH SS, VI, p. 415.

[49] Hildegard of Bingen, St, *Epistolae*, no. XXVIII, P.L. 197, cols. 187–8. The new edition of Hildegard's letters in Corpus Christianorum does not yet include her correspondence with laymen.

[50] Thierry went on crusade in 1139, 1148, 1157 and 1164: WT, XV, 6, XVII, 1, XVIII, 16–19, 21, 24, XIX, 10–11, pp. 681, 760–1, 833–42, 846 and 866–8; Sibyl of Flanders's death at Bethany: Continuator of Sigebert of Gembloux, *Chronographia*, MGH SS, VI, p. 412.

[51] See p. 90 above.

[52] Roger of Howden, *Gesta Regis Henrici Secundi*, p. 101.

[53] Robert of Torigni, *Chronicon*, ed. R. Howlett, RS 82(iv), (London, 1889), pp. 271–2.

Henry II of England had viewed Philip's crusading plans with misgivings. The reasons for this are not entirely clear. It is true that Philip had supported the 'young king' Henry of England in his unsuccessful revolt in 1173, but normal relations had been restored between Philip and Henry II in 1175.[54] It is also true that Henry, like Philip, had a claim to the regency of Jerusalem during Baldwin IV's minority, but by 1176 the king had come of age and that potential source of discord was no longer relevant. The *Gesta Henrici* relates that 'the King of England had been informed that the aforesaid Count of Flanders was intending to go to Jerusalem in order to make himself king there'.[55] What Henry may have had in mind was this: that although Philip had no claim to the throne of Jerusalem himself, he was the guardian of his two nieces, Ida and Matilda of Boulogne, the daughters of his brother Matthew who had died in 1173. Matthew had married Mary, the daughter and only surviving legitimate descendant of King Stephen of England. Her mother had been Matilda, the daughter and heiress of Eustace III of Boulogne, the elder brother of Godfrey of Bouillon and of King Baldwin I of Jerusalem.[56] When Baldwin I died in 1118 Eustace had been summoned by one party in the High Court of Jerusalem to accept the kingship, and had agreed to this, but had been turned back when he reached Calabria by the news that Baldwin II had been enthroned.[57] Arguably Eustace's granddaughter, Mary dowager-countess of Boulogne, and her daughters had a better claim to the throne of Jerusalem than Baldwin IV and his sisters, and that theoretical claim might have significance in the troubled and uncertain situation which existed in Jerusalem, after King Amalric's death. Baldwin IV was an Angevin, and if Philip of Flanders were to use his crusade to restore the house of Boulogne as rulers of Jerusalem, Angevin interests would be damaged. This seems the most likely reason for Henry II's concern, but if it was, his anxieties would appear to have been unfounded, because there is no evidence that Philip had any plans to promote his nieces' interests.

In 1176 Henry II sent a high-powered mission to Flanders to

---

[54] G.G. Dept, *Les influences anglaise et française dans le comté de Flandre au début du XIIIe siècle* (Ghent, 1928), pp. 21–2; W.L. Warren, *Henry II* (London, 1973), pp. 22, n. 3, 118–38 and 224.

[55] Roger of Howden, *Gesta Regis Henrici Secundi*, p. 116.

[56] J.H. Round, 'The counts of Boulogne as English lords', in *Studies in Peerage and Family History* (Westminster, 1901), pp. 147–80; see Genealogy V.

[57] WT, XII, 3, p. 550.

request the count to delay his departure until Easter 1177, assuring him that he would subsidise his expedition and would either join it himself or attach a contingent of troops to it.[58] Philip was willing to agree to these proposals because the death of his brother Peter made it essential for him to place his lands under the protection of some powerful ruler during his absence and the choice lay between the kings of France and England. He believed that Louis VII was seeking to arrange marriages between Philip's nieces, the heiresses of Boulogne, and his own son Philip and his nephew Louis, son of Theobald of Blois.[59] That would increase the power of the French crown at the expense of the count of Flanders and would not be in the interests of Henry II either, for Ida and Matilda had inherited a claim to the Honour of Boulogne in England.[60] At Henry's suggestion, Philip swore under oath that he would not marry his nieces to anybody without the consent of the English king.[61] This meant, in effect, that the lands of the count of Flanders and his wards were taken under the protection of the English crown during his absence. The corollary was, of course, that Philip could not act while in the Crusader Kingdom in ways which were contrary to the wishes of Henry II and the interests of the House of Anjou by promoting the claims of his nieces to the crown of Jerusalem, and the presence of English representatives on the crusade made that certain. Louis VII of France did not object to Philip's understanding with Henry II, but remained on good terms with him and instructed him to discuss the possibility of a French–Byzantine alliance with Manuel Comnenus on his return journey.

In the spring of 1177 Philip came to England and prayed at the shrine of St Thomas at Canterbury, where he was joined by a group of English crusaders led by William de Mandeville, earl of Essex, and Hugh de Lacey, earl of Meath. King Henry contributed 500 marks towards Philip's expenses and sent an equal sum to Baldwin IV 'to sustain the land of Jerusalem' and a further 500 marks in alms to the Hospital of Jerusalem.[62]

---

[58] Roger of Howden, *Gesta Regis Henrici Secundi*, pp. 116 and 132–3; Continuator of Sigebert of Gembloux, *Chronographia*, MGH SS, VI, p. 415; H.-E. Mayer, 'Henry II of England and the Holy Land', EHR 97 (1982), pp. 721–7. On Henry's crusading penance see p. 75 above.

[59] Roger of Howden, *Gesta Regis Henrici Secundi*, p. 133.

[60] Round, 'Counts of Boulogne', pp. 147–80.

[61] Roger of Howden, *Gesta Regis Henrici Secundi*, pp. 132–3 and 136.

[62] Gervase of Canterbury, *Opera Historica*, ed. W. Stubbs, 2 vols., RS 73 (London, 1879–80), I, p. 262; Roger of Howden, *Gesta Regis Henrici Secundi*, pp. 158–9.

William of Tyre gives a very detailed account of Philip's activities, and as chancellor of the kingdom he was certainly in a position to know what took place, but because of the need to preserve state secrets his account is extremely allusive and difficult to interpret.[63] Moreover, it is not impartial. He was concerned to show that the Franks in the East were not to blame for the failure of Philip's crusade, because the Crusader Kingdom stood in great need of military aid and William did not wish to dissuade other western princes from taking the cross. The interpretation of William's account offered here has been built up with the help of other contemporary sources. It is, of necessity, conjectural, but it does, in my view, provide an explanation of all the known facts.

As explained above, because of the situation in Flanders Philip could only stay in the East for a limited time, and when he set out that did not appear problematic because the succession in Jerusalem seemed to be stable. Yet by the time he reached Acre the whole situation had changed because William of Montferrat had recently died. Had William lived, Philip would have been under no pressure to accept any military or administrative responsibilities because there would have been no power vacuum. Philip must have set out on crusade in the expectation of undertaking some military operation which would make the Christian position more secure and increase his own prestige. His father's personal crusades had all been of that kind. Instead he found himself greeted as the solution to the kingdom's problems. Despite his illness the king had himself carried in a litter from Ascalon to Jerusalem and convened a *curia generalis* attended by the members of the High Court, the patriarch and the senior clergy, and the masters of the military Orders. Acting on their advice Baldwin offered Philip the regency:

He should have full jurisdiction, both inside and outside the kingdom, over all men, both small and great, in time of peace and during war; and he should have complete control over the treasury and the revenues of the kingdom.[64]

Philip was a close kinsman of the king but he had no claim to the throne and he was not aligned with any group in the kingdom. He was therefore well suited to take command at a time when the king was seriously ill, the heir to the throne was his widowed and

---

[63] WT, XXI, 13–18, pp. 979–87 and 24, pp. 994–6.
[64] *Ibid.*, XXI, 13, p. 979.

pregnant sister, and a major war with Egypt was imminent. Reynald of Châtillon, whom Baldwin had appointed as his executive regent a few weeks earlier, did not complain about being demoted in favour of Philip and did not harbour any resentment towards the king on that score, but always remained loyal to him. Philip declined the honour, because the situation in Flanders made it impossible for him to accept a commitment which might keep him in the East for several years. He replied that:

He had not come to acquire power of any kind, but to offer himself to the service of God through Whose grace he had come: nor did he intend to bind himself to administration of any kind, since he wished to be free to return to his own country when its needs demanded this of him. But let the lord king appoint whom he liked as regent and he would be willing to take orders from him for the well-being of the kingdom, just as he would do from his own lord, the King of France.

William of Tyre reports that when the king asked him to take command of the entire Christian army, which was about to attack Egypt, the count gave the same answer. Baldwin then reinstated Reynald of Châtillon as 'regent of the kingdom and of the armies [*regni et exercituum procuratorem*] who, if the lord king was unable to be present in person, should administer the business of state, yet should be ruled in all things by the advice of the lord count'. It would appear from William of Tyre's account that at this point the king's illness became worse so that he was unable to talk to the count directly and all business had to be transacted in his name by intermediaries who were members of the High Court. It soon became apparent that there were members of the Court who resented the presence of this great western lord in the kingdom, and misunderstandings arose between them and the count. William reports that Philip protested that it was unnecessary to appoint Reynald of Châtillon as the king's deputy for the Egyptian campaign. The king should instead appoint a responsible commander, who should shoulder the blame if things went wrong and receive the government of Egypt if the campaign were successful. William of Tyre, who was one of the intermediaries between the king and the count, was indignant about this proposal, alleging that 'the king could not appoint such a regent unless he made the man king'. In regard to Egypt that was surely what Philip had in mind.

The political status of newly conquered territories was a perennial source of tension between the government of Jerusalem and crusaders from the West. The assumption by the kings of Jerusalem that all newly conquered lands would form part of their dominions was not shared by the crusaders. It was alleged that one of the reasons for the failure of the Second Crusade had been that the western leaders wished to give Damascus, if it were captured, as an independent appanage to Thierry of Flanders, Count Philip's father;[65] and certainly in 1157 Thierry had abandoned the siege of Shaizar because he refused to hold it as a fief from the prince of Antioch if he captured it.[66] Philip therefore had ample precedent in his own family tradition for reacting in the way he did to King Baldwin's proposals. Egypt was, of course, a far greater prize than Damascus, and there was no reason why, if conquered, it should form part of the Kingdom of Jerusalem. Philip was not unique in thinking this, for in 1219 the papal legate quarrelled with John of Brienne about that precise point when Damietta was captured by the Fifth Crusade.[67]

From what William of Tyre tells us it would appear that although Philip was unwilling to stay in the East to be regent of Jerusalem, or to deputise for the king as his commander on the Egyptian campaign, he was prepared to lead an attack on Egypt if that were to give him an opportunity of ruling all or part of it. There was no inconsistency in this. The regency would give him no long-term security to offset any losses he might thereby sustain in the West, whereas it would be worth sacrificing his interests in Flanders in order to gain a kingdom in Egypt. Its conquest would give him immense prestige and its government would place him on a par with the great rulers of the Christian world. Such an ambition was not completely unrealistic: Philip's nephew, Baldwin IX of Flanders, was presented with just such a choice during the Fourth Crusade and appointed a regent in Flanders in order to become Latin emperor of Constantinople.[68] What Philip had no intention of doing was acting as deputy commander for Baldwin IV on the Egyptian campaign; taking the blame if it was a failure; handing over the conquests to the crown of Jerusalem and the Byzantine emperor if it was a success; and returning home at the end of it.

But Philip was not satisfied either about the appointment of

---

[65] *Ibid.*, XVII, 7, p. 768.
[66] *Ibid.*, XVIII, 18, p. 837.
[67] J.M. Powell, *Anatomy of a Crusade, 1213–1221* (Philadelphia, 1986), pp. 126–7.
[68] J. Longnon, *Les compagnons de Villehardouin* (Paris, 1978), pp. 137–40.

Prince Reynald, or, it would seem, any other man, as executive regent for the king. He considered that the right course of action would be to arrange a new marriage for Sibyl, the heir to the throne. Her second husband would automatically become regent, and there would be no need to appoint an executive regent. As a close kinsman of the king, Philip considered that he had a right to be consulted about the succession. The High Court tried to parry the count's proposal by declaring that the custom of the kingdom allowed a widow a year of mourning before requiring her to remarry and that this rule was particularly appropriate in Sibyl's case because she was pregnant. The Court nevertheless professed its readiness to consider any suitable candidate whom the count might suggest. Philip would only agree to this if the members of the Court would first swear to accept his nominee, arguing that it would be disparaging to any nobleman whom he might name if his candidature was rejected. There was an issue of principle here: the count saw the High Court's function merely as confirmatory, whereas its members supposed that the final decision rested with them. The Court therefore refused to accept the count's unnamed nominee and the discussions were terminated.[69]

The *Chronicle* of Ernoul gives a more detailed description of this debate than William of Tyre, and is independent of him. Opposition to Philip, it relates, was led by Baldwin of Ibelin, 'who had separated from his wife because he hoped to marry this lady [Sibyl]'. He opposed Philip's proposal and insulted the count, and as a result Philip left the kingdom refusing to take any further part in the campaign. This report was based on the oral traditions of the Ibelin family and was not written down until many years later and can be faulted in points of detail.[70] Baldwin of Ibelin's first wife, Richendis of Bethsan, is not mentioned after 1167. If he had separated from her in the hope of marrying Sibyl, as this source suggests, this must have occurred in King Amalric's reign, and the king did not countenance his suit, for by 1175 he had married Elizabeth, or Isabel, the widow of Hugh of Caesarea. She bore him a son named Thomas, but was dead by 1176. Baldwin did not marry again until after 1180, and

---

[69] WT, XXI, 14, pp. 980–1.

[70] For example, Ernoul places the count of Flanders's visit before Sibyl's marriage to William of Montferrat and Baldwin's marriage to Elizabeth of Caesarea after the count's visit: Ernoul, pp. 33 and 48.

Ernoul may therefore be correct in asserting that he aimed to marry Sibyl in 1177.[71]

William of Tyre and Ernoul are in agreement that Philip of Flanders's candidate for Sibyl's hand was Robert, the eldest son of the advocate of Béthune, and William adds that Philip also wanted the king's younger sister, Isabel, to marry the advocate's second son, William. Both sons were adult and had accompanied their father on Count Philip's crusade. The archbishop of Tyre accuses Henry II's representative on the crusade, William de Mandeville, of brokering a deal whereby Robert V of Béthune offered to surrender his allodial lands in Flanders to Count Philip in return for arranging these two prestigious marriages for his sons.[72] Why de Mandeville thought that Henry II would approve of these marriages can only be conjectured, but Robert V had helped to negotiate peace between Henry II and Philip of Flanders and was therefore in good standing with the English king, and he and his sons had received generous grants of land in England.[73] The proposed marriage was in no sense the *mésalliance* that William of Tyre implies it would have been. The family of Béthune was among the high nobility of Flanders and some of Robert V's sons were later to attain distinction. Baldwin, count of Aumâle, became a close friend of Richard I of England, while his brother Conon took part in the Fourth Crusade and became lord of Adrianople, protovestiarius, and later regent, of the Latin Empire of Constantinople.[74] Robert and William of Béthune arguably had greater international standing in 1177 than either Baldwin of Ibelin, who wished to marry Sibyl, or Humphrey of Toron who later did marry Isabel. Indeed, the proposed marriages had much to commend them, for they would have ended any uncertainty about the future government of the Kingdom of Jerusalem. Robert of

---

[71] Edbury examines the circumstances in which Baldwin's first marriage was dissolved, *John of Ibelin*, p. 9. Elizabeth of Caesarea is recorded as his wife in 1175, *CGOH*, nos. 470, 489, but was dead by 1176 because, unlike the rest of her family, she was not associated with her husband in the sale of Bethduras, CGOH, no. 495. Her son Thomas is first mentioned in 1181, CGOH, no. 603; *Lignages*, c. 8, RHC Lois II, p. 448 state that Thomas was the son of Baldwin's first wife, Richildis, but Ernoul, p. 48, deriving his information from Ibelin sources, is more likely to be correct in stating that he was Elizabeth's child.

[72] WT, XXI, 14, pp. 980–1.

[73] Dept, *Les Influences*, p. 55.

[74] E. Warlop, *The Flemish Nobility before 1300*, 4 vols. (Courtrai, 1975–6), vol. II, pt. I, Table 21, pp. 658–63. Baldwin of Aumâle was one of the hostages who acted as a guarantor for the payment of Richard I's ransom in 1194, J. Gillingham, *Richard the Lionheart* (London, 1978), p. 126. For Conon see P.W. Lock, *The Franks in the Aegean 1204–1500* (London, 1995), pp. 41, 57, 165, 175, 185 and 190.

Béthune, as heir to the throne, would have had the support of the count of Flanders and the king of England, both of whom were committed to the defence of the Latin Kingdom. But the High Court of Jerusalem was hostile to the count's proposals because it considered that he was infringing its prerogative rights.

At this point a Byzantine fleet of seventy war galleys, together with transport ships, put into the port of Acre.[75] It was commanded by Andronicus Angelus, a kinsman of Manuel, who headed a distinguished delegation which had come to implement the treaty negotiated by Prince Reynald. It certainly involved the recognition of the Byzantine protectorate over the Latin Kingdom to which Amalric had formerly agreed, and the Orthodox patriarch of Jerusalem, Leontius, whose restoration was the subject of one of the key clauses of the agreement, came to Acre probably in the company of the imperial envoys. But though welcomed there by the Orthodox population, he did not go straight to Jerusalem because difficulties arose about the implementation of the treaty.[76]

Again, it was Philip of Flanders who caused the problems. This was not because he felt any antipathy towards Byzantium: he had been entrusted by the king of France with a diplomatic mission to the court of Constantinople, and that should have furnished him with an incentive to co-operate with the Byzantines in their attack on Egypt, but when he was shown the text of the imperial chrysobull he began to raise difficulties. It was presumably stipulated that any lands conquered by the Franks in Egypt should be held under Byzantine suzerainty, and Manuel may also have claimed direct rule over certain named cities.[77] This would have shown Philip conclusively that there was no possibility of his being allowed to have sovereignty over any territory that he might conquer in Egypt. The terms of the treaty were not negotiable, and Philip did not challenge

[75] WT, XXI, 16, p. 983.
[76] *Life*, cc. 80–1, pp. 126–9. His biographer tells us that 'the Latins who held power over Palestine did not permit him to set foot on [sic] Jerusalem': *ibid.*, p. 129. The editor accepts that these events formed part of the Byzantine embassy of 1177, *ibid.*, n. 80.1, p. 201, n. 81.1, p. 202.
[77] Mayer has suggested that that may have been one of the conditions in the treaty of alliance against Egypt between Amalric and Manuel in 1168, 'Le service militaire des vassaux à l'étranger et le financement des campagnes en Syrie du nord et en Egypte au XIIe siècle', in *Mélanges sur l'histoire du royaume latin de Jérusalem*, Mémoires de l'Académie des Inscriptions et Belles-Lettres, n.s., 5 (Paris, 1984), pp. 145–58; Lilie, *Byzantium*, pp. 309–20, is in part a critique of Mayer's monograph, but both authors agree that the treaties between Byzantium and the Franks must have made provision for a partition of Egyptian conquests.

them, but found excuses for not taking part in the campaign. For example, he protested that the Nile floods made the autumn season a perilous time for campaigning, and also raised difficulties about the commissariat of his troops. Philip professed his readiness to campaign elsewhere, but such an offer was obviously pointless, because there was no Muslim territory except Egypt that was accessible to the Byzantine fleet. The Franks, who had no wish to offend the emperor and lose his protection, therefore decided to go ahead with their attack on Egypt without the count's participation, but Philip was not prepared to accept this. Finally the Byzantine ambassadors agreed to delay their attack on Egypt until April 1178.[78]

William of Tyre's account makes Philip's conduct appear totally irrational, whereas it was quite coherent. He did not intend to campaign in Egypt on the conditions specified in the chrysobull. Yet it was not consistent with his honour to stay in Jerusalem with his army through the winter while the host of the kingdom was attacking Saladin. The problem was that his army, though sizable, was not huge, and in order to campaign anywhere else he needed the support of at least some of the local Franks, and that would not be available if the Egyptian expedition went ahead. But if it were to be deferred until the spring, then Philip could campaign in Syria during the winter with Frankish help and return to the West in the spring of 1178 before the launching of the attack on Egypt.

William of Tyre reports that:

There were many who blamed the Lord Prince of Antioch who was present and the Lord Count of Tripoli for the Count of Flanders's opposition to serving in Egypt. It was said that they tried to entice him to their own lands, hoping with his help to undertake something which would benefit their states.[79]

The northern princes may plausibly have argued that because Saladin had left few troops in Syria it would be good sense to attack Damascus and his other possessions there, for with a Byzantine war-fleet stationed at Acre and threatening Egypt he would be unable to send any troops to their assistance. Having destroyed or reduced his power in Syria during the winter months, a full-scale attack on Egypt could be launched in the spring. But they could not act without Philip's support. Turan-Shah, governor of Damascus, had made a truce with the Franks earlier in the year and was so anxious

---

[78] WT, XXI, 15–16, pp. 981–4.   [79] WT, XXI, 17, p. 985.

to maintain peaceful relations that he sold grain to them despite the famine which Syria was then experiencing.[80] But the truce contained a clause stipulating that the Franks would not be bound by its provisions should any great prince come from the West and wish to fight against Islam, and Philip's participation would allow that clause to be invoked.[81]

At this stage Philip paid a visit to Nablus. The only reason he can have had for going was to consult King Amalric's widow, the Byzantine Queen Maria Comnena, who lived there, and Philip no doubt wanted her advice about the Byzantine court and how best to forward his mission on behalf of Louis VII.[82] Maria would certainly have been in communication with the Byzantine ambassadors and was therefore probably aware that they were about to call off the entire expedition because of a general lack of Frankish co-operation. The inference is that she persuaded Philip that the High Court would place the entire blame for this on him, which would reflect adversely on his honour and would create a very unfavourable impression on the Emperor Manuel, for Philip immediately sent a delegation to Jerusalem announcing that he was, after all, prepared to set out for Egypt whenever necessary. Nevertheless, he did this in a very offhand way: he did not go to Jerusalem himself, although the distance from Nablus was trifling, but chose as his principal envoy the advocate of Béthune, the man least likely to have a calming effect on the sensibilities of the High Court. No doubt William of Tyre is correct in saying that this was merely a token gesture, that Philip had not undergone any real change of heart, but was wishing to shift possible blame for the failure of the Egyptian expedition on to the High Court.[83]

The Byzantine ambassadors were sceptical about Philip's sincerity and required him to take a solemn oath that he would take part in the expedition, or that he would send his army if he were prevented by ill-health from going in person; and also to swear, and to require his men to swear, that:

he would work for the good of Christianity throughout the entire expedition, in good faith and without deceit or evil intent; and that he would not break the agreement which had been made in discussion and in

[80] Lyons and Jackson, *Saladin*, p. 126.
[81] AS, RHC Or, IV, pp. 191–2.
[82] WT, XXI, 16, p. 984; Ernoul, p. 31.
[83] WT, XXI, 16, p. 984

writing between the lord king and the lord emperor either by his actions or by his advice.

This oath was framed in such a way that Philip could not take it because it cast doubt on his honour and on his good faith as a crusader. The Byzantine ambassadors therefore broke off negotiations and returned to Constantinople, while the sea-lanes were still open before the onset of winter, taking the Byzantine war fleet with them.[84] Philip almost immediately afterwards went to campaign in north Syria.[85]

William of Tyre has carefully constructed his account in order to place the whole blame for this failure on Philip of Flanders, yet it seems obvious that the Byzantine commanders did not call off the Egyptian expedition simply because the count was unco-operative, for it must have been planned without any certainty that an army from Flanders would be in the East then. But as William of Tyre makes clear, the prince of Antioch, and the count of Tripoli, who was also prince of Galilee, did not approve of the attack on Egypt, and the new master of the Knights of St John seems to have shared their views. Master Jobert, who had fully supported Baldwin IV's Egyptian policy, is last recorded in January 1177.[86] His successor, Roger des Moulins, although he was to prove to be one of the greatest masters of the Order, was, in the summer of 1177, comparatively inexperienced.[87] Two years before, he had been a serving brother in the Hospitaller preceptory at Antioch and it was, perhaps, natural that he should have considered the defence of the northern states a priority and have been influenced by the advice of Bohemond III.[88] Bearing in mind the fate of his recent predecessor, Gilbert d'Assailly,[89] he was no doubt also worried about the costs of involvement in Egypt. Although William of Tyre does not say that Bohemond III, Raymond III and Roger des Moulins refused to take part in the Egyptian expedition, all the evidence points to the fact

[84] The Byzantine fleet was only half the size of that reported by John Cinnamus as mustering to attack Egypt in 1176 (see pp. 112–13, above). Consequently the Byzantine commanders could not proceed without the support of Frankish land forces, whereas in 1176 a solely Byzantine attack seems to have been planned.

[85] WT, XXI, 17, pp. 984–5.

[86] CGOH, no. 508.

[87] J. Riley-Smith, *The Knights of St John in Jerusalem and Cyprus (1050–1310)* (London, 1967), p. 64; G. Ligato, 'Il *Magister* ospedaliero Ruggero des Moulins nella crisi finale del regno Latino di Gerusalemme', *Antonianum* 71 (1996), pp. 495–522.

[88] In March 1175 'Fr Roggerius de Molendinis' witnessed: CGOH, no. 474.

[89] See p. 37, above.

that their opposition to it was the real reason for Byzantine withdrawal.

There were those who regretted the breakdown of the Byzantine alliance. The king was one of them and, as will be seen, he sought to rebuild it. William of Tyre was outspoken in his condemnation of the breach of treaty obligations:

Furthermore, it was neither safe nor honourable for us to fail in our treaty obligations . . . We did not consider that it was safe to disregard the help which the emperor was now offering us, for we feared his anger which could be very dangerous to us.[90]

Another critic of Count Philip and his supporters was the master of the Temple, Odo of St Amand. The continuator of Sigebert of Gembloux's *Chronicle* reports that the count of Flanders quarrelled with the Templars 'about certain state business', and William of Newburgh says that Philip went to Antioch because he had been offended by the Templars.[91] These reports, which are independent of each other, reflect news that had reached the West of some estrangement between the count and the Order. Odo of St Amand was not a tactful or slow-tempered man and if he disapproved of Philip's behaviour he was probably at no pains to conceal his opinion.

In retrospect it can be seen that Philip and his friends failed to seize the best opportunity that the Franks were ever to have of breaking Saladin's power. The combined armies of the Crusader States and of Count Philip, in conjunction with Byzantine forces, could at the least have caused serious damage to Saladin's hold on Egypt and would also have prevented him from taking any action in Syria had the Zengid princes counter-attacked there. The threat which he posed to the Franks might not have been removed altogether but it would certainly have been weakened. As it was, Byzantium had been alienated, while Saladin remained as powerful as before. Moreover, this policy was also hazardous in the short term, for the Byzantine fleet had returned to Constantinople, while Saladin's army had been marshalled near the Egyptian frontier to repel a Frankish invasion, and the departure of Philip and his allies for the north left the Kingdom of Jerusalem with very few troops.

---

[90] WT, XXI, 16, p. 983.
[91] Continuator of Sigebert of Gembloux, *Chronographia*, MGH SS, VI, p. 416; William of Newburgh, *Historia Rerum Anglicarum*, ed. R. Howlett, III, 11, RS 82(1), p. 243.

CHAPTER 7

The victor of Mont Gisard

Philip of Flanders led his army to Tripoli in late September 1177, where they met up with Raymond III and his vassals, together with Roger des Moulins, the master of the Hospital, and most of the Knights of St John from the Kingdom of Jerusalem, as well as a number of Templars, and some 100 knights and 2,000 infantry from the kingdom, perhaps representing the levy from Raymond's principality of Galilee.[1] In November the army moved against Hama.[2] The city was ill prepared for a siege, for the governor was sick and no reinforcements had come from Damascus; nevertheless, the Franks withdrew after four days in response to an appeal from Bohemond III.[3]

Gumushtekin of Aleppo had been overthrown and executed that autumn, but the garrison of Harim refused to acknowledge the new rulers and offered the castle to Bohemond III.[4] According to Michael the Syrian, who was living near Antioch at that time and was therefore well placed to know the truth, the negotiations foundered because Bohemond wished to replace the existing garrison by a Frankish one. He then called on the Franks besieging Hama to help him capture Harim.[5] Harim was strategically important and both Philip of Flanders and Raymond of Tripoli had a personal

[1] WT, XXI, 17, p. 985; John of Ibelin, *Livre des Assises*, c. XIII, ed. Edbury, *John of Ibelin*, p. 118.

[2] WT, XXI, 18, p. 986; M.C. Lyons and D.E.P. Jackson, *Saladin. The Politics of the Holy War* (Cambridge, 1982), pp. 126–7.

[3] Ibn al-Athir attributes the withdrawal to popular resistance, which is unsubstantiated, RHC Or I, pp. 630–1; AS, RHC Or IV, p. 191; al-Maqrizi, p. 57.

[4] Kamal ad-Din, ROL 4 (1896), pp. 150–1; C. Cahen, *La Syrie du nord à l'époque des croisades et la principauté franque d'Antioche* (Paris, 1940), p. 418.

[5] MS, XX, vii, III, pp. 375–6; cf. *Anonymi Auctoris Chronicon ad Annum Christi 1234 pertinens*, c. 473, tr. A. Abouna, CSCO *Scriptores Syri*, ser. 3, 154 (Louvain, 1974), p. 142; WT, XXI, 18, p. 986.

interest in it.[6] Philip's father, Thierry of Flanders, had helped Baldwin III to recover Harim for the Franks in 1158, and Philip wished to emulate his father's prowess,[7] while Raymond had been taken prisoner by Nur ad-Din in 1164 when attempting unsuccessfully to defend Harim, had been held captive for ten years, and wished to avenge himself by capturing the fortress from Nur ad-Din's son.[8]

Saladin must have been amazed by this turn of events, for he had begun to move his army towards the Frankish border in the hope of deflecting the projected attack on Hama by forcing the Frankish armies to come south to defend Jerusalem.[9] The departure of the Frankish forces to Antioch left the way open for him to invade the Latin Kingdom. Odo of St Amand, master of the Temple, took eighty of his knights to garrison Gaza.[10] An anonymous Christian writer in north Syria described how in this crisis 'everyone despaired of the life of the sick king, already half dead, but he drew upon his courage and rode to meet Saladin'.[11] Baldwin had little military experience and would normally have relied on the advice of the constable, Humphrey II of Toron, but he was gravely ill at this time.[12] The campaign was therefore organised by Prince Reynald, the king's executive regent. This is known from Arabic sources,[13] for William of Tyre and the *Chronicle* of Ernoul merely mention that he was present with the host.[14] According to Ernoul, in the autumn of 1177 there were only 600 knights left in the whole kingdom, including the members of the military Orders, and this seems to be approximately correct.[15] The patriarch, Amalric of Nesle, was left in charge

---

[6] On the site of the castle, Cahen, *La Syrie*, p. 134; W, Müller-Wiener, *Castles of the Crusaders* (London, 1966), p. 65, plates 88, 89; P. Deschamps, *Les châteaux des croisés en Terre Sainte* III, *La défense du comté de Tripoli et de la principauté d'Antioche* (Paris, 1973), p. 23.

[7] WT, XVIII, 19, pp. 838–40. Nur ad-Din had captured it in 1164, N. Elisséeff, *Nur ad-Din, un grand prince musulman de Syrie au temps des croisades (511–569H/1118–1174)*, 3 vols. (Damascus, 1967), pp. 590–5

[8] WT, XIX, 9, pp. 874–5; M.W. Baldwin, *Raymond III of Tripolis and the Fall of Jerusalem (1140–1187)* (Princeton, 1936), pp. 10–11.

[9] al-Maqrizi, p. 56.   [10] WT, XXI, 21, p. 990.

[11] *Chronicon . . . 1234*, c. 472, p. 141.   [12] WT, XXI, 19, p. 988.

[13] Abu Shama, citing Ibn Shaddad, RHC Or IV, p. 188; Baha al-Din, RHC Or III, p. 63; al-Maqrizi, p. 56.

[14] WT, XXI, 21, p. 990; Ernoul, p. 54.

[15] Ernoul, p. 34; the knight-service of the kingdom in Baldwin IV's reign was c.675 men, see pp. 54–5 above. One hundred knights had accompanied Philip of Flanders to the north, together with most of the Knights of St John and many Templars. Eighty Templars are known to have remained in the kingdom (see n. 10 above), and together with the remaining secular knights this makes a total of c.655.

of Jerusalem, which was stripped of troops, while the host marched to Ascalon.[16] The bishop of Bethlehem carried the Holy Cross and among those present were Joscelin of Courtenay, Reynald of Sidon, Baldwin and Balian of Ibelin, and Hugh and William of St Omer, the stepsons of Raymond of Tripoli.[17] When he reached Ascalon, Baldwin issued the *arrière ban*. This obligation on all able-bodied men to serve in the host was very seldom invoked and its use is an index of how desperate the situation appeared to be.[18]

Saladin left his heavy baggage train at al-Arish, and bypassing Gaza, reached Ascalon on 22 November. The king led his forces out to meet him, but soon withdrew into the city again when he realised how hopelessly outnumbered he was.[19] Saladin considered that the royal army posed no threat, and determined to leave it in his rear and to march straight on to Jerusalem: this is confirmation that the Frankish estimates of the size of Baldwin's army were approximately correct, not just exaggerations designed to make the Christian victory appear miraculous.

As Saladin's troops scattered to plunder the fertile coastal regions they met parties of men hurrying on foot to join the king at Ascalon in obedience to the *arrière ban*; they were taken prisoner and strapped to camels in Saladin's baggage train to be sold as slaves.[20] The vanguard of the sultan's army marched on Ramla, whose population fled to Jaffa, while another detachment burnt the small hill settlement of Mirabel. The vanguard then attacked Lydda, where the people took refuge in the fortress-like cathedral of St George. Jerusalem had not been threatened for decades. Its walls were in a ruinous state, and the terrified population sought refuge in the Tower of David.[21]

Saladin did not expect the Franks to leave the safety of Ascalon and was so confident of this that he had not bothered to station a

---

[16] The master of the Hospital of Jerusalem wrote that only civilians were left to defend the city. It may be inferred that the patriarch was placed in charge of them, R. Röhricht (ed.), *Beiträge zur Geschichte der Kreuzzüge*, 2 vols. (Berlin, 1874–8), II, pp. 127–8, no. 45.

[17] WT, XXI, 21, p. 990; Ernoul, pp. 44–5.

[18] Ernoul, p. 43; R.C. Smail, *Crusading Warfare 1097–1193*, 2nd edn (Cambridge, 1995), pp. 92–3; J.L. Lamonte, *Feudal Monarchy in the Latin Kingdom of Jerusalem 1100–1291* (Cambridge, Mass., 1932), p. 159.

[19] WT, XXI, 19, pp. 987–8; AS dates this 22 or 23 November, RHC Or IV, p. 184, a date more consonant with William of Tyre's account than that of 18 November given by IA, RHC Or I, p. 628.

[20] Ernoul, p. 43.

[21] WT, XXI, 20, p. 989 and 24, p. 996.

detachment of men to watch the city and bring him news of troop movements. This lack of elementary caution cost him dearly, for the king and Prince Reynald were able to liaise with the Templars of Gaza and to lead their combined forces along the coast, unperceived by Saladin's men. By 25 November the sultan and his main army had reached the hill of Mont Gisard, or Tell Jazar, near Ibelin and his troops were about to ford a small stream when they were quite unexpectedly confronted by the Frankish host.[22] Many of his men had dispersed to raid the countryside and consequently he lost the advantage of overwhelmingly superior numbers, though he still had a larger force than the Franks.[23] William of Tyre says that Baldwin's army consisted of only 375 men of all ranks, but that must be a deliberate underestimate since the master of the Hospital put the number of Frankish dead in the battle at nearly three times that figure.[24]

The sultan himself later admitted that he had been caught unawares and that the Franks had charged before he had succeeded in disposing his troops satisfactorily around the Tell.[25] Prince Reynald seized his opportunity and directed the main Frankish cavalry charge at the centre of the sultan's army while its two wings were carrying out a complicated manoeuvre to take up their positions. The result was a rout. One of Saladin's great-nephews was killed in the mêlée, while the sultan himself barely escaped with his life.[26] The Frankish captives from the *arrière ban*, taking advantage of the general confusion, escaped and killed the attendants of the sultan's baggage train.[27]

Battle had not been joined until the afternoon,[28] so darkness soon overtook the sultan's army as it fled and it was unable to hold any semblance of formation. It proved relatively easy for the Franks to

---

[22] On the site of the battle, D. Pringle, 'Jazar, Tall al', in *The Churches of the Crusader Kingdom of Jerusalem. A Corpus*, 2 vols. (Cambridge, 1993, 1998) I, pp. 273–4; C. Clermont-Ganneau, *Recueil d'archéologie orientale*, 8 vols. (Paris, 1888–1924), I, pp. 351–91. The different location suggested by Lyons and Jackson, *Saladin*, p. 123, is not convincing in the light of contemporary evidence: WT, XXI, 22, pp. 991–2; AS, RHC Or IV, p. 185; al-Maqrizi, pp. 56–7; Baha al-Din, RHC Or III, p. 64 (who dates the campaign wrongly).

[23] Lyons and Jackson, *Saladin*, p. 122.

[24] WT, XXI, 21, p. 990; Röhricht, *Beiträge*, II, p. 128, no. 45.

[25] Baha al-Din, RHC Or III, p. 64; Cf. AS, RHC Or IV, p. 190; Lyons and Jackson, *Saladin*, pp. 123–4.

[26] Taqi al-Din's son Ahmad, IA, RHC Or I, p. 628; AS, RHC Or IV, p. 185.

[27] Ernoul, p. 45.

[28] 'Erat autem hora diei quasi octava' (i.e. c. 2 p.m.), WT, XXI, 21, p. 990.

round up and kill, or take prisoner, the raiding-parties of Muslims who had fanned out towards Lydda and Jerusalem earlier that day.[29] The next day the winter rains began and continued for ten days, which made it impossible for Saladin to regroup his forces. The Franks captured more stragglers and, to make matters worse, when news of the defeat reached the Beduin of eastern Sinai they plundered the sultan's base camp at al-Arish, so that he and the other survivors had to make their way back to Cairo with few supplies.[30] Saladin reached Cairo on 8 December.[31] He recognised the seriousness of the defeat and years later said to Ibn Shaddad: 'Although it was so great a disaster, God, blessed be His name, made it good in the end by the famous victory at Hattin.' But as Abu Shama, who records that conversation, remarks, that only happened ten years later.[32]

There is no doubt that Mont Gisard was a great Frankish victory. When the kingdom seemed about to be lost, the courage of the young leper king and the good leadership of Prince Reynald had enabled its small army to inflict a crushing defeat on the invading forces. Yet the cost had been high. Raymond, the brother in charge of the Hospital of St John at Jerusalem, reported that 1,100 Christians were killed in the battle, while a further 750 were severely wounded and were admitted to the Hospital for treatment.[33]

The king led his army to Jerusalem to give thanks to Almighty God for the victory, for neither he nor his troops doubted that their success had been due to divine aid.[34] St George, whose shrine at Lydda was being besieged by Saladin's vanguard when the battle took place, was said to have been seen on the field of Mont Gisard fighting alongside his fellow Christians.[35] As an act of thanksgiving the Franks built a Benedictine monastery on the site of the battle, dedicated to St Catherine of Alexandria on whose feast it had been fought.[36]

Bohemond III, Raymond III and Philip of Flanders began to

---

[29] IA, RHC Or I, p. 629.   [30] WT, XXI, 23, pp. 993–4.
[31] IA, RHC Or I, p. 629.   [32] AS, RHC Or IV, p. 189.
[33] Röhricht, *Beiträge*, II, p. 128, no. 45.
[34] WT, XXI, 23, pp. 993–4.   [35] Ernoul, p. 44.
[36] Prior Peter of St Catherine's *de Campo belli* in Jerusalem is named in a Trani charter of 1187, A. di G. Prologo (ed.), *Le carte . . . nell'Archivio del Capitolo . . . di Trani* (Barletta, 1877), no. 78, pp. 165–6. John of Ibelin records the prior of St Catherine's of Mont Gisard among the suffragans of the Bishop of Lydda, *Livre*, c. VIII, ed. Edbury, *John of Ibelin*, p. 113; Pringle, 'Jazar, Tall al: No. 122. Priory Church of St Catherine', *Churches*, I, p. 274.

besiege Harim in early December.[37] It was a difficult fortress to assault, and they later enlisted the help of Rupen III of Cilicia.[38] The siege dragged on inconclusively throughout the winter. The weather was bad, and because the Frankish nobility rode into Antioch to sample the various kinds of dissipation offered by its baths, brothels and taverns,[39] the common soldiers became demoralised, while the people of Antioch, who were expected to provision this large force in a year of famine, became mutinous.[40] Then, when the Franks appeared to be on the point of success, Bohemond III negotiated peace with Aleppo. It was agreed that the Aleppans should keep the castle, but indemnify the Franks for the expenses incurred by the siege, and half the villages of the fief of Harim may also have been ceded to Bohemond.[41] It would appear that this settlement was made because Philip of Flanders wished to keep Holy Week in Jerusalem and then return home.[42]

His crusade can only be judged an anticlimax, yet he cannot be entirely blamed for this. He had brought an army to the Levant in order to protect the Holy City at considerable financial cost and in the knowledge that he was neglecting his European interests by doing so. But though he was a royal kinsman he had been slighted by the members of the High Court who were jealous of their prerogatives. This quarrel had then been exploited by Bohemond III and Raymond III so that the count's crusade had in the end achieved nothing. Yet the sincerity of Philip's commitment to the Crusader Kingdom cannot be doubted: despite his unhappy experiences in 1177–8, he returned on the Third Crusade and died at the siege of Acre.[43]

He returned to the West by way of Constantinople, and discussed with Manuel the possibility of marrying the emperor's only son

[37] *Chronicon . . . 1234*, c. 473, p. 143 says the siege began in December 1177; Ibn al-Athir says the Franks went to Harim before 25 November but that may refer to the time at which they left Hama: RHC Or I, p. 632.

[38] 'With them was the son of Leo', Kamal ad-Din, ROL 4 (1896), p. 151.

[39] WT, XXI, 24, pp. 994–5.

[40] *Chronicon . . . 1234*, c. 473, pp. 142–3.

[41] Kamal ad-Din, ROL 4 (1896), p. 153; MS, XX, vii, III, p. 376; AS, RHC Or IV, p. 193; IA, RHC Or I, p. 193; WT, XXI, 24, p. 995; *Chronicon . . . 1234*, c. 473, p. 143, states that as-Salih offered Bohemond '50,000 dinars and half the villages of the citadel [of Harim]'.

[42] Baha al-Din, RHC Or III, p. 64, places the end of the siege in the last ten days of Ramadan (14–23 March). Count Philip kept Holy Week in Jerusalem and Palm Sunday fell on 2 April in 1178; WT, XXI, 24, p. 996; Kamal ad-Din, ROL 4 (1896), p. 153; IA, RHC Or I, p. 632.

[43] Roger of Howden, *Gesta Regis Henrici*, RS 49(II), p. 171.

Alexius to a Capetian princess. The discussions went well, and Manuel sent envoys back with Philip to the French court.[44] Manuel was anxious to find new allies in the West to counteract the hostility of Frederick Barbarossa, Venice and Sicily. But if his western diplomacy was to succeed, he recognised that it was important that he should not antagonise the papacy, and this may account for his decision not to try to force the restoration of an Orthodox patriarch in Jerusalem.

Leontius II had remained in the Latin Kingdom after the departure of the Byzantine fleet in 1177, and his *Life* relates how in the autumn he visited Nazareth and Jerusalem. This must have occurred with the assent of Baldwin IV, who was concerned to preserve the Byzantine protectorate despite the collapse of the projected attack on Egypt, and who was continuing to treat the patriarch as Manuel's representative. Leontius's biographer claims that the Latin patriarch hired assassins to kill him, but they were frustrated by the power of the supernatural Light that shone about him. The emir of Damascus then invited him to live in that city and offered him the Church of the Mother of God there. When they learned of this exchange the Frankish authorities at first agreed to allow Leontius to celebrate the Divine Liturgy publicly in the Church of the Holy Sepulchre, but in the end he was merely allowed 'to enter the church with a group of monks, to pay their respects at the holy shrine'. Having been recalled by the emperor, he then returned to Constantinople.[45]

This narrative, despite the hagiographical terms in which it is couched, is plausible, though uncorroborated. Saladin was the emir of Damascus, and had Leontius accepted his invitation it would have been an acknowledgement that the Byzantine protectorate of the Crusader States was at an end. The king was anxious to avoid that, but could not overcome the hostility of the Latin patriarch. Although it is unlikely that Amalric of Nesle tried to have Leontius assassinated, it is very probable that he would only bow to royal pressure so far as to allow him to celebrate the Divine Liturgy in the Church of the Holy Sepulchre privately, in the presence of the Orthodox canons alone.[46] It may reasonably be supposed that Manuel recalled

[44] Robert of Torigni, *Chronicon*, ed. R. Howlett, RS 82(iv), p. 279; Ernoul, pp. 46–7.
[45] *The Life of Leontios Patriarch of Jerusalem*, tr. D. Tsougarakis (Leiden, 1993), cc. 82–90, pp. 129–41.
[46] B. Hamilton, *The Latin Church in the Crusader States. The Secular Church* (London, 1980), p. 171. There were five Orthodox canons there in King Amalric's reign, CGOH, no. 443.

Leontius to Constantinople in order to avoid a conflict with the Latin patriarch, and through him with Alexander III, which would have jeopardised negotiations with Louis VII.

During the winter of 1177–8 Princess Sibyl had given birth to William of Montferrat's posthumous son, who was named Baldwin after the king.[47] Her official period of mourning came to an end in the following June and it then became possible to discuss her remarriage with propriety. No consideration was given to the suit of Baldwin of Ibelin, although if Ernoul's account is to be believed his ambition to marry Sibyl was public knowledge by this time. But it may have been with a view to conciliating the Ibelins that the king had allowed Baldwin's younger brother Balian the unusual privilege of marrying the dowager-queen Maria Comnena in the autumn of 1177.[48] She brought with her the dower fief of Nablus and consequently the Ibelin brothers became the greatest feudatories in the kingdom except for Raymond of Tripoli.[49] As a result of his marriage Balian became the stepfather of the king's younger sister, Isabel, and this powerful family became part of the extended royal kin group.

From 1 July 1178 Baldwin IV began to associate his sister with him in some of his public acts,[50] just as his great-grandfather, Baldwin II, had associated his daughter Melisende with him towards the end of his reign, thereby designating her as his heir.[51]

William of Tyre relates that 'we had unanimously agreed that we should give in marriage to [the lord Duke of Burgundy] the king's sister, who had previously been married to the marquis [of Montferrat], and upon the same conditions'. The negotiations were

---

[47] Baldwin cannot have been conceived much later than April 1177 as his father died in June having been critically ill for two months and Sibyl's pregnancy had been diagnosed by then: WT, XXI, 12, p. 978. When he was crowned co-king in November 1183 he was said to have been five, WT, XXII, 30, p. 1058; when he died in the late summer of 1186 he was said to have been nine, Arnold of Lübeck, *Chronica Slavorum*, IV, 2, ed. I.M. Lappenberg, MGH SS, XXI, p. 164. These data suggest that he was born in December 1177 or January 1178 and was in his ninth year at the time of his death. R. Hiestand, 'Chonologisches zur Geschichte des Königsreiches Jerusalem. 3. Das Alter Balduins V', *Deutsches Archiv* 35 (1979), pp. 553–5.

[48] WT, XXI, 17, p. 986.

[49] They owed service of 135 knights to the crown: eighty-five for Nablus, forty for Ramla and Mirabel, and ten for Ibelin, John of Ibelin: *Livre*, c. XIII, XIV, ed. Edbury, *John of Ibelin*, pp. 118, 122.

[50] Delaville Le Roulx, 'Inventaire de pièces de Terre Sainte de l'Ordre de l'Hôpital', no. 125, ROL 3 (1895), p. 63, of 1 July 1178; E. Strehlke (ed.), *Tabulae Ordinis Teutonici* (Berlin, 1869), no. 11, pp. 11–12, of 22 October 1179.

[51] Kohler, no. 21, ROL 7 (1899), p. 128. Cf. H.-E. Mayer, 'Studies in the history of Queen Melisende of Jerusalem', DOP 26 (1972), p. 99.

entrusted to Bishop Joscius of Acre, who was a member of the delegation from the Latin Church in the Crusader States to the Third Lateran Council, which Alexander III had summoned to meet in Rome in March 1179. Because of the problems of sea travel during the winter months, this meant that the delegates had to leave in October 1178.[52] Hugh III was thirty years old and had been ruling Burgundy since 1162; he was a nephew of Queen Adela of France, and was known to some members of the High Court because he had visited Jerusalem in 1171.[53] He had married Alix of Lorraine in c.1165 and she had borne him two sons, Eudes and Alexander.[54] Although there is some doubt about when this marriage was dissolved, Richard is surely correct in supposing that this must have happened before 1178 because Bishop Joscius would, as a matter of course, have discovered whether there was any canonical impediment to the proposed marriage with Sibyl.[55]

It was almost certainly at this time that Baldwin IV wrote to Louis VII:

To be deprived of the use of one's limbs is of little help to one in carrying out the work of government. If I could be cured of the disease of Naaman, I would wash seven times in Jordan, but I have found in the present age no Elisha who can heal me. It is not fitting that a hand so weak as mine should hold power when fear of Arab aggression daily presses upon the Holy City and when my sickness increases the enemy's daring . . . I therefore beg you that, having called together the barons of the kingdom of France, you immediately choose one of them to take charge of this Holy Kingdom. For We are prepared to receive with affection whomever you send Us, and We will hand over the kingdom to a suitable successor.

There seems no reason to doubt the validity of this letter, even though it only survives in a late thirteenth-century *ars dictaminis* collection, for the bulk of the material that this contains is genuine and relates to late twelfth-century France.[56] The letter, it would seem,

---

[52] William of Tyre wrongly calls the Duke Henry: WT, XXI, 25, pp. 996–7.

[53] *Ibid.*, XX, 25, p. 947. See Genealogy No. II.

[54] J. Richard, *Les ducs de Bourgogne et la formation du Duché du XIe au XIVe siècle* (Paris, 1954), pp. 158 and 207; E. Petit, *Histoire des ducs de Bourgogne de la race capétienne*, 9 vols. (Dijon, 1885–1905), II, pp. 150–1.

[55] Alberic of Trois-Fontaines wrote that Hugh only left Alix in 1184 (*recte* 1183) in order to marry Beatrice d'Albon, *Chronica*, MGH SS, XXIII, p. 858. For Richard's counterargument, *Ducs de Bourgogne*, pp. 158–9 and n. 4.

[56] The manuscript was written for the chancery of the archbishop of Salzburg in 1284–90. The date of Baldwin's letter has not been transcribed in the copy, which is addressed merely *regi Francie*, but Cartellieri who edited it and Röhricht who calendared it agree in assigning it to 1178–9. This is supported by the fact that the two letters which immediately follow this

formed part of the negotiations relating to Sibyl's second marriage. There was no guarantee that Hugh of Burgundy would accept the invitation to come to Jerusalem, but if he did Louis VII's approval would be needed to allow him to leave the kingdom permanently and transfer the duchy to his son. If he did not accept, then the urgency of determining the succession was so great that the king of France was given freedom to choose an alternative husband for Sibyl.

In the Frankish East 1178 was a relatively peaceful year. In April Saladin moved his main army back to Damascus, leaving his capable brother, al-Adil, as viceroy of Egypt.[57] The Franks did not attempt to intercept Saladin, but soon after this they attacked the fortress of Qalat Guindi, which had a crucial role in his lines of communication because it was the last source of water on the Sinai crossing from Egypt before Eilat. The Franks were unable to take the castle because they had too few men.[58] It seems likely that this expedition was led by Prince Reynald and Odo of St Amand, because Reynald's fief of Hebron and the Templar fief of Gaza bordered the Sinai desert.

In the late spring a Sicilian fleet of forty ships captured and sacked Tinnis, but they only held it for four days before returning to Sicily with many captives and much plunder.[59] The Franks made no attempt to support them. Part of their army had only just disbanded from the long winter campaign at Harim, while those who had remained in the south were still recovering from the heavy losses they had suffered at Mont Gisard.

The Franks spent the summer of 1178 strengthening the defences of their kingdom. Preparations were made for restoring the walls of Jerusalem, and Humphrey of Toron rebuilt the fortress of Chastel-neuf in Upper Galilee, which had been abandoned since 1167.[60]

---

in the collection undoubtedly date from 1179–80. There are also empirical reasons for accepting this date for Baldwin's letter. It can only have been written when there was no designated, male heir to the throne: i.e. after the death of William of Montferrat in 1177 and before 1180 when Sibyl married Guy of Lusignan. When Guy was excluded from the succession in 1183 Sibyl's son, Baldwin V, was designated heir. A. Cartellieri (ed.), *Ein Donaueschinger Briefsteller. Lateinische Stilübungen des XII Jahrhunderts aus der orleanischen Schule*, no. 148 (Innsbruck, 1898), p. 33; RRH, no. 569c, II, p. 35.

[57] AS, RHC Or, IV, p. 193; al-Maqrizi, p. 57; Lyons and Jackson, *Saladin*, p. 128.

[58] AS, RHC Or IV, p. 193; al-Maqrizi, p. 57.

[59] al-Maqrizi, *Kitab al Muwa'iz, A.H. 573*, tr. M. Amari, *Biblioteca Arabo-Sicula*, 2 vols. (Turin and Rome, 1880–9), I, p. 297.

[60] WT, XXI, 24, p. 996 and 26, p. 999; AS, RHC Or IV, p. 111; Baha al-Din, RHC Or III, p. 45.

Then in the autumn a major project was begun, almost certainly through the initiative of the Templars – the building of the castle of Le Chastellet at Jacob's Ford.[61] This was a massive fortification, and was considered a work of such importance that throughout the winter of 1178–9 the army of the kingdom and the king himself remained at Jacob's Ford to protect the workforce.[62] Le Chastellet was finally completed in April 1179 and entrusted to the Templars.[63] Saladin had made no attempt to prevent its being built. The drought which had afflicted Syria for some years was continuing and that made it difficult for him to keep a large army in the field, and he was also preoccupied by a revolt at Baalbek which had the support of Raymond of Tripoli;[64] but Lyons and Jackson are surely right in their conjecture that after Mont Gisard Saladin was afraid to risk another pitched battle with the Franks in case he should lose it and this should encourage the Zengid princes to break the uneasy truce that they had made.[65] Nevertheless, Le Chastellet was a threat to the security of Damascus. There were eighty Templar knights in the garrison and a total fighting force of almost 1,000 men. So unless Saladin kept a substantial body of men at Damascus, the garrison of Le Chastellet would be able to raid his territory at will and cause substantial damage. This would be a very effective check to any attempt he might wish to make to extend his power in north Syria.[66]

---

[61] Ernoul, pp. 51–4, who wrongly dates the building of Le Chastellet to 1182–3, claims it was constructed in breach of a truce between Baldwin IV and Saladin. There is no evidence in contemporary sources that such a truce existed in 1178, although Saladin did make truces then with Raymond of Tripoli and Bohemond of Antioch to protect his interests in north Syria. This is known because he later complained that they had been infringed, AS, RHC Or IV, p. 198. As Prawer has pointed out, it is anachronistic to consider that in Baldwin IV's reign the fortification of a frontier would be construed as a breach of a truce (even had a truce existed at that time). All examples of such truces date from after the Third Crusade, when Ernoul wrote: *Histoire du royaume latin de Jérusalem*, 2 vols. (Paris, 1969), I, p. 555, n. 20. Sir Hamilton Gibb supposed that the truce made between Saladin and Raymond of Tripoli in 1175 remained in force unless a foreign prince, such as Philip of Flanders, came on crusade. There is no warrant for this strange assumption: H.A.R. Gibb, *The Life of Saladin from the Works of Imad ad-Din and Baha' ad-Din* (Oxford, 1973), p. 22 (and elsewhere).

[62] WT, XXI, 25, pp. 996–8; cf. the royal diplomas issued at Jacob's Ford on 17 November 1178 and 4 April 1179, RRH, nos. 562 and 577, I, pp. 149 and 154. For all that follows about the building and loss of this castle, M. Barber, 'Frontier warfare in the Latin Kingdom of Jerusalem: the campaign of Jacob's Ford, 1178–1179', in J. France and W.G. Zajac (eds.), *The Crusades and their Sources. Essays presented to Bernard Hamilton* (Aldershot, 1998), pp. 9–22.

[63] WT, XXI, 29, p. 1003.

[64] al-Maqrizi, p. 57; IA, RHC Or I, p. 633; MS, XX, viii, III, p. 379.

[65] Lyons and Jackson, *Saladin*, pp. 133–4.

[66] AS, RHC Or IV, p. 194; MS, XX, viii, III, p. 378; Barber, 'Jacob's Ford', p. 11.

By the spring of 1179 the Franks were looking reasonably strong and Baldwin IV led some of his men to the forest of Banias to pillage the cattle of Damascus that were sent to graze there. Saladin's nephew, Farrukh Shah, came upon the Franks by chance and in the ensuing fracas the king's horse bolted and, while trying to rescue him, the elderly constable, Humphrey of Toron, was mortally wounded. The king escaped unharmed, but Humphrey died a few days later.[67] He had been constable for twenty-seven years and one of the ablest Frankish commanders. A generation later the great Islamic historian Ibn al-Athir wrote of him: 'His name was a byword for bravery and courage in battle. He was a kind of affliction unleashed by God against the Muslims.'[68]

A few weeks later the king, learning that Syrian Beduin were raiding the lordships of Beirut and Sidon where the harvest had just been gathered, mustered the host and marched to Toron to intercept them.[69] Saladin sent a party of cavalry to raid the outskirts of Sidon on 10 June. This led the king to march to the hills of the Marj Uyun, accompanied by the master of the Temple and Raymond of Tripoli.[70] Although this force had no difficulty in routing Saladin's raiding party as it was fording the Litani river, the Franks were themselves routed by Saladin who brought his main army against them. The royal bodyguard succeeded in fighting its way to safety, although the king was unhorsed during the battle and, being unable to remount without help, had to be carried from the field on the back of a Frankish knight.[71] The count of Tripoli escaped to Tyre, while other Frankish fugitives were rescued by Reynald, lord of Sidon, but many Franks were taken prisoner, including Odo of St Amand, the master of the Temple, Baldwin of Ibelin, and Raymond of Tripoli's stepson, Hugh of St Omer.[72]

---

[67] The battle occurred on 10 April 1179, WT, XXI, 26, pp. 998–9; AS, RHC Or IV, pp. 195–6; al-Maqrizi, p. 59.

[68] IA, RHC Or I, p. 635.

[69] al-Imad, cited by AS, RHC Or IV, p. 197; Lyons and Jackson, *Saladin*, p. 138.

[70] Raymond's truce with Saladin as count of Tripoli would not have precluded his supplying the king with the knight-service he owed for Galilee and perhaps also Tripoli: John of Ibelin, *Livre*, cc. X and XIII, ed. Edbury, *John of Ibelin*, pp. 114 and 118. A brother of 'the prince of Gibelet' was among the prisoners taken by Saladin, but he had married one of the co-heiresses of Henry the Buffalo and was perhaps serving on behalf of his wife as a vassal of the king of Jerusalem, not on his own behalf as a vassal of the count of Tripoli, *Lignages*, c. 16, RHC Lois II, p. 454; al-Maqrizi, p. 60; AS, RHC Or IV, p. 198.

[71] AS, RHC Or IV, p. 202.

[72] WT, XXI, 28, pp. 1001–2; IA, RHC Or I, p. 636; AS, RHC Or IV, pp. 198–9; al-Maqrizi, p. 60; Ernoul, pp. 49–50.

Meanwhile, the Third Lateran Council had met in Rome in March 1179. This was the most important council to be held in the western Church for forty years, and was attended by some 300 bishops and 700 other delegates.[73] The Latin patriarchs of Jerusalem and Antioch did not attend in person, perhaps on account of their age. Amalric of Nesle was represented by Peter, prior of the Holy Sepulchre, and Aimery of Limoges by the bishop of Jabala. The other delegates from the Crusader States were William, archbishop of Tyre, Heraclius, archbishop of Caesarea, the bishops of Sebastea, Bethlehem and Tripoli and the abbot of Mount Sion.[74] None of these men had the weight needed to influence the decisions of the council. Had the two patriarchs been in attendance, they might have been able to present the needs of the Latin East in a more forceful way because they would have taken precedence over all other clergy except the pope himself. As it was, the council ignored the needs of the Latin East and, instead of launching a new crusade, offered a partial indulgence to all those who would fight against heretics and *routiers* in Languedoc.[75]

From the point of view of the Latin Kingdom the diplomatic activity which followed the council proved more valuable than the council itself. Bishop Joscius of Acre visited Burgundy and successfully discharged his mission. Hugh III accepted the proposal to come to Jerusalem and Louis VII gave his assent.[76] Hugh arranged for his elder son, Eudes III, who was about fifteen, to take over the duchy.[77] Eudes was given his own ducal seal and on 14 January 1180 issued a confirmation of a privilege given by his father to the Church of St Maurice, Sémur. Dom U. Plancher, who first drew attention to this confirmation, and who was not aware of Hugh's plans to leave the kingdom, was very surprised by it:

Ce prince est le premier et même l'unique des enfans des Ducs de Bourgogne qui, plusieurs années avant la mort de son père, et avant d'être

---

[73] C.J. Hefèle, ed. and tr. H. Leclercq, *Histoire des Conciles d'apres les documents originaux*, 11 vols. (Paris, 1907–52), V(II), p. 1087.

[74] WT, XXI, 25, p. 996; Mansi, XXII, p. 215.

[75] Canon XXVII, Mansi, pp. 1106–7.

[76] Richard has found evidence of his presence in Burgundy in the summer of 1179, *Les Ducs de Bourgogne*, p. 158, n. 4; WT, XXI, 25, p. 997; when Louis VII's brother and son-in-law reached the Holy Land in August 1179 they knew about Hugh's decision and it had royal approval: *ibid.*, XXI, 29, p. 1004.

[77] Hugh III had not married until c.1165 and Eudes III was probably not born before the end of that year at the earliest: Richard, *Ducs de Bourgogne*, p. 158.

duc, a donné des chartes particulières scellées de son sceau, où il est representé à cheval comme les Ducs . . .[78]

Hugh was intending to leave for Jerusalem with the spring sailing of 1180.

A distinguished group of French crusaders came to Jerusalem in early July 1179. It was led by Louis VII's brother, Peter of Courtenay, his nephew, Philip, bishop-elect of Cambrai, and his brother-in-law, Henry of Troyes, count of Champagne.[79] They were present when Saladin launched an attack on Le Chastellet. The sultan was anxious to return to north Syria where his interests were being threatened by Kilij-Arslan of Iconium,[80] but he could not leave Damascus inadequately defended against attacks from the Templars of Le Chastellet. Ibn abi Tayy reports that Saladin had offered the government of Jerusalem first 60,000 and then 100,000 dinars if they would demolish the fortress, but that the Templars had refused.[81] Odo of St Amand, master of the Order, who had been taken prisoner at Marj Uyun, would certainly never have agreed to this. He believed so strongly that it was wrong for his brethren to pay money to the infidel that he refused to allow them to pay his own ransom and died in prison a few months later.[82] In any case, there would have been no point in agreeing to Saladin's proposals, since the castle was clearly fulfilling its intended function admirably.

In order to resolve this problem, Saladin laid siege to Le Chastellet on 24 August. Izz ad-Din Chauli, the senior *mamluk* of his late uncle Shirkuh, and one of the sultan's most trusted staff officers, advised an immediate assault rather than a regular siege. The outer defences were stormed at the first attack and the Muslims were then able to mine the inner walls. A breach was effected on 29 August and the castle fell on the same day. The Templars and the Frankish archers were executed on Saladin's orders, and some 700 other

---

[78] U. Plancher, *Histoire générale et particulière de Bourgogne*, 4 vols. (Dijon, 1739–81), I, p. 368.

[79] WT, XXI, 29, p. 1003.

[80] al-Maqrizi, p. 60; IA, RHC Or I, pp. 639–40.

[81] AS, RHC Or IV, p. 197; IA, RHC Or I, p. 638; al-Maqrizi, pp. 60–1.

[82] Robert of Torigni, *Chronicle*, RS 82(IV), p. 288; cf. WT, XXI, 28, p. 1002; AS, RHC Or, IV, p. 200; al-Maqrizi, p. 60. The obituary of the Temple of Rheims records his death on 9 October presumably in 1179: E. de Barthélemy, 'Obituaire de la commanderie du Temple de Reims', *Collection des documents inédits sur l'histoire de France. Mélanges historiques. Choix de documents*, IV (Paris, 1882), p. 328. Alexander III knew about it by February 1180, but assumed that Odo had died in battle: M. d'Albon, 'La mort d'Odon de Saint-Amand, grand maître du Temple (1179)', ROL 12 (1911), pp. 279–82.

members of the garrison were taken prisoner, although many of them were later killed by Saladin's troops. The sultan remained at Le Chastellet for a fortnight during which the castle was razed to the ground and the bodies of the Christian dead flung into the well.[83]

When Baldwin IV had learned of Saladin's invasion he had summoned the host to Tiberias. William of Newburgh, whose account is based on Templar sources, says that 'the Christian army assembled at Tiberias, but not with the speed which was customary', and goes on to relate how the host refused to march without the relic of the True Cross, which had to be fetched from Jerusalem, and how by the time it arrived Le Chastellet had already fallen.[84] The king, of course, had no reason to think that haste was necessary, because Le Chastellet had been built to withstand a long siege. Nevertheless, the fact that the army was slow to answer the summons, and that the Holy Cross was not present as a matter of course, suggests that there had been a breakdown in organisation, perhaps produced by the recent deaths of the constable and the marshal, whose offices were still vacant.[85]

This no doubt led to the rapid appointment of a new marshal, Gerard of Ridefort, a Flemish knight formerly in the service of Raymond of Tripoli.[86] According to a story later recorded in one version of the *Eracles*, Raymond III had promised Gerard the hand in marriage of the first heiress in his gift, but had reneged on this agreement when the lordship of Botrun passed to a woman, by granting the bride to a Pisan merchant called Plievan (or Pleban) in return for her weight in gold. Gerald, angered by this breach of faith, went to Jerusalem and became a Templar. Despite what Ruth Morgan justly called its 'folkloristic character', this story may have

---

[83] IA, RHC Or I, pp. 637–8; al-Maqrizi, p. 61; AS, RHC Or IV, pp. 204–5.

[84] William of Newburgh, *Historia Rerum Anglicarum*, ed. R. Howlett, III, xi, RS 82(1), p. 244; WT, XXI, 29, pp. 1003–4; Ernoul, pp. 53–4.

[85] The marshal, Gerard of Pugi, is last mentioned in a document of 1 May 1179: RRH, no. 582, I, p. 155.

[86] Gerard first appears as marshal on 22 October 1179, Strehlke, *Tabulae*, no. 11, pp. 11–12. Ernoul, p. 114, asserts he was a Fleming; J.H. Round, 'Some English crusaders of Richard I', EHR 18 (1903), pp. 475–8, suggested that the family was of Anglo-Norman origin; Gerald first appeared in Raymond of Tripoli's service in c.1175: Delaville Le Roulx, 'Chartes de Terre Sainte', ROL 11 (1905–8), no. 4, pp. 187–9. There is no evidence that Aimery of Lusignan was constable before March 1181: RRH, no. 601, I, p. 160: although Ernoul, p. 59, says that he was constable in the early months of 1180, but this source was written at least twenty years later, and the author may have supposed that Aimery succeeded Humphrey of Toron immediately.

been partly true.[87] William Dorel, lord of Botrun, died before November 1179, and by March 1181 a Pisan named Pleban had married William's daughter and heiress.[88] As Gerard came to Jerusalem in 1179, and later became a Templar, and as he was very hostile to Raymond III, the *Eracles* may have preserved a true tradition.

In October 1179 an Egyptian fleet blockaded the harbour of Acre for two days.[89] Before Saladin came to power the Fatimid navy had been allowed to decline. Saladin's conquests in Libya and Cyrene gave him access to timber supplies and to experienced seamen from the north African ports, and he had built up an Egyptian navy initially in response to the Sicilian threat. By 1179 he had a fleet of sixty war galleys and twenty transports.[90] This attack on Acre does not seem to have caused much damage, but the fact that it happened at all alarmed the Franks, who had no navy of their own.

Saladin was in no position to follow up his victory at Le Chastellet, for a severe epidemic had broken out among his troops, which killed ten emirs. It was probably caused by the putrefying Christian corpses which on his orders had been thrown into the well of Le Chastellet during the height of summer while the demolition work was in progess.[91] To add to his problems, Syria was still beset by drought, while in Egypt, the chief source of his wealth, the Nile failed to rise.[92]

Although the destruction of their prize fortress must have damaged Frankish morale, their situation did not appear particularly bleak in the winter of 1179–80. The French crusaders stayed on, awaiting the arrival of Hugh of Burgundy in the following spring. As Baldwin had announced his intention of abdicating, they were presumably hoping to assist at Sibyl and Hugh's coronation.

Meanwhile William of Tyre was in Constantinople, where he stayed from late August 1179 until 23 April 1180. He does not specify

[87] M.R. Morgan (ed.), *La continuation de Guillaume de Tyr (1184–1197)*, DRHC 14 (Paris, 1982), c. 33, pp. 45–6 and n. 1.

[88] William Dorel died before November 1179, when his widow remarried, Strehlke, *Tabulae*, no. 12, p. 12; Pleban is first mentioned as lord of Botrun in March 1181: Müller, *Documenti*, no. 15, pp. 17–18; CGOH, no. 596.

[89] AS, RHC Or IV, p. 211.

[90] A.S. Ehrenkreutz, 'The place of Saladin in the naval history of the Mediterranean Sea', *Journal of the American Oriental Society* 75 (1955), pp. 100–16. Saladin also sought shipbuilding materials from Pisa: M. Amari, *I diplomi arabi del R. Archivio Fiorentino*, no. X (Florence, 1863), p. 264.

[91] AS, RHC Or IV, p. 206.   [92] al-Maqrizi, p. 61.

what his business was, but presumably he had been charged by Baldwin IV to restore the Byzantine protectorate, in abeyance since the fiasco of 1177.[93] He received a cordial welcome from the emperor, who was constructing a new system of western alliances which combined very well with those which had been made by the Franks of Jerusalem. In the early months of 1180, Manuel's only daughter Maria married Rainier, the youngest son of William V of Montferrat.[94] William had been one of Frederick Barbarossa's most loyal allies in his wars with the Lombards, but was dissatisfied because his interests were not well protected by the terms of the Peace of Venice.[95] He was won over to Manuel's cause by the honour which a marriage to a purple-born princess conferred on his family: no Byzantine emperor's daughter had ever before married a man who was not of royal birth. This alliance soon produced results, for on 29 September 1179 William's eldest surviving son, Conrad, seized and imprisoned Barbarossa's chancellor, Christian of Mainz, who was trying to impose imperial rule in Tuscany.[96] On 11 March 1180 Manuel's ten-year-old son, the co-emperor Alexius II, was married to Louis VII's youngest daughter, the eight-year-old Agnes.[97] Both marriages were solemnised with great splendour: William of Tyre was overwhelmed by the display of rich vestments, gold furnishings and elaborate public games in the hippodrome.[98] Agnes of France was first cousin to Hugh III of Burgundy, who was about to become king of Jerusalem, while Rainier of Montferrat was the uncle of Sibyl's son, Baldwin of Montferrat, the next heir to the throne of Jerusalem.[99] These links seemed guaranteed to ensure the continuance of the Byzantine protectorate of the Crusader States in the foreseeable future. Charles Brand has pointed out that there is some evidence that Manuel also required the Franks of Antioch and Jerusalem in the event of his death to pledge their support to his young son, Alexius II.[100]

[93] He stayed in Constantinople for seven months and left on 23 April 1180 ('quarta post Pascha feria').

[94] Choniates, *Historia*, ed. van Dieten, I, p. 200; WT, XXII, 4, p. 1010.

[95] C.M. Brand, *Byzantium Confronts the West, 1180–1204* (Cambridge, Mass., 1968), pp. 18–19.

[96] Choniates, *Historia*, ed. Van Dieten, I, p. 201; Roger of Howden, *Gesta Regis Henrici Secundi*, ed. W. Stubbs, 2 vols., RS 49(I), pp. 243–4.

[97] WT, XXII, 4, p. 1010.   [98] *Ibid.*, XXII, 4, p. 1011.

[99] See Genealogy VI.

[100] Brand, *Byzantium Confronts the West*, pp. 26–7; Eustathius of Thessalonica, *The Capture of Thessaloniki*, c. 48, Greek text with English tr. by J.R. Melville-Jones, Byzantina Australiensia 8 (Canberra, 1988), pp. 56–7.

William of Tyre left the capital for Syria in Easter Week accompanied by imperial envoys and with an imposing escort of four Byzantine galleys. The emperor had entrusted him with a special mission to Bohemond III and to Aimery of Limoges, the Latin patriarch of Antioch. In part this must have concerned the Byzantine protectorate, but William also says that his mission was 'very useful to us and to our church', by which he presumably means the Catholic Church in the Crusader States.[101] It is possible that William had succeeded in convincing the emperor that the Byzantine protectorate of the Crusader States should not be accompanied by any attempt to reinstate the Orthodox patriarchs of Jerusalem and Antioch. Alexander III had made his opposition to this policy publicly known, and Manuel had to give weight to the pope's views if he wished to form alliances with the western powers.[102] There are two indications that Manuel made a commitment of this kind, at least in the case of Antioch. First, Aimery of Limoges immediately after this became a strong supporter of the Byzantine alliance. Secondly, in the years immediately following these discussions the eastern Christian communities in the Levant began to treat Aimery as though he were the sole patriarch of Antioch ruling over both Latin Catholics and Byzantine Orthodox.[103]

In the winter of 1179–80 the future of the Crusader States was looking more assured than it had done since the death of King Amalric, but that apparent security proved illusory. In 1179 Louis VII planned to associate his only son, the fourteen-year-old Philip, in power with him on All Saints' Day, 1 November, but before this happened Louis had a stroke which rendered him semi-paralysed. Philip when crowned thus became effectively sole king of France, although the old king did not die until 18 September 1180. Louis commended his young son to Count Philip of Flanders who became virtual regent of France, but his power was viewed with grave alarm by Queen Adela and her brothers, Theobald, count of Blois and William, archbishop of Reims, who threatened to withdraw their obedience from the young king.[104]

---

[101] WT, XXII, 4, p. 1011.

[102] Alexander III in c.1178 warned the people of Antioch against any attempt to restore an Orthodox patriarch there: R. Hiestand (ed.), *Papsturkunden für Kirchen im Heiligen Lande*, no. 111 (Göttingen, 1985), pp. 278–9.

[103] See pp. 166–7 below.

[104] A. Cartellieri, *Philipp II August, König von Frankreich*, 4 vols. (Leipzig, 1899–1922), I, pp. 29–63; M. Pacaut, *Louis VII et son royaume* (Paris, 1964), pp. 218–19; M. Bur, 'Rôle et

Philip II wrote to his uncle, Henry the Liberal, begging him to return and mediate peace between his mother and himself. Henry replied, agreeing to return at once, 'although we had previously intended to offer our services freely by fighting for God'.[105] This correspondence survives only in later copies which are undated, but Philip's letter must have been written between his coronation on 1 November 1179 and the Peace of Gisors on 28 June 1180, when Henry II of England successfully mediated peace between the king and his mother.[106] This letter reached Henry while he was still in the Holy Land, for urgent messages were sometimes conveyed there by sea even during the winter months.[107] Henry travelled home by the land route through Anatolia and was taken captive by the sultan of Iconium. He had to be ransomed by the Emperor Manuel, and consequently did not reach France until Lent 1181.[108] Peter of Courtenay also returned to France on hearing the news and was present at the Peace of Gisors on 28 June 1180.[109] Hugh of Burgundy did not come to Jerusalem as expected with the spring sailing in 1180, probably because he felt unable to leave his young and inexperienced son in sole charge of the duchy of Burgundy when the kingdom appeared to be on the verge of civil war.

There are two quite different accounts of what happened in the Holy Land at Easter 1180. One is by William of Tyre, who although he was not an eyewitness, returned to the kingdom a few weeks later and had excellent sources of information. He considered the events of Easter 1180 so important that he began a new Book of his *Chronicle* at that point, but his account makes better sense if this division is disregarded and the reader begins at the last section of Book XXI, which leads straight into the opening of Book XXII:

---

place de la Champagne dans le royaume de France au temps de Philippe Auguste', and T. de Hemptinne, 'Aspects des relations de Philippe Auguste avec la Flandre au temps de Philippe d'Alsace', both in R.-H. Bautier (ed.), *La France de Philippe Auguste* (Paris, 1982), pp. 236–49 and 255–8 respectively.

[105] A. Cartellieri (ed.), *Ein Donaueschinger Briefsteller. Lateinische Stilübüngen des XII Jahrhunderts aus der orleanischen Schule* (Innsbruck, 1898), nos. 149–50, pp. 33–4.

[106] Cartellieri, *Philipp II August*, I, pp. 75–82.

[107] E.g. Frederick II was informed of the papal invasion of the Regno while he was in the Holy Land in the winter of 1228–9: *Eracles*, XXXIII, vii, RHC Occ II, pp. 373–4.

[108] Robert of Auxerre, *Chronicon*, ed. O. Holder-Egger, MGH SS, XXVI (Hanover, 1872), p. 244; Continuator of Sigebert of Gembloux, *Chronographia*, ed. D.L.C. Bethmann, MGH SS, VI, pp. 418–19; Ernoul, p. 54; Cartellieri, *Philipp II August*, I, p. 97.

[109] Cartellieri, *Philipp II August*, I, p. 77.

Figure 3 Baldwin IV gives Guy of Lusignan Sibyl's hand in marriage.

[Book XXI, c. 29.] At the same time the discussion, which in the year which had just passed had been initiated with the duke of Burgundy, was resumed with the lord Count Henry his uncle. It was hoped that [the duke] would arrive with the next sailing, but, as was afterwards only too obvious, he declined to come here for certain reasons which are unknown. [Book XXII, c.1.] At that time the lord Prince Bohemond of Antioch and the lord Count Raymond of Tripoli, entering the kingdom with an army, terrified the lord king who feared lest they should attempt to organise a revolution by deposing the king and laying claim to the kingdom for themselves. For the king was afflicted more grievously than usual by his illness and day by day the symptoms of leprosy became more and more evident. The sister of the king, who had been the wife of the marquis, had still not remarried but was awaiting the arrival of the duke [of Burgundy], as we have already said. When the king knew that these noblemen had come, although both of them were his kinsmen, he viewed them with suspicion and hastened his sister's marriage. Although there were men in the kingdom who were more noble, more brave and more wealthy, both among his own subjects and among the visitors from overseas, to whom he might more fittingly for reasons of state have given his sister's hand, he did not give sufficient weight to the maxim that 'acting on impulse causes harm to everything'. Nevertheless, because certain things had happened [*causis quibusdam intervenientibus*], she was unexpectedly married to a certain young man [*adolescenti*] called Guy of Lusignan. He came from quite a good family and was the son of Hugh the Brown in the diocese of Poitiers. The marriage took place in Holy Week, which was highly irregular.[110] The aforementioned noblemen, seeing that their presence was viewed with distrust by the king and his court, returned home when they had completed their religious devotions in the normal way.[111]

Ernoul gives a quite different account of these events, which has been quite widely accepted by distinguished scholars.[112] He relates that when Baldwin of Ibelin was held prisoner by Saladin, Princess Sibyl sent a message to him saying that if he would arrange his ransom she would persuade the king to allow him to marry her. Saladin fixed his ransom at 200,000 bezants and threatened to pull out Baldwin's teeth if he did not agree to the terms. Ernoul continues: 'Quant on l'en ot II trais, si ot grant engousse, qu'il cria merchi, et dist qu'il paieroit le rancon . . .'. He was then released on bail, hostages being given on his behalf; but Sibyl refused to discuss their marriage until the ransom was fully paid. Baldwin went to Constantinople to ask for the Emperor Manuel's help. Manuel willingly paid the ransom, but during Baldwin's absence Aimery of Lusignan had persuaded Sibyl and her mother, Agnes of Courtenay, of the charms of his younger brother Guy, and had fetched him

---

[110] 'infra Paschalia preter morem sollempnia' must refer to Holy Week, not to the octave of Easter when there would have been no canonical irregularity in solemnising marriages.

[111] WT, XXI, 29, XXII, 1, pp. 1004, 1007.

[112] E.g. R. Grousset, *Histoire des Croisades et du royaume franque de Jérusalem*, 3 vols. (Paris, 1934–6), II, pp. 686–9; Runciman, *Crusades*, II, pp. 423–4, do not even mention William of Tyre's more sober account. Prawer, *Royaume Latin*, I, pp. 588–9, inclines to accept Ernoul's account though with certain reservations.

from France. The king was persuaded by his mother and sister to allow Guy to marry Sibyl, and when Baldwin of Ibelin returned and found what had happened he was heartbroken, but later married the daughter of the constable of Tripoli.[113]

As Ruth Morgan pointed out, the *Chronicle* of Ernoul is in part a skilful work of propaganda, designed to show the members of the Ibelin family in the best light. One criticism that must have been levelled against Baldwin of Ibelin, to which Ernoul obliquely refers, was that by refusing to serve under Guy when he became king he had weakened the defence of the kingdom on the eve of Hattin.[114] Ernoul wrote his account of the Lusignan marriage in such a way as to exculpate Baldwin from this charge. This involved him in falsifying the chronology, for he alleged that Baldwin was in Constantinople when Sibyl married Guy. Baldwin had indeed been taken prisoner by Saladin in June 1179, but he had been released on bail and was in Jerusalem at the time of Sibyl's wedding and only went to Constantinople later in the year.[115] The story told by Ernoul is couched in the genre of a courtly love romance with which his audience would have been familiar and omits entirely the political considerations that must of necessity have surrounded the marriage of the heir to the throne. Sibyl is shown as an emotional and inconstant woman, swayed by a passing fancy for a handsome young man, and unmindful of the devotion and sufferings of her faithful knight, Baldwin. Blame for her unfortunate marriage is placed on her mother, Agnes of Courtenay, portrayed as a silly, scheming woman, and on Aimery of Lusignan, who is reputed to have once been Agnes's lover and is shown as intent on promoting the fortunes of his family. Nothing is said about the attempt to dethrone the king, or about Sibyl's betrothal to Hugh of Burgundy. Any mention of that betrothal would have spoiled the story, since it would have made it clear that Sibyl was not free to marry Baldwin, and that Baldwin, who had been a member of the High Court in 1178 when her remarriage was discussed, had known this. This picture bears little relation to the known facts. Sibyl had been trained to rule; Agnes was centrally interested in political power and was hated because she was successful in wielding it. Neither woman would have behaved in the halfwitted way in which Ernoul portrays them.[116] Nevertheless,

---

[113] Ernoul, pp. 56–60.
[114] Morgan, *Chronicle*, pp. 42 and 136.   [115] CGOH, no. 582; see below p. 160.
[116] Hamilton, 'Women in the Crusader States: the queens of Jerusalem 1100–1190', in

the story served its purpose. Ernoul provided an explanation of Baldwin's hatred of Guy which was acceptable within the terms of the chivalric code: Baldwin had been inspired not by ambition but by love; Princess Sibyl had trifled with his affections and rejected his suit. Courtly romances contained many similar stories, and Ernoul's account has been widely believed until the present day.

There is no reason to question William of Tyre's statement that Bohemond of Antioch and Raymond of Tripoli were trying to stage a *coup d'état* in 1180. If, as William implies, they wished to depose Baldwin, then Sibyl would become queen. The object of the *coup* would seem to have been to find her a husband acceptable to Raymond and Bohemond. Unless that had been so, their *coup* would not have failed when Baldwin IV married his sister to Guy. The revolt was obviously prompted by the news that had reached the Latin East of near anarchy in France, and by the inference that could be drawn from this that Hugh of Burgundy would not come to Jerusalem in the immediate future. This raises two questions: why did Bohemond and Raymond object to him, and whom did they wish Sibyl to marry? In regard to the first question, they may have been motivated by two considerations. First, they wished to restore authority to Baldwin IV's paternal kin, of whom they were the chief representatives in the East, and to drive the Courtenays from power. Secondly, they did not want a prince from overseas as their new king, but preferred a member of the local nobility. It is also possible that the presence in the kingdom of Peter of Courtenay had alarmed them. It is not fanciful to suggest that he had come on crusade because he wished to form closer links with his kindred in the Latin Kingdom, where his young cousin Sibyl was about to marry his nephew, Hugh of Burgundy. This connection made it likely that the Courtenays of Edessa would continue to occupy a dominant place at the court of the new king, who would be dependent on their advice when he first came to the East, and that Raymond and Bohemond would not exercise any great influence in Hugh's reign.

The answer to the second question – whom should Sibyl marry – is clearer. Neither Raymond nor Bohemond could marry her themselves because they were already married; moreover, Raymond had no son, and Bohemond's two sons were related to Sibyl within

D. Baker (ed.), *Medieval Women* (Oxford, 1978), pp. 159–73; B. Hamilton, 'The titular nobility of the Latin East: the case of Agnes of Courtenay', in CS, pp. 197–203.

the prohibited degrees. The evidence suggests that their preferred candidate was Baldwin of Ibelin. He had already made plain his ambition to marry Sibyl in 1177 and had not yet remarried. Indeed, he had many of the qualities desirable in a king of Jerusalem. He was a respected military commander of mature years who seems to have enjoyed the reputation among his peers of being loyal and trust-worthy, while as lord of Ramla and Ibelin he had been a member of the High Court for many years and was therefore trained in dealing with affairs of state. Saladin must have heard, perhaps through his spy network, something about this conspiracy, for when Baldwin of Ibelin was released his ransom was fixed at 150,000 dinars and the freeing of 1,000 Muslim prisoners of war, which was a king's ransom.[117]

The king and his advisers reacted decisively by arranging his sister's marriage before Raymond and Bohemond reached the capital with their army. As Prawer shrewdly remarked, the marriage of Sibyl presented the rebels with a *fait accompli* and put an end to their intrigues.[118] It was, of course, in the Courtenays' interest to take this action, but the king's role may not have been a passive one. It is true that he wished to relinquish the throne because he was ill; but he was a knight, not an ascetic, and, as Guy of Lusignan later discovered, Baldwin wished to abdicate on his own terms, not to have terms forced on him. If he had approved of Baldwin of Ibelin as a suitable husband for his sister he could have allowed him to marry her in 1178 when the matter was discussed by the High Court, but he had not done so. The Ibelins were a parvenu family and for that reason alone Baldwin IV may have considered them unsuitable candidates for the throne of Jerusalem. Baldwin of Ibelin can have looked no more desirable as a potential brother-in-law in 1180, not least because his ransom, equivalent to the money fiefs of 300 knights, had not been paid, and would be a drain on the treasury.[119]

If the king and his supporters were to foil the attempted *coup*, they had to find a husband for Sibyl who fulfilled four conditions: he must not be disparaging to her in rank; he must be canonically free to marry her (that is, he must not be married already or related to her

---

[117] AS, RHC Or IV, p. 199; IA, RHC Or I, p. 636.

[118] Prawer, *Royaume Latin*, I, p. 589.

[119] 'A normal fief, whether in land or money, assured a knight an income of some 450 to 500 gold bezants annually. This . . . equalled the annual income from an average village': Prawer, *Latin Kingdom*, p. 73.

within the prohibited degrees); he must be present in Jerusalem; and he must be old enough to take over the regency or the crown itself when Baldwin IV became too ill to rule. Apart from Baldwin of Ibelin, no man native to the Kingdom of Jerusalem met those conditions.[120]

In any case marriage to the heiress of Jerusalem was an important diplomatic asset. It is extremely unlikely that the king chose the new heir to the throne without any thought of the political consequences.[121] What was significant about Guy of Lusignan was that he came from Poitou, which formed part of the continental dominions of Henry II of England.[122] Now that France had a boy king and was racked by internal divisions there was no likelihood of a new French crusade being launched for some years. The only western ruler who might realistically be expected to come to the help of the Holy Land was Henry II of England, who owed a penitential pilgrimage there and who had deposited considerable sums of money with the military Orders in Jerusalem to defray his expenses when he reached Palestine.[123] The presence of a Poitevin as heir to the throne of Jerusalem was arguably calculated to stimulate Angevin interest in the Latin East. It is true that the Lusignans were troublesome vassals to Henry II, yet when Richard I went on the Third Crusade he supported the claims of the discredited Guy of Lusignan to the throne of Jerusalem against those of Conrad of Montferrat, until it became apparent that Guy lacked adequate local support.[124] This would suggest that Baldwin IV and his advisers had sound political judgment: a western king would rather see on the throne of

---

[120] Humphrey IV of Toron was not yet fifteen; Hugh of St Omer, who would become prince of Galilee when his mother died, was ruled out because he was in prison, having been captured at Marj Uyun (WT, XXI, 28, p. 1002), and also because he was Raymond of Tripoli's stepson.

[121] William of Tyre says there were visitors from the West 'more valiant, more noble and more wealthy' than Guy, whom the king might have chosen, but he does not name them: WT, XXII, 1, p. 1007.

[122] C. Farcinet, *L'ancienne famille de Lusignan*, 2nd edn (Vannes, 1899); J.L. Lamonte, 'The houses of Lusignan and Châtellerault, 1150–1250', *Speculum* 30 (1955), pp. 374–84; S. Painter, 'The lords of Lusignan in the eleventh and twelfth centuries', *Speculum* 32 (1957), pp. 27–47; M. Maupilier, 'Les Lusignans de Bas-Poitou et l'Outre-mer' in P.J. Arrignon (ed.), *Les Lusignans d'Outremer* (Poitiers, 1995), pp. 190–200.

[123] H.-E. Mayer, 'Henry II of England and the Holy Land', EHR 97 (1982), pp. 721–39; Warren considers it possible that Henry had been released from his crusade vow in 1176, but that is not certain: *Henry II* (London, 1973), p. 538, n. 1.

[124] J. Gillingham, *Richard the Lionheart* (London, 1978), pp. 54 and 165–216.

Jerusalem one of his own turbulent vassals than some other ruler's exemplary vassal.

It is not known when Guy had come to Jerusalem. No credence should be given to Ernoul's story that Aimery of Lusignan went to fetch him from France in the winter of 1179–80.[125] Such a journey would have been pointless, because everybody, including Aimery, expected that Sibyl would marry Hugh of Burgundy at Easter 1180. Roger of Howden relates that in 1168 the Lusignan brothers had ambushed Eleanor of Aquitaine as she was on her way to Poitiers and Guy had killed the commander of her escort, Patrick, earl of Salisbury:

King Henry of England was angered by this and expelled him from Poitou. Taking the cross he set out for Jerusalem and stayed there in the service of King Baldwin the Leper, and was much loved and honoured by the king and princes because of his integrity.[126]

He was still in France in 1173,[127] and it is impossible to determine how soon after that he went to Jerusalem. Perhaps he came there with the French crusaders in 1179.[128]

Although William of Tyre describes him as *adolescens*, Guy, who had been of fighting age in 1168, must have been at least twenty-seven, and probably some years older, in 1180. He obviously would have been considered old enough to cope with the duties of kingship when Baldwin abdicated. Once Sibyl's marriage to Guy had been consummated the pope alone had the power to dissolve it. Consequently, when the northern rulers reached Jerusalem they were unable to do anything: they could only keep the Easter triduum in the Holy City and then go home.[129]

If this interpretation of what happened in Jerusalem at Easter 1180 is correct, it would explain why Baldwin of Ibelin bore such deep emnity to Guy of Lusignan that he refused to do homage to him when he became king, and left Jerusalem to take service with Bohemond III of Antioch.[130] Baldwin of Ibelin was an ambitious

---

[125] Ernoul, p. 60.
[126] Roger of Howden, *Chronica*, RS 51(i), pp. 273–4. The *Itinerarium Peregrinorum* says that Guy went to Jerusalem on a pilgrimage, 'sepulcri visitator advenerat', but does not specify when, ed. H.-E. Mayer, MGH Schriften 18, p. 336.
[127] Roger of Howden, *Gesta Regis Henrici Secundi*, RS 49(i), p. 46.
[128] The fact that Guy is not mentioned in any of the quite plentiful records of the Kingdom of Jerusalem before Easter 1180, although his brother was prominent there, inclines me to think that he had not been there for very long before he married Sibyl.
[129] WT, XXII, 1, p. 1007.   [130] See below p. 223.

man. He had aspired to marry Sibyl since the death of William of Montferrat, and Guy had not merely thwarted him in this ambition, but had also left him with a king's ransom to pay to Saladin.

Any marriage of the heir to the throne made in such circumstances was bound to prove divisive. Bohemond III, Raymond III and the Ibelins may have been outwitted but they were not reconciled to the prospect of Guy of Lusignan as the next king. It has for a long time been common to speak of a division in the leper king's reign between the native baronage and newcomers from the West, but this classification has never been sustainable and has recently been effectively demolished by Peter Edbury.[131] There is no evidence of serious divisions in the kingdom before 1180, but after Sibyl and Guy's marriage they undoubtedly existed. On the one side was the young king, his mother, his uncle Joscelin, his stepfather, Reynald of Sidon, his sister Sibyl and her husband Guy, together with the king's cousin, Prince Reynald. On the other side were Bohemond III and Raymond III, the king's cousins, supported by Baldwin of Ibelin, his brother Balian, and Balian's wife, the dowager-queen Maria Comnena. The military Orders were not at this stage involved: the Templars lacked a master, and the Knights of St John held aloof from the dispute. The division was not between native barons and newcomers from the West, but between the king's maternal and paternal kin.

But the consequence was that Baldwin IV could not abdicate as he had hoped to do. Guy could not become king while the rulers of Antioch and Tripoli and some of the barons of the kingdom were so hostile to him. It was essential for the well-being of the kingdom that Baldwin should remain in office until unity had been restored.

---

[131] P.W. Edbury, 'Propaganda and faction in the Kingdom of Jerusalem: the background to Hattin', in M. Shatzmiller (ed.), *Crusaders and Muslims in Twelfth-century Syria* (Leiden, 1993), pp. 173–89.

CHAPTER 8

Prince Reynald's initiative

Because of the deep divisions in his kingdom, Baldwin IV sought a two-year truce with Saladin in the late spring of 1180, but whereas Islamic rulers had normally paid the Franks tribute in order to obtain a truce, on this occasion both sides agreed to the terms unconditionally.[1] Saladin was not interested in exploiting Frankish divisions, perhaps because he feared lest that should provoke fresh Byzantine intervention, but welcomed Baldwin's proposal because he wanted to be free to campaign in north Syria and check the growing power of Kilij-Arslan II of Iconium.[2] For that reason he also forced Raymond III of Tripoli to make a truce by invading his county and by mounting a naval assault on Tortosa.[3] Saladin was feeling insecure at this time because the Abbasid Caliph al-Mustadi and his vizier, Zahir al-Din Ibn al-Athir, on whose support Saladin could rely, had died within a few days of each other in the early spring of 1180. He needed the caliph's assent to legitimise his seizure of Zengid lands, and was uncertain whether he would enjoy the same degree of co-operation from the new Caliph al-Nazir and his vizier, Majd al-Din Ibn al-Sahib.[4]

King Baldwin was anxious to give an official explanation to the Emperor Manuel of what had happened in Jerusalem at Easter 1180 and to assure him that the Franks still stood in need of his protection. He sent his most important minister and his closest kinsman, Joscelin of Courtenay, to Constantinople, which is an indication of how

---

[1] WT, XXII, 1, p. 1008. It was concluded after 15 April 1180 (when Farrukh-Shah attacked Safad, M.C. Lyons and D.E.P. Jackson, *Saladin. The Politics of the Holy War* (Cambridge, 1982), p. 145), but before 1 June 1180 (when Saladin's fleet, observing the truce, did not attack Beirut: WT, XXII, 3, pp. 1008–9). It was to last for two years, *ibid.*, XXII, 8, p. 1017; al-Fadil cited by Lyons and Jackson, *Saladin*, p. 147,

[2] Saladin had told the Caliph al-Mustadi that he would have to seek a truce with the Franks because of the Seljuk threat, Lyons and Jackson, *Saladin*, p. 144.

[3] WT, XXII, 2, 3, pp. 1008–9.   [4] Lyons and Jackson, *Saladin*, p. 146.

important he considered this mission. Before this business had been finished, Manuel died on 24 September 1180 and Joscelin had to spend the winter in the Byzantine capital to complete the negotiations with the new government. Manuel was succeeded by his eleven-year-old son, Alexius II, for whom his mother, Mary of Antioch, was regent, assisted by Manuel's nephew, the protosebastus Alexius.[5] Mary of Antioch wished to maintain close links with the Crusader States, and the alliance made with Manuel was renewed.[6] Baldwin of Ibelin had also come to Constantinople to seek help with the payment of his ransom. Although he was of no political consequence, the regent granted his request, perhaps because the protosebastus Alexius was the uncle of Maria Comnena, Balian of Ibelin's wife, and therefore regarded Baldwin as part of his kin-group.[7] Joscelin and Baldwin did not reach Jerusalem again until the summer of 1181.[8]

One consequence of Joscelin's long absence was that the king had to carry out the work of government alone even though his health was deteriorating.[9] Moreover, Reynald of Châtillon, who had been his executive regent since 1177, could no longer hold that position because it would be disparaging to Guy of Lusignan, who was heir to the throne.[10] The king seems at this time particularly to have relied on the advice of his mother, Agnes of Courtenay.

Baldwin's first concern was to make the succession more secure by

---

[5] M. Angold, *The Byzantine Empire 1025–1204. A Political History*, 2nd edn (London, 1997), pp. 295–6.

[6] I infer this from the statement of Eustathius of Thessalonica, when writing of Andronicus I's seizure of power, that Bohemond III and Baldwin IV 'owed genuine friendship and help after Manuel's death to his unjustly treated son Alexius', tr. J.R. Melville-Jones, *The Capture of Thessaloniki*, c. 48, p. 57.

[7] Ernoul, p. 60; see Genealogy VI.

[8] Baldwin of Ibelin had returned before 23 September 1181, H.-E. Mayer, *Die Kanzlei der lateinschen Könige von Jerusalem*, 2 vols., MGH Schriften, 40 (Hanover, 1996), II, pp. 898–9; Joscelin is first recorded there again on 8 November 1181, F. Wilken, *Geschichte der Kreuzzüge*, 7 vols. (Leipzig, 1807–32), III, pp. 33–4; RRH, no. 606, I, p. 161.

[9] 'Premebatur enim solito acrius rex egritudine sua et singulis diebus lepre signum magis et magis evidens prominebat': WT, XXII, 1, p. 1007.

[10] From 1177–80 Reynald took precedence over all other witnesses in a group of royal diplomas: S. Paoli (ed.), *Codice diplomatico*, 2 vols. (Lucca, 1733–7), no. lxiii, I, p. 63 (1177); CGOH, nos. 516 and 518 (1177); Strehlke, no. 11, pp. 11–12 (22 October 1179); CGOH, no. 582 (28 April 1180) He does not appear in the witness lists of any royal diplomas between 28 April 1180 and 24 February 1182 (Strehlke, no. 14, pp. 13–14). In the latter Guy and Sibyl were present, but were associated with the king in the confirmation, and so did not appear on the witness list, which Reynald headed. On 27 April 1182 Reynald was listed after Raymond of Tripoli and Count Joscelin (Strehlke, no. 15, pp. 14–15); and on 28 August 1182 he was listed after Guy of Lusignan and Count Joscelin (Müller, no. 19, p. 23).

arranging the marriage of his eight-year-old half-sister, Isabel, to Humphrey IV of Toron, who was about fifteen. His intention was to prevent Guy of Lusignan's opponents from putting Isabel forward as an alternative heir to the throne, and marrying her to a candidate of their choice. Isabel and Humphrey were solemnly betrothed in Jerusalem in October 1180.[11] The religious marriage did not take place for another three years, presumably because the princess had not yet reached the canonical age of twelve and the king did not want any impediment to be urged against the legality of the marriage.[12] Isabel went to live with her future mother-in-law, Stephanie of Milly, at Kerak, one of the most impregnable fortresses in the kingdom, and Stephanie prevented the child from paying visits to her mother at Nablus.[13] In so far as was possible Isabel had been placed beyond the reach of any conspirators who might seek to make her queen.

Humphrey was Reynald of Châtillon's stepson and this marriage was further evidence of the confidence that the king had in Prince Reynald. Humphrey has a reputation of having been effeminate. This is based on a passage in the *Itinerarium Regis Ricardi* in which he is described, when he was in his late twenties, as 'more like a woman than a man, gentle in his dealings and with a bad stammer'.[14] This writer was seeking to justify the questionable divorce of Humphrey and Isabel, and his insinuations must therefore be treated with caution. All that can be said with certainty about Humphrey's sexuality is that his marriage to Isabel was childless.

William of Tyre, who drew up the marriage contract, makes an enigmatic reference to its terms:

Humphrey. . . exchanged his hereditary lands [Toron, Chastelneuf and his claim to Banias] . . . with the lord king, upon certain conditions, the text of which agreement, drawn up by us in our official capacity, has been deposited in the royal archive.[15]

From later evidence it appears that the exchange that Humphrey received was the rather meagre one of a money fief of 7,000 Saracen

---

[11] WT, XXII, 5, p. 1012.

[12] Isabel was considered Humphrey's wife in the law of Jerusalem from 1180; Delaborde, no. 41, pp. 88–9, in which she is called 'the king's daughter Elisabeth'.

[13] 'Car quant Hanfrei espousa sa fille, il comenca a hair la reyne Marie sa mere, et ne voleit que ele veist sa fille, et ce faiseit il par le conseill sa mere Estefenie, qui esteit dame dou Crac': M.R. Morgan (ed.), *La continuation de Guillaume de Tyr (1184–1197)*, DRHC 14 (Paris, 1982), c. 104, p. 106.

[14] I, 63, RS 38(1), p. 120.   [15] WT, XXII, 5, p. 1012.

bezants. The king was no doubt anxious that two great fiefs, Toron and Transjordan, should not be held by one man, just as King Amalric had been concerned about the fiefs of Transjordan and Beirut, but Steven Tibble is surely right to see also in this exchange evidence of royal concern for the defence of the realm, although the timing of the exchange suggests that the king wished to defend himself against Raymond of Tripoli rather than Saladin. Beirut was a royal fief, Sidon was held by the king's stepfather, and by adding Toron and Chastelneuf to the royal demesne Baldwin cut Raymond of Tripoli off from contact with his power-base in the kingdom, his wife's fief of Galilee.[16]

The patriarch of Jerusalem, Amalric of Nesle, died on 6 October 1180. William of Tyre gives no information about the subsequent election beyond stating that Heraclius, archbishop of Caesarea, was the successful candidate.[17] Two slightly different accounts of what happened are contained in the *Chronicle* of Ernoul and one text of the *Eracles*. Both sources agree that the choice of the canons of the Holy Sepulchre lay between William of Tyre and Heraclius. They were men with very similar career structures: both had been educated in the schools of western Europe; both had become archdeacons in Amalric's reign, and both had been appointed to archbishoprics while Raymond of Tripoli was regent. William of Tyre had enjoyed a greater distinction in public service than his rival, as tutor to the king and chancellor of the kingdom. Heraclius, moreover, is accused of irregularity of life in both texts. He is said to have formerly been

---

[16] In 1186 Guy of Lusignan granted the fiefs of Toron and Chastelneuf to Joscelin of Courtenay, together with the fief of Maron and its six estates, and guaranteed that 'if the agreements made between the Lord Baldwin, sixth Latin King of Jerusalem and the Lord Humphrey the Young should happen to come into effect [and you should have to restore Toron and Chastelneuf to him] you and your heirs will forever hold and possess Maron with its aforementioned estates, together with that exchange for Toron and Chastelneuf which the Lord Humphrey the Young holds and possesses': Strehlke, no. 21, p. 19. From this it is clear that Maron did not form part of the exchange granted to Humphrey IV. Maron had been a crown fief since 1161, Strehlke, no. 3, p. 4; it was briefly granted by Baldwin IV to Count Joscelin in 1182 (*ibid.*, no. 14, p. 14) but was resumed by the king in 1183 (*ibid.*, no. 17, p. 16). In 1229 when Frederick II enfeoffed Humphrey's heirs with Toron and Chastelneuf, newly recovered from the Ayyubids, he explained that the exchange had consisted of a money fief of 7,000 Saracen bezants, but assumed wrongly that it also included the fief of Maron and its estates: J.L.A. Huillard-Bréholles (ed.), *Historia Diplomatica Friderici Secundi*, 6 vols. in 12 (Paris, 1852–61), III, pp. 123–5. I should like to thank Steven Tibble who first drew my attention to this evidence, though I do not completely agree with his interpretation of it: Tibble, *Monarchy and Lordships in the Latin Kingdom of Jerusalem 1099–1291* (Oxford, 1989), pp. 97–8.

[17] WT, XXII, 4, p. 1012.

the lover of Agnes of Courtenay and, while patriarch, to have publicly kept a mistress, Pasque de Rivieri, wife of a merchant of Nablus, who bore him a child.[18] Although the first of these rumours may merely be malicious gossip directed against the king's mother, the account of the lady said to have been known as *madame la patriarchesse* is too circumstantial to be readily dismissed. There was nothing particularly unusual about a concubinary bishop in the twelfth century, and the Patriarch Arnulf among Heraclius's prede-cessors in the see of Jerusalem had been accused of sexual irregular-ities.[19] It should be added that although William of Tyre is universally described by modern historians as a man of upright life, and may well have been so, there is no evidence for this outside the Lyons manuscript of the *Eracles*.[20]

Ernoul's *Chronicle* relates that the names of both men were submitted to the king, and both versions agree that he delegated the choice to his mother.[21] In this he was following precedent. At the previous patriarchal election in 1157, Baldwin III had delegated the choice to his mother, Queen Melisende, who had been advised by a committee of other royal ladies.[22] Agnes's choice of Heraclius was not irresponsible. He has had a bad press, based entirely on the pejorative accounts of him in, or deriving from, Ernoul's *Chronicle*, and as Kedar has observed, when using these sources 'historians have exhibited a tendency to opt at every juncture for the alternative least complimentary to the patriarch's reputation, as if in response to some variety of Gresham's law'. He was learned and energetic and was to prove a resourceful diplomat.[23]

During the summer of 1180 the new master of the Templars reached Jerusalem. He was a Catalan nobleman, who had been master of the Order in Spain and Provence since 1167 and had taken an active part in the wars of the *reconquista*. Malcolm Barber's suggestion that he may have been nominated master by Pope

---

[18] Ernoul, p. 82; Morgan, *Continuation*, c. 38, pp. 50–1.

[19] B. Hamilton, *The Latin Church in the Crusader States. The Secular Church* (London, 1980), p. 63; B.Z. Kedar, 'The Patriarch Eraclius', in *Outremer*, pp. 177–204 at pp. 182–3.

[20] 'Guillaume l'arcivesque de Sur, qui mout estoit preudom et douteit mout Dieu et l'amoit': Morgan, *Continuation*, c. 37, p. 49.

[21] Ernoul, pp. 83–4; Morgan, *Continuation*, c. 37, p. 50; P.W. Edbury and J.G. Rowe, 'William of Tyre and the patriarchal election of 1180', EHR 93 (1978), pp. 18–25; Kedar, 'Eraclius', p. 188.

[22] WT, XVIII, 20, pp. 840–1.

[23] Kedar, 'Eraclius', pp. 177–204, has rehabilitated the patriarch. See also, Hamilton, *Latin Church*, pp. 80–4.

Alexander III is convincing.[24] The pope was concerned about the situation in the Holy Land and may have wanted to appoint somebody there who would be able to submit authoritative but independent reports about the state of the Latin East. This was a role that Arnold of Toroja sustained, and it is one that would help to explain this otherwise enigmatic choice of a master who had no previous links with the Holy Land.

Alexander III made his concerns about the Crusader Kingdom public in his encyclical *Cor nostrum* of 16 January 1181, calling for a new crusade. In it he relates how 'The sinister rumours which have reached Us from the region of Jerusalem through the common report of travellers have troubled Our heart and those of Our brethren . . .' But what seems to have troubled him was not the divisions in the Latin Kingdom, but the state of the king's health. He shows no compassion for the king's sufferings, but simply restates the view, widely held in western Europe, about the causes of leprosy:

the king is not such a man as can rule that land, since he, that is to say Baldwin who holds the government of the realm, is so severely afflicted by the just judgment of God, as We believe you are aware, that he is scarcely able to bear the continual torments of his body.[25]

This was a matter about which Alexander felt strongly, for the Third Lateran Council had legislated about the need to segregate lepers.[26] This bull must have been disheartening to Baldwin the Leper, who was remaining head of state at great personal cost in the interests of Frankish unity, while as a means of raising help for the Latin East it proved ineffective. Alexander died on 30 August 1181 and his successor, Lucius III (1181–5), was preoccupied with Italian affairs and showed no interest in the Crusader Kingdom.

There was fresh trouble there in the winter of 1180–1 and Baldwin IV had to act as a mediator. Bohemond III of Antioch divorced his Byzantine wife Theodora and married Sibyl, sister-in-law of his vassal, the lord of Burcey.[27] His marriage to Theodora had been

---

[24] M.L. Bulst-Thiele, *Sacrae Militiae Templi Hierosolymitani Magistri. Untersuchungen zur Geschichte des Templerordens 1118/1119–1314* (Göttingen, 1974), pp. 99–105; M. Barber, *The New Knighthood. A History of the Order of the Temple* (Cambridge, 1994), pp. 109, 353, n. 138.

[25] P.L. 200, cols. 1294–6; Roger of Howden, *Gesta Regis Henrici Secundi*, RS 49(1), pp. 272–4. Cf. the pope's letter to the clergy on the same theme, *Cum Orientalis terra*, RS 49(1), p. 275; P.L. 200, cols. 1296–7.

[26] Canon XXIII, Hefèle tr. Leclercq, *Conciles*, V(II), pp. 1103–4.

[27] R. Grousset, *Histoire des Croisades et du royaume franque de Jérusalem*, 3 vols. (Paris, 1934–6), II, pp. 692–5; C. Cahen, *La Syrie du nord à l'époque des croisades et la principauté franque d'Antioche*

forced on him by the Emperor Manuel, and he was able to repudiate her without fear of reprisals once Manuel was dead and his own sister Mary had become regent of the empire. His new wife was a controversial choice. William of Tyre said she was a witch, Michael the Syrian called her a prostitute, while Ibn al-Athir and al-Imad claimed that she was a secret agent in the service of Saladin.[28] Opposition to the marriage was led by the patriarch, Aimery of Limoges, who had the support of an influential section of the baronage, although whether they had political as well as personal reasons for objecting to Sibyl is not clear. Aimery excommunicated Bohemond, who retaliated by confiscating church property, and this led the patriarch to place the principality under an interdict and retire with some of his clergy to his castle of Cursat. It was, no doubt, inevitable that the dispute should extend to include control of church property, for the Church of Antioch was rich, whereas the secular government was comparatively poor and had inadequate resources to meet its defence commitments. This was not a new issue – it had embittered relations between Aimery of Limoges and Reynald of Châtillon when he had been prince of Antioch.[29] The dispute then escalated into a civil war; some of the nobility, headed by Reynald Masuer, lord of al-Marqab, sided with the patriarch, while Bohemond laid siege to the patriarch's castle.[30]

When news of this reached Jerusalem, Baldwin IV sent Heraclius at the head of a delegation to mediate peace. The other envoys were the archbishop-elect of Caesarea, the bishop of Bethlehem, the abbot of Mount Sion, the prior of the Holy Sepulchre, Roger des Moulins, master of the Hospital, and Arnold of Toroja, master of the Temple. The only lay member of the group was Reynald of Châtillon, whose advice and assistance were particularly needed because he was Bohemond III's stepfather as well as being a former prince of Antioch. As the envoys passed through Tripoli Heraclius invited Count Raymond to join them because he was a cousin and close friend of Bohemond's and might be able to influence him.

(Paris, 1940), pp. 422–3. Bohemond cannot have separated from Theodora before Manuel's death. In September 1180 his diploma in favour of the Master of the Order of Santiago was witnessed by the patriarch and Reynald Masuer, and at that time clearly they were at peace: A.F. Aguado de Cordova, A.A. Aleman et Rosales and I.L. Agurleta (eds.), *Bullarium Equestris Ordinis S. Iacobi de Spatha* (Madrid, 1719), pp. 22–3.

[28] WT, XXII, 5, p. 1012; MS, XXI, 2, III, p. 389; IA, RHC Or I, pp. 729–30; AS, RHC Or IV, p. 374.

[29] Hamilton, *Latin Church*, pp. 43 and 46.   [30] WT, XXII, 6, pp. 1013–15.

That the mission was successful is perhaps evidence of Heraclius's diplomatic skills. After holding preliminary and independent meetings at Latakia with the prince and the patriarch, the envoys persuaded them to attend a joint meeting at Antioch, at which it was agreed that the prince would restore confiscated church property while in return the patriarch would lift the interdict. The prince, nevertheless, would remain excommunicate unless he put away Sibyl and returned to Theodora. On these terms peace was re-established; but Bohemond later banished some of his his most determined lay opponents – the constable, the chamberlain and three other great lords – who sought refuge with Rupen III of Cilicia;[31] and Bohemond also remained married to Sibyl who was associated with him in his public acts for the next twenty years.[32] Despite this he and the patriarch henceforth worked together in relative harmony.[33]

Aimery of Limoges no doubt wished to maintain the Byzantine protectorate of Antioch, which Bohemond's divorce had placed in jeopardy, because Manuel's recognition of him as sole patriarch had increased his authority, and he feared that if Byzantine suzerainty were rejected the empire might appoint a new Orthodox patriarch. That would not only have undermined the obedience of Byzantine Orthodox Christians to Aimery, but would also have diminished the respect in which he had come to be held by the non-Chalcedonian churches.

Aimery had capitalised on imperial recognition to open negotiations about Church unity with the Maronite Church of the Lebanon, and these were nearing a successful conclusion at the time of Bohemond's divorce. In fact the union was achieved in c.1181. William of Tyre implies that it was monolithic,[34] but from Maronite sources it is clear that whereas the patriarch and some members of the hierarchy, together with those Maronites who lived in the coastal cities and were familiar with the Franks, supported the union, those who lived in the mountain areas and had little contact with the Frankish settlers were for a long time bitterly opposed to what they saw as a betrayal of their own traditions.[35] The Maronite Patriarch

---

[31] WT, XXII, 7, pp. 1015–16; Cahen, *La Syrie*, p. 423.

[32] RRH, nos. 610, 611b (1181); 629 (1183); 648, 649 (1186); 657c (1187); 680 (1189); 689, 695 (1190); 753 (1199); I, pp. 162, 166, 171–2, 181, 183, 185, 200; II, pp. 39, 44.

[33] Cahen, *La Syrie*, p. 507.   [34] WT, XXII, 9, pp. 1018–19.

[35] K.M. Salibi, 'The Maronite Church in the Middle Ages and its union with Rome', *Oriens Christianus* 42 (1958), pp. 92–104 at p. 94.

Peter, who took part in the initial negotiations, died in 1183 and was succeeded by Jeremias al-Amshitti during whose long reign the details of reunion were finally worked out in 1203 and endorsed by Innocent III in 1215. The Maronites became the earliest example of a uniate Church. They were required to bring their faith and practice into conformity with Catholic norms in those matters of significance in which they differed from them, but they retained their own hierarchy, liturgy and canon law, and were not subject to the Latin patriarch of Antioch, but to the pope alone. How much the details of the final settlement owed to Aimery of Limoges it is difficult to determine.[36] Though imperfect at first, the Maronite union was a model of how closer relations might be achieved between the western Church and the eastern Churches, and such growth of Christian unity could only be beneficial to the stability of Frankish rule in the Levant.

Rupen III of Cilicia also drew closer to the Franks at this time. He came to Jerusalem in 1181 and married Isabel of Toron, Humphrey IV's sister, and thus was linked to the royal kindred.[37]

During the time of truce Baldwin IV strengthened the position of his own family. Joscelin the seneschal received various royal gifts, the most important of which were the fiefs of Maron and Chastelneuf in February 1182.[38] It is possible that at this same time the king granted the usufruct of Toron to his mother: she certainly held those revenues in 1184.[39] From March 1181 Guy of Lusignan began to take precedence over all other laymen in the witness lists of royal diplomas,[40] and he and Sibyl began to be associated with the king in some public acts, which is evidence that he was being publicly acknowledged as heir to the throne.[41] His brother Aimery was appointed constable of the kingdom at about this time.[42] Although unity seemed to have been restored, there was one important exception: Raymond of Tripoli had not been reconciled with the king. In the spring of 1182 Raymond was turned back at the frontier when he tried to enter the kingdom because Baldwin IV believed that he was hatching a fresh plot to depose him. In his account of

---

[36] P. Dib, 'Maronites', *Dictionnaire de Théologie Catholique*, X(I), cols. 1–142 at cols. 40–120.

[37] G. Dédéyan (ed.), *La Chronique attribuée au Connetable Smbat*, DRHC 13 (Paris, 1980), c. 15, p. 57; cf. Vahram of Edessa, *Chronique rimée des rois de la Pétite-Armenie*, RHC Arm I, p. 509; *Lignages*, cc. 14, 15, RHC Lois II, pp. 452–4; Ernoul, p. 31.

[38] Strehlke, nos. 13, 14, pp. 13–14.   [39] Ibn Jubayr, p. 316.

[40] CGOH, II, p. 909, no. xx.   [41] *Ibid.*, no. 607.

[42] He is first named as constable on 24 February 1182: Strehlke, no. 14, pp. 13–14.

this episode, William of Tyre, a good crown servant, did not directly criticise the king, but held the Courtenays responsible:

> It was the true intention of those deceivers that in the absence of the count [of Tripoli] who was a hardworking man and gave his full attention to all matters, they should conduct the business of state as they pleased, and should use the king's illness for their own profit. Among them were the king's mother, a woman totally hateful to God and relentless in her greed, and her brother, the king's seneschal, who together with a few of their minions, who were wicked men, shamelessly drove the king to take this course of action.[43]

In view of the attempted *coup* of 1180 the king had every reason for distrusting Raymond without any prompting from his mother and uncle. In this connection William of Tyre's comment that Baldwin 'was very mindful of the benefits he received and also of the injuries which were done to him' may be relevant.[44] In any case, William's picture of a sick king manipulated by an unscrupulous cabal is unacceptable, since, as William himself relates, Baldwin was still able to lead the army of the kingdom and to take important military decisions a few weeks after his quarrel with Raymond III.[45] William was not an impartial observer of events at court: he was a loyal supporter of the count of Tripoli to whom he owed his preferment and he hated Agnes of Courtenay who had thwarted him in his ambition to become patriarch.

Presumably the king's intention was to charge Raymond with treason and remove Galilee from his control and entrust it to his stepson, Hugh II of St Omer. Under the terms of the *Assise sur la ligèce* Baldwin would have needed the High Court's assent to this, since a vassal could not be deprived of his fief without judgment of peers.[46] The High Court advised that the king should be reconciled with the count of Tripoli and, as William of Tyre reports, the king very reluctantly agreed to this.[47] The Court had made a wise decision. The truce with Saladin was about to expire, and an attempt to deprive Raymond of Galilee might have led to civil war. Raymond, as count of Tripoli, had renewed his own truce with Saladin perhaps in order to be free to fight for his rights should the need arise.[48] Reconciliation with the king meant that Raymond also

---

[43] WT, XXII, 10, p. 1019.   [44] *Ibid.*, XXI, 1, p. 962
[45] *Ibid.*, XXII, 15, pp. 1026–8; see below pp. 172–6.   [46] See Chapter 3 n. 85, above.
[47] 'rege invito sed tamen permittente': WT, XXII, 10, pp. 1019–20.
[48] al-Maqrizi, p. 68.

had to be reconciled with Guy of Lusignan, and they began to take their places together at court.[49]

Baldwin IV was in fact governing Jerusalem very effectively, but he was extremely ill and Guy of Lusignan was unpopular with a substantial section of the baronage. Some people in the kingdom were disquieted about the future, and news of this reached the West. At Eastertide 1182 a conference was held near Senlis attended by Henry II of England and the papal legate, the bishop of Albano, to mediate peace between Philip Augustus and Philip of Flanders, at which envoys arrived from the Holy Land:

King Baldwin of Jerusalem being wasted by the royal illness and shrinking from the greatness of kingship, the Templars and knights beyond the seas sent envoys beseeching the kings of France and England that they should take charge of the Kingdom of Jerusalem, send help to defend it, and dispose of the crown as they wished.[50]

It seems likely that this delegation had been sent by the new Master of the Temple, Arnold of Toroja, who was not subject to the King of Jerusalem, and could make independent approaches to the rulers of Western Europe, and that it also had the support of some of the Frankish barons. The appeal met with no response. It is important only as an index of the strength of opposition to Guy of Lusignan's succession.

The truce with Saladin was due to expire in May 1182. The sultan had made very little use of those two years to build up his own power. In 1180 he had taken his army to Raban and stayed there throughout the summer, and his presence had led both Kilij-Arslan and the new prince of Mosul, Izz ad-Din, to make peace with him;[51] but at the end of the year he had to return to Egypt where his brother, Turan-Shah, whom he had left as governor, had died.[52]

Saladin spent the whole of 1181 in Egypt. News had reached him that William II of Sicily was preparing an armada, which the sultan feared would be directed against the ports of the Nile delta, even though William had opened peace negotiations with Cairo in the

---

[49] They first appeared together on 25 August 1182. Raymond took precedence over Guy in the witness list because he was a head of state: Müller, no. 19, p. 23.

[50] Continuator of Sigebert of Gembloux, *Chronographia*, MGH SS, VI, p. 420; A. Cartellieri, *Phillip II August, König von Frankreich*, 4 vols. (Leipzig, 1899–1922), I, p. 126.

[51] MS, XX, 2, III, p. 388; IA, RHC Or I, pp. 640–3; AS, RHC Or IV, pp. 211, 213; Baha al-Din, RHC Or III, pp. 65–6.

[52] Saladin reached Cairo on 2 January 1181: al-Maqrizi, p. 63; Baha al-Din, RHC Or III, p. 63; Lyons and Jackson, *Saladin*, pp. 151–3.

summer of 1180.[53] It was only when Saladin learned that the Sicilian war fleet had been wrecked in a great storm off Ventimiglia on its way to attack the Almoravids of Majorca, that he became convinced that William II's desire for peace was sincere and sent ambassadors to Palermo in August 1181 to arrange a ten-year truce.[54]

In the summer of 1181 Mary of Antioch sent an embassy to Cairo to negotiate peace with the sultan, whose help she hoped to enlist against the growing power of Kilij-Arslan of Iconium.[55] This did not, of course, prejudice the Byzantine protectorate of the Crusader States, except in so far as Byzantium would not join with the Franks in an attack on Egypt.

On 18 November 1181, while Saladin was still in Egypt, the young Prince as-Salih of Aleppo became seriously ill. Before he died on 4 December, he designated his cousin, Izz ad-Din Mas'ud, lord of Mosul, as his successor, saying that the combined power of Aleppo and Mosul would be great enough to prevent further inroads by Saladin into Zengid territory.[56] When news of this reached Saladin he ordered his nephews, Farrukh-Shah at Damascus and Taqi ad-Din at Hama, to prevent any force from Mosul taking over Aleppo, but in the event they were unable to carry out his instructions;[57] for at some time after the start of the heavy rains in the month of Rajab (mid-November to mid-December) Prince Reynald led a cavalry force from his lands in Transjordan towards Eilat. He did not attack it, even though its defences were in a ruinous state, but instead struck into the Arabian desert, and al-Maqrizi implies that he reached Tarbuk, 130 miles south of Eilat.[58] In order to undertake an expedition of that kind he needed the help of the Beduin of Transjordan and the Hijaz who were familiar with the route and, as is known from Arabic sources, Saladin was in serious doubt at precisely this time about whether he could count on their loyalty.[59] Normally the Franks could not operate in the deep desert, which was not suitable for use by

[53] Lyons and Jackson, *Saladin*, p. 147 (citing the Mosul MS of al-Fadil).

[54] WT, XXII, 8, pp. 1017–18; *Annales Casinenses*, ed. G.H. Pertz, MGH SS, XIX (Hanover, 1866), p. 312.

[55] In the month of Safar (16 June–14 July); the terms were finally agreed in Jumada al-Akhira (16 October–15 November 1181), al-Maqrizi, p. 64; C. Cahen, *Pre-Ottoman Turkey. A General Survey of the Material and Spiritual Culture and History c.1071–1330*, tr. J. Jones-Williams (London, 1968), pp. 105–6.

[56] IA, RHC Or I, pp. 647–8; AS, RHC Or IV, p. 213; Kamal ad-Din, ROL 4 (1896), pp. 154–5.

[57] Lyons and Jackson, *Saladin*, p. 160.   [58] al-Maqrizi, p. 66

[59] Lyons and Jackson, *Saladin*, pp. 156–7.

horses, for they had never learned how to use camels in warfare. But a raid proved practical at that time, for the heavy rains which had washed away the mud-bricks of Eilat caused the Syrian desert to be covered with grass and thus able to support Frankish cavalry.[60]

Tarbuk was on the pilgrimage route from Damascus to Mecca, and the Frankish presence there, which was unprecedented, alarmed the Muslim world. Saladin, with some degree of hyperbole, reflected this concern when he wrote to the Caliph about Reynald's attempt to attack Teïma, 'the vestibule of Medina', which is 200 miles south-east of Tarbuk, although there is no reason to suppose that Reynald travelled so far. Saladin's nephew, Farrukh-Shah, governor of Damascus, had no alternative but to lead his troops in an attack on Transjordan, and news of this caused Reynald to return.[61] But this, of course, meant that at the vital time of the interregnum in Aleppo Farrukh-Shah was in Transjordan with the main army of Damascus monitoring Reynald's movements, while Taqi ad-Din was unable to intervene at Aleppo because he had too few troops. Izz ad-Din of Mosul was therefore able to take peaceful possession of Aleppo on 29 December 1181 and Saladin had, for the time being, lost the opportunity of gaining control of the city.[62]

Reynald carried out this raid on Tarbuk while the truce was still in force. The fact that he frustrated Saladin's plans so neatly was arguably more than a coincidence. The lines of communication between Damascus and Cairo ran through Transjordan, so that Reynald could intercept couriers and learn about Saladin's plans, a matter about which Saladin had complained to Turan-Shah a few years before.[63] If this explanation is correct, then Reynald, far from being a maverick robber-baron when he broke the truce, was in fact seeking to preserve an independent Aleppo, which had been a keystone of royal policy since 1176.

It must have been during the raid on Tarbuk that Reynald seized a caravan travelling from Egypt to Damascus, imprisoned its members, and refused to free them or make restitution even though the king asked him to do so when Saladin lodged a protest. Ernoul, who seeks to place the blame for the loss of the kingdom on Reynald's inability to observe truces, recounts this episode twice.[64]

[60] AS, RHC Or IV, p. 215.   [61] *Ibid.*, p. 214.
[62] Kamal ad-Din, ROL 4 (1896), pp. 156–7.   [63] Lyons and Jackson, *Saladin*, p. 116.
[64] WT, XXII, 15, p. 1026; Ernoul, pp. 54–6 and 96–7: the first account is dated to a time of truce when Saladin was in Yemen, and must be intended to relate to the truce of 1175–6

In fact, Saladin himself did not wish to renew the truce. In the spring of 1182, while it was still in force, a Christian vessel from Apulia was wrecked near Damietta and he seized the cargo and imprisoned the 1,676 passengers. Baldwin IV lodged a formal complaint about this, but the sultan made what William of Tyre describes as impossible demands and added that unless the king 'gave satisfaction in all these matters, he wished to retain the aforementioned ship and also to break the peace which had been established between them'.[65]

Saladin wished to return to Damascus partly in order to secure his lines of communication between Syria and Egypt. When he left Cairo on 11 May his army was swollen with non-combatants, merchants who wished to trade in Damascus and tribesmen from Syria who had come to Egypt in the years of drought and now wished to return home. Their presence is an index of the fear which Prince Reynald's seizure of the caravan had inspired.[66]

When news reached Jerusalem that the sultan was mustering his army, the king summoned a *curia generalis* at which Reynald of Châtillon persuaded his peers to march the host to Kerak in order to block the passage of the Egyptian army. Raymond of Tripoli's protest that this would leave the rest of the kingdom, and notably his own dominions in eastern Galilee, undefended, was ignored, presumably because it was considered unwise to divide the army.[67]

When Saladin reached Eilat he sent the non-combatants, under the command of his brother, Taj al-Muluk Buri, into the deep desert to follow the main pilgrim road that ran north from Maan to Damascus. After spending a few days raiding the lands around Montréal he marched on Kerak, but the Franks did not give battle. They wished, of course, to defend the fortresses of Transjordan, but their chief concern was to preserve the cornlands from attack, because they were ready to be harvested, and that was vital to the economic well-being of the kingdom. Saladin did not wish to give battle either and, after skirting the Frankish camp at Kerak, took his forces to the castle of al-Azrak, fifty miles to the east in the Syrian desert, where he met up with the non-combatants.[68]

when Saladin's armies were conquering Yemen. This account must be disregarded for Reynald did not become lord of Transjordan until 1177.

[65] WT, XXII, 15, p. 1026; AS, RHC Or IV, pp. 216–17.
[66] IA, RHC Or I, p. 651.   [67] WT, XXII, 15, pp. 1026–7.
[68] AS, RHC Or IV, p. 218; WT, XXII, 16, p. 1029; C. Clermont-Ganneau, 'La marche de Saladin du Caire à Damas avec démonstration sur Kerak', *Revue biblique internationale*, n.s., 3 (1906), pp. 464–71.

While Saladin was on the march Raymond III's fears were realised. Farrukh-Shah, with the army of Damascus, entered Galilee and, having sacked the village of La Burie near Mount Tabor, crossed the Jordan and, after a siege lasting only five days, captured the cave fortress of al-Habis Jaldak on the south side of the River Yarmuk, which guarded the plains of eastern Galilee. This stronghold had been considered impregnable, and its speedy reduction was blamed on the spinelessness of its eastern Christian garrison.[69]

Saladin reached Damascus on 22 June.[70] By that time news must have reached him of the change of government in Constantinople, where in April 1182 Mary of Antioch had been overthrown in a revolt led by Andronicus Comnenus, an elderly cousin of the Emperor Manuel. Andronicus was well known in the Latin East. Appointed governor of Cilicia in 1166, he had caused scandal by seducing the empress's sister, Philippa of Antioch, and had fled to Jerusalem. There King Amalric gave him the fief of Beirut, but he added to his misdemeanours by eloping to the court of Nur ad-Din with Baldwin III's widow, the Dowager-queen Theodora. After living in exile in Muslim territory for many years he had been reconciled to Manuel shortly before the emperor's death and allowed to return to Pontus.[71]

Andronicus came to power on a wave of anti-Latin feeling. The Westerners, who had occupied a privileged position in the empire during Manuel's reign, had aroused great resentment among the Byzantines. When Andronicus advanced on Constantinople there was a spontaneous uprising by the mob, who massacred all the Latins in the city, regardless of age and sex, and cut off the head of the papal legate. Even the hospital of St John was sacked and its sick inmates murdered. Some Latins escaped by boarding western merchant ships in the Golden Horn and some of them sailed to the Crusader States. It was from them that William of Tyre learned of the tragedy and he gives the fullest account of it.[72]

---

[69] WT, XXII, 15, 16, pp. 1028–9; IA, RHC Or I, p. 652; AS, RHC Or IV, p. 218; D. Nicolle, 'Ain al-Habis. The "cave de Sueth"', *Archéologie medievale* 18 (1988), pp. 113–40; H. Kennedy, *Crusader Castles* (Cambridge, 1994), pp. 52–4; D. Pringle, *Secular Buildings in the Crusader Kingdom of Jerusalem. An Archaeological Gazetteer* (Cambridge, 1997), no. 10, p. 18.

[70] AS, RHC Or IV, p. 218; IA wrongly dates this 16 June, RHC Or I, p. 651.

[71] B. Hamilton, 'Women in the Crusader States, the queens of Jerusalem 1100–90', in D. Baker (ed.), *Medieval Women* (Oxford, 1978), pp. 161–2; C. Diehl, 'Les romanesques aventures d'Andronic Comnène', in *Figures byzantines*, 5th edn (Paris, 1918), pp. 107–33.

[72] WT, XXII, 11–14, pp. 1020–5.

Andronicus speedily eliminated potential rivals: Manuel's daughter Maria and her husband Rainier of Montferrat were murdered and so, a few months later, was Mary of Antioch.[73] The influential figures at the court of Constantinople who had ensured the continued Byzantine protectorate of the Holy Land had all been swept away, leaving a regent for the child emperor, Alexius II, who was virulently anti-Latin. Since 1158, when Baldwin III had married Theodora Comnena, the Franks in the Latin East had relied on Byzantine protection as their chief means of defence, first against Nur ad-Din and later against Saladin. Although this policy had not always been popular, no viable alternative to it had been found.

Saladin therefore was able to launch a spirited attack on the Latin Kingdom secure in the knowledge that the Byzantines would not retaliate and that the Sicilians with whom he was at peace would not attack Egypt. On 13 July 1182 a detachment of his army laid siege to the castle of Bethsan in southern Galilee. The king, who had expected Saladin to invade, and who had already assembled the host at Saffuriya, marched to its relief. The Franks met with Saladin near Le Forbelet in south-eastern Galilee. His strength was formidable. William of Tyre reports that the older Frankish princes said that they had never before faced a Muslim army of such size. It is not known whether the king fought on this occasion, but he was certainly present at the battle.[74] All sources agree that it was fought in intense heat and it must have required considerable willpower for a man as ill as Baldwin to stay in the field; indeed, on the return march the canon of the Sepulchre who was carrying the Holy Cross collapsed and died from sunstroke. The Christian army was smaller than Saladin's force: William of Tyre reports that there were only about 700 knights present. Nevertheless, although there was considerable slaughter of Christian infantry, few knights were killed, whereas Muslim losses were substantial. Saladin conceded defeat and withdrew across the Jordan, while the king ordered the host to return to the more temperate region of Saffuriya.[75] This battle was fought on 15 July, the eighth anniversary of Baldwin IV's coronation, and

[73] O. Jurewicz, *Andronikos I Komnenos* (Amsterdam, 1970); C.M. Brand, *Byzantium Confronts the West, 1180–1204* (Cambridge, Mass., 1968), pp. 31–75; M. Angold, *The Byzantine Empire, 1025–1204. A Political History*, 2nd edn (London, 1997), pp. 296–7.

[74] 'Domino igitur rege cum suis expeditionibus ad [fontem Sephoritanum] reverso . . .': WT, XXII, 18, p. 1032; Pringle, *Secular Buildings*, no. 228, p. 104.

[75] WT, XXII, 16, 17, pp. 1030–2; al-Maqrizi, p. 69; IA, RHC Or I, pp. 652–3; AS, RHC Or IV, pp. 218–22.

although Muslim writers understandably tried to disguise the fact, Le Forbelet was a Frankish victory: a far larger Muslim army had been forced to retreat with heavy losses by a determined Frankish cavalry force. Credit for this must be given, at least in part, to the leper king, for he commanded the respect and loyalty of all his vassals and was able to hold in check the factions that were to prove so damaging to the Frankish host once he became too ill to lead it.

While he was in Egypt during the truce Saladin had completed the organisation of the naval *diwan* of Cairo, and had built up a fleet of between thirty and forty war galleys.[76] He planned a joint attack on Beirut, the weakest point in Frankish control of the Syrian coast, by this fleet and his army. Immediately after the battle of Le Forbelet he marched his forces to the Beka'a and posted scouts in the hills above Beirut to watch for the arrival of his fleet. It appeared at the beginning of August and blockaded the city while Saladin moved his forces to besiege it by land. At the same time the Egyptian army invaded the region of Darum, Gaza and Ascalon and defeated the small Frankish force which tried to intercept it. When news of these events was brought to the king, who was still with the host at Saffuriya, he kept his nerve. He decided that it would be fatal to divide the army, since that was clearly what the sultan was hoping to achieve, but that he should concentrate on the defence of Beirut and let events in the south run their course. This showed a proper sense of priorities: the loss of Beirut would seriously damage Frankish security, whereas the smaller Egyptian army would be unable to do much long-term harm.[77]

The king moved the host to Tyre, which became his operational headquarters. He immediately set about recruiting a fleet to relieve Beirut and within a week had secured thirty-six ships from the ports of Acre and Tyre. These ships almost certainly belonged to Italian maritime powers who were trading with the Franks. The Pisans appear to have taken a major part in this expedition, for on 25 August 1182, after Beirut had been relieved, the king granted that commune a square at Acre, with the right to erect there any buildings that they wished.[78] The crown of Jerusalem was almost certainly in this instance a beneficiary of the Latin massacre at

[76] A.S. Ehrenkreutz, 'The place of Saladin in the naval history of the Mediterranean Sea', *Journal of the American Oriental Society* 75 (1955), pp. 100–16; Lyons and Jackson, *Saladin*, p. 170.

[77] WT, XXII, 18, pp. 1032–4.   [78] Müller, no. 19, p. 23.

Constantinople earlier in the year, as a result of which the Pisans had lost their trading privileges in the Byzantine Empire and needed to find alternative markets in the eastern Mediterranean.[79] The defence of Beirut was directed by the bishop and the king's governor. The assault, though intense, lasted for only three days; Saladin was hampered by a lack of siege-engines and although he tried to mine the walls the defence frustrated this by springing countermines. Saladin intercepted a messenger from the king, sent to inform the Beirut garrison that relief was on its way by land and sea, and he ordered his fleet to withdraw. Shortly after this his army also withdrew. Thus when the Christian fleet reached Beirut they found that the siege had ended so that there was no need for the host to march north from Tyre.[80]

Saladin had publicly announced his commitment to the conquest of Beirut, and his precipitate abandonment of the siege was damaging to his prestige.[81] This was particularly serious because it followed immediately after the Frankish victory at Le Forbelet. Unable to make any headway against the Franks, Saladin moved his army to north Syria in the late summer. King Baldwin and his advisers were disturbed because, contrary to previous practice, he did not make a truce with them on this occasion.[82] The situation in 1182 was different from that in earlier years because, lacking naval support from Sicily or Byzantium, the Franks would not have been able to mount an effective attack on Egypt during Saladin's absence in the north; and he must have supposed that the risks involved in remaining at war with the Crusader Kingdom in those circumstances would be offset by the money he would save by not having to pay them tribute. Certainly the campaign he was planning would be expensive, for not only would he have to pay his army, he would also have to make lavish gifts to the rulers of cities whose recognition he hoped to obtain.

In late September he reached al-Bira, one of the crossing points on the Euphrates, which submitted to him in return for his protection against the Artuqids of Mardin. He then moved eastwards,

---

[79] Brand, *Byzantium Confronts the West*, pp. 207–13; see also G.W. Day, *Genoa's Response to Byzantium, 1155–1204. Commercial Expansion and Factionalism in a Medieval City* (Urbana and Chicago, 1988), pp. 55–9.

[80] WT, XXII, 19, pp. 1034–6; IA, RHC Or I, p. 653; AS, RHC Or IV, p. 223; Baha al-Din, RHC Or III, p. 68; Kamal ad-Din, ROL 4 (1896), pp. 159–60.

[81] 'He resolved not to go away until he had captured [Beirut]': IA, RHC Or I, p. 653.

[82] WT, XXII, 21, p. 1038.

receiving the submission of Harran, Edessa, Rakka and Nisibin, and
by 10 November was encamped outside Mosul, the Zengid capital,
where he remained until February 1183.[83] The city was commanded
by Izz ad-Din who, under pressure from the Aleppans, had ceded
that city to his brother, Imad ad-Din Zengi, who had been Nur
ad-Din's favourite nephew.[84] The brothers had foreseen Saladin's
impending campaign against the Zengid territories and had made
alliances with the Franks. One of Imad ad-Din's first acts when he
reached Aleppo in May 1182 was to make peace with Bohemond III
of Antioch and Rupen III of Cilicia.[85] Then at some time between
late June and mid-August Izz ad-Din of Mosul, the senior Zengid
prince, sent envoys to the court of Jerusalem. Baldwin IV and his
advisers made an eleven-year truce with Mosul, and in return Izz
ad-Din agreed to pay the Franks an annual subsidy of 10,000 dinars,
and the first payment was made immediately. In addition the Mosul
government agreed to release all Frankish prisoners of war and, if
they recovered Damascus, to restore to the king of Jerusalem Banias
and the cave fortresses of Tyron and al-Habis Jaldak.[86]

As soon as Saladin's army left for the north, King Baldwin led a
cavalry force into Damascene territory, accompanied by Count
Raymond and the Patriarch Heraclius, an indication of the degree
to which he had restored unity among his subjects. Ibn al-Muqaddam, the governor of Damascus, had too few troops to risk
giving combat, and the Franks were able to burn the harvest with
impunity. The king then led his forces to Bosra, some ninety miles to
the south, the first major settlement on the desert road from
Damascus to Egypt. If the Franks had captured it, Saladin's lines of
communication would have been seriously disrupted, but the inhabitants had blocked all the wells outside the walls and as there was no
alternative water supply it was impossible to lay siege to it.

The royal army rode back through the Yarmuk valley to the
fortress of al-Habis Jaldak, captured by Farrukh-Shah a few months

[83] AS, RHC Or IV, pp. 223 and 227; IA, RHC Or I, pp. 654–5; Baha al-Din, RHC Or III,
p. 68; Lyons and Jackson, *Saladin*, pp. 173–83.

[84] N. Elisséeff, *Nur ad-Din, un grand prince musulman de Syrie au temps des croisades (511–569H/
1118–1174)*, 3 vols. (Damascus, 1967), II, pp. 657–62; Kamal ad-Din, ROL 4 (1896), pp. 155,
158–9; AS, RHC Or IV, p. 214; IA, RHC Or I, pp. 649–50.

[85] Kamal ad-Din, ROL 4 (1896), p. 159; Lyons and Jackson, *Saladin*, p. 171.

[86] AS, RHC Or IV, p. 225. This treaty was made after the fall of al-Habis Jaldak in June 1182
and before the end of the siege of Beirut in August 1182: Kamal ad-Din, ROL 4 (1896),
p. 160; Baha al-Din, RHC Or III, p. 68.

Figure 4 The citadel of Bosra.

before. It consisted of three fortified, interconnecting caves, set one above the other in a hillside, which could only be approached by a single, narrow, steeply angled path. Baldwin knew that no relief force could be sent from Damascus and laid siege to it. Part of the Frankish force fought its way to the hilltop above the caves and sappers began to cut an entrance into the fortress through the rock, while the main body of the army remained in the plain to block the access road. At the end of three weeks the garrison surrendered in return for a safe conduct to Bosra. Frankish control over eastern Galilee was thus restored.[87] The total distance covered during the campaign was about 200 miles and the king's health must have stabilised as he was able to ride so far.

Since the beginning of Baldwin's personal rule the Franks had prevented Saladin from extending his power to any great extent in north Syria and this remained their chief objective. Their military activities during the winter of 1182–3 were directed to that end, but their strategy is only comprehensible if William of Tyre's account is used in conjunction with the Islamic sources. William relates that in

[87] WT, XXII, 21, 22, pp. 1038–42.

December 1182 the king summoned a council to Caesarea to debate how best to exploit Saladin's absence in Mosul. It was decided that Raymond of Tripoli should lead a raiding party against Bosra, while the king led the main army against Damascus. Both campaigns were brief and inconclusive. The king threatened to destroy the great mosque at Darayya, but was dissuaded by a deputation of Christians who told him that if he did so Ibn al-Muqaddam would destroy all the Christian churches in the province.[88] There was no fighting and the king returned in time to keep Christmas at Tyre.[89]

These raids, which in themselves are not impressive, make good military sense in the context of Prince Reynald's campaign in the Red Sea during the winter of 1182–3. In 1181 Reynald had been forced to return from Tarbuk because the army of Damascus had invaded the lands of Kerak using the desert road. Bosra was the first main settlement on that road to the south of Damascus and Raymond of Tripoli's raid there in early December should be seen as a reconnaissance expedition to discover whether a relief force had set out from Damascus to reinforce the garrison of Eilat. Similarly the demonstration against Damascus by the royal army was intended to confirm that no fresh troops had reached the city since September. Once that had been established Prince Reynald's expedition could go ahead without fear of Damascene intervention.

Reynald's campaign is known about only from Arabic sources. The only Christian source to mention it, the *Chronicle* of Ernoul, says merely:

On the shores of [the Red] Sea Prince Reynald once built five galleys. When they were completed, he launched them and placed knights and sergeants aboard, with enough provisions to go and find out what kind of people lived on the further shore. When they were rigged, they ventured on the high seas, but after that nothing was heard of them and nobody knows what became of them.[90]

This makes the enterprise sound like an early scientific exploration of the coast of Nubia. William of Tyre does not mention it at all. He says very little in his work about Prince Reynald, of whom he did not approve because he was a Courtenay supporter.

Reynald's initiative was not a private enterprise. It could not have

---

[88] IA, RHC Or I, p. 655. Stevenson pointed out that this source has conflated this attack with the Frankish raid on Damascus in September 1182, *The Crusaders in the East* (Cambridge, 1907), p. 228, n. 3.
[89] WT, XXII, 23, pp. 1042–3.   [90] Ernoul, pp. 69–70.

been kept secret, and it would have needed a royal subsidy. Reynald commanded a fleet of five warships. Ibn al-Athir relates that they were built in sections in the fief of Kerak, and all Muslim writers agree that they were transported on the backs of camels to the Gulf of Aqaba where they were assembled and launched.[91] According to a letter of Saladin it had taken Reynald two years to construct this flotilla.[92] This must have entailed the employment of skilled ship-wrights, presumably recruited from the coastal cities. The cost of hiring these men and of buying and transporting the raw materials for the vessels must have been considerable. The ships were galleys, and although Muslim prisoners could have been forced to man them it seems unlikely that they were used, for the success of the expedition depended on the full and willing co-operation of all the personnel. Yet freemen used as rowers would have had to be paid. The Red Sea was notoriously difficult to navigate and al-Fadil reports that Reynald engaged Arab pilots, who would also have had to be paid well. The galleys also carried trained fighting men. Exact numbers are not known, but al-Fadil reports that 170 prisoners were taken from the three ships that penetrated the Red Sea after some Franks had been killed in battle, and this suggests that the total fighting force aboard the five galleys was in the region of 300 men.[93] These were almost certainly mercenaries, for Reynald needed his own men from Kerak and Montréal to besiege Eilat by land. In addition bribes had to be paid to the Beduin, whose co-operation was essential to the success of the undertaking, for they were able to supply reliable information about the Red Sea area. The lordship of Montréal and Hebron did not possess resources commensurate with financing an undertaking on that scale, and some part of the cost must have been borne by the crown.

Saladin, who had a good spy network, was aware that Reynald was preparing some kind of offensive, of which the razzia to Tarbuk had been a foretaste, but he made a false diagnosis, supposing that Reynald planned to bring Eilat and the Sinai peninsula once more under Frankish control. That would have been a sound policy, for it would have severed communications between the two halves of the sultan's dominions. The main road from Eilat to Egypt ran through Qalat Guindi in the north of the Sinai, at the head of the *wadi*

---

[91] IA, RHC Or I, p. 658; AS, RHC Or IV, pp. 230–1; Ibn Jubayr, p. 52.
[92] Lyons and Jackson, *Saladin*, p. 185.   [93] AS, RHC Or IV, pp. 232 and 235.

al-Arish. This important station on the Sinai crossing had already
been the object of a Frankish attack in 1178.[94] Presumably before
he left Egypt, Saladin ordered this fortress to be strengthened with
a curtain wall, for this work, undertaken by his brother al-Adil, was
completed in March 1183. It was a considerable technical achievement: the fortress stands on a 400-foot cliff in the middle of the
desert. The curtain-wall is built of dressed stones, is between 4 and
8 feet thick, 145 yards long and 87 yards wide at its broadest
point.[95]

Reynald was indeed intending to attack Eilat, for its loss would
create serious problems for Saladin when he wished to move troops
between Syria and Egypt. However, Reynald was not intending to
occupy the Sinai, but to launch part of his fleet on the Red Sea,
where no Christian vessel had been seen since the Islamic conquest
of Egypt some 500 years before. Consequently no Muslim warships
were stationed there and most of the coastal cities were unwalled.
Reynald's intention was to disrupt trade between Egypt and the
Yemen (and thus with eastern Asia), and dislocate pilgrim traffic
from Egypt and the Maghrib to Mecca.

Saladin claimed to be the defender of Islam and justified his war
against the Zengids on the grounds that he needed the resources of
Syria in order to drive the Franks from the Crusader States. His
credibility would have been severely damaged in the eyes of the
entire Islamic community if the Franks had succeeded in preventing
pilgrims from reaching the holy cities of which he was the protector
while he and his armies were fighting Sunnite princes in Iraq. It was
presumably Reynald's hope that Saladin would be forced to return
from Mosul to counter this threat. The Franks would thus be aiding
their Zengid allies while protecting their own interests by restraining
the growth of Saladin's power in Syria.

Reynald's expedition showed a remarkable degree of initiative for
which he is seldom given credit. Modern historians, with the notable
exception of Prawer, have been almost unanimous in treating this
campaign as a wild and ill-considered venture on the part of the lord
of Kerak, which succeeded only in uniting the entire Muslim world
in hatred of the Franks for threatening the security of Mecca and

---

[94] See above p. 141.
[95] J. Barthaux, 'Description d'une forteresse de Saladin découverte au Sinai', *Syria* 3 (1922),
pp. 44–57; Rothenberg, *God's Wilderness*, plates 28, 29.

Medina.[96] Reynald's plan had the initial advantage of taking his
enemies completely by surprise, because the Franks had never
launched ships from Eilat in the fifty years that they had held the
port before Saladin took it from them. The expedition was launched
in December 1182.[97] Two ships were detailed to blockade Pharoah's
Island, the fortified island in the Gulf of Aqaba. Reynald did not
take part in the naval campaign, but probably mounted a land
blockade of Eilat.[98] The remaining three warships sailed into the
Red Sea. Their potential for causing havoc was soon evident: they
captured sixteen merchant ships, burned some of them and added
the remainder to their own fleet. They then sailed to Aidhab on the
Egyptian coast, where pilgrims from Egypt and the Maghrib, unable
to use the route through the Sinai because of Reynald's siege of
Eilat, took ship for Jedda, the port of Mecca.[99] There they captured
a pilgrim ship and two merchant ships from Aden. They sacked the
town, which was unwalled, and captured the supplies that had been
stored there to feed the large influx of pilgrims expected later in the
year, and sent a raiding party inland, which captured a caravan from
Qus and slaughtered all its members. The fleet then crossed the Red
Sea and sent a raiding party ashore to attack the oasis of Rabigh,
near the coast between Medina and Mecca, before sailing to
al-Haura, north of Jedda. al-Fadil described the fear which the
Franks inspired at Mecca, while Ibn Jubayr, who reached Alexandria
from Granada a few weeks later, was told that the Franks had
intended to attack Medina and destroy the tomb of the prophet.[100]
This seems unlikely, for the Franks did not have horses and could
therefore not raid far inland.

---

[96] E.g. G. Schlumberger, *Renaud de Châtillon, Prince d'Antioche, Seigneur de la terre d'Outre-Jourdain*,
   3rd edn (Paris, 1923), pp. 199–222; Grousset, *Histoire des Croisades*, II, pp. 732–6; S.
   Runciman, *A History of the Crusades*, 3 vols. (Cambridge, 1951–5), II, pp. 436–7; Lyons and
   Jackson, *Saladin*, p. 185; but see J. Prawer, *Histoire du royaume latin de Jérusalem*, tr. G. Nahon,
   2 vols. (Oxford, 1968), I, pp. 612–15, and 'Crusader security and the Red Sea', in *Crusader
   Institutions* (Oxford, 1980), pp. 471–84.
[97] al-Imad says the expedition was defeated in Shawal (28 January–26 February) 1183: AS,
   RHC Or IV, p. 230; Ibn Jubayr says that the Frankish ships had been operating for some
   six weeks before the Egyptian fleet began to track them down: pp. 53–5. This suggests that
   the campaign began in December 1182. Reynald had returned to Acre by 19 March 1183:
   Strehlke, no. 16, pp. 15–16.
[98] All the members of the fleet which raided in the Red Sea were captured: AS, RHC Or IV,
   pp. 231 and 233–4; IA, RHC Or I, p. 658; al-Maqrizi, p. 70.
[99] Ibn Jubayr, pp. 63–8.
[100] AS, RHC Or IV, p. 233; Ibn Jubayr, p. 52.

The governor of Egypt, al-Adil, the most capable of all the Ayyubid princes, ordered warships from Alexandria to be sent to Cairo and then to be carried overland to the Red Sea. Within six weeks of the launching of Prince Reynald's ships, this Egyptian flotilla, commanded by Husam al-Din Lu'lu, was in operation.[101] It sailed first to the Gulf of Aqaba and destroyed the two Frankish galleys blockading Pharoah's Island, though some crew members escaped to land and made their way back to Kerak, perhaps escorted by Prince Reynald, who abandoned the land siege. The Egyptian fleet then tracked down the other Frankish vessels at al-Haura and penned them in the harbour. Recognising that they could not defeat this numerically superior force, the Franks abandoned their ships, together with their plunder and their captives, and fled inland on foot. It was some time before the Egyptians could commandeer enough horses from the local Arabs to set out in pursuit. They overtook the Franks on the fifth day of their march and succeeded in trapping them in a narrow ravine. In the ensuing fight many Franks were killed but the remainder appear to have surrendered voluntarily. al-Imad relates that this happened in the month of Shawal (28 January–26 February 1183) when the Franks were within a day's march of Medina.[102]

al-Adil wrote to inform Saladin of what had happened and the sultan ordered that all the prisoners should be executed because they had knowledge of the Red Sea routes.[103] The captives were distributed to various parts of Saladin's dominions to publicise his victory and exemplify his justice and were put to death,[104] but a more sinister fate was reserved for two of them. They were taken to Mecca where, during the great annual pilgrimage, they were led outside the city to Mina. This is a stage in the pilgrimage at which the faithful offer animals for slaughter and give their flesh to feed the poor. There, among a zealous and hostile crowd of thousands of pilgrims, the two Christian prisoners were slaughtered 'like animals for sacrifice', presumably by having their throats cut.[105] These two unknown Franks have a tolerable claim to have been the first western Christians to set foot in the holy city of Islam, four centuries before Varthema. al-Adil felt misgivings about executing all these

[101] al-Maqrizi, p. 70.
[102] IA, RHC Or I, p. 658; AS, RHC Or IV, pp. 230–5; al-Maqrizi, p. 70; Ibn Jubayr, pp. 51–3.
[103] AS, RHC Or IV, p. 232.   [104] Ibn Jubayr, pp. 51–2.
[105] Letter of al-Imad in AS, RHC Or IV, p. 231; cf. IA, RHC Or I, p. 659; al-Maqrizi, p. 70.

prisoners, for in accordance with Islamic law their lives should have
been spared because they had surrendered voluntarily, but Saladin
had no scruples of this kind.[106] He was concerned to emphasise that
he truly was the champion of Islam even though he had to break
Islamic law in order to do so.

Throughout the time of Reynald's campaign, Saladin and his
army had remained at Mosul. Izz ad-Din refused to submit to him
and the sultan did not have enough troops to invest the city. He had
no legitimate title to the Zengid lands and needed the co-operation
of the caliph to authorise his annexation of them. But an-Nasir
feared the growth of Saladin's power in Iraq and sent the head of the
Baghdad *ulema* to beg him to desist from attacking Mosul, while the
Shah-Arman of Akhlat and Shams al-Din al-Pahlawan of Azerbaijan
supported the caliph in this.[107] In February 1183 Saladin withdrew
to Harran and, having conquered Amida and received the submission of Mardin, crossed the Euphrates and reached Tell Khalid near
Aleppo on 17 May 1183.[108] His power had been augmented considerably as a result of his expedition to Iraq, but while Mosul
remained independent his position there was not secure: a military
setback elsewhere could jeopardise his recent conquests, which were
fragile in so far as they were based for the most part on the
recognition of his suzerainty by independent rulers.

It is difficult to determine whether Prince Reynald's activities had
any effect on events in Iraq. By the time Saladin left Mosul in
February news would have reached his enemies about the Frankish
attack on the Red Sea but not about al-Adil's containment of it.
This may well have encouraged Izz ad-Din and his allies, and
indeed the caliph himself, to take a firm stand against Saladin, for if
the Frankish threat could not be contained the sultan would have
no alternative but to return to Syria and deal with it himself.
Certainly Saladin treated Reynald of Châtillon as his principal
enemy from this time. He may, as his admirers argue, have been
motivated by simple piety and a desire to exact vengeance on this
infidel prince who had sacrilegiously threatened the holy places of
Islam, but that argument would have greater force if Reynald had
attempted to attack Medina or Mecca. What the prince had done

---

[106] Lyons and Jackson, *Saladin*, p. 187.
[107] Baha al-Din, RHC Or III, pp. 69–70; IA, RHC Or I, pp. 656–7.
[108] A full account of Saladin's campaign in Iraq is in Lyons and Jackson, *Saladin*, pp. 173–95.

was to prove that Saladin was unable to protect the *haj* because of his political ambitions in Iraq, and this injured the sultan's public image, because it called in question his entire politico-religious policy.

CHAPTER 9

The dying king

The events of 1182 had placed a great strain on the financial resources of the kingdom, and at a *curia generalis* held at Jerusalem in February 1183, to which representatives of the Frankish burgesses were also summoned,[1] it was enacted that a 1 per cent tax should be levied on all property with a value of 100 bezants or more, and a 2 per cent tax on all annual incomes of 100 bezants or more. Households whose property or income was below those thresholds should normally be charged a flat rate of 1 bezant. This tax was to be paid by the entire population 'of whatever tongue, of whatever race, of whatever creed and of both sexes'. Arrangements were made for the assessment and collection of this tax at a local and regional level, and it was stipulated that the money should be spent solely for defence purposes and not used to defray the general expenses of government. This was one of the earliest provisions made in the Christian world for the collection of income tax, and it ended with a pious expression of hope, which sadly has proved ill founded: 'And let this be done once and not taken as a precedent by later generations.'[2]

Benjamin Kedar has pointed out that the form of the tax and the procedures for its collection were modelled very closely on those used by Henry II of England and Louis VII of France when levying a general tax for the support of the Holy Land in 1166. He justly observes that it would indeed be surprising if this revolutionary fiscal policy had originated in the administratively backward Latin Kingdom of Jerusalem, and has suggested that Stephen of Sancerre, who brought the money raised in France in 1166 to Jerusalem in 1171, may have supplied information about how it had been

---

[1] Representatives of the burgesses had previously been summoned to the council of Nablus in 1166: WT, XIX, 13, p. 882.
[2] *Ibid.*, XXII, 24, pp. 1044–6.

collected.[3] It is equally possible that the members of the *curia generalis* learned of this system from some distinguished western visitor present in the kingdom in 1183.[4] It is not known how much money was raised, but Prawer rightly noted how 'in the year it was imposed and the four following years we regularly see on the battlefield large armies, exceeding in number the troops recruited on a feudal basis alone'.[5]

Kedar has pointed out that there is no mention of the king in the taxation decree of 1183, which is issued in the name of the *principes regni*.[6] It is possible that Baldwin was too ill to attend the assembly, but if so this was a temporary setback, because on 19 March he presided at a meeting of the High Court at Acre.[7] Nevertheless, William of Tyre reports that there was a severe deterioration in the king's health in 1183:

the leprosy which had affected him since the beginning of his reign . . . became much worse than usual. He had lost his sight and the extremities of his body became completely diseased and damaged, so that he was unable to use his hands and feet. Yet although some people suggested to him that he should abdicate and lead a retired life, drawing an income from the royal demesne, he had refused to surrender either the royal office or the government of the kingdom, for although his body was weak and powerless, yet he was strong in spirit, and made a superhuman effort to disguise his illness and shoulder the burdens of kingship.[8]

In mid-May Saladin brought his army to Aleppo. As a result of his conquests in Iraq the city was cut off from the Zengids of Mosul and Prince Imad ad-Din lacked financial and military resources, for when Izz ad-Din had agreed to allow his brother to rule there, he had first stripped the arsenal of its weapons and emptied the treasury.[9] Imad ad-Din therefore offered to surrender Aleppo to Saladin in return for his former fief of Sinjar, together with Nisibin and al-Khabur. Saladin formally took possession of Aleppo on

---

[3] B.Z. Kedar, 'The general tax of 1183 in the crusading kingdom of Jerusalem: innovation or adaptation?', EHR 89 (1974), pp. 339–45.

[4] E.g. Ralph of Mauléon from Poitou who was in the kingdom in September 1182 and may have been present when these discussions were held: WT, XXII, 28, p. 1054.

[5] J. Prawer, *Histoire du royaume Latin de Jérusalem*, tr. G. Nahon, 2 vols. (Paris, 1969), I, p. 618.

[6] Kedar, 'General tax', p. 343.

[7] Strehlke, nos. 16 and 17, pp. 15–16.

[8] WT, XXII, 26, p. 1054.

[9] Kamal ad-Din, ROL 4 (1896), pp. 158–9; AS, RHC Or IV, p. 214; IA, RHC Or I, pp. 649–50.

12 June 1183 and subsequently received the surrender of the remaining Zengid fortresses in the province.[10]

The fall of Aleppo caused anxiety to the Franks of Antioch. The abbot of St Paul's reached an agreement with the abbot of the Mount Tabor monastery in Galilee that his community would give shelter to the brethren of St Paul's, 'if the land of Antioch should fall into the hand of the Turks'.[11] Bohemond III sold the city of Tarsus to Rupen III of Cilicia, presumably in order to raise money for defence purposes.[12] In fact there was no immediate threat, since before Saladin left for Damascus in August 1183, he made peace with Bohemond III, although this treaty may have contained a clause recognising that Bohemond had a duty to fight in defence of the king of Jerusalem if required to do so.[13] However, Saladin had no wish to make peace with the rest of the Franks.[14]

When he learned that Saladin was bringing his army south once again, the king summoned the host to Saffuriya. Raymond III and Bohemond III brought troops to the muster, and the proceeds of the general tax were used to hire additional soldiers. William of Tyre estimates that there were 1,300 cavalry present and 15,000 infantry, a figure broadly confirmed by al-Imad.[15] The court was staying nearby at Nazareth, where the king was attended by his mother and the Patriarch Heraclius, but Baldwin developed a fever and was not expected to live, and it became imperative to appoint a regent. The High Court, most of whose members were with the host at Saffuriya, was summoned to the king's bedside. Among those present were Joscelin of Courtenay, Raymond III of Tripoli, Reynald of Châtillon, Reynald of Sidon, Baldwin and Balian of Ibelin, Walter of Caesarea and Guy of Lusignan.

Baldwin designated Guy of Lusignan as his regent. There was no

[10] M.C. Lyons and D.E.P. Jackson, *Saladin. The Politics of the Holy War* (Cambridge, 1982), p. 195; IA, RHC Or I, pp. 661–3; al-Maqrizi, p. 72; Baha al-Din, RHC Or III, pp. 71–3; Kamal ad-Din, ROL 4 (1896), pp. 164–8; AS, RHC Or IV, pp. 235–7.

[11] CGOH, no. xxii, II, p. 910.

[12] He may have received the city from Manuel Comnenus as a dowry for his wife Theodora: WT, XXII, 25, pp. 1047–8; C. Cahen, *La Syrie du nord à l'époque des croisades et la principauté franque d'Antioche* (Paris, 1940), p. 423; S. Der Nersessian, 'The Kingdom of Cilician Armenia', in Setton, *Crusades*, II, p. 644.

[13] AS, RHC Or IV, p. 239. Bohemond was present in the royal host later that year, see below, p. 194.

[14] For details of ineffectual attempts by Raymond III to negotiate peace with Saladin for the county of Tripoli, Lyons and Jackson, *Saladin*, pp. 197–8.

[15] WT, XXII, 28, p. 1053; Ernoul, p. 98; Lyons and Jackson, *Saladin*, p. 206.

alternative since Guy was the heir apparent. This was a different situation from that of 1177 when Baldwin had appointed Reynald of Châtillon as his executive regent on the understanding that he would resume power when he was well enough. In 1183 the king's health had deteriorated to such an extent that he needed to appoint a permanent regent:

[The king] appointed Guy of Lusignan . . . regent of the kingdom, reserving to himself the royal title, and keeping for himself only Jerusalem and an annual income of 10,000 gold pieces; he gave him free and general control over the other parts of the kingdom, ordering all his liegemen and all the princes in general, that they should become his vassals and do him manual homage. And this was done. But first, by the king's command, Guy was made to swear that during [Baldwin's] lifetime he would never seek to make himself king and that he would neither give to anyone else, nor alienate from the royal treasury, any of the cities and castles which the king at present possessed.

William of Tyre reports that these conditions were imposed because it was rumoured that Guy had tried to gain popularity by promising his supporters substantial portions of the royal demesne when he came to power. William, who became his chancellor, had a very low opinion of him: 'He was unequal in strength and wisdom to the great burden he had taken upon himself.'[16]

As regent, Guy automatically became commander-in-chief of the army, and his future thus depended on the way in which he handled the invasion. If he showed himself to be a capable commander he would silence many of his critics, and his right of succession to the throne would be strengthened. His main problem was lack of experience, for the king had never delegated any responsibilities to him for fear of causing a rift among his vassals. So the new regent, who had never before been asked to take charge even of a large-scale raiding party, was singularly ill equipped to take command of the host on the eve of a major invasion.

On 17 September Saladin began to muster his army to the south of Damascus and the Frankish command sent appeals for reinforcements to the coastal cities. The Genoese, Pisan and Venetian colonies all sent troops (although they were not obliged to contribute to the defence of the kingdom unless the cities in which they were

---

[16] 'inpar enim et viribus et prudentia pondus importabile humeris imposuit': WT, XXII, 26, pp. 1048–50; the members of the High Court present are listed *ibid.*, XXII, 28, pp. 1053–4.

living were attacked), and able-bodied pilgrims, waiting to return to the west with the autumn sailing, were also recruited.[17]

The Frankish and Muslim sources are in general agreement about the course of this campaign. The sultan crossed the Jordan on 29 September and marched on Bethsan, whose garrison fled to Tiberias leaving the settlement to be pillaged by the Muslims. On the following day an advance party of *mamluks* encountered troops from Kerak and Montréal led by Humphrey IV of Toron marching down the Nablus road to join the main army and, in the ensuing skirmish, took 100 of the troops prisoner. Meanwhile, the Frankish host advanced towards La Fève and Saladin sent a troop of 500 men to harass them. The Franks kept good discipline, with the cavalry in the centre, flanked by the infantry, and refused to break ranks. As they drew level with Saladin's main army the sultan withdrew, though a minor skirmish took place between troops commanded by the constable, Aimery of Lusignan, and those of Saladin, but Aimery received support from the Ibelin brothers and beat off the attack, and the Franks camped at the springs of La Tubanie about a mile away from Saladin's camp. The entire campaign from that point on may best be described as lacking in incident, for the Franks remained in their camp and Saladin was unable to provoke them into attacking him. On 7 October he moved his army to Mount Tabor in the hope that they would pursue him, but they did not do so and, as his own supplies were running low, he withdrew across the Jordan and was back in Damascus by 14 October. The Frankish host then returned to Saffuriya.[18]

In strictly military terms the campaign had not gone badly for the Franks. As R.C. Smail argued, Saladin was convinced that the Franks had deliberately adopted a successful strategy which he had been unable to weaken: Muslim sources are unanimous about that. A huge Muslim army had invaded Galilee but had made no territorial gains, while the Franks had sustained no losses worth mentioning. Both William of Tyre and Ernoul are critical of the way the campaign was handled, leaving Saladin's forces unscathed while the largest army that the Franks had ever put in the field had not struck a single blow against the enemy; but, as Smail has rightly pointed out, both sources are bitterly hostile to Guy and endorse the

---

[17] *Ibid.*, XXII, 28, p. 1053.
[18] Ernoul, p. 99; WT, XXII, 27–8, pp. 1050–5; Baha al-Din, RHC Or III, pp. 74–6; Kamal ad-Din, ROL 4 (1896), pp. 169–70; IA, RHC Or I, pp. 663–4; AS, RHC Or IV, pp. 242–4.

views of his opponents.[19] All of this is true, yet some legitimate complaints could have been made about the way in which the Frankish high command conducted the campaign. For example, no thought had been given to the protection of the Holy Places. Muslim raiders sacked the Orthodox monastery on Mount Tabor and were only repelled from the fortified Latin abbey by the combined efforts of the brethren and of local people who had sought refuge there; while a party of Muslims even appeared on the hill above Nazareth, which was unwalled, terrifying the population. Moreover, although the host had ample warning of Saladin's approach, no adequate thought was given to provisioning the army. Food had to be brought to the camp at La Tubanie under armed escort from nearby towns. Some of these convoys were ambushed by detachments of Saladin's troops and it would appear that only the discovery of an abundant supply of fish in the pools of La Tubanie saved the rank and file from starving to death.[20]

It was not uncommon in the Middle Ages for an inexperienced ruler to find himself unexpectedly in charge of an army, as Guy had on this occasion. The leper king had been in just such a situation at the battle of Mont Gisard where Prince Reynald had assumed effective military command. Guy's problem was that he could not count on the support of the other great lords. William of Tyre says quite bluntly that it was widely believed that Guy of Lusignan's enemies refused to co-operate with him because they feared that if the campaign were a success they would be unable to dislodge him from power. William does not name them beyond describing them as 'those who were best placed to take action in the present situation'.[21] A successful commander in the Kingdom of Jerusalem needed to be able to work harmoniously with other military leaders, not all of whom were subject to him: the masters of the military Orders were in that category, while the rulers of Antioch and Tripoli were virtually autonomous heads of state. Guy seems to have had little talent for personal relations of this kind. One certain outcome of the campaign of La Tubanie, and the one which Guy's opponents most desired, was that he had been made to appear totally incompetent as a field commander and to lack the capacity to inspire respect in his

---

[19] Smail, 'The predicaments of Guy of Lusignan 1183–87', in *Outremer*, pp. 159–76.
[20] Ernoul, p. 100; WT, XXII, 27–8, pp. 1050–5.
[21] 'Qui negocia presentia videbantur maxime promovere potuisse': WT, XXII, 28, p. 1054.

equals or loyalty in his vassals, qualities that were essential in any twelfth-century king.

King Baldwin recovered from his fever and returned to Jerusalem, but he soon asked Guy to exchange Jerusalem for Tyre. Sir Steven Runciman is assuredly right in his suggestion that the king found the climate of the coast more congenial to his health; certainly he had spent most of the previous year, since he had become dangerously ill, at Acre and Tyre.[22] Guy refused this request, perhaps because Tyre, a great commercial centre, was an important source of royal revenue, which Jerusalem was not, but his conduct appeared churlish, and the king, who was sensitive about his honour, did not take this insult lightly.[23]

The religious marriage of Humphrey IV of Toron and the king's sister Isabel had been arranged for the autumn of 1183, for the bride was now in her twelfth year and old enough to contract a canonical marriage. This took place at Kerak, and had evidently been planned well in advance, for the castle was filled with professional entertainers who had come from all the region round, which meant that Saladin was almost certainly aware of what was happening. It is therefore likely that he planned his attack on Kerak to coincide with the festivities, for if it succeeded not merely would he be avenged on Prince Reynald for his Red Sea campaign, he might also take some important prisoners whose ransoms would defray the costs of the campaign.

Saladin set out from Damascus on 22 October. The most vivid account of the siege is that of Ernoul, which probably derives from the bride's mother, Maria Comnena, wife of Ernoul's patron, Balian of Ibelin.[24] This relates how, when the siege began, Stephanie de Milly sent food to Saladin from the wedding banquet, and he

---

[22] Runciman, *A History of the Crusades*, 3 vols. (Cambridge, 1951–5), II, p. 439; RRH, nos.624, 625, I, pp. 165–6; WT, XXII, 25, p. 1047.

[23] WT, XXII, 30, p. 1057.

[24] The author was aware that Kerak had been besieged twice by Saladin, but he did not know the dates. He places one siege in the years preceding the truce of 1180: pp. 80–2. It is clear from Arab historians, who in some places corroborate his account in points of detail, that this description relates to the second siege in 1184, see below, p. 201. The author places his account of a second siege immediately after the campaign of Saffuriya in 1183; the date and the information he gives, much of which is concordant with that of William of Tyre and the Arab historians, show that this relates to the first siege of Kerak in 1183: pp. 102–6. Ernoul's story that Saladin had in his youth been a prisoner at Kerak when Philip de Milly was lord seems implausible, since it does not fit into the known pattern of the sultan's early career: *ibid.*, pp. 35–6 and 103.

Figure 5 Reynald of Châtillon's castle of Kerak.

courteously instructed his engineers not to range their mangonels on the tower in which the bride and groom were lodged. There may be some truth in this story, for Saladin would not have wished to kill the two most important potential prisoners. Kerak was built on the side of a steep escarpment and could only be approached from one direction, where there was a walled settlement separated from the castle by a deep fosse.[25] Reynald was forced after a while to abandon the *faubourg* and evacuate the population to his already overcrowded castle. Saladin had eight mangonels in his siege train, which he was then able to range on the castle, causing severe damage to the fabric and preventing the garrison from manning the walls and firing at his men.[26]

From William of Tyre's account it would appear that the king had already summoned a council to meet in Jerusalem in order to advise

---

[25] P. Deschamps, *Les châteaux des croisés en Terre Sainte*. II, *La défense du royaume de Jérusalem* (Paris, 1939), pp. 80–98; H. Kennedy, *Crusader Castles* (Cambridge, 1994), pp. 45–52; D. Pringle, *Secular Buildings in the Crusader Kingdom of Jerusalem. An Archaeological Gazetteer* (Cambridge, 1997), no. 124, pp. 59–60.

[26] WT, XXII, 29, 31, pp. 1055–7, 1059–60; Baha al-Din, RHC Or III, pp. 76–7; IA, RHC Or I, p. 664; AS, RHC Or IV, p. 248; Kamal ad-Din, ROL 4 (1896), p. 170; al-Maqrizi, p. 72.

him about the government of the kingdom before news reached him of the siege of Kerak.[27] Bohemond III and Raymond III attended, as did Guy of Lusignan, Reynald of Sidon, and Baldwin and Balian of Ibelin. Agnes of Courtenay was also present, but some of the most important men in the kingdom, such as Prince Reynald, and perhaps Joscelin of Courtenay, were at Kerak. Baldwin dismissed Guy from the regency and resumed sovereignty. Although Guy had offended him by his refusal to exchange Jerusalem for Tyre, Baldwin was not motivated solely by personal animosity. It was a matter of record that while Guy had been in command during the campaign of La Tubanie the other leaders had refused to work with him. For that reason he could not responsibly be left in charge of the army sent to the relief of Kerak. Yet the fortress was in urgent need of help and was vital to the security of the kingdom. It was also important that the king's sister and her guests should not fall into the hands of Saladin.

The removal of Guy from the regency was a public admission that he was not fit to be king. The question of who should take his place as Baldwin IV's heir might best have been deferred until after the relief of Kerak, and the fact that the council insisted on settling this question even though that delayed the relief expedition suggests that Guy's enemies wished to exploit their position of dominance. The men who were to be the chief supporters of Princess Sibyl's rights in 1186, Joscelin of Courtenay and Prince Reynald, were not present; while the claims of Princess Isabel and Humphrey of Toron could not be considered either, because they were in danger of becoming Saladin's prisoners. Perhaps Raymond of Tripoli was attempting to use the council to have himself designated as Baldwin IV's heir, with the support of Bohemond III and the Ibelins. If so, he was foiled by Agnes of Courtenay who, as William of Tyre relates, suggested that the king's nephew, Baldwin, the son of Sibyl and William of Montferrat, should be crowned co-king.[28] This met with general approval, since, apart from his mother, Prince Baldwin had the best claim to the throne. On 20 November 1183 he was crowned and anointed co-king in the Church of the Holy Sepulchre, was acclaimed by the assembled clergy and people, and received the homage of all the royal vassals except his stepfather, Guy of

---

[27] WT, XXII, 30, 31, pp. 1057–60; Ernoul, p. 104.
[28] 'suggerente hoc et ad id penitus hortante regis matre': WT, XXII, 30, II, p. 1058.

Lusignan. The chief difficulty about this solution was that King Baldwin V was only five years old.

It is sometimes said that Raymond of Tripoli was appointed regent at this time.[29] The evidence cited for this is the account of Baldwin V's coronation given by Ernoul, which was wrongly dated to 1183 by Mas Latrie, but which relates to a solemn crown-wearing which took place in 1185 shortly before Baldwin IV's death. This will be examined in more detail later in the chapter.[30] William of Tyre, who gives the only account of the coronation of 1183, concludes in this way:

> It was the general wish that a regent should be appointed to conduct public business, and specially to lead the army into battle in the usual way against the growing threat of the enemy; and it was the opinion of almost everybody that only the Count of Tripoli was suited to hold this office and that nobody else could carry out those duties satisfactorily.[31]

Nevertheless, he does not say that Raymond was made regent then, but places his appointment later in the reign.[32]

The problem of the appointment of a regent did concern the leper king. During his lifetime he could, at need, appoint whom he wished as his executive regent, but when he died Sibyl and Guy would have the best claim to be regents for the child king, Baldwin V. The only sure way of preventing this was to secure the annulment of their marriage, and the king discussed this with the Patriarch Heraclius.[33]

Before that could be arranged it was essential to relieve Kerak and towards the end of November the king ordered the beacon to be lit on top of the Tower of David as a sign that help was on its way.[34] Whether this would have been visible in distant Kerak seems doubtful, but it may well have been the first of a chain of beacons which would be seen by and hearten the defenders. They were in need of encouragement, for they suffered from extreme over-crowding and Saladin's mangonels kept up an intensive bombardment, which caused considerable damage. Then on 22 November Saladin's brother, al-Adil, joined him at Kerak with the army of Egypt. This was prearranged. al-Adil had asked to be made governor of Damascus, and Saladin had ordered him to join with him in the attack on Kerak; he would then appoint a new governor for Egypt

[29] E.g. R. Grousset, *Histoire des Croisades et du royaume franque de Jérusalem*, 3 vols. (Paris, 1934–6), II, p. 731; Prawer, *Royaume latin*, I, p. 624.

[30] Ernoul, pp. 115–19; see below, pp. 207–9.   [31] WT, XXII, 30, pp. 1058–9.

[32] *Ibid.*, XXIII, 1, p. 1064.   [33] *Ibid.*, XXIII, 1, pp. 1062–3.   [34] Ernoul, pp. 104–5.

and send him back with the Egyptian army after the siege had ended. Their combined forces could make no progress, because the deep fosse of Kerak formed an insuperable barrier between the fortress and their camp in the *faubourg*.[35]

The king accompanied the host to Kerak. He was almost certainly too ill to ride, and would have had to be carried in a litter, but his presence was important to the deeply divided baronage. Even Guy of Lusignan, despite his recent humiliation, rode in the host at the head of the men of Jaffa and Ascalon.[36] But Baldwin was too ill to take part in the fighting, and when the army reached La Palmerie he appointed Raymond of Tripoli field-commander. Nobody could reasonably take exception to this, as he was an experienced general, a prince of the blood royal and the senior-ranking crown vassal. In the event there was no fighting. Islamic writers record that when Saladin's scouts told him that the army of Jerusalem was moving towards Hebron he became alarmed for the safety of Egypt, which had been stripped of its troops. He appointed his nephew Taqi ad-Din as new governor and sent him back to Cairo on 3 December with the Egyptian army. Saladin's forces were thus depleted and, as the host of Jerusalem approached, he declined to give battle, but abandoned the siege on 4 December and returned to Damascus.[37] The king was thus able to enter Kerak in triumph.[38]

Guy of Lusignan did not accompany the main army back to Jerusalem, but led his troops directly to Ascalon and asked Sibyl to join him there. Kedar has suggested that Heraclius, who was a friend of Guy's, may have forewarned him of the king's intention to have his marriage annulled, and this may have been so, but in any case the king had made no secret of his aims.[39] Baldwin, it would seem, had reckoned without Sibyl's great attachment to her husband, which was constant throughout her life.[40] She joined Guy at Ascalon in 1183 and because they both refused to attend the patriarch's court

---

[35] al-Maqrizi, p. 72; Kamal ad-Din, ROL 4 (1896), p. 170.

[36] William of Tyre later describes how Guy 'ab expeditione rediens, a reliquo exercitu segregatus . . . Ascalonem profectus est': XXIII, 1, pp. 1062–3.

[37] Baha al-Din, RHC Or III, p. 77; Kamal ad-Din, ROL 4 (1896), p. 170; AS, RHC Or IV, p. 248; al-Maqrizi, pp. 72–3; IA, RHC Or I, pp. 664–5; Lyons and Jackson, *Saladin*, p. 204. Ernoul, p. 106 states that Saladin returned to Damascus by way of Samaria, but that is a confusion with the events of the second siege of Kerak in 1184, see below, p. 203.

[38] WT, XXII, 31, p. 1060.

[39] Kedar, 'The Patriarch Eraclius', in *Outremer*, pp. 177–204 at p. 191.

[40] She was instrumental in his becoming king, and in 1188 left the safety of Tripoli to share with him the hardships of the siege of Acre at which she died: B. Hamilton, 'Women in the

no action could be taken about annulling their marriage. William of Tyre gives no information about the grounds on which the king proposed to 'accuse' their marriage, though it is possible that he intended to claim that Sibyl had been forced by him to marry Guy against her will at a time when she was betrothed to Hugh III of Burgundy.

Baldwin summoned Guy as his vassal to attend him in Jerusalem. Guy excused himself on the grounds of ill-health and, after this procedure had been followed several times, the king, in accordance with Jerusalem custom, was carried to Ascalon, attended by members of the High Court, to require the count's attendance in Jerusalem in person. Guy closed the gates of the city against him and the inhabitants stood on the battlements and towers to watch as the king raised his hand to knock on the gates and demand admission, but the gates remained shut. King Baldwin had observed the legal forms and his vassal had defied him. The king then went straight to Jaffa, where the citizens received him ceremonially, and he installed a royal governor in the castle, thus depriving Guy of half of his fief. He next went to Acre and summoned a *curia generalis*.[41]

Prawer has argued convincingly that Baldwin, in accordance with the *Assise sur la ligèce*, wanted the agreement of this assembly to dispossess Guy of Lusignan of his fief of Jaffa and Ascalon for failing to answer the royal summons.[42] William of Tyre says nothing directly about this, but relates how the Patriarch Heraclius, flanked by the masters of the Temple and the Hospital, knelt before the king and begged him to receive Guy back into favour. This was sound political sense, since it was obvious that Guy would only surrender Ascalon if forced to do so and the kingdom could not afford a civil war. The king would not allow this proposal to be considered. This does not imply that illness had warped his judgment: no twelfth-century king could have pardoned a vassal who had so publicly defied him. Nevertheless, the patriarch and the masters, who evidently thought that some compromise should be possible, were exasperated by the king's intransigence, stormed out of the assembly and rode away from Acre; but it would appear that their inter-vention had swayed the *curia generalis*, for the king took no further action against Guy, who remained in undisturbed possession of

Ascalon.[43] William of Tyre relates that as a result of this quarrel the main business of the assembly – that of sending a mission to the West to seek military aid – remained undiscussed.

This meeting was held in the early weeks of 1184. Immediately after his account of it, William writes about Guy of Lusignan's attack on Beduin in the royal fief of Darum, and his *Chronicle* ends with these words:

> When he learned of this, the king, having reconvened the chief men, handed over the government of the kingdom and its general administration to the count of Tripoli, placing his hope in his courage and benevolence. In doing this he appeared to satisfy the wishes of all the people and of most of their leaders; for the only safe course of action seemed to everybody to be that the conduct of royal business should be placed in the hands of the aforesaid count.[44]

The opinion of most scholars has been that these events took place in the early months of 1184, although there is a minority that is rightly more cautious.[45] All other evidence shows that Guy's attack on the Beduin and the appointment of Raymond as regent occurred after 6 October 1184.[46] This is compatible with what is known about the date at which William wrote the last entries in his *Chronicle*. He wrote the general preface to the whole work in 1184, and in it he states that he has divided the *Chronicle* into twenty-three Books. As it has come down to us, Book XXIII consists of a separate preface and a single chapter.[47] In that preface William implies that he knew about events that occurred later than 1184. He says that he had

---

[43] He was still count of Jaffa and Ascalon in December 1185: H.-E. Mayer, 'Sankt Samuel auf dem Freudenberge und sein besitz nach ein unbekannten Diplom König Balduins V', QF 44 (1964), pp. 35–71 at p. 71.

[44] WT, XXIII, 1, pp. 1062–4

[45] W.B. Stevenson, *The Crusaders in the East* (Cambridge, 1907), p. 237; M.W. Baldwin, 'The decline and fall of Jerusalem, 1174–1189', in Setton, *Crusades*, I, p. 601; Prawer, *Royaume Latin*, I, p. 628; H.-E. Mayer extends the timespan slightly, but places Raymond's appointment as regent at the same time as the authorisation of Heraclius's mission to the West, that is in the late spring of 1184: *The Crusades*, tr. J. Gillingham 2nd edn (Oxford, 1988), p. 132, an opinion shared by J. Riley-Smith, *Feudal Nobility and the Kingdom of Jerusalem, 1174–1277* (London, 1973), p. 107; Grousset, *Histoire des Croisades*, II, pp. 740–5, spreads the events throughout the last year of Baldwin's reign, but with a certain lack of specificity; Lamonte writes, 'The ordering of the *bailliage* to Raymond was the last act of Baldwin IV. Consumed by leprosy [he died] on 16 March 1185 . . .': *Feudal Monarchy in the Latin Kingdom of Jerusalem, 1100–1291* (Cambridge, Mass., 1932), p. 33; Runciman, while placing Guy's revolt and the 'parlement' of Acre too early, in the summer of 1183, dates Guy's attack on Darum in the autumn of 1184 and Raymond's appointment as regent 'early in 1185', *Crusades*, II, pp. 439–43.

[46] See below, pp. 204–5.   [47] WT, Prologue, pp. 100–1; see above, p. 6, n. 3.

intended to stop writing at the end of Book XXII (which concludes with an account of the relief of Kerak in December 1183) because 'we who used frequently to triumph over our enemies and bring back the palm of victory with glory, now, in almost every conflict, being deprived of Divine grace, are the losers'. Nevertheless, he had been persuaded to follow the example of historians such as Livy and Josephus and record the bad as well as the good.[48]

It is difficult to determine precisely when William died. The following account of his last years is given in the *Eracles*:

When Heraclius was patriarch he was at the Church of Mount Sion on Maundy Thursday to bless the holy oils and excommunicated the archbishop of Tyre. He did this without warning and without right of appeal by which he might appear before him to defend himself. The aforesaid archbishop appealed to Rome against this, so that he might go and defend himself before Pope Alexander at the council which he was about to hold. He made preparations to leave. The patriarch bribed a doctor and gave him money so that he should go to Archbishop William and poison him. He did as he was asked and poisoned him. The patriarch went overseas to Marseilles and from there went to his home in Gévaudan. When he heard that Archbishop William was dead, he returned to Jerusalem and led a worse life than he had done before.[49]

The author is wrong to date the excommunication before the Third Lateran Council of 1179 because Heraclius was not patriarch then; but Peter Edbury and John Rowe have argued that the story may be true in substance because excommunication without right of appeal would have made it impossible for William to continue to act as chancellor. He was still chancellor when he wrote the prologue to his *Chronicle* early in 1184, but by 16 May 1185 that office was held by Peter, archdeacon of Lydda.[50] This implies that William was excommunicated on Maundy Thursday 1184 because Heraclius was in western Europe during Holy Week 1185.[51]

The *Eracles* alleges that William was excommunicated because he

---

[48] WT, Prologue to Bk XXIII, pp. 1061–2.

[49] M.R. Morgan (ed.), *La continuation de Guillaume de Tyr (1184–1197)*, DRHC 14 (Paris, 1982), c. 39, pp. 51–2.

[50] WT, Prologue, p. 100; Peter of Lydda is first recorded as chancellor in Delaborde, no. 43, pp. 91–2; RRH, no. 643, I, p. 170; P.W. Edbury and J.G. Rowe, 'William of Tyre and the patriarchal election of 1180', EHR 93 (1978), pp. 9–11; H.-E. Mayer, *Die Kanzlei der lateinischen Könige von Jerusalem*, 2 vols., MGH Schriften 40 (Hanover, 1996), I, pp. 247–53 and 255–64.

[51] Heraclius kept Easter 1185 at Rouen with Henry II: R.W. Eyton, *Court, Household and Itinerary of King Henry II* (London, 1878), p. 263.

criticised the patriarch's concubinage, but Edbury and Rowe are surely right in claiming that the true reason was probably political.[52] If the excommunication occurred in Holy Week 1184, that was a time when Heraclius was about to leave on a mission to western Europe. During his absence William would, as next senior-ranking prelate, become spokesman for the Catholic Church in the kingdom. As this was a very uncertain time in the history of the Latin East because of the king's poor health, Heraclius, who was a firm supporter of the Courtenays, may not have wanted the Church to be represented by William of Tyre, who was committed to their chief opponent, Raymond of Tripoli. It would not have been difficult to find some areas of contention. William was very sensitive about the rights of the church of Tyre and its subjection to the patriarchate of Jerusalem, which had involved loss of control over the suffragan sees of Tyre in the county of Tripoli.[53] A dispute over some jurisdictional issue of that kind could have provided the patriarch with the excuse he needed to excommunicate William, and, once he had been disqualified, Heraclius was able to appoint Bernard, bishop of Lydda, as his vicar before he left for the West.[54]

Hiestand has found evidence that William died on 29 September, but his source does not give the year.[55] His death occurred before 21 October 1186 for on that day his successor as archbishop of Tyre, Joscius, the former bishop of Acre, witnessed a group of royal charters.[56] Because of his knowledge of events in the winter of 1184–5 William cannot have died before 29 September 1185, but many scholars have accepted Mayer's argument that he died on that same day in 1186. If he survived until the beginning of Guy of Lusignan's reign this would explain why he takes so gloomy a view of

---

[52] P.W. Edbury and J.G. Rowe, *William of Tyre. Historian of the Latin East* (Cambridge, 1988), p. 21.

[53] 'We blame the Roman Church, and not without reason, for this evil, for while ordering us to obey the Church of Jerusalem, it has allowed us to be unlawfully cut off from the Church of Antioch. If our fullness of jurisdiction were restored to us, we would be prepared to obey either master without cavilling or making any difficulty about it, like the obedient sons [of holy Church] that we are': WT, XIV, 14, pp. 650–1; J.G. Rowe, 'The papacy and the ecclesiastical province of Tyre', BJRL 43 (1960–1), pp. 160–89.

[54] B. de Broussillon, 'La charte d'André II de Vitré et le siège de Kérak en 1184', BHCTH (1899), pp. 50–3.

[55] The necrology of St Maurice at Chartres, R. Hiestand, 'Zum Leben und zur Laufbahn Wilhelms von Tyrus', *Deutsches Archiv* 34 (1978), pp. 345–80 at p. 351, n. 28. Hiestand agrees with Mayer's argument that William died in 1186: H.-E. Mayer, 'Zum Tode Wilhelms von Tyrus', *Archiv für Diplomatik* 5–6 (1959–60), pp. 182–201; cf. WT, p. 1.

[56] Strehlke, nos. 21–3, pp. 19–21.

the future of the kingdom in the preface to Book XXIII, but the evidence for this date is not without difficulties.[57] The allegation in the *Eracles* that William was poisoned may almost certainly be discounted because sudden and unexplained deaths were frequently attributed to poison in the twelfth century.[58]

The king was reconciled to Heraclius and the masters of the military Orders, for at some time after the beginning of June they left on a mission to seek help from the rulers of the West. There seems no doubt that the king sent them, for he wrote to them in September 1184 saying that he had heard that they had reached Brindisi safely.[59] He went on to tell them that Saladin had launched a fresh attack on the castle of Kerak during that summer. The *Chronicle* of Ernoul contains a quite detailed account of this siege, although it is placed in the wrong chronological sequence; but the passage undoubtedly relates to the siege of 1184 because the author describes, just as the Muslim accounts do, how Saladin, learning from his failure of 1183, tried to fill in the fosse before attempting an assault on the castle.[60]

Saladin was joined by forces from north Syria and Mesopotamia, led by his brother al-Adil and the princes of Mardin and Hisn Kaifa, and also by the Egyptian army commanded by his nephew Taqi ad-Din. The latter was accompanied by al-Adil's family who wished

---

[57] Mayer originally based his conclusion about the date of William of Tyre's death on the fact that he is recorded in a document of 17 October 1186. It is known only through an eighteenth-century calendar entry: Delaville Le Roulx, 'Inventaire de Pièces de Terre Sainte de l'Ordre de l'Hôpital', ROL 3 (1895), p. 69, no. 162, which concerns a dispute between the master of the Hospital and the bishop of Valania, adjudicated by William, archbishop of Tyre, and Odo, bishop of Beirut, papal judges delegate, in the presence of R., patriarch of Jerusalem. Since the patriarch in 1186 was Heraclius, the calendarist evidently found the hand difficult to read. I would not wish to place too much weight on the fact that the name of the archbishop of Tyre has been correctly transcribed, since it also may have been represented by an initial in the original, and the archbishop named may have been J[oscius]. This indeed seems likely, since William is known to have died on 29 September, no later than 1186.

[58] Mayer has rightly drawn attention to the parallel between this account of William's death and William's account of the death of Ralph of Domfront, patriarch of Antioch (WT, XV, 17, pp. 698–9), which he considers may have been the model for the *Eracles* story: 'Zum Tode Wilhelms von Tyrus', p. 200.

[59] Part of the letter is preserved by Ralph de Diceto, *Ymagines Historiarum*, ed. W. Stubbs, 2 vols., RS 68 (London, 1876), II, pp. 27–8; some names have been glossed by Ralph for the benefit of English readers (e.g. 'Gerinum, quae villa Templi erat . . .'), but there is no reason to doubt that the letter is genuine. Information derived from this letter is also found in Roger of Wendover, *Flores Historiarum*, ed. H.G. Howlett, 2 vols., RS 84 (London, 1886), I, p. 133; RRH, no. 638, I, p. 169; Kedar, 'Eraclius', p. 193.

[60] pp. 80–1.

to join him at Aleppo, and among their effects was a pet giraffe, which made the crossing of the Sinai desert.[61] The siege of Kerak began on 23 August. On this occasion it was not crowded with guests, so Prince Reynald was able to evacuate the *faubourg* in an orderly way and withdraw to the castle. This left Saladin free to set up his camp in the *faubourg* and to range nine mangonels on the walls of the keep. They caused considerable damage, but the sultan had learned from his experience in the siege of 1183 that he could not exploit any breaches which he made in the defences unless he filled in the fosse. He therefore constructed two covered walkways in the *faubourg* so that volunteers from his army could throw earth into the fosse without danger of being shot by the garrison.[62]

When news of the attack reached Jerusalem the host was mustered and the patriarch's vicar, the bishop of Lydda, together with the seneschal of the Temple, recruited visiting knights to serve on the campaign. The seneschal was Gerard of Ridefort, the former marshal of the kingdom, who had become a Templar and, as seneschal, was acting head of the Order in the absence of the master.[63] According to Ernoul the king was present with the army.[64] This is possible, though it is unlikely that he was able to ride, so he would have been carried in a litter. The Franks approached Kerak from the north end of the Dead Sea, crossing the Jordan at St John's ford. Saladin promptly abandoned the siege. Burning his siege-engines, he marched north to Heshbon.[65] According to Ernoul the king gave orders for the fosse of Kerak to be cleared. This work

---

[61] This is found only in Blochet's translation of al-Maqrizi, *Histoire d'Egypte*, ROL 9 (1902), p. 12.

[62] Ernoul, pp. 80–1; IA, RHC Or I, p. 666; AS, RHC Or IV, p. 254; Kamal ad-Din, ROL 4 (1896), p. 172; Lyons and Jackson, *Saladin*, p. 217.

[63] This is known from a charter of André de Vitré, a third cousin of Baldwin IV, who took part in the campaign: M. Bar, *La formation du comté de Champagne* (Nancy, 1977), pp. 452–3; de Broussillon, 'La charte d'André II de Vitré', pp. 50–3. Gerard of Ridefort first appears as a Templar in 1183, Delaborde, no. 42, pp. 89–90; RRH, no. 631, I, p. 167; cf. M.L. Bulst-Thiele, *Sacrae Domus Militiae Templi Hierosolymitani Magistri. Untersuchungen zur Geschichte des Templerordens 1118/19–1314*, Abhandlungen der Akademie der Wissenschaften in Göttingen Philologisch – Historische Klasse, Dritte Folge, No. 86 (Göttingen, 1974), pp. 108 and 360; F.M. Abel, 'Lettre d'un Templier trouvée recemment à Jérusalem', *Revue Biblique*, 35 (1926), pp. 288–95; on the role of the seneschal, *La Règle du Temple*, (ed.) H. de Curzon, c. 99 (Paris, 1886), p. 87.

[64] Ernoul, p. 81; in his letter to the envoys in Western Europe Baldwin describes the host's arrival at Kerak as 'adventus noster': Ralph de Diceto, RS 68(II), p. 28.

[65] al-Maqrizi, p. 74; Kamal ad-Din, ROL 4 (1896), p. 172; IA, RHC Or I, pp. 666–7; AS, RHC Or IV, p. 251; Baha al-Din, RHC Or III, pp. 80–2; Ibn Jubayr, pp. 313–14; Ralph de Diceto, RS 68(II), pp. 27–8; Lyons and Jackson, *Saladin*, pp. 217–18.

could have been carried out quite rapidly by volunteers from a large army if they were given suitable donatives. Ernoul further relates that Baldwin IV gave Prince Reynald a large subsidy so that he could make good the damage caused to the fortifications of Kerak.[66]

Saladin returned to Damascus by way of Samaria, knowing that all the Frankish forces were at Kerak. Between 8 and 10 September he attacked the unwalled city of Nablus. As its lord, Balian of Ibelin, was serving with the host, his wife Maria Comnena presumably took charge of the defence. Although she could not prevent Saladin from sacking the town, there were no Frankish casualties because she organised the entire population to take refuge in the citadel. The Catholic bishop of neighbouring Sebastea received an *aman* from Saladin's commander in return for releasing eighty Muslim prisoners of war, and his city was spared the horrors of a sack. Other places were less fortunate: the Saracens attacked Samaritan villages, killing some of the peasantry, and laid waste the Templar settlement at Zarin before crossing the Jordan near Belvoir. Soon after returning to Damascus Saladin disbanded his army.[67]

The Moorish pilgrim, Ibn Jubayr, left Damascus for Acre on 13 September 1184. He was surprised that trade was not affected by the war but that Muslims continually journeyed 'from Damascus to Acre [through Frankish territory] and likewise not one of the Christian merchants was stopped or hindered [in Muslim territory]'.[68] He stayed in Acre from 18 September to 6 October 1184 seeking a ship which would take him to al-Andalus. He records that Baldwin IV was living in the city at that time:

The pig, the lord of Acre whom they call king, lives secluded and is not seen, for God has afflicted him with leprosy. . . His chamberlain and regent is his maternal uncle, the count, the controller of the treasury, to whom all dues are paid and who supervises all with firmness and authority. The most considerable amongst the accursed Franks is the accursed count, the lord of Tripoli and Tiberias. He has authority and position among them. He is qualified to be king, and indeed is a candidate for the office. He is described as being shrewd and crafty. . .[69]

---

[66] Ernoul, p. 81.
[67] Lyons and Jackson, *Saladin*, p. 219; Ibn Jubayr, p. 314; Ralph de Diceto, RS 68(II), p. 28; Kamal ad-Din, ROL 4 (1896), p. 172; IA, RHC Or I, p. 667; AS, RHC Or IV, pp. 251 and 256; al-Maqrizi, p. 74; Baha al-Din, RHC Or III, pp. 81–2.
[68] Ibn Jubayr, p. 301.
[69] *Ibid.*, p. 324. For the dates of his stay at Acre, pp. 317 and 325.

The king's maternal uncle was Joscelin of Courtenay who, as seneschal, was able to deputise for Baldwin in all the routine business of state. At that time Raymond of Tripoli had not been appointed regent.

The Lyons manuscript of the *Eracles*, the Old French translation and continuation of William of Tyre's *Chronicle*, gives a faithful rendering of William's last chapter, but immediately after the account of the raid by Guy of Lusignan on the Beduin of Darum inserts a sentence not found in the original:

> The king received the news of Count Guy of Jaffa's raid on the beduin in the fief of Darum who were under his protection as he was returning from Acre to Jerusalem. He was very distressed by this, and subsequently contracted the illness which caused his death.

The author then translates William's concluding words about the appointment of Raymond of Tripoli as regent. This passage shows that Guy's raid took place after 6 October, when the king was still at Acre.[70]

Guy's attack on the Beduin was a serious matter. A minor raid of this kind in the course of a quarrel would have been unremarkable in his home in Poitou, but in the Crusader Kingdom it was an act of wanton folly which can only have confirmed his opponents in their belief that he was unfit to govern. Beduin were under the protection of the crown, and because they were well treated they were on the whole friendly towards the Franks, a fact which Saladin deplored but was unable to remedy.[71] Darum was a royal fief on the edge of the Sinai desert and the Beduin played a key role in its security by supplying the Franks with information about Egyptian troop movements. It is entirely comprehensible that Guy's activities should have caused the king grave anxiety.

As Piers Mitchell has explained, 'developing lepromatous leprosy before adulthood', as Baldwin had done, 'increases the likelihood of premature death', but it would not in itself have been the immediate cause of death, and he suggests a variety of infections which might have produced the fever that caused the king's death.[72] His illness

---

[70] Morgan, *Continuation*, c. 1, p. 18; P.W. Edbury, 'The Lyons *Eracles* and the Old French *Continuations* of William of Tyre', in *Montjoie*, pp. 146–7, cites this as an example of the unwarranted expansions of the text characteristic of the Lyons compiler, but I can see no reason why this piece of information, which accords very well with all the rest of the evidence, should not be accurate.

[71] Lyons and Jackson, *Saladin*, pp. 156–7.   [72] See below, Appendix, p. 253.

made it necessary for him to appoint a regent, which he did after he had returned to Jerusalem. The Lyons *Eracles* accurately translates William of Tyre's statement about this: 'At once he sent for the count of Tripoli, because he had confidence in his intelligence and loyalty, and appointed him regent with full power over the land and the kingdom.'[73] This took place at the earliest in October 1184, but more probably early in 1185, for in the Colbert-Fontainebleau family of *Eracles* manuscripts, the translation of William's last sentence, describing the appointment of Raymond as regent, is followed by the words: 'Ce fu en l'an de l'Incarnacion de nostre Seignor mil et cent et quatre vinz et cins anz.'[74]

The king had had illnesses of this kind twice before and had recovered from them, and he was not at this stage arranging for the succession, but appointing an executive regent whom he could dismiss when he became well enough to resume power. It was a personal choice and he did not consult the High Court. Nevertheless, it was an unexpected choice, because since he came of age he had refused to give Raymond any public position in the kingdom, but the appointment should be seen in the context of Heraclius's mission to the West. The king received no news during the winter months of how that embassy was progressing, but he hoped that the delegates would succeed in persuading a western prince to come and take over the regency on behalf of himself and his little nephew. Raymond's appointment was therefore a stopgap measure. Because there was no truce with Saladin, the regent needed to be an experienced field commander, and the only alternative to Raymond among the royal kin was Prince Reynald, who was needed in Transjordan, which was the chief object of Saladin's attacks.

After some weeks it became evident that the king was dying, and he summoned the High Court to his bedside. The succession was already determined, as Baldwin V had been anointed co-king in 1183, but it was necessary to appoint a regent for him, and that choice lay with the High Court, not with the king alone. Ernoul claims that the members of the High Court said:

We do not wish when the child has been crowned that his stepfather [Guy of Lusignan] should be regent because we know that he would have neither the knowledge nor the ability to govern the kingdom. Then the king said:

[73] Morgan, *Continuation*, c. 1, p. 18.
[74] *Eracles*, XXIII, 1, RHC Occ II, p. 3. On 6 October as Ibn Jubayr attests, Raymond of Tripoli had not yet been appointed regent: see n. 69 above.

'Decide among yourselves whom I should appoint as regent for the child.' They decided that nobody could rule as well as the Count of Tripoli. So the king sent for the count and asked him to act as regent of the kingdom and of the child [king] for ten years until the child came of age.[75]

From this point the text of Ernoul becomes the basis for the Old French continuations of William of Tyre, which exist in a variety of versions.[76] There are no significant differences between those versions in the account that they give of the appointment of Raymond of Tripoli as regent, and the account given below is that found in the Lyons text. This relates that when offered the regency the count of Tripoli replied that he would accept the office only if four conditions were met. This account is attempting to show that Raymond III's appointment was unopposed and that the restrictions imposed on him as regent were entirely of his own choosing. The nature of some of them makes this improbable. The first was that a personal guardian should be appointed for the young king so that Raymond should not be held responsible for his death should this occur while he was still a minor. This is proof that some influential members of the Court distrusted Raymond. Joscelin of Courtenay was appointed guardian: he was Baldwin V's great-uncle, but had no claim to the throne and had every reason to wish to keep the child alive because the power of the Courtenays would be diminished if he were to die. But Joscelin was a political enemy of Raymond's and this choice was not designed to conciliate the regent. The second condition was that the royal castles should be placed in the hands of the military Orders during the regency. This was unprecedented and amounted to a lack of confidence in Raymond's integrity, for it implied that, without this safeguard, he might try to usurp sovereign power. The Orders were trusted by all parties in the kingdom because they were independent of royal control and subject only to the pope. The fourth condition agreed by the High Court is strangely worded:

The count asked for an assurance that he would have and hold the regency for ten years, but that if the child were to die during that time, then the regency should revert to those who were the most rightful heirs, until such

---

[75] Ernoul, pp. 115–16. The Lyons *Eracles* gives a slightly different account of this debate. It reports that Baldwin IV ordered the High Court to accept Raymond of Tripoli as regent for Baldwin V until he came of age, but that if his nephew should die before reaching his majority, the Court should either accept Raymond as king, or be advised by him about seeking a king from the West: Morgan, *Continuation*, c. 2, p. 19.

[76] M.R. Morgan, *The Chronicle of Ernoul and the Continuations of William of Tyre* (Oxford, 1973), p. 117.

time as on the advice of the pope of Rome, the emperor of Germany, the king of France and the king of England the crown should be conferred on one of the two sisters, either on Sibyl who was the daughter of Countess Agnes, or on Isabel who was the daughter of Queen Maria. . .

This means that the High Court had rejected the proposals which Baldwin IV is said to have made about the government of the kingdom in the event of his nephew's death as a minor. Instead, it was decided that the whole question of the regency should then be reopened, and the succession adjudicated by the four great leaders of Catholic Europe. This solution proved, in the event, unenforceable, and the other terms of this provision are extremely vague: who were 'those who were the most rightful heirs' to whom the regency should revert? This provision bears all the marks of a proposal that has been accepted to end a deadlock. The only one of the four conditions which was in any way favourable to Raymond was the third, which stipulated that he should be granted the fief of Beirut to defray his expenses.[77]

It is evident that the High Court wished to restrict Raymond's power. The reason for this may only be conjectured, but would seem to have been the belief, which was widely held, that he wished to make himself king. Ibn Jubayr had heard rumours to that effect when he was staying at Acre in the previous autumn, and similar rumours also reached the Angevin Empire and were recorded in the Latin *Continuation* of William of Tyre, a work strongly influenced by pro-Lusignan sources.[78]

When the debate about the regency had ended, Baldwin IV ordered all his vassals to do homage to the little King Baldwin and to Count Raymond as his regent and to swear that they would keep the terms of the agreement that they had made about the succession.[79] He then commanded that Baldwin V should perform a

---

[77] Morgan, *Continuation*, c. 4, p. 20. Baldwin V was seven in 1185 and would only have needed a regent for eight years. The compiler of the *Eracles* presumably calculated his age from the time he became co-king in 1183.

[78] Ibn Jubayr, p. 324. The opinion is attributed in the Latin *Continuation* of William of Tyre to Guy of Lusignan, reflecting on the acccession of Baldwin V: 'Querebatur, quod rege puero nomen inane portante, comes regno ad libitum uteretur, illum dici regem, istum re vera esse regem, qui regiam haberet potestatem, nichil iam superesse nisi rege aut expulso aut extincto, comes post regnum etiam coronam sibi assumeret': Salloch (ed.), *Die lateinische Fortsetzung Wilhelms von Tyrus*, I, i, p. 51.

[79] 'Devant ce que li rois fust mors et que li enfes ot porte corone li fist il faire a touz les barons de la terre feauté et homage com a seignor et a roi. Et apres fist il faire homage au conte de Triple com a baill. . .' Morgan, *Continuation*, c. 6, p. 22.

Figure 6 Baldwin IV on his deathbed passes the crown to Baldwin V in the
presence of the High Court.

solemn crown-wearing at the Holy Sepulchre. The *Eracles* relates
that when the child king left the cathedral to go to his banquet in the
Temple he was carried on the shoulders of Balian of Ibelin because
he was the tallest of the great lords present.[80] This statement is

[80] Mas Latrie dated this passage 1183, Ernoul, pp. 117–19. This is exactly the same text as that
    of the *Eracles* (Morgan, *Continuation*, c. 5, p. 21), and refers to events in 1185, but Mas Latrie's
    dating has misled some modern scholars, e.g. Prawer, *Royaume Latin*, I, p. 624; M.W.

politically naive: public ritual gestures in the Middle Ages, as now, were seldom fortuitous. Balian of Ibelin was not chosen for his height alone but because of who he was. The most important fact about him was that he was not Guy of Lusignan, Baldwin V's stepfather, but one of his declared opponents. He was also the husband of Maria Comnena, whose daughter Isabel was the only other possible contestant for the throne, and Balian's gesture signified that Isabel's family supported the child king.

Baldwin IV had made such provision for the future of the kingdom as he could. He had sent to ask for help from western rulers, and specially from his Angevin kinsmen, to care for the realm during the minority of his nephew, and had made a superhuman effort to remain head of state until that help arrived, but his bodily strength had not proved commensurate with his strength of will. When he knew that he was dying he had tried to ensure that the government would continue to function smoothly after his nephew came to power.

After Baldwin V's crown-wearing the members of the High Court stayed in Jerusalem since it was evident that the leper king was dying. Even Prince Bohemond came there from Antioch.[81] On the day he died the king summoned his vassals for the last time, and they came to pay their respects to the young man who had ruled Jerusalem for eleven years.[82] The good-looking child whom William of Tyre had tutored and who loved riding had become blind, crippled and deformed. Yet he had never sheltered behind his illness in order to escape from the duties of state: he had led his army in battle until he could no longer ride and had then been carried in a litter at the head of his host. Until within a few days of his death he had been present at meetings of the High Court and been concerned

Baldwin, 'The decline and fall of Jerusalem, 1174–1189', in Setton, *Crusades*, I, pp. 590–621 at p. 600. Runciman accepts the sequence of events given in the *Eracles*, and is therefore inclined to think that William of Tyre may have been mistaken in placing Baldwin V's coronation in November 1183: *Crusades*, II, p. 443, n. 2; but the *Eracles* text makes clear that this crown-wearing happened in 1185: 'Ne demora puis gaires que li rois ot portee corone que li Rois Meziaus fu mors': Morgan, *Continuation*, c. 5, p. 21.

81 Hiestand has drawn attention to his presence at Acre in April 1185 (RRH, no. 642a, II, p. 42) and has rightly inferred that he was on his way to or from King Baldwin's deathbed, 'Chronologisches . . . 2. Die Todesdaten König Balduins IV . . .', *Deutsches Archiv* 35 (1979), p. 551.

82 'Et devant ce que il morust manda il tos ses homes que il venissent a lui en Jerusalem. Et il i vindrent tuit. A cel point que il i vindrent, trespassa li rois de cest siecle, si que tuit li baron de la terre furent a sa mort': Morgan, *Continuation*, c. 5, p. 21.

with arrangements for the succession. Few rulers have remained executive heads of state when handicapped by such severe physical disablilities or sacrificed themselves more totally to the needs of their people.

Baldwin died at some time before 16 May 1185.[83] He was buried near his father in the chapel of the Latin kings in the Church of the Holy Sepulchre at the foot of Mount Calvary, the most holy place in Christendom, which he had striven successfully to defend throughout his reign.[84] He was not quite twenty-four years old.

[83] Hiestand argued, citing the necrology of St Niçaise de Meulan, that Baldwin IV died on 15 April 1185: 'Chronologisches . . . 2. Die Todesdaten König Balduins IV . . .', p. 551; but Thomas Vogtherr has shown that this evidence is not secure, 'Die Regierungsdaten der lateinischen Könige von Jerusalem', ZDPV 110 (1994), pp. 51–81 at pp. 65–7. Baldwin V had become sole king by 16 May 1185: Delaborde, no. 43, pp. 91–2; RRH, no. 643, I, p. 170.

[84] Morgan, *Continuation*, c. 5, p. 21; J. Folda, 'The Tomb of King Baldwin IV', in *The Art of the Crusaders in the Holy Land, 1098–1187* (Cambridge, 1995), p. 461.

CHAPTER 10

The heirs of the leper king

The author of the Latin *Continuation* of William of Tyre's *History* remarks that during Raymond of Tripoli's second regency 'the land was free from external battles, but not from those within'.[1] Raymond, when he became regent, had, in the last days of Baldwin IV's reign, entered into negotiations with Saladin 'with a request about the Antioch truce', which Lyons and Jackson suggest was an attempt to extend to the other Frankish states the truce which Antioch had had with Saladin since 1183.[2] It would seem that these negotiations were successful, for Saladin concluded a truce with the Kingdom of Jerusalem soon after this, which the *Eracles* claims was to last for four years.[3]

Saladin was anxious to return to Iraq, where his recent gains were threatened by Izz ad-Din of Mosul, who had formed a coalition with al-Pahlawan, *atabeg* of Azerbaijan, and the Shah Arman of Akhlat.[4] He was not willing to leave his other dominions unprotected as he had done in 1182, possibly because he was aware of the mission that had been sent to the West to seek military aid, and in addition to his truces with the Crusader States he also tried to negotiate peace with the Byzantine Emperor Andronicus Comnenus, and with Rupen III of Cilicia.[5] Saladin left Damascus in the early spring of 1185 and did not return until May 1186.

---

[1] Salloch, I, 1, p. 51.

[2] M.C. Lyons and D.E.P. Jackson, *Saladin. The Politics of the Holy War* (Cambridge, 1982), pp. 221–2.

[3] 'So the Sultan made an armistice with the Franks and left Damascus in the month of Dhu'l-Qa'da 580' (6 February–6 March 1185), Kamal ad-Din, ROL 4 (1896), p. 173; M.R. Morgan (ed.), *La continuation de Guillaume de Tyr (1184–1197)*, DRHC 14 (Paris, 1982), c. 9, pp. 23–4.

[4] Lyons and Jackson, *Saladin*, pp. 220–7.

[5] Magnus of Reichersberg, *Chronica*, ed. W. Wattenbach, MGH SS, XVII (Hanover, 1861), p. 511; cf. F. Dölger (ed.), *Regesten der Kaiserurkunden des oströmischen Reiches*, 5 vols. (Munich and Berlin, 1924–65), nos. 1563, 1607; RRH, no. 688, I, p. 183; C.M. Brand, 'The Byzantines and Saladin, 1185–92', *Speculum* 37 (1962), pp. 167–81; Lyons and Jackson, *Saladin*, p. 222.

Frankish morale received a severe blow when it became known, either from the Patriarch Heraclius in person, or from messages sent by him, that no western prince would be coming to help the kingdom.[6] This was not through any lack of zeal on the part of the envoys. The embassy first visited Pope Lucius III at Verona, where, on 31 October 1184, Arnold of Toroja, master of the Temple, died.[7] There Heraclius and Roger des Moulins met with Pope Lucius III and the Emperor Frederick Barbarossa, and the pope issued the bull *Cum cuncti praedecessores*, commending the embassy to Henry II of England and urging him to give help to the Holy Land.[8]

The envoys left for France, and the fact that they crossed the Alps in winter gives some indication of their sense of urgency. Heraclius, who was one of the most distinguished sons of France at that time, was received with great honour by Philip Augustus when the embassy reached Paris on 16 January 1185. The king had come to power too recently to be able to leave his kingdom for a long period of time, but he instructed his bishops to preach the crusade in their dioceses and undertook to send knights and infantry to defend the Christian East.[9]

The patriarch and the master of the Hospital spent less than a fortnight in Paris and, crossing the Channel in winter, reached Canterbury on 29 January.[10] As in France, they were received with great honour. Henry II was at Nottingham, travelling towards York, when he learned of their arrival, but he immediately turned back and met them at Reading.[11] The envoys had been empowered to

---

[6] The precise date of the envoys' return is not known. Roger des Moulins was present at al-Marqab on 1 February 1186 (RRH, no. 647, I, p. 171), and is likely to have reached the East by the previous autumn; Heraclius had returned before Baldwin V's death, see below, p. 218.

[7] The day and the month are recorded in the obituary of the Temple of Rheims, E. de Barthelémy, 'Obituaire de la commanderie du Temple de Reims', *Collection de documents inédits sur l'histoire de France, Mélanges historiques*, IV (Paris, 1882) p. 327; the year is given by Ralph de Diceto *Ymagines Historiarum*, ed. W. Stubbs, 2 vols., RS 68(II), p. 32.

[8] P.L. 210, cols. 1312–13. On 4 November Lucius III also confirmed amendments to the Rule of the Hospital for Roger des Moulins, ed. J. von Pflugck-Harttung, *Acta Pontificum Romanorum Inedita*, II, p. 389, no. 441; cf. R. Hiestand (ed.), *Papsturkunden für Templer und Johanniter*, no. 172 (Göttingen, 1972), p. 361.

[9] Rigord, *Gesta Philippi Augusti*, c. 30, ed. H.-F. Delaborde, *Œuvres de Rigord et Guillaume le Breton*, 2 vols. (Paris, 1882–5), I, pp. 46–8; *Anonymi Laudunensis, Chronicon universale*, ed. G. Waitz, MGH SS, XXVI, p. 450; A. Cartellieri, *Philip II August König von Frankreich*, 4 vols. (Leipzig, 1899–1922), II, pp. 20–2.

[10] Gervase of Canterbury, *Opera Historica*, ed. W. Stubbs, 2 vols., RS 73(I), p. 325.

[11] Roger of Howden, *Gesta Regis Henrici Secundi*, ed. W. Stubbs, RS 49(I), pp. 335–7; R.W. Eyton, *Court, Household and Itinerary of King Henry II* (London, 1878), p. 261.

offer the keys of the Holy Sepulchre, those of the Tower of David and the banner of the Kingdom of Jerusalem to any ruler who would come to protect the Latin East,[12] but there is little doubt that the mission was directed chiefly to Henry II, who, as Anglo-Norman historians were aware, was the grandson of King Fulk of Jerusalem. Heraclius was an excellent public speaker and, as a Frenchman, could talk to the Angevin court without an interpreter. At his first audience his eloquence reduced the entire court to tears, and Henry II convoked a council to discuss the needs of the Holy Land. This met in London at the Hospitaller priory of Clerkenwell on 18 March 1185,[13] the patriarch's request was debated at length, but the king alleged that the oath which he had sworn at his coronation to defend the realm of England inhibited him from undertaking the government of Jerusalem, nor would he agree to any of his sons doing so. Nevertheless, as he had often done before, he offered to send money to help with the defence of the Crusader States. This led Heraclius to exclaim in exasperation, 'We have come in search of a sovereign, not a subsidy.' It was finally decided that Henry should cross to France to take counsel with Philip Augustus about the Holy Land. Some of those present at Clerkenwell were nevertheless moved by the patriarch's eloquence and received the cross at his hands.[14]

The envoys had to wait in England until the king was ready to leave for France in the middle of April.[15] The joint meeting with Philip Augustus was not helpful. The kings of France and England promised to send men and money to Jerusalem, but would make no further commitment and the *Gesta Henrici* records how:

[12] Rigord relates that Heraclius brought the keys of the city of Jerusalem and of the Holy Sepulchre to the West; *Gesta Philippi*, c. 30, I, p. 46; the *Gesta Henrici* adds to the two sets of keys the royal banner of Jerusalem, I, p. 336; as does Gerald of Wales, *Expugnatio Hibernica*, II, xxvi, ed. J.F. Dimock, RS 21(v) (London, 1867), pp. 360–1. Only the annalist of Laon, writing in the early thirteenth century, speaks of the patriarch bringing the 'diadema regni Ierosolimitani', and this is confirmed in no contemporary source: *Anonymi Laudunensis*, p. 450.

[13] Eyton, *Itinerary of Henry II*, p. 261.

[14] Ralph de Diceto, pp. 32–4; Roger of Howden, *Gesta Henrici*, pp. 335–7; William of Newburgh, *Historia Rerum Anglicarum*, ed. R. Howlett, RS 82(i), p. 247; Roger of Howden, *Chronica*, ed. W. Stubbs, 4 vols., RS 51(ii) p. 302, names those who took the cross; Gerald of Wales, *Expugnatio Hibernica*, II, 26–7, pp. 360–4, *Liber de Principis Instructione*, Dist. II, cc. 24–5, 27, RS 21(viii), pp. 202–3, 206 and 208–9.

[15] Although Gervase of Canterbury places the crossing after the feast of St Augustine of Canterbury, 26 May (RS 73(i), p. 326), Ralph de Diceto says it occurred in April and that the king and patriarch kept Easter at Rouen, (RS 68(ii), p. 34). Eyton considers Ralph's date more compatible with the other evidence about Henry's movements: *Itinerary of Henry II*, pp. 263–4.

The patriarch . . . hastened home; he was indeed much distressed that he had achieved so little . . . for he had hoped that he would bring back with him for the defence of that land the King of England or one of his sons.[16]

No doubt the chief obstacle to the success of this mission had been that the envoys could only offer a western prince the post of regent until Baldwin V came of age in eight years' time, whereas such a prince would only be willing to live in the Crusader Kingdom if he were offered the crown, which it was not within their power to give.

Because the mission was a failure, Raymond of Tripoli's appointment as regent remained unchallenged, but he had little real power. Although Agnes of Courtenay had died,[17] Joscelin remained seneschal and controlled the financial and civil administration of the kingdom, while the Latin Church was governed by Heraclius, who was a Courtenay supporter. The new chancellor, Peter, archdeacon of Lydda, was a strong supporter of Guy of Lusignan;[18] while the Knights Templar elected as their new master their new seneschal, Gerard of Ridefort, who was hostile to the regent.[19]

When Baldwin V became sole king, his grandfather, William V of Montferrat, surrendered his dominions to his eldest son and came to live in the Holy Land. He was an old man, and had taken part in the Second Crusade, though he was still vigorous enough to fight at Hattin. He was given the castle of St Elias in Judaea, which formed part of the crown lands, and although he held no official position in the kingdom his presence there was a further restraint on Raymond and a guarantee that the rights of Baldwin V would be fully respected.[20] Raymond, it would seem, restored Jaffa to Guy of

[16] Roger of Howden, *Gesta Henrici*, p. 328.

[17] She was still alive in September 1184 (Ibn Jubayr, p. 316) and had died before 21 October 1186 (Strehlke, no. 22, p. 20). Mayer has argued that her death occurred before 1 February 1185, 'Die Legitimität Balduins IV von Jerusalem und das Testament der Agnes von Courtenay', *Historisches Jahrbuch* 108 (1988), pp. 88–9. This is borne out by the fact that she is not mentioned in any account of the disputes about the appointment of a regent for Baldwin V.

[18] He was probably appointed in Baldwin IV's reign before Raymond became regent, although he is first attested as chancellor on 16 May 1185: Delaborde, no. 43, pp. 91–2; H.-E. Mayer, *Die Kanzlei der lateinischen Könige von Jerusalem*, 2 vols., MGH Schriften 40 (Hanover, 1996), I, pp. 255–71.

[19] M.L. Bulst-Thiele, *Sacrae Domus Militiae Templi Hierosolymitani Magistri. Untersuchungen zur Geschichte des Templerordens 1118/9–1314*, Abhandlungen der Akademie der Wissenschaften in Göttingen Philologische-Historische Klasse, Dritte Folge, No. 86 (Göttingen, 1974), pp. 106–22.

[20] Morgan, *Continuation*, c. 10, p. 24; D. Jacoby, 'Conrad Marquis of Montferrat and the Kingdom of Jerusalem (1187–92)', in L. Balletto (ed.), *Dai Feudi Monferrini e dal Piemonte ai nuovi mondi oltre gli oceani* (Alessandria, 1993), p. 189.

Lusignan, but according to the Latin Continuation of William of Tyre, that did not reconcile Guy to the fact that he was not regent for his own stepson.[21]

Meanwhile, Saladin's attempts to subdue Mosul had met with no success. He arrived there in July 1185 and was initially encouraged by the death of the Shah Arman, but al-Pahlawan of Azerbaijan remained powerful and continued to support Izz ad-Din of Mosul in his resistance to Saladin. Although Saladin camped outside the city until December, he was unable to blockade it effectively because of its great size. On 3 December he fell ill and withdrew to Harran, and the siege of Mosul had to be lifted and his army disbanded. His doctors could find no remedy and he was thought to be dying, and this news caused unrest throughout his empire, for he had no son of mature age to take over the government, and some of his kinsmen began to assert their independence. His nephew, Taqi ad-Din, governor of Egypt, began to behave like an autonomous ruler, according to Kamal ad-Din.[22] There was also an escalation in the strife that had broken out in 1185 between the Turkmen, transhumant shepherds who wintered in the Syrian desert and came north into the mountains in the spring, and the Kurds of Mardin; this developed into a full-scale war, which spread westwards to Anatolia in 1186.[23]

This would have been an excellent opportunity for the Franks to intervene had they not been prevented from doing so by the truce. Indeed, when western knights reached Jerusalem at Eastertide 1186 in response to the appeals made by the Patriarch Heraclius while he was touring the West, they were not allowed to fight and most of them returned home having completed a purely religious pilgrimage, although a few, such as Hugh Beauchamp and Roger de Mowbray, both veterans of the Second Crusade, stayed on in the hope that things would change.[24] This was bad publicity because it discour-

---

[21] Guy was styled count of Jaffa and Ascalon on 30 December 1185: H.-E. Mayer, 'Sankt Samuel auf dem Freudenberge und sein besitz nach ein unbekannten Dipiom König Baluins V', QF 44 (1964), p. 71; Salloch, I, c. 1, p. 51.

[22] al-Maqrizi, p. 79; Baha al-Din, RHC Or III, pp. 82–5; Kamal ad-Din, ROL 4 (1896), pp. 173–5.

[23] MS, XXI, vi, III, pp. 400–2; C. Cahen, *Pre-Ottoman Turkey. A General Survey of the Material and Spiritual Culture and History c.1071–1330*, tr. J. Jones-Williams (London, 1968), pp. 110–11; *Anonymi auctoris Chronicon ad Annum Christi 1234 pertinens*, ed. J.B. Chabot, tr. A. Abouna, CSCO, Scriptores Syri, 154 (Louvain, 1974), pp. 146–7.

[24] Salloch, I, 6, p. 57; Roger of Howden, *Gesta Henrici*, pp. 359–60; cf. Vincent of Beauvais, *Bibliotheca Mundi*, IV, *Speculum Historiale*, XXIX, 38 (Douai, 1624), p. 1198; C.J. Tyerman, *England and the Crusades 1095–1588*, (Chicago and London, 1988), p. 52.

aged western rulers from taking the defence needs of the Latin Kingdom with the seriousness which they merited.

Saladin's health began to improve in March 1186 and so did his fortune. al-Pahlawan of Azerbaijan died in the early months of that year. He was the chief ally of Mosul, his death led to anarchy in his dominions and, deprived of his support, Izz ad-Din made his submission to Saladin. On 4 March 1186 Saladin concluded a treaty with Mosul whereby Izz ad-Din undertook to recognise his conquests, to acknowledge him as his overlord and to give him military support when required. He had completed his conquest of the empire of Nur ad-Din and by 23 May he was once again in Damascus.[25]

The little King Baldwin V died at Acre in 1186. The exact date of his death is not known, but it occurred sometime between May when Raymond III was still regent, and mid-September, the latest date for Guy of Lusignan's coronation.[26] The cause of Baldwin's death is not known, though William of Newburgh's assertion that Raymond of Tripoli poisoned him seems implausible, coming as it does from a source very hostile to Raymond, since the child was in the care of Joscelin of Courtenay who had a vested interest in keeping him alive.[27] He was buried alongside the six other Latin kings in the Church of the Holy Sepulchre, where an elaborate tomb was erected (presumably by his mother, Queen Sibyl) bearing this epitaph:

> Septimus in tumulo puer isto tumulatus
> Est Baldevinus, regum de sanguine natus,
> Quem tulit e mundo sors primae conditionis,
> Ut paradisiacae loca possideat regionis.[28]

---

[25] al-Maqrizi, p. 79; Baha al-Din, RHC Or III, pp. 85–7 (Baha al-Din was one of the negotiators from Mosul); Kamal ad-Din, ROL 4 (1896), pp. 175–6; Lyons and Jackson, *Saladin*, pp. 238–9 and 243.

[26] J. Delaville Le Roulx (ed.), 'Inventaire de pièces de Terre Sainte de l'Ordre de l'Hôpital', no. 157, ROL 3 (1895), p. 69. For the date of Guy's coronation see p.221, below. R. Hiestand, 'Chronologisches zur Geschichte des Königreichs Jerusalem im 12 Jahrhundert. 2. Die Todesdaten König Balduins IV und König Balduins V', *Deutsches Archiv* 35 (1979), pp. 545–53.

[27] William of Newburgh, *Historia*, III, xvi, RS 82(1), p. 255.

[28] The tomb was destroyed in the fire of 1808 and is only known from engravings, S. de Sandoli (ed.), *Corpus Insciptionum Crucesignatorum Terrae Sanctae* (Jerusalem, 1974), p. 61; Z. Jacoby, 'The tomb of Baldwin V, king of Jerusalem (1185–6), and the workshop of the Temple area', *Gesta* 18 (1979), pp. 3–14; J. Folda, *The Art of the Crusaders in the Holy Land 1098–1187* (Cambridge, 1995), pp. 467–9.

The fullest account of the succession disputes that followed is that of the *Eracles*, which is hostile to Guy of Lusignan, but which can be controlled by the briefer reports in western and Islamic sources, among whom the Anglo-Norman historians and the Latin *Continuation* of William of Tyre are particularly helpful because they are, for the most part, sympathetic to Guy.

The *Eracles* tells how, when Baldwin V died at Acre, Joscelin of Courtenay persuaded Raymond of Tripoli to go to Tiberias while the Templars took the king's body to Jerusalem for burial. Joscelin then seized the regent's fief of Beirut. From Tiberias Raymond summoned the barons to meet at Nablus and they all attended except Guy of Lusignan, Reynald of Châtillon and Joscelin of Courtenay. Meanwhile Sibyl, Guy and William of Montferrat had gone to Jerusalem to attend the young king's funeral.[29] This account is implausible. The funeral of a king is not a private occasion. Raymond as regent should have informed all the important men in the kingdom of Baldwin's death, and summoned them to the burial in Jerusalem, where a *curia generalis* could then have been held to discuss the succession. By absenting himself from the funeral and sending out invitations to a *curia generalis* at Nablus, the home of his supporter Balian of Ibelin, Raymond was trying to seize the initiative from his opponents led by Joscelin of Courtenay.

Three writers, widely separated in space and time, Ibn al-Athir, Arnold of Lübeck, and the Genoese author of the *Brevis Historia* all assert that Raymond was scheming to become king, and this shows how widely that view was held.[30] If that was the truth, then Raymond must have been intending to gain the support of the members of the High Court favourable to himself while the Courtenays and their supporters were assisting at the king's funeral. It is not known for sure who Raymond of Tripoli's supporters were, since the *Eracles* refers to them merely as 'li baron qui estoient a Naples'. Raymond's stepsons

---

[29] Morgan, *Continuation*, cc. 17–20, pp. 31–5.
[30] IA, RHC Or I, p. 674; Arnold of Lübeck, *Chronica Slavorum*, ed. I.M. Lappenberg, IV, 2, MGH SS, XXI, p. 165. Raymond is alleged to have claimed that his mother, Hodierna, had been born after Baldwin II became king and therefore had had a better right to the throne than her eldest sister, Melisende, from whom both Sibyl and Isabel traced their descent: *Regni Iherosolymitani Brevis Historia*, ed. L.T. Belgrano, *Caffaro e suoi continuatori del MXCIX al MCCXCIII*, Fonti per la storia d'Italia, 5 vols. (Rome, 1890–1929), I, p. 136. If Raymond made such a claim it was not true; only Yveta, abbess of Bethany, was born to Baldwin II after his coronation: WT, XII, 4, p. 551; the Latin *Continuation* of William of Tyre asserts that some people in the Latin East wanted Raymond to be king: Salloch, c. 6, pp. 57–8.

were presumably there, and Baldwin and Balian of Ibelin certainly were, and also Balian's stepdaughter, Princess Isabel, and her husband, Humphrey of Toron. It is not known whether other great lords such as Reynald of Sidon and Walter of Caesarea were there, or whether they remained neutral in the conflict.[31]

Nevertheless, Raymond had underestimated the level of support that Sibyl enjoyed. She and Guy went to Jerusalem for Baldwin's funeral and placed a garrison there. They were joined by the late king's grandfather, William of Montferrat, and by Prince Reynald. The Patriarch Heraclius and the master of the Temple, Gerard of Ridefort, who were avowed supporters of Sibyl, were already in the city, as was Roger des Moulins, the master of the Hospital. Sibyl also had the support of the constable, Aimery of Lusignan, and of the chancellor, Peter of Lydda, although it is not known whether they were present in Jerusalem, and, of course, of Joscelin the seneschal, who remained at Acre. Sibyl's support did not come from a narrow family clique as the *Eracles* suggests, and she would not have been successful if it had done.

The nobles and prelates present in Jerusalem were agreed that it was necessary to settle the succession immediately and were also agreed that Sibyl had the best claim to the throne, but they were divided about the position of Guy of Lusignan. For although some of them held that Guy should succeed to the throne because he had married Sibyl in the expectation of becoming king, others had reservations about this, both because they thought him unequal to the responsibilities of office and because Baldwin IV had excluded him from the succession.

Benjamin Kedar has rightly drawn attention to sources independent of the *Eracles* and derived from informants on the whole favourable to Guy of Lusignan, which relate that Sibyl's supporters in 1186 required her to divorce Guy before they would agree to recognise her as queen.[32] As Kedar points out, there was a good

---

[31] After Agnes of Courtenay's death, Reynald of Sidon married Helvis, the daughter of Balian of Ibelin and Maria Comnena: *Lignages*, c. 18, RHC Lois II, p. 456. J.L. Lamonte argues that this happened before July 1187: 'The lords of Sidon in the twelfth and thirteenth centuries', *Byzantion* 17 (1944–5), pp. 183–211 at pp. 199–200. If this marriage took place before Baldwin V's death, Reynald of Sidon may have been present at Nablus.

[32] Notably Roger of Howden, *Gesta Henrici*, pp. 358–9; Roger of Howden, *Chronica*, pp. 315–16; Roger of Wendover, RS, 84(1), pp. 138–9; Guy of Bazoches in Alberic of Trois-Fontaines, *Chronica a monacho novi monasterii Hoiensis interpolata*, ed. P. Scheffer-Boichorst, MGH SS, XXIII, p. 859; B.Z. Kedar, 'The Patriarch Eraclius', in *Outremer*, pp. 177–204 at pp. 196–7.

auant ꞇ receues ceste corone · car ic
ne sai ou ie la puisse miex emploier.
Oil s'agenolla deuant lui · ꞇ celebruist
la corone ē la teste. si furois ꞇ cle fu roi
ne · Inapit liber · rrvi.

fu de robe de moine uit ce si s'en re
torna par la posterne ou il estoit ue
nu · les malades le mistrent hors si se
reunt a naples la ou li baro estoiet ·
ꞇ lor conta tout ce quil auoit ueu ·
Quit bauduin de rames oi ce que gui
de lusagnē estoit roi de iherslm · si dist
cest p · i · couenant quil nē sera pas
· i · an roi · ꞇ il ne fu · car · il fu comes ē
mi setembre · ꞇ por terre a la s'ait mar
tin le boillant · qui est deuant aost ·

Figure 7 The Patriarch Heraclius crowns Sibyl, secretly watched by
Cistercian monks sent by the barons at Nablus.

precedent for this, because the High Court had required Amalric to divorce Agnes of Courtenay before he was crowned. Moreover, in 1183 Baldwin IV had discussed with Heraclius the possibility of having Sibyl's marriage dissolved, and the patriarch had therefore had ample time to consider the grounds for an annulment. The Latin *Continuation* of William of Tyre relates that Sibyl agreed to a divorce in 1186 on three conditions: that the children of her marriage should be legitimised (she had borne Guy several daughters); that Guy should remain count of Jaffa and Ascalon; and that she should have the right to choose a new husband herself. Her supporters agreed to those conditions.[33] The *Eracles* does not contradict this account. It relates that Prince Reynald urged the people of Jerusalem to accept Sibyl as queen, without naming a consort, because she was 'le plus droit heir dou reaume'.[34] An invitation was sent from Jerusalem to the barons at Nablus to attend the coronation, and according to the *Eracles* it was issued in Sibyl's name alone. Perhaps her supporters supposed that her candidacy would prove acceptable to the whole kingdom if she were no longer married to Guy.

Raymond of Tripoli and his supporters not merely refused to attend the coronation, but sent a delegation to Jerusalem to forbid Sibyl to be crowned.[35] Her supporters disregarded this protest, and although Roger des Moulins refused to be present at her coronation, Arnold of Lübeck may be right in stating that this was because he considered himself bound by the agreement about the succession made by the High Court before Baldwin IV's death, not because he was opposed in principle to Sibyl's becoming queen. The *Eracles* relates that Heraclius crowned Sibyl and then asked her to bestow a second crown on a regent to share the work of government with her, whereupon she called Guy of Lusignan forward and placed the crown on his head and the patriarch subsequently anointed him king.[36] As Kedar remarks, this story as it stands is nonsensical, since Sibyl could not have chosen a man other than her husband to share the throne with her, but the account becomes comprehensible if it is

[33] Salloch, c. 10, pp. 64–5.
[34] Morgan, *Continuation*, c. 18, pp. 32–3.
[35] 'Conseill lor aporta que la contesse [de Japhe] mandast au conte de Triple et as barons qui estoient a Naples que il venissent a son coronement quar li roiaumes li estoit escheuz': *ibid.*, c. 17, p. 31.
[36] Arnold of Lübeck, IV, 2, p. 165; Morgan, *Continuation*, c. 18, p. 33.

assumed, as the other sources relate, that Sibyl had previously agreed to divorce Guy.[37] It would appear that she outwitted her supporters by choosing Guy as king, and they could not object to this because they had agreed to her condition that she should have the right to choose her new husband. Sibyl never wavered in her attachment to Guy and Roger of Wendover later held her up for admiration as an example of a virtuous woman: 'A most praiseworthy woman, to be commended both for her virtue and for her courage. She so arranged matters that the kingdom obtained a ruler while she retained a husband.'[38]

There is a conflict of evidence about the date of Guy and Sibyl's coronation. Arnold of Lübeck says it took place on the Sunday when the introit 'Omnes gentes plaudite manibus' is sung.[39] This is the introit of the Mass for the seventh Sunday after Pentecost, which in 1186 fell on 20 July. Ralph de Diceto says that Guy was crowned in August,[40] while the *Eracles*, which is a local source and likely to be well informed about this, dates the event to a Friday in mid-September.[41] Any of these dates is consonant with the earliest record from Guy's reign, which is dated 17 October 1186.[42]

When news of the coronation reached Nablus, Raymond III proposed to the barons there that they should proclaim Humphrey and Isabel of Toron king and queen. This plan was a piece of criminal folly since, had it succeeded, it would have plunged the kingdom into civil war, and to his credit Humphrey of Toron refused to be a party to it. Leaving Nablus secretly by night he made his submission to Guy.[43] Part of his reason for doing so may have been that his mother and stepfather, Stephanie of Milly and Reynald of Châtillon, were on the opposite side and he did not wish to fight against them, but it is also arguable that, unlike Count Raymond, he placed the security of the realm above his own advantage. Yet despite Humphrey's acceptance of Guy, some of the barons at Nablus remained hostile to him and wished to attack him before his power was firmly established.[44] Peace was mediated by the Patriarch

[37] Kedar, 'Eraclius', p. 196.   [38] *Flores Historiarum*, RS 84(1), p. 139.
[39] IV, 2, MGH SS, XXI, p. 165.   [40] *Ymagines Historiarum*, p. 47.
[41] Morgan, *Continuation*, c. 18, p. 33.   [42] Delaville Le Roulx, 'Inventaire', no. 162, p. 69.
[43] Morgan, *Continuation*, c. 19, p. 34.
[44] 'Pauci cum rege, multi vel pene omnes cum comite Tripolitano et cum sociis suis, parati erant invicem inter se inire certamen': *De Expugnatione Terrae Sanctae*, RS 66, p. 209. Weight must be given to this account which from internal evidence appears to have been written by an eyewitness of events in the Latin Kingdom in 1186–7.

Heraclius and the master of the Hospital, Roger des Moulins, and the advice of the latter no doubt carried special weight because he had taken no part in the coronation of Sibyl and Guy.[45] The majority of the barons at Nablus then went to Jerusalem and did homage to Guy, but there were two notable absentees, Baldwin of Ibelin and Raymond of Tripoli.[46]

When Guy of Lusignan became king and Raymond of Tripoli led the opposition to him, the truce which Raymond had made with Saladin needed to be renegotiated. The deep divisions among the Franks were potentially very dangerous, because throughout the summer of 1186 Saladin was at Damascus, well placed to intervene. The *Gesta Henrici* reports that in 1186:

When Saladin had proposed to enter the land of Jerusalem with his army, the Templars and Hospitallers with other leading men of the kingdom gave 60,000 bezants to Saladin in return for a truce from that time to the octave of the following Easter [5 April 1187].[47]

Saladin certainly acted on the assumption that his truce with the Franks would expire in the spring of 1187, and although this information is uncorroborated, like Jean Richard, I find it convincing.[48]

Saladin had no wish to mount a major campaign against the Franks in 1186. He was still convalescent, and he also wanted to place Egypt, his chief source of money and manpower, in more secure hands than those of Taqi ad-Din, whose loyalty seemed doubtful. He finally persuaded his brother al-Adil to return to Cairo, and gave Taqi ad-Din fiefs in Mesopotamia instead, but this exchange was not completed until November 1186.[49]

An apocalyptic atmosphere prevailed throughout the Near East in the summer of 1186, for astronomers had calculated that on

---

[45] *Regni Iherosolymitani Brevis Historia*, I, p. 138.   [46] Morgan, *Continuation*, c. 20, pp. 34–5.

[47] Roger of Howden, *Gesta Henrici*, pp. 341–2. The Latin Continuation of William of Tyre puts the sum at 40,000 bezants, but Salloch points out that the author derives this figure from the *Gesta* and that it must have been wrongly transcribed, c. 5, p. 56 and n. 54. The *Gesta Henrici* later reports that: 'After Guy became king he began to display such qualities as a military leader that Saladin . . . asked that those truces which had been granted until Easter should be extended for another three years. The king, acting on the advice of the Templars, granted this request' (p. 359). Given everything that is known about Guy's brief reign this cannot be true, and is presumably a misunderstanding on the part of the author about the status of the four-year truce negotiated by Raymond of Tripoli with Saladin in 1185.

[48] J. Richard, *The Latin Kingdom of Jerusalem*, tr. J. Shirley, 2 vols. (Amsterdam, 1979), p. 149, n. 19.

[49] Lyons and Jackson, *Saladin*, pp. 244–6.

16 September all five planets would gather in the house of Libra and that, since Libra was an airy sign, this conjunction would produce a great wind which would destroy all life on earth. Their concern transcended all cultural and religious frontiers and letters about this were exchanged between Muslim and Christian scientists. The devout in both traditions were sceptical about these predictions, since neither the Christian nor the Islamic revelation foretold that the world would end in this way, and they therefore noted with some satisfaction that although the conjunction occurred on the appointed day nothing whatever untoward happened.[50]

The depth of Baldwin of Ibelin's hatred of Guy became evident when he attended the first meeting of the High Court in the new reign held in the Cathedral of the Holy Cross at Acre. When he was required to do homage to the king, he replied: 'My father never did homage to yours and I will not do homage to you.' He then gave his lands into Guy's charge, asking him to enfeoff his son Thomas with them when he came of age, and appointing his brother Balian as the boy's guardian. Then together with some of his vassals Baldwin left the kingdom to take service with Bohemond of Antioch.[51] Although Guy's power was increased by receiving the administration of Ramla and Mirabel, his prestige and his honour were damaged because of this public insult by one of his greatest vassals.

Raymond of Tripoli posed a more intractable problem. According to the *Eracles*, when Raymond refused to do homage to him, Guy, acting on the advice of Gerard of Ridefort, assembled the host and marched on Tiberias intending to disseize Raymond of Galilee by force, but this frightened Raymond into placing himself under Saladin's protection and admitting Muslim troops into Tiberias to strengthen the garrison.[52] This led Guy to withdraw his forces, because he was not prepared to go to war with Saladin while his kingdom was so divided.

The *Eracles* is so hostile to Guy that it tries to portray Raymond's

---

[50] MS, XXI, iv, III, pp. 397–400; Lyons and Jackson, *Saladin*, p. 246.
[51] Morgan, *Continuation*, cc. 20, 21, p. 35. Thomas first appears as a charter witness in 1181, which suggests that he was then about seven years old: CGOH, no. 603. According to the *Eracles*, Raymond of Tripoli advised King Guy to summon Baldwin of Ibelin back on the eve of the Hattin campaign: Morgan, *Continuation*, c. 30, p. 44; 'et post breve tempus lumen vite clausit extremum', *Brevis Historia*, ed. Belgrano, I, pp. 138–9.
[52] Morgan, *Continuation*, c. 23, pp. 36–7. Ibn al-Athir's report that Guy demanded that Raymond should account for the public money he had spent while regent is uncorroborated: RHC Or I, p. 675.

action as a legitimate defence against Guy's oppression. This opinion, though defended by Marshall Baldwin, was not shared by most of Raymond's contemporaries.[53] Arnold of Lübeck reports that Raymond swore under oath to Saladin that he would allow the sultan's army to pass through his lands if Saladin would make him king, and an almost identical statement is found in Ibn al-Athir. Kamal al-Din was shocked by the count of Tripoli's behaviour, saying that he 'had made agreements with the sultan in violation of his duties towards the Franks', while James of Vitry, writing a generation later, says bluntly that Raymond allied with Saladin because he wished to become king.[54] The plain name for Raymond's action is treason. He may not have been guilty of treason towards King Guy, to whom he had refused homage, but by allowing Saladin's troops to garrison Tiberias he was betraying his fellow Franks. He appears to have been hoping that if he helped Saladin to overthrow Guy he would be allowed to become king because he was prepared to live at peace with the sultan; an aspiration which was not compatible with Saladin's desire to lead a *jihad* that would restore the holy city of Jerusalem to Islam.

Although his kingdom was so disunited, Guy did little to increase the loyalty of those barons who had hitherto supported him. In the six years since his marriage he had built up a Poitevin retinue, and the *Eracles* relates how when he became king his supporters annoyed the native Franks by going through the streets of Jerusalem shouting:

> Maugre li Polein
> Avrons nous roi poitevin.[55]

Once he became king, Guy sought to build up a power-base for his own family in the Holy Land. One of his first acts was to arrange that Joscelin of Courtenay should make his two daughters his co-heiresses (apparently irrespective of whether Joscelin should later have a son), and that the elder should marry Guy's own brother, William of Valence, while the younger should marry one of Guy's nephews. He further stipulated that when his brother William came to the East Joscelin should immediately pay him 4,000 bezants a

---

[53] Baldwin, *Raymond III*, pp. 82–3; also 'The decline and fall of Jerusalem, 1174–1189', in Setton, *Crusades*, I, pp. 605–6.

[54] Arnold of Lübeck, IV, iii, p. 166; IA, RHC Or I, p. 675; Kamal ad-Din, ROL 4 (1896), p. 178; James of Vitry, *Libri duo, quorum prior Orientalis sive Hierosolimitana, alter Occidentalis Historiae nomine inscribuntur,* (Douai, 1597), c. 95, p. 232.

[55] Morgan, *Continuation*, c. 41, p. 53.

year and after the marriage should either continue the payment or give his son-in-law some share of his lands during his own lifetime.[56] Such acts were bound to cause resentment among the nobility of the kingdom whose own marriage prospects were thereby diminished.

The *Eracles* relates how in the winter of 1186–7 Prince Reynald attacked a caravan travelling from Cairo to Damascus through his lands in Transjordan, and how, when Saladin protested to Guy about this contravention of the truce, Reynald refused the king's demand that he should make restitution asserting that 'he was king in his lands just as Guy was in his own, and he had no truce with the Saracens'. The *Eracles* adds: 'The reason for the loss of the Kingdom of Jerusalem was the seizure of this caravan.'[57]

Although this source is very hostile to Reynald and this account contains minor errors (it wrongly claims, for example, that Saladin's sister was among the prisoners), it is substantiated by Arabic historians. Ibn al-Athir and al-Imad (cited by Abu Shama), claim that Reynald's crime was particularly serious because he had made a personal treaty with Saladin in 1186 and had received an *aman* for his territory, subjects and family. This seems unlikely to be true. Reynald lacked the temperament to seek special favours from the Muslims, and there would have been no need for him to make any private truce because he would have been included in the general truce between Saladin and the Kingdom of Jerusalem. It is possible that the sultan's advisers spread this story in order to justify the summary execution of Reynald after the battle of Hattin, for some Muslim jurists, such as al-Fadil, certainly disapproved of Reynald's execution because it was contrary to Islamic law to kill a prisoner who had surrendered.[58] It is in any case extremely unlikely that Saladin would have granted an *aman* to Reynald, whom he regarded as his chief enemy among the Franks. In 1184–5 he had commissioned the Emir Izz ad-Din Usama to build a castle at 'Ajlun in the no-man's-land of Jerash. As C.N. Johns commented, its chief purpose was 'to check Reginald of Kerak by bringing northern Trans-Jordan under the control of Damascus'.[59] Because of the truce negotiated by

[56] Strehlke, nos. 21–3, pp. 19–21.   [57] Morgan, *Continuation*, c. 22, p. 36.

[58] AS, RHC Or IV, p. 259; IA, RHC Or I, p. 676; Baha al-Din, RHC Or III, pp. 39–40, 96–7; Lyons and Jackson, *Saladin*, p. 264.

[59] C.N. Johns, 'Medieval 'Ajlun', *Quarterly of the Department of Antiquities in Palestine* 1 (1931), pp. 21–33; reprinted, and annotated by D. Pringle, in *Pilgrims' Castle ('Atlit), David's Tower (Jerusalem) and Qal'at ar-Rabad ('Ajlun). Three Middle Eastern Castles from the Time of the Crusades* (Aldershot, 1997).

Raymond of Tripoli and renewed by Guy, Reynald had no opportunity to prevent or hinder this work although it was a threat to his
lordship.

All the indications were that Saladin would not be prepared to
renew the truce when it expired during Eastertide 1187. The
submission of Mosul had left him free to concentrate on the *jihad*.
Although this had been his official objective since his seizure of
Damascus in 1174, he had devoted very little time to it, as Lyons and
Jackson point out: 'Since the autumn of 1174 he had spent some
thirteen months in fighting the Franks and thirty-three in campaigns
against his fellow Muslims.' But after his recovery from his near-fatal
illness he became personally committed to driving the Franks from
Syria.[60] It is plain from Muslim sources that he was intending to
attack the Franks during the campaign season of 1187. Lyons and
Jackson comment that he 'had at his disposal troops from Egypt,
Syria, the Euphrates and the Tigris, and for the sake of his
reputation he needed a victory against the Franks'.[61] On 13 March
1187 he moved from Damascus to Ras al-Ma', where he began to
muster troops from all over his empire for what was clearly going to
be an attack on the Frankish states.[62] Reynald's seizure of the
caravan should be seen in this context. Ibn al-Athir reports that the
caravan was accompanied by a large armed escort, and Reynald
may have supposed that Saladin was using the truce to move troops
through Frankish territory and have considered this a breach of the
truce.[63] In any case, as Lyons and Jackson justly observe, 'The
seizure of the caravan may have envenomed Saladin's relations with
Reynald, but it was obvious that even without this the Holy War was
about to be resumed.'[64]

Saladin did not himself break the truce. In mid-March 1187 he
took a detachment of troops to Bosra to deter Reynald of Châtillon
from attacking the caravan in which his sister was returning to
Damascus from making the *haj*.[65] He also wished to effect a liaison
with the Egyptian army, which was marching to join his host, and to
mount a fresh attack on Kerak as soon as the truce ended.

---

[60] Lyons and Jackson, *Saladin*, p. 239.   [61] *Ibid.*, p. 248.   [62] al-Maqrizi, pp. 81–2.
[63] RHC Or I, p. 676.   [64] Lyons and Jackson, *Saladin*, p. 248.
[65] IA, RHC Or I, pp. 677–8; AS, RHC Or IV, p. 261. The Lyons *Eracles* wrongly states that
the sultan's sister was in the caravan that Reynald captured: Morgan, *Continuation*, c. 22,
p. 36. That story grew with the telling: the Latin *Continuation* of William of Tyre relates that
Saladin's mother had been in the caravan but had evaded capture: Salloch, c. 6, pp. 58–9.

When the truce was about to end (on 5 April 1187) and it became apparent that Saladin would not renew it, King Guy sought the advice of the High Court. Those present persuaded him to seek peace with Raymond of Tripoli, and appointed as arbitrators the masters of the military Orders, Joscius, the new archbishop of Tyre who, when bishop of Acre, had shown considerable talent as a diplomat, Reynald of Sidon, and Balian of Ibelin.[66] This was the only sensible course, for the kingdom could not be defended while Saladin had free access to Galilee.

By the time the delegation left Jerusalem on 30 April, Saladin had already declared war. On 26 April he had attacked Kerak for the third time, once more capturing the *faubourg*. As he had no siege-train he posed no threat to the castle, although he did cause a good deal of damage to the surrounding countryside. He also ordered his son al-Afdal, who had remained at Ras al-Ma', to take a raiding party through Galilee to attack the lands around Acre.[67] The raid was planned for 1 May, by coincidence the day on which the mediators appointed by the High Court had agreed to meet Raymond III. Reynald of Sidon travelled to Tiberias by a separate route, Balian of Ibelin spent the night of 30 April at Nablus, but the masters of the military Orders and the archbishop of Tyre rode ahead to the Templar castle of La Fève, a few miles south of Nazareth. A very circumstantial report of the crisis is given in the anonymous *Libellus de Expugnatione Terrae Sanctae*, apparently the work of someone living in the kingdom in 1187. This relates that the watchmen of Nazareth sent word to La Fève that Muslim raiders had entered their territory and both masters resolved to resist them. Nazareth was an independent ecclesiastical lordship, not included in Raymond of Tripoli's truce with Saladin. Gerard of Ridefort and Roger des Moulins were bound to respond to this appeal because the *raison d'être* of their Orders was the defence of the Holy Places, but they had few men at their disposal: Roger des Moulins was accompanied by ten knights and Gerard of Ridefort by eighty Templar knights from the castles of La Fève and Caco. They were joined by the forty royal knights garrisoning Nazareth and in

---

[66] This meeting is dated 'pres de la Pasque': in 1187 Easter fell on 29 March: Morgan, *Continuation*, c. 24, p. 37.

[67] Although Saladin countermanded this order, his instructions were disregarded. Letters of al-Fadil, cited by Lyons and Jackson, *Saladin*, p. 249; IA, RHC Or I, pp. 678–9; AS, RHC Or, IV, p. 262.

addition were accompanied by some 300 sergeants; but the enemy numbered about 7,000 and when the small Frankish force attacked them at the springs of Cresson it was hugely outnumbered. The Franks fought bravely, but only Gerard of Ridefort and three other knights escaped from the battle alive. Among the dead was Roger des Moulins. After their victory the Muslims withdrew with their prisoners and with the heads of dead Christians on the points of their lances.[68]

The loss of men in this battle weakened the Christian army when it fought at Hattin ten weeks later. The *Eracles* sought to place the blame for this on Gerard of Ridefort, claiming that Count Raymond had sent messengers to warn the envoys of the impending Muslim invasion, but that Gerard had insisted on fighting even though Roger des Moulins protested that it would be folly to do so. This account has been widely accepted partly because Ernoul, the author of the lost chronicle, claims to have been present as a page in the service of Balian of Ibelin. While there is no reason to doubt this, Balian and his retinue did not reach La Fève until after the battle had occurred and were not eyewitnesses of the discussions that preceded it. Ernoul did not write his account until some years later, and the contemporary evidence of the *Libellus* is to be preferred.[69]

The following day the surviving envoys, accompanied by the archbishop of Nazareth, reached Tiberias and talked to Count Raymond, who agreed to expel the Muslim garrison and to do homage to the king.[70] That this change of heart was not inspired simply by remorse at what had happened is made plain by Muslim writers. Ibn al-Athir relates that Raymond's vassals both in Galilee and in Tripoli threatened to renounce their allegiance to him because of the events at Cresson, and both he and Kamal ad-Din report that Raymond was threatened with excommunication and with the annulment of his marriage unless he broke off his relations with Saladin.[71] Raymond's vassals do not seem to have objected to his refusing homage to Guy or even to his making an alliance with Saladin, but they would not stand by and see fellow Christian knights killed in their territory by Saracens. Raymond had to pay

---

[68] *De expugnatione Terrae Sanctae*, RS 66, pp. 211–17; Morgan, *Continuation*, cc. 25–6, pp. 37–40.

[69] [Balian] 'fist descendre i sien varlet qui avoit a non Ernous. Ce fu cil qui cest conte fist metre en escript', Ernoul, p. 149. See above, pp. 7–9.

[70] Morgan, *Continuation*, c. 28, pp. 41–2; *De Expugnatione*, p. 217.

[71] IA, RHC Or I, p. 680; Kamal ad-Din, ROL 4 (1896), p. 178.

special attention to the views of the Knights of St John and the Knights Templar because they had a very important role in the defence of his county of Tripoli.

Yet although the defeat at Cresson had led to the unification of the kingdom at a speed which would not perhaps otherwise have been possible, it had nevertheless weakened Frankish fighting capacity at a critical time. Gerard of Ridefort wrote to inform Pope Urban III of the disaster, and he relayed this news to England in his bull *Dum attendimus* of 3 September 1187, but by that time the kingdom had been lost.[72]

Saladin remained in Transjordan where he ravaged the lands around Montréal and met up with the Egyptian army at al-Karietin, and it was not until 27 May that he rejoined his main army at Ashtara.[73] There he was joined by Taqi ad-Din with the army of Aleppo and additional contingents from Mesopotamia. Before he left for the south Taqi ad-Din had made a truce with Bohemond III, but even so Bohemond was only able to send fifty knights to help King Guy. This was because the Turkmen war, which had been escalating and spreading west since its inception in 1185, reached Antioch in 1187.[74] The Turkmen attacked Latakia, ravaged the plain of Antioch, and even pillaged the monasteries of the Black Mountain before they were routed and stripped of most of their plunder by Bohemond III's troops.[75]

The Frankish host, as was customary, mustered at Saffuriya. Gerard of Ridefort had released the money deposited with his Order by Henry II of England to meet the costs of his projected crusade and this had been used to hire mercenaries.[76] All the king's vassals were present, and castles and cities throughout the realm were stripped of all but token garrisons. Even so, Saladin's forces outnumbered those of Guy by at least a third.[77]

It is not necessary to describe the campaign of Hattin again since the strategy has been admirably treated from the Frankish side by

---

[72] Gerald of Wales preserves the text, but wrongly ascribes it to 1186, *Liber de Principis Instructione*, Dist. II, c. 23, RS 21(VIII), pp. 201–2.

[73] AS, RHC Or IV, p. 261; Baha al-Din, RHC Or III, pp. 91–2.

[74] Kamal ad-Din, ROL 4 (1896), p. 177; AS, RHC Or IV, p. 261; Morgan, *Continuation*, c. 28, p. 42.

[75] Robert of Auxerre, *Chronicon*, ed. O. Holder-Egger, MGH SS, XXVI, p. 251.

[76] Morgan, *Continuation*, c. 29, p. 43.   [77] Lyons and Jackson, *Saladin*, pp. 251–2.

Kedar and from the Muslim side by Lyons and Jackson.[78] When Saladin invaded Galilee the Frankish high command was divided about what strategy to adopt; Raymond of Tripoli advised the king not to fight a pitched battle, whereas Gerard of Ridefort urged him to do so.[79] The final decision rested with Guy of Lusignan, and R.C. Smail rightly drew attention to the difficult position in which he was placed. In 1183, on the only other occasion when he had been in supreme command, he had been widely criticised for allowing Saladin to range freely through Galilee while he kept the host in camp at La Tubanie. He was therefore under considerable moral pressure to fight in 1187, even though he might have been more successful had he repeated the 1183 strategy.[80] He led his army to a crushing defeat at Hattin on 4 July 1187. Lyons and Jackson have argued that Guy's strategy was not ill conceived even though it proved a failure, but the divisions in the Frankish high command, coupled with Guy's lack of experience, cannot have helped the Frankish cause.[81]

Saladin's victory at Hattin enabled him to conquer almost all the Frankish East. Stripped of their garrisons, few of the Frankish cities and fortresses were able to resist the sultan's armies and within a few months only Tyre, Tripoli, Antioch and a few castles remained in Christian hands. The leaders who had dominated the political life of the kingdom during the leper king's reign met various fates. Prince Reynald, who was captured at Hattin, had the doubtful distinction of being executed by Saladin himself after having, in accordance with Islamic law, been offered his life if he would embrace the Muslim faith. This he scorned to do and he came to be regarded as a Christian martyr in Angevin circles, with some justice since he represented traditional crusading values.[82] It is a striking testimony to the spirit of dedication to the Holy War with which he had inspired his men, that the garrison of Kerak did not surrender for

---

[78] B.Z. Kedar, 'The battle of Hattin revisited', in HH, pp. 190–207; Lyons and Jackson, *Saladin*, pp. 255–66.

[79] Morgan, *Continuation*, cc. 30–2, 34, pp. 43–5, 46–7. H.-E. Mayer has pointed out that Gerard needed to justify spending Henry II's money: 'Henry II of England and the Holy Land', EHR 97 (1982), pp. 735–7.

[80] R.C. Smail, 'The predicaments of Guy of Lusignan', in *Outremer*, pp. 159–76.

[81] Lyons and Jackson, *Saladin*, p. 258.

[82] B. Hamilton, 'The elephant of Christ: Reynald of Châtillon', SCH 15 (1978), pp. 97–108 at p. 107 and n. 75 (listing sources); Peter of Blois, *Passio Reginaldis Principis Antiocheni*, P.L. 207, cols. 957–76; M. Markowski, 'Peter of Blois and the conception of the Third Crusade', in HH, pp. 261–9.

more than a year after the battle of Hattin, while the castle of Montréal held out until April/May 1189. In both cases it was obvious from the start that no relief force could reach the Frankish garrisons.[83] Reynald of Châtillon was the only prisoner of note to be killed after Hattin, although the sultan bought all the surviving members of the military Orders from their captors in order to indulge in a barbaric custom whereby men of piety, unskilled in the use of weapons, were allowed to try their hand at executing the prisoners. This spectacle, we are told, made Saladin smile.[84] The only exception was Gerard of Ridefort, the master of the Temple, who like all the other important prisoners was subsequently released in return for a ransom.[85]

Raymond of Tripoli, Reynald of Sidon and Balian of Ibelin fought their way through Saladin's lines at Hattin. Lyons and Jackson argue that they were not deserting the king, but were trying to obey his orders and break the Muslim encirclement, but that they lost most of their men in the attempt and were too weak to force their way back in order to rejoin the king.[86] Count Raymond went to Tripoli where he fell ill and died in September 1187, pursued to the grave by his evil reputation as a traitor.[87]

Guy of Lusignan, who had been taken prisoner at Hattin, was released by Saladin in 1188. He rallied most of the Frankish fighting men who were still at liberty and led them to besiege Acre, where his courage and pertinacity laid the foundation for the limited success of the Third Crusade. The siege lasted for two years and many Frankish leaders died in the course of it, including Queen Sibyl and her children and the Patriarch Heraclius, who were victims of an epidemic, and Gerard of Ridefort, who was killed in the fighting.[88]

When the news of Hattin reached the West a new crusade was preached, but there were considerable delays before it could set out. The great German army, led by the seventy-year-old Emperor Frederick Barbarossa, followed the land route, but disbanded after he died in Cilicia in 1190, and only a small part of the force went on

---

[83] Baha al-Din, RHC Or III, pp. 119 and 122.   [84] AS, RHC Or IV, pp. 277–8.

[85] Morgan, *Continuation*, c. 49, p. 62.   [86] Lyons and Jackson, *Saladin*, pp. 262–3.

[87] Baldwin, *Raymond III*, p. 138, n. 16; Robert of Auxerre, *Chronicon*, MGH SS, XXVI, pp. 250–1; *Anonymi . . . Chronicon . . . 1234*, c. 483, p. 149; Roger of Howden, *Chronica*, RS 51(II), p. 322.

[88] Roger of Howden, *Gesta Henrici*, pp. 94 (death of Gerard of Ridefort) and 147 (victims of the epidemic). Sibyl and Guy had had four daughters, *Itinerarium Peregrinorum*, ed. H.-E. Mayer, MGH Schriften 18 (Stuttgart, 1962) p. 336.

to Acre. The combined armies of Richard I of England and Philip II of France finally reached Acre by sea in 1191, and the city was soon captured. But Philip returned to the West later that summer, and although Richard I remained in the Holy Land for more than a year the result was a stalemate, since neither he nor Saladin could decisively defeat the other's army. In September 1192 peace was made between them, under the terms of which a strip of coastal territory extending from Jaffa to Tyre, together with most of the county of Tripoli and part of the principality of Antioch, were secured to the Franks.[89]

As a result of Sibyl's death and that of her children, Guy was adjudged to have forfeited the kingship, but Richard I, who had a sense of loyalty to his Lusignan vassals, secured for him the lordship of Cyprus, which he had annexed on his way to the Holy Land. Guy proved a competent ruler there, and when he died in 1194 was succeeded by his brother, Aimery the Constable, from whom the Lusignan kings of Cyprus were descended.[90] Baldwin the Leper's younger sister Isabel was recognised as queen of the reconstituted Kingdom of Jerusalem in exile. Her marriage to Humphrey of Toron had been annulled in 1190 and she was married three more times before her death in 1205.[91] Among the survivors of the First Kingdom were Reynald, lord of Sidon, Balian of Ibelin, and perhaps Joscelin of Courtenay, although the date of his death is disputed.[92] Bohemond III continued to rule what remained of the principality of Antioch until his death in 1201, and his son Bohemond took over the county of Tripoli after Raymond III's death.[93] But the longest surviving member of the ruling class from the leper king's reign was

---

[89] S. Painter, 'The Third Crusade: Richard the Lionhearted and Philip Augustus', in Setton, *Crusades*, II, pp. 45–85.

[90] P.W. Edbury, *The Kingdom of Cyprus and the Crusades 1191–1374* (Cambridge, 1991), pp. 23–9.

[91] B. Hamilton, 'King consorts of Jerusalem and their entourages', in H.-E. Mayer (ed.), *Die Kreuzfahrerstaaten als multikulturelle Gesellschaft. Einwandere und Minderheiten im 12 und 13 Jahrhundert*, Schriften des Historischen Kollegs, Kolloquien 37 (Munich, 1997), pp. 14–18.

[92] Balian of Ibelin lived until c. 1193, RRH, no. 716, I, p. 191; Reynald of Sidon was still alive in 1200: *ibid.*, no. 776, I, p. 207; the date of Joscelin's death is uncertain: R.L. Nicholson places it in 1199–1200, *Joscelin III of Edessa and the Fall of the Crusader States (1134–1199)* (Leiden, 1973) pp. 195–8; Edbury argues that Joscelin should be identified with the *comes Iocelinus* whose death is recorded at the siege of Acre in the *Itinerarium Peregrinorum*, ed. Mayer, p. 317: P.W. Edbury, 'The "Cartulaire de Manosque": a grant to the Templars in Latin Syria and a charter of King Hugh I of Cyprus', *Bulletin of the Institute of Historical Research* 51 (1978), p. 176.

[93] J. Richard, *Le Comté de Tripoli sous la dynastie toulousaine (1102–87)* (Paris, 1945), p. 8; C. Cahen, *La Syrie du nord à l'époque des croisades et la principauté franque d'Antioche* (Paris, 1940), pp. 579–95.

Figure 8 An illustration to the Lamentations of Jeremiah, interpreted as a prophecy of Saladin's conquest of Jerusalem.

his stepmother, Maria Comnena, who died in 1217 when her great-granddaughter, Isabel II, was queen of Jerusalem.[94]

The new kingdom, brought into being by the peace of 1192 and sometimes known as the Kingdom of Acre, was very different from that over which the leper king had ruled. It was a kingdom without Jerusalem, the goal to which the entire crusading movement had been directed, the holiest city in the Christian world. That kingdom effectively ended when after the battle of Hattin the Holy Cross was derisively carried into Damascus, in Saladin's triumph, lashed upside down to a Saracen lance.[95]

[94] B. Hamilton, 'Women in the Crusader States: the queens of Jerusalem', in D. Baker (ed.), *Medieval Women* (Oxford, 1978), pp. 161–74 at p. 173.

[95] Lyons and Jackson, *Saladin*, p. 265.

Epilogue

The defeat of Hattin and the loss of the kingdom have cast a shadow on the reign of Baldwin IV in the minds of historians ever since Ernoul wrote his *Chronicle*. Attention has focused on those aspects of the reign which contained the seeds of future Frankish weakness and aided Saladin's victory. It is important to remember that this is not a view which people living at the time would have shared. The leper king's subjects recognised that they faced great dangers, but they did not expect to be defeated, and, indeed, while Baldwin lived they were not. Under his leadership they frustrated for some six years Saladin's plans to take over Nur ad-Din's empire and encircle the Crusader States; while Saladin's direct attacks on Frankish territory were for the most part ineffective. He suffered a disastrous defeat at Mont Gisard in 1177, and a decisive defeat at Le Forbelet in 1182; his newly formed navy did not cause the Franks any serious problems, and when he tried to capture Beirut by a joint land and sea operation he was driven off. He twice failed to capture the fortress of Kerak even though he brought huge forces against it. His victories in the forest of Banias and at Marj Uyun in 1179 were fortuitous and for that reason were not followed through. Indeed, the only important successes that he achieved against the Franks in Baldwin IV's reign were his capture and demolition of Le Chastellet in 1179, and the destruction of Prince Reynald's fleet in 1182, and neither of these victories led to any loss of Frankish territory.

The society of the Latin East in Baldwin's reign showed no symptoms of decline. On the contrary, it appeared vigorous and self-confident. The Franks themselves would have considered the devout practice of the Christian faith the most reliable index of a flourishing society. Despite the strictures of the *Chronicle* of Ernoul, which was written after the loss of the kingdom and sought to account for the withdrawal of divine support from the Christians, the Catholic

235

Figure 9 A Nazareth capital, showing two apostles.

Church in the Crusader States was in a sound spiritual condition in the years before 1187.[1] The Franks were assiduous in the care of the Holy Places, which they considered their primary duty, and the eightfold Divine Office according to the Latin rite was sung each day in all the shrines of the kingdom. This achievement, while in part supported by donations from all over the Christian West, was chiefly made possible by the generosity with which the Frankish population of the Crusader Kingdom contributed to the service of God.[2]

Throughout Baldwin IV's reign, work was undertaken to restore the cathedral church of the Annunciation at Nazareth, damaged by an earthquake in 1170. This restoration was still in progress at the time of Saladin's conquest in 1187, and a set of sculptured capitals, which had not been put in place, were buried, and have therefore been preserved in almost mint condition as one of the chief glories of the art of the Crusader Kingdom.[3] At the same time the chapel of the *Cenaculum* (the Upper Room in which Christ was believed to have celebrated the Last Supper) in the Church of Mount Sion at Jerusalem, administered by Austin Canons, was rebuilt in graceful early Gothic style. That work had been completed by 1185.[4]

Frankish piety also found expression in an impressive range of good works, of which the most notable were the activities of the Hospital of St John in Jerusalem. The statutes drawn up in 1182 for the administration of the Hospital during the mastership of Roger des Moulins are a model of Christian concern for the sick and destitute, and the spirit that informs them is encapsulated in the precept that the brethren are to serve the sick poor 'with zeal and devotion as if they were their lords'.[5] St Nerses of Lampron, Armenian archbishop of Tarsus, writing in 1177, has this to say of his Catholic neighbours in the Crusader States: 'We cannot compete at all with their piety, their charitable works, their zealous regard for canon law, the regularity with which they publicly celebrate the

---

[1] See p. 47, above.
[2] B. Hamilton, 'Rebuilding Zion: the Holy Places of Jerusalem in the twelfth century', SCH 14 (1977), pp. 105–16.
[3] J. Folda, *The Nazareth Capitals and the Crusader Shrine of the Annunciation* (University Park, Pa., and London, 1986); J. Folda, *The Art of the Crusaders in the Holy Land, 1098–1187* (Cambridge, 1995), pp. 414–41.
[4] Folda, *Art of the Crusaders*, pp. 469–71.
[5] CGOH, no. 627, I, pp. 425–9. The need for caution in interpreting these Rules is stressed by A. Luttrell, 'The Hospitallers' medical tradition: 1291–1530', in Barber (ed.), *The Military Orders*. I. *Fighting for the Faith and Caring for the Sick* (Aldershot, 1994), pp. 64–81 at pp. 64–7.

Divine Office.' This evidence cannot lightly be set aside, since it comes from a writer who was by no means uncritical of the Catholic clergy in other ways.[6]

A twentieth-century observer would tend to judge the health of a society less by its religious vigour than by its economic vitality. In this regard also the Latin East was in a flourishing condition. Under Frankish rule the ports of the Syrian coast had developed into important commercial centres. The fleets of the great Italian maritime powers came there each year to trade with the Franks and with the Muslim hinterland of Aleppo and Damascus.[7] It is also possible that commerce in the Frankish East benefited towards the end of Baldwin IV's reign from the dislocation of Italian trade with the Byzantine Empire, which resulted from the massacre of the Latins in Constantinople in 1182, for the loss of access to the luxury trade of the East through Constantinople would have made their trading relations with the Crusader States more important to the Italian maritime cities. As Ibn Jubayr bore witness, war did not disrupt trade between the Italians working out of the Syrian ports and merchants from Saladin's empire.[8]

As the pressure from Saladin increased, the Franks responded in a number of positive ways. The defence tax of 1183 is a pragmatic example of this, but they also seem to have become aware for the first time of the need to create a sense of solidarity between themselves and their eastern Christian subjects. The lead in this was taken by the Latin patriarch of Antioch, Aimery of Limoges, who in c.1182 negotiated the agreement whereby the Maronite Church entered into full communion with the Roman See.[9] Aimery also cultivated good relations with the patriarch of the Syrian Orthodox (or Jacobite) Church, the learned Syriac historian Michael III. Michael visited Jerusalem in 1178 and was received by Baldwin IV who confirmed the rights of the Syrian Orthodox Church in the

---

[6] 'Our secular clergy have learned from them [Frankish clergy] intemperate eating habits and the impure excesses of sexual incontinence': St Nerses of Lampron, *Reflections on the Institutions of the Church and Explanation of the Eucharistic Mystery*, extracts ed. with French tr., RHC Arm I, pp. 569–603 at pp. 574–5.

[7] E. Ashtor, 'Il regno dei crociati e il commercio di Levante', in G. Airaldi and B.Z. Kedar, *I comuni italiani nel regno crociato di Gerusalemme* (Genoa, 1986), pp. 15–56.

[8] Ibn Jubayr, p. 317.

[9] B. Hamilton, 'Aimery of Limoges, patriarch of Antioch: ecumenist, scholar and patron of hermits', in E.R. Elder (ed.), *The Joy of Learning and the Love of God. Essays in Honour of Jean Leclercq* (Kalamazoo, Mich., 1995), pp. 269–90 at pp. 281–2.

kingdom.[10] Although no formal union was effected between the two Churches at this time, Michael III's goodwill towards the Franks was unfeigned and lasted until his death, despite the Frankish defeat at Hattin, and it was reciprocated by the Franks, for neither Aimery of Antioch nor Heraclius of Jerusalem would recognise Theodore bar-Wahboun, who set himself up as rival patriarch to Michael, even though he offered to unite his followers with the western Church in return for their support.[11]

In 1184, the catholicus of Armenia, Gregory IV, sent one of his bishops to Pope Lucius III with a profession of faith. This was certainly understood by the pope as evidence of a desire to enter into full communion with the Latin Church, and he sent the catholicus a pallium, thereby acknowledging Gregory as a properly accredited Catholic metropolitan, together with a copy of the *Rituale Romanum* which St Nerses of Lampron translated into Armenian. Although it is doubtful whether the pope and the catholicus understood Catholic unity in the same sense, it is certain that the Armenians thought it desirable to establish closer links with the Western Church.[12] In this case the initiative may have come from Rupen III of Cilicia, who had a Catholic wife, Isabel of Toron.

The extent of Baldwin's own contribution to the achievements of his reign is difficult to determine. He was certainly responsible for choosing the Courtenays and Prince Reynald as his chief advisers rather than Raymond of Tripoli, and this must mean that he shared their views about the importance of curbing the growth of Saladin's power and the inadvisability of trying to live at peace with him. Baldwin almost certainly did not plan singlehandedly the strategies of the campaigns which were fought in his name, or the diplomacy which was designed to support them; the influential men in military affairs were Humphrey of Toron, Prince Reynald and the masters of the military Orders. It is not known how far Baldwin was responsible for decisions about domestic policies. He seems to have delegated Church patronage very largely to his mother, while Joscelin of Courtenay was responsible for the royal finances, but other matters

---

[10] MS, XX, viii, III, p. 379.

[11] B. Hamilton, *The Latin Church in the Crusader States. The Secular Church* (London, 1980), pp. 197–8.

[12] B. Hamilton, 'The Armenian Church and the papacy at the time of the crusades', *Eastern Churches Review*, 10 (1978), pp. 61–87 at p. 69.

seem to have been resolved by the king on the advice of the High Court.

Baldwin's importance to the kingdom lay in his willingness to remain at its head throughout his life. In his early years, as his illness became more serious, he hoped to be able to retire from public life. When William of Montferrat reached Jerusalem in 1176 Baldwin offered to abdicate, but William's unexpected death left Baldwin as head of state. When negotiating with the king of France about a new husband for Sibyl in 1178–9 Baldwin again expressed his desire to abdicate, but because Hugh of Burgundy did not come to the East he was unable to do so. In 1180 he made a wrong decision by arranging the marriage of the heiress to the throne to Guy of Lusignan without ascertaining whether that marriage commanded general support. The circumstances in which he made this decision were not of his own making; nevertheless, the decision was mistaken. The consequence was that Baldwin had to remain king, even though his health made this an almost intolerable burden. William of Tyre tells us that he was urged to abdicate at that time, but he refused to plead illness in order to evade his responsibilities, because he hoped that in time the chief men in the kingdom would come to accept Guy.[13] But when the combination of illness and state security forced the king to appoint Guy as regent in 1183, Guy's failure to command respect made it necessary for Baldwin to resume power. He then associated his young nephew, Baldwin V, in the kingship and sought to find a western prince who would act as regent for him. In this he was not successful, and he died in office.

Because of his illness Baldwin must have found his royal duties very burdensome; even if his civil functions were chiefly ceremonial and the main business of state was discharged by his ministers, he had to preside at meetings of the High Court, give audience to foreign envoys, receive the homage of vassals and carry out all the normal public duties of a king. This must have been troublesome even in his early years when his leprosy first became apparent, but towards the end of his reign, when he could no longer see, or walk unsupported, or use his fingers, such state occasions must have been intolerable.

Baldwin initially enjoyed his role as battle leader, but by the time he rode on his last long-distance razzias in 1182, when the disease

---

[13] WT, XXII, 26, p. 1049.

had attacked his hands and feet, he must have found the experience anything but pleasurable. When finally he had to be carried into battle in a litter slung between two horses, unable even to see what was occurring around him, as happened when he went to the relief of Kerak in 1183 and again in 1184, only sheer willpower can have enabled him to stay the course.[14]

It would appear that Baldwin judged rightly that there was nobody except himself who could hold the kingdom together unless some powerful western ruler would come and take on the task. For although William of Tyre tells us often how popular Raymond of Tripoli was, on both occasions when he tried to seize power he failed to command enough support. Nobody refused to serve Baldwin IV, who was the anointed king, and despite the divisions among the baronage, unity was preserved as long as he lived. As the events in the two years following his death show, no one else was capable of holding in check the divisions among the Franks which did so much to facilitate Saladin's victory in 1187.

Baldwin's subjects accepted his illness and did not fear it, even though leprosy was then thought to be highly contagious, which is why lepers were normally segregated. The Muslim scholar Imad al-Din was surprised by this:

In spite of [Baldwin's] illness the Franks were loyal to him, they gave him every encouragement . . . being satisfied to have him as their ruler; they exalted him . . . they were anxious to keep him in office, but they paid no attention to his leprosy.[15]

Christian opinion in the twelfth century was divided about the theological significance of leprosy, chiefly because the Old Testament contains conflicting evidence on this subject. In some cases leprosy is said to be a punishment sent by God for sin: the leprosy of Moses's sister Miriam, of Elisha's servant Gehazi and of King Azariah are examples of this.[16] On the other hand Isaiah's description of the Suffering Servant, universally accepted in the Middle Ages as a prophecy of Christ's Passion, placed leprosy in a quite different context. This passage is familiar to English readers in the Authorised Version of 1611:

---

[14] B. Hamilton, 'Baldwin the leper as war leader', in A.V. Murray (ed.), *From Clermont to Jerusalem. The Crusades and Crusader Society 1095–1500* (Turnhout, 1998), pp. 119–30.

[15] Imad ad-Din al-Isfahani, *La conquête de la Syrie et de la Palestine par Saladin*, tr. H. Massé, DRHC 10 (Paris, 1972), p. 18.

[16] Numbers, 12, vv. 1–5; 2 Kings, 5, vv. 21–7; 2 Kings, 15, vv. 1–5.

He is despised and rejected of men; a man of sorrows and acquainted with grief; and we hid as it were our faces from him; he was despised, and we esteemed him not. Surely he hath borne our griefs and carried our sorrows: yet we did esteem him stricken, smitten of God and afflicted.

The Vulgate text reads:

Despectum et novissimum virorum, virum dolorum et scientem infirmitatem, et quasi absconditus vultus eius et despectus, unde nec reputavimus eum. Vere languores nostros ipse tulit et dolores nostros ipse portavit, et nos putavimus eum *quasi leprum* et percussum a Deo et humiliatum.[17]

This prophecy encouraged men to see Christ in those suffering from leprosy, just as they could see Him in the poor. It was this perception that led healthy men to devote their lives to the service of lepers in the Order of St Lazarus and in leper houses, and such attitudes were quite widespread. As Nicole Bériou and François-Olivier Touati have shown, there developed in the Latin Church during the twelfth century a school of thought which considered that leprosy, if accepted in the right spirit, could be the occasion of a vocation to the religious life, and that the leper house might then become a quasi-monastic institution.[18]

Although Pope Alexander III described Baldwin IV as stricken with leprosy by the just judgment of God, Baldwin's subjects did not share this view.[19] One reason for this may have been that he remained chaste.[20] It was widely believed by learned physicians as well as by the general public that lepers were extremely lecherous. Indeed, this became a literary *topos*.[21] Moreover, when kings or great noblemen lived chastely this was regarded by their contemporaries as a sign of supernatural grace. That Baldwin, who was both a leper and a king, remained chaste, must therefore have been seen as evidence of unusual sanctity of life. Even more persuasive was Baldwin's success in war against the Saracens. The participants in

[17] Isaiah, 53, vv. 3–4 (emphasis added).
[18] N. Bériou and F.-O. Touati, *Voluntate Dei Leprosus. Les lépreux entre conversion et exclusion au XIIème et XIIIème siècles*, Testi, Studi, Strumenti 4, Centro Italiano sull'alto medioevo (Spoleto, 1991).
[19] 'He lived among them for some ten years. He commanded obedience as their king, and he was cherished by them since he was concerned to keep peace between them': Imad ad-Din, *La conquête de la Syrie*, pp. 18–19.
[20] '. . . celibem agens vitam, in castitate perseverans, virgo in evum permansit': Arnold of Lübeck, *Chronica Slavorum* ed. I.M. Lappenberg, IV, 2, MGH SS, XXI, (Hanover, 1869), p. 164.
[21] E.g. In Beroul's *Romance of Tristan* King Mark hands Yseut over to a band of lepers as punishment for her supposed adultery, tr. A.S. Frederick (Harmondsworth, 1970), pp. 73–5; S.N. Brody, *The Disease of the Soul. Leprosy in Medieval Literature* (Ithaca, 1974), pp. 52–5.

the First Crusade had been convinced that they were fulfilling God's will, and the failure of subsequent crusades was attributed to the sin of those who took part, which incurred God's displeasure. It therefore followed that Baldwin's success against Saladin was a sign that he enjoyed God's favour. Indeed, long after his death he was remembered as the last successful Christian defender of the Holy City of Jerusalem. John of Joinville, who completed his *Life of St Louis* in 1309, relates how when Louis IX was staying at Acre in 1252 after his catastrophic defeat in Egypt, he sent his armourer to Damascus during a truce to buy materials for making crossbows. The armourer fell into conversation in the *suq* with an old man who told him:

I have seen a time when King Baldwin of Jerusalem, the one who was a leper, beat Saladin although he only had 300 armed men against Saladin's 3,000. But now your sins have brought you to such a pass that we round you up in the fields like cattle.[22]

Yet although in many ways Baldwin was a Christ-like figure, suffering in the service of God and the defence of the Holy Land, he did not conform to the conventional twelfth-century picture of a royal saint. Edward the Confessor, for example, canonised in Baldwin's lifetime, was revered because of his monastic way of life. Baldwin, on the contrary, although he stated his desire to abdicate, never showed any desire to enter the cloister. There is no evidence that he was particularly devout. Indeed, apart from his foundation of the abbey of St Catherine's *in campo belli* as thanksgiving for his victory at Mont Gisard, he was not a generous benefactor of the Church.

Baldwin was by training and temperament a knight, whose primary vocation was to lead his army in battle and to fight in defence of the Holy Places. The most distinctive character traits that he displayed, according to the reports of eye-witnesses, were knightly ones: great physical courage and a highly developed sense of honour. His courage is shown in his willingness to ride into battle even though he was unable to remount if he were unhorsed. His sense of honour is seen in his refusal for two years to be reconciled with Raymond of Tripoli after he had rebelled against him, and in his refusal ever to be reconciled with Guy of Lusignan after he had denied him service.

---

[22] John of Joinville, *Histoire de Saint Louis*, c. 466, p. 159, cited in the translation of R. Hague, *The Life of St Louis* (London, 1955), p. 137; on sin as the reason for the failure of crusades, see E. Siberry, *Criticism of Crusading 1095–1274* (Oxford, 1985).

What most commands our admiration is Baldwin's strength of will, which enabled him to discharge his royal duties despite the severity of his illness. His contemporaries admired him for that too, but they admired him even more because, despite his disabilities, he was a successful ruler. When he died Sicard of Cremona wrote this encomium:

Although he suffered from leprosy from childhood, yet he strenuously preserved the frontiers of the Kingdom of Jerusalem and won a remarkable victory over Saladin at Mont Gisard, and as long as he lived he was victorious.[23]

---

[23] Sicard of Cremona, *Chronicon*, P.L., 213, col. 512.

An evaluation of the leprosy of King Baldwin IV of Jerusalem in the context of the medieval world

Piers D. Mitchell

INTRODUCTION

Baldwin IV was perhaps one of the more remarkable kings in the medieval Christian world. He is not remembered for great military campaigns, despite the fact that he beat the infamous Saladin on the battlefield on several occasions.[1] Nor is his name associated with a long and illustrious reign as he died at a young age. He is renowned because he developed leprosy. Perhaps more to the point, he developed leprosy and still maintained his position on the throne, becoming a successful ruler. Many kings over the ages have suffered with disease and continued to rule. Hardly any have managed to do so if their illness was leprosy.[2] It was so feared in the medieval world and associated so closely with severe social consequences that to overcome these obstacles was an incredible feat.

There were a number of reasons why developing leprosy was seen as such a disaster in the medieval period. First, it can be a disfiguring disease leading to ulceration and deformity of the face, hands, feet and skin elsewhere. Disfigurement and disability have always had powerful effects on how a person is viewed by others. This may be related to fear of developing the same disease after contact with the sick person or the guilt from being healthier or luckier than them. While it is difficult to tell exactly how many people had leprosy at this time, it may well have been the most common disease to cause such major disfigurement. Secondly, there were strong religious

---

[1] B. Hamilton, 'Baldwin the leper as war leader', in A.V. Murray (ed.), *From Clermont to Jerusalem: The Crusades and Crusader Society, 1095–1500* (Turnhout, 1998), pp. 119–30.

[2] J.G. Andersen, 'Studies in the medieval diagnosis of leprosy in Denmark', *Danish Medical Bulletin* 16 (suppl.) (1969), pp. 1–142.

overtones attached to the disease.[3] This is thought to have originated from a poor translation of the Hebrew word *Tsar'ath*, used in biblical texts to refer to any disfiguring skin disease. As disease in the biblical period was often thought to be punishment for the sins of the patient or his ancestors, those with skin lesions were forbidden entry to the synagogue and were ostracised from the community. Ironically, leprosy may not even have been present in the eastern Mediterranean at the time of these Old Testament records, and it is believed that the diseases described would have been other conditions. Unfortunately, medieval translators of older medical texts did not always choose the most appropriate word when translating Arabic, Hebrew or Greek texts into Latin. Constantinus Africanus (c. 1018 AD) produced a version of a book by al-Majusi and entitled it *Liber Pantegni*. In it he used the word *lepra* for the Arabic word *judhām*, which was a description of true leprosy. However, *lepra* was a word used in the Hippocratic Corpus of classical times for a non-specific skin lesion and in translations of the Old Testament for the Hebrew *Tsar'ath*. Consequently, those countries that used Latin as the major written language (most of Europe) were given the impression that, as stated in the Bible, people with leprosy should be excluded from society. For the same reasons there were strong religious overtones of impurity and sin associated with the disease and many thought the disease was spread by sexual activity.[4]

Despite his fame, it is only in recent years that assessment of Baldwin's disease has advanced beyond merely listing his symptoms. This is partly because most authors have come from a historical background rather than a medical one. Recent advances in the understanding of leprosy have also allowed a greater insight into his case.[5] The clear and detailed description of the symptoms he developed and the age they occurred enables an assessment of the progression of his disease. We can determine the subtypes of leprosy he had at different ages, estimate how his symptoms would have

---

[3] E.V. Hulse, 'The nature of biblical "leprosy" and the use of alternative medical terms in modern translations of the Bible', *Palestine Exploration Quarterly* 107 (1975), pp. 87–105.

[4] E. Campbell and J. Colton (ed. and tr.), *The Surgery of Theodorich ca. AD 1267*. 2 vols. (New York, 1955–60), I, p. 17 and II, pp. 167–73; M.E. Duncan, 'Leprosy and procreation – a historical review of social and clinical aspects', *Leprosy Review* 56 (1985), pp. 153–62.

[5] P.D. Mitchell, 'Leprosy and the case of King Baldwin IV of Jerusalem: mycobacterial disease in the Crusader States of the 12th and 13th centuries', *International Journal of Leprosy and Other Mycobacterial Diseases* 61(2) (1993), pp. 283–91.

affected him and explain how the disease caused the damage it did to his body.

THE BASICS OF LEPROSY

Leprosy is often poorly understood by those historians and archaeologists who do not come from areas of the world where the disease is prevalent today. A brief summary should enable those less familiar with its effects to see Baldwin's symptoms in a clearer light.

It is caused by a bacterium known as *Mycobacterium leprae*.[6] In modern times it is found in the tropics and subtropics but in the past the disease has been a problem in all areas from the arctic to antarctic circles. It is thought to be spread mainly through the air in droplets of water but may also be contracted via direct contact with bacteria in ulcerous skin. Contrary to popular belief, it is difficult to transmit from person to person and usually close contact is required for months or years before the disease is passed from one person to another. In consequence of this low infectivity it often runs in families as they have plenty of close contact with one another. Of the various forms of the disease lepromatous leprosy is relatively more infectious than tuberculoid. The bacterium is so slow growing that it often takes several years of incubation time before any symptoms are noticed. Unlike most infectious diseases, few of the symptoms produced are actually caused by the growth of *M. leprae* itself. It lives within the cells of the body and fails to produce significant amounts of any toxic substances. The major problems result from the attempts by the body to kill the bacteria. Different people react in different ways to the disease and the type of response has been shown to depend on both genetic and environmental factors.[7]

At one extreme, in tuberculoid leprosy, white blood cells attack the bacteria. This results in the destruction of most of the organisms, but unfortunately the fragments of dead bacteria may cause inflammation and damage to local tissues. This means that the nerves containing the bacteria can be damaged, leading to muscle weakness and the development of areas of skin which are without sensation or

---

[6] B. Ji and J. Grosset, 'Leprosy', in P.D. Hoeprich, M.C. Jordan and A.R. Ronald, *Infectious Diseases. A Treatise of Infectious Processes*, 5th edn (Philadelphia, 1994), pp. 1008–17; WHO, *Epidemiology of Leprosy in Relation to Control*. Technical Report Series no. 716 (Geneva, 1985).

[7] R.R.P. de Vries, W. van Eden and J.J. van Rood, 'HLA-linked control of the course of *M. leprae* infections', *Leprosy Review* 52 (Suppl. 1) (1981), pp. 109–19.

the ability to sweat. Consequently damage to the hands and feet goes unnoticed because of the loss of feeling, so wounds break down to form ulcers. Where the skin cannot sweat it becomes dry and cracks, also forming ulcers. In each case infection may develop, which can destroy the bones and deep tissues leaving a useless, deformed hand or foot. Few bacteria are present in the skin as many are killed by the white blood cells, so this subtype of leprosy is not associated with nodules and plaques in the skin, although the skin is typically discoloured. Most cases of tuberculoid leprosy heal spontaneously, but nerve damage and the consequences may persist. At the other extreme of response, lepromatous leprosy, the body attacks the bacteria with antibodies. In many infections antibodies break holes in bacterial cell walls causing them to die, but *M. leprae* are mainly found within cells of the body, hiding from these antibodies. In consequence, the mycobacteria slowly multiply to form nodules and plaques in the skin, which causes significant disfigurement. Other changes noted in the lepromatous subtype include loss of eyebrow hair, a hoarse voice and destruction of the nose. Nerve damage is a late problem, so that anaesthetic skin and ulcers occur only after a number of years. Unlike tuberculoid leprosy, lepromatous leprosy does not typically heal spontaneously, and the disease slowly leads to more progressive disfigurement and deformity. In modern times only a minority of cases are lepromatous.

Between the two extremes of tuberculoid (TT) and lepromatous leprosy (LL) are various subtypes of the disease, arbitrarily used to describe the spectrum of symptoms seen. They are determined by the degree to which the reaction to the bacteria resembles TT or LL. For example, borderline tuberculoid (BT) has less nerve damage than TT, borderline (BB) has even less, and borderline lepromatous (BL) has more characteristics of LL but not enough to be classed as true LL. A further subtype is primary polyneuritic (PP), which is associated with nerve damage (leading to anaesthetic skin and muscle weakness), but not colour change in the skin as occurs in TT and BT. Over time the situation can change, typically with downgrading towards the lepromatous end of the spectrum. It is known that physiological stresses such as puberty, pregnancy and infections can trigger downgrading. This means a person may start off with nerve involvement and areas of anaesthetic skin (BT or PP) and change to develop skin nodules and facial disfigurement (BL or LL). TT is not thought to downgrade as it is more immunologically stable.

When leprosy is first introduced into an area it is said to be epidemic. Statistics from the first half of the twentieth century, before the development of effective antibiotics that cure leprosy, showed that during the epidemic phase the disease affects around 10 to 30 per cent of the population in all age groups. When leprosy has been present in a population for many years it is said to be endemic. If someone is going to develop the disease then symptoms typically develop in childhood or as young adults, with peak age at presentation today between ten and twenty years old. Around 1 to 5 per cent of a susceptible community develop the disease once it has become endemic.

Leprosy itself and its direct complications does not cause death if developed as an adult, although the social consequences which may result from the diagnosis in the past may have shortened the lifespan of the patient. However, if lepromatous leprosy has developed in childhood, the direct complications of the disease have been shown to increase the likelihood of premature death.[8]

THE COURSE OF KING BALDWIN'S DISEASE

Baldwin was born in the early summer of 1161, the son of Amalric and Agnes of Courtenay. It was only when Amalric's brother, King Baldwin III, died in 1163 that Amalric was proclaimed king and Baldwin became heir to the throne. There is no evidence that either Amalric, Agnes or Amalric's second wife Maria Comnena had leprosy, but someone who spent plenty of time with the young prince must have had the disease as he clearly caught it from somebody. It is possible that either a member of his family, a wet nurse or other staff from the royal household had the disease with mild or easily concealed symptoms and that the disease spread from them. Whatever the source, the disease was contracted by Baldwin at a young age. William of Tyre was tutor to Prince Baldwin from the age of nine to thirteen and he gives a vivid description of the symptoms in his *Chronicle*.[9] He tells us:

he was playing one day with his companions of noble rank when they began, as playful boys often do, to pinch each other's arms and hands with

---

[8] D.G. Smith and R.S. Guinto, 'The association between age of onset and mortality in lepromatous leprosy', *International Journal of Leprosy* 46 (1978), pp. 25–9.
[9] William of Tyre, *A History of Deeds done beyond the Sea*, ed. and tr. E.A. Babcock and A.C. Krey, 2 vols. (New York, 1943), II, pp. 398, 417 and 492.

their nails. The other boys often gave evidence of pain by their outcries, but Baldwin, although his comrades did not spare him, endured it all to patiently, as if he felt nothing. After this had occurred several times it was reported to me. At first I supposed that it proceeded from his capacity for endurance and not from lack of sensitivity. But when I called him and began to enquire what it meant I discovered that his right arm and hand were partially numb, so that he did not feel pinching or even biting in the least. I began to be uneasy, remembering the words of the wise man, 'There is no question that a member which is without feeling detracts greatly from the health of the body and one who does not realise that he is sick is in great danger.'

Clearly the first symptom is anaesthetic skin in his arm. There is no mention of skin discolouration or nodules, destruction of the nose, hoarse voice, loss of eyebrow hair or other signs of lepromatous leprosy. The subtypes of leprosy that present in this way are PP, TT and BT. With PP there are no visible skin lesions, just nerve involvement, but TT and BT are associated with raised plaques and patches of discoloured skin. As no such skin lesions were mentioned in William of Tyre's very detailed description, PP appears to be the most likely form that Baldwin developed initially. TT or BT are possible alternatives if it is argued that William may not have thought it necessary to mention all of Baldwin's symptoms at that time.

At this point the court was mobilised into action. It seems likely that in the early years of his disease Baldwin was not actually diagnosed as having leprosy.[10] While all the medical texts of the period mention loss of sensation among the symptoms of leprosy, we do not know how many of these symptoms a person was required to have before a diagnosis of leprosy could be made. A misdiagnosis of the disease would have been unforgivable due to the dire social consequences, so clearly his doctors would have held back from making this diagnosis until they were convinced this was correct. However, any physician would have known that leprosy was a possible cause for the loss of sensation. It became of the utmost importance that the heir to the throne should be cured if at all possible. William described how,

The lad's father was informed of his condition and physicians were consulted. Repeated fomentations, oil rubs and even poisonous remedies were employed without result in the attempt to help him. For, as we

---

[10] S. Lay 'A leper in purple: the coronation of Baldwin IV of Jerusalem', JMH 23 (1997), pp. 317–34.

Figure 10 Schoolboys pinching Prince Baldwin's affected arm and the examination
by William of Tyre

recognised in the process of time, these were the premonitory symptoms of
a most serious and incurable disease which later became plainly apparent.

One of the physicians called for an opinion was a Christian named
Abū Sulaymān Dawūd. He was a native of Jerusalem who had
emigrated to Fatmid Egypt where he became renowned for his
medical knowledge and clinical skill. He then returned to Jerusalem
to work for King Amalric in the late 1160s.[11] With the death of his

---

[11] C. Cahen, 'Indigènes et croisés. Quelques mots a propos d'un médecin d'Amaury et de
Saladin', *Syria* 15 (1934), pp. 351–60. E. Kohlberg and B.Z. Kedar, 'A Melkite physician in

father in July 1174, Baldwin was crowned, aged just thirteen. There was no mention in the records of his being diagnosed as having leprosy at that time, which would have been a significant impediment to his ascendancy to the throne. It appears that up to that point his problems had been limited to the loss of sensation in his right arm. However, William went on to describe the progression of Baldwin's symptoms in the years after his coronation. He noted,

It is impossible to refrain from tears while speaking of this great misfortune. For as he began to reach the age of maturity it was evident that he was suffering from the terrible disease of leprosy. Day by day his condition became worse. The extremities and face were especially attacked, so that his faithful followers were moved with compassion when they looked at him.

In the fourth year and second month of the reign of King Baldwin IV, about the first of August, Philip, count of Flanders, whose arrival had been expected for a long time, landed at Acre. The king, although still ill, caused himself to be carried in a litter from Ascalon to Jerusalem . . .

[In 1183,] while the army was waiting in this state of suspense at the Fountain of Sephorie, the king was suffering from a severe attack of fever at Nazareth. In addition, the leprosy which had begun to trouble him at the beginning of his reign – in fact, in very early youth – became much worse than usual. His sight failed and his extremities were covered with ulcerations so that he was unable to use either his hands or his feet. Yet up to this time he had declined to heed the suggestion offered by some that he lay aside his kingly dignity and give up the administration of the realm, so that with a suitable provision for his needs from the royal venues he could lead a tranquil life in retirement.

Although physically weak and impotent, yet mentally he was vigorous and, far beyond his strength, he strove to hide his illness and support the cares of the kingdom. When he was attacked by the fever, however, he lost hope of life.

Baldwin managed to survive some time, however, as he died in the spring of 1185 in Jerusalem,[12] aged twenty-three. When he was a child he had developed PP or BT leprosy but after his coronation his symptoms changed. It is possible that puberty triggered Baldwin's downgrading to the lepromatous form of the disease in his teenage years. This downgrading makes a diagnosis of TT unlikely for his original presentation as TT is thought to be immunologically stable,

Frankish Jerusalem and Ayyubid Damascus: Muwaffaq al-Dīn Ya'qūb b. Siqlāb', *Asian and African Studies* 22 (1988), pp. 113–26.

[12] P.W. Edbury, *The Conquest of Jerusalem and the Third Crusade. Sources in Translation* (Aldershot, 1996), p. 15.

not prone to downgrading. By his early twenties the nerve damage had led to muscle weakness so he was unable to walk and had to be carried on a litter. The most likely cause of his blindness was that due to weakness in the muscles of the eyes he had lost the ability to blink, so that the cornea had dried and the eye become damaged. The loss of sensation in his limbs, also from the nerve damage, had led to unnoticed wounds turning into chronic ulcers. The bacteria had multiplied in the skin of the limbs and face to form disfiguring plaques and nodules and destroyed the nose. It is not possible to say for sure what caused his death. It is known that developing lepromatous leprosy before adulthood increases the likelihood of premature death, and Baldwin's death was certainly premature even for the medieval period. While it is known that he developed a fever back in 1183, there were many diseases present in the medieval eastern Mediterranean which typically do this. Possibilities include infectious diseases such as malaria, typhoid, a chest infection or perhaps septicaemia from an infected foot wound, common in untreated leprosy patients.

TREATMENT OF LEPROSY IN THE CRUSADER STATES

It is known that leprosy was present in the eastern Mediterranean for at least a thousand years before the crusades. Archaeological excavation of human skeletal remains has recovered examples from 200 BC Egypt[13] and the Judean desert around 600 AD.[14] Evidence from excavations and medical texts suggests that at this early time, several diseases causing similar skin rashes and deformity of the hands and feet may have been grouped together by doctors and thought of as 'leprosy'.[15] In the following centuries physicians in the Levant became much more aware of the symptoms of leprosy that differentiated it from other apparently similar diseases.[16] For example, the twelfth-century Syrian chronicler Ousāma ibn Moun-kidh (1095–1188) described how his great-grandfather thought his

---

[13] T. Dzierzykray-Rogalski, 'Paleopathology of the Ptolemaic inhabitants of the Dakhleh Oasis (Egypt)', *Journal of Human Evolution* 9 (1980), pp. 71–4.

[14] J. Zias, 'Leprosy and tuberculosis in the Byzantine monasteries of the Judean desert', in D.J. Ortner and A.C. Aufderheide (eds.), *Human Paleopathology: Current Syntheses and Future Options* (Washington, 1991), pp. 197–9.

[15] J. Zias and P.D. Mitchell, 'Psoriatic arthritis in a fifth-century Judean Desert monastery', *American Journal of Physical Anthropology* 101 (1996), pp. 491–502.

[16] Anderson, 'Diagnosis of leprosy'; M.W. Dols, 'Leprosy in medieval Arabic medicine', *Journal of the History of Medicine and Allied Sciences* 36 (1979), pp. 314–33.

son had leprosy and was so desperate that he was prepared to pay his physician Ibn Botlān over 500 dinars to cure him. Ibn Botlān reassured the man that his son had a skin disease common in childhood which would clear up as the child became older and that it was not leprosy.[17] Medical manuscripts of the twelfth and thirteenth centuries identify that changes to the nose, eyes and voice, the skin lesions, the loss of sensation and deformity in the hands and feet may all be caused by leprosy.[18] However, it is not known how many of these symptoms were required to be present in a patient in the twelfth century before a diagnosis of leprosy could be made. People thought to have leprosy were often segregated into institutions known as leprosaria. While analysis of the bones from a leprosarium cemetery of the period would clarify the accuracy of diagnosis at that time, none of the sites from the Crusader States where human skeletal remains have been excavated[19] have been leprosaria. In consequence, some have suggested that patients with some of the symptoms noted in the manuscripts, which can also be caused by other diseases such as psoriatic arthritis, Reiter's syndrome or treponemal disease,[20] may still have been classed as having leprosy. To avoid misunderstanding, the term 'leprosy complex disease' can be used to refer to those diagnosed as having leprosy in the medieval period where the degree of accuracy of that diagnosis is not known.

The general approach to the treatment of those with leprosy complex disease in the crusader period was by modification of diet, bathing in hot springs, the use of drugs, bloodletting, avoidance of sexual activity and segregation in leprosaria.[21] Diet was modified in the treatment of all disease at that time as it was believed that illness

---

[17] G.R. Potter (ed. and tr.), *The Autobiography of Ousāma* (London, 1929), pp. 240–1.

[18] Campbell and Colton, *Surgery of Theodorich*; C. Singer, 'A thirteenth-century description of leprosy', *Journal of the History of Medicine and Allied Sciences* 4 (1949), pp. 237–9.

[19] P.D. Mitchell, 'Pathology in the crusader period: human skeletal remains from Tel Jezreel', *Levant* 26 (1994), pp. 67–71; P.D. Mitchell, 'Further evidence of disease in the crusader period population of Le Petit Gerin (Tel Jezreel, Israel)', *Tel Aviv* 24(1) (1997), pp. 169–79; J.C. Rose, 'Crusader period disease in Jordan', in *Abstracts of the XIIth European Meeting of the Paleopathology Association, August 26–29, 1998 in Prague-Pilsen, Czech Republic* (Prague, 1998), p. 77; P.D. Mitchell, 'The archaeological approach to the study of disease in the Crusader States, as employed at Le Petit Gerin', in H. Nicholson (ed.), *The Military Orders*. II. *Welfare and Warfare* (Aldershot, 1998), pp. 43–50.

[20] E.H. Hudson, 'Historical approach to the terminology of syphilis', *Archives of Dermatology* 84 (1961), pp. 545–62; E.H. Hudson, 'Treponematosis and pilgrimage', *American Journal of the Medical Sciences* 246 (1963), pp. 645–56.

[21] Campbell and Colton, *Surgery of Theodorich*.

was a response to an imbalance in the 'humours' of the body and that the balance could be returned to normal by changing the food and drink consumed. Bathing in hot springs had been a popular treatment for those with skin disease for hundreds of years in the eastern Mediterranean and sulphurous pools were thought particularly effective.[22] Drugs used in leprosy varied from syrups containing a wide range of herbs, to enemas, to the topical application of ointments. One popular ointment for use 'in the early stage of the disease' was the 'saracenic ointment'[23] which was rubbed into the skin. Theodorich Borbognoni outlined several prescriptions for the ointment, although all were based on mixing quicksilver (mercury) and herbs with fats and oils. Oil rubs were one of the treatments William of Tyre mentioned as having been used on Baldwin, but we do not know the constituents of the medication. Bloodletting was a common treatment that was believed to help both in preventing many diseases from occurring in a healthy person and in treating those who were already unwell. While it has been suggested that the bloodletting may have been useful in the management of some infectious diseases, by causing an iron deficiency which would have impaired the growth of some bacteria,[24] the slow-growing leprosy bacillus is unlikely to have been affected. Many in the medieval period believed that leprosy was spread by sexual activity,[25] but this is not accepted as a significant source of transmission by clinicians today. The *M. leprae* bacillus has been found in the semen of lepromatous leprosy patients[26] but it is not thought to be a cause of disease spread. Segregation into leprosaria was implemented widely in the Crusader States, as was the case across Europe in the medieval period. There is no evidence that segregation of leprosy patients has any effect on the prevalence of the disease in a community[27] as the patient will have had the disease for

---

[22] M. Avi-Yonah, 'The bath of the lepers at Scythopolis', *Israel Exploration Journal* 13 (1963), pp. 325–6; H.D. Isaacs, 'A medieval Arab medical certificate', *Medical History* 35 (1991), pp. 250–7; J. Wilkinson, 'The Piacenza pilgrim', in *Jerusalem Pilgrims before the Crusades* (Warminster, 1977), p. 81.

[23] Campbell and Colton, *Surgery of Theodorich*.

[24] N.W. Kasting, 'A rationale for centuries of therapeutic bloodletting: antipyretic therapy for febrile diseases', *Perspectives in Biology and Medicine* 33 (1990), pp. 509–16; P. Brain, 'In defence of ancient bloodletting', *South African Medical Journal* 56 (1979), pp. 149–54.

[25] Campbell and Colton, *Surgery of Theodorich*; Singer, 'Description of leprosy'.

[26] A. Abraham, S. Kaur, and V.K. Sharma, 'Acid-fast bacilli in semen: correlation with bacterial index', *International Journal of Leprosy* 58 (1990), pp. 466–8.

[27] WHO, *Epidemiology of Leprosy*.

many years before obvious symptoms develop. However, this was not realised in the medieval period.

Segregation of those thought to have leprosy was a common practice within the Crusader States.[28] Nobles of the kingdom diagnosed as having leprosy were obliged by laws within the *Livre au Roi*,[29] drawn up between 1196 and 1205, to join a specific military Order established to accommodate those with the disease, the Order of St Lazarus. Even those already in a military Order, such as the Order of St John or the Order of the Temple, were encouraged to join the Order of St Lazarus if they were later believed to have leprosy.[30] The chronicler Gerard of Nazareth[31] wrote in his work *De Conversatione Servorum Dei* of the hermits and religious in twelfth-century Crusader States. He mentions two pilgrims who cared for the patients in the leprosarium outside Jerusalem at that time, Alberic and Bartholomew. Alberic was a colourful character who wore a rough goat-hair shirt and cut his hair and beard asymmetrically. He would whip himself until he drew blood and shout biting remarks at laymen as they travelled past the leprosarium. He did, however, help the patients by looking after their daily needs, carrying the weak on his shoulders and washing their ulcerous feet. This was particularly important as the nerve damage in leprosy led to wounds in the feet remaining unnoticed as the skin was numb and they often became infected. Washing the feet identified new wounds early and ensured they were bandaged and cared for properly until they healed. Leprosaria in the early years of the kingdom were typically located outside towns,[32] while hospitals for those with other diseases were found inside the walls.[33] It is particularly ironic as many of the diseases that would have been found in these hospitals, such as

---

[28] S. Shahar, 'Des lepreux pas comme les autres: l'Ordre de Saint-Lazare dans le royaume latin de Jérusalem', *Revue Historique* 267 (1982), pp. 19–41.

[29] RHC Lois I, p. 636; II, p. 18.

[30] J. Delaville le Roulx (ed.), *Cartulaire générale de l'Ordre des Hospitaliers Saint Jean de Jérusalem (1110–1310)*, 4 vols. (Paris, 1894–1906), III, cartulaire 3396, statute 17, pp. 225–9; J.M. Upton-Ward, *The Rule of the Templars* (Woodbridge, 1992), p. 118.

[31] B.Z. Kedar, 'Gerard of Nazareth. A neglected twelfth-century writer in the Latin east', DOP 37, (1983), pp. 55–78.

[32] Theodoric, *Description of the Holy Places*, tr. A. Stewart, Palestine Pilgrims' Text Society 5 (London, 1896), p. 34; D. Bahat, 'New discoveries in Jerusalem', *Bulletin of the Anglo-Israel Archaeological Society* (1984–5), pp. 50–3.

[33] John of Wurzburg, *Description of the Holy Land (AD 1160–1170)*, tr. A. Stewart, Palestine Pilgrims' Text Society (London, 1896), p. 440; A. Ovadiah, 'A crusader church in the Jewish quarter of the old city of Jerusalem', in Y. Tsafir (ed.), *Ancient Churches Revealed* (Jerusalem, 1993), pp. 136–9.

dysentery, smallpox and tuberculosis,[34] would have been a much greater risk for disease spread to the town inhabitants than was leprosy. This segregation outside towns was also practised in most of Europe at that time.[35]

However, by the thirteenth century there appears to have been increasing tolerance to the disease in the Crusader States.[36] The Order of St Lazarus began to include healthy knights in its ranks and the leprosaria for both men and women in Acre were located inside the city walls, no longer isolated outside. The order was even given the responsibility of defending a section of the city walls of Acre.[37] The laws of the states appear to have softened as the *Livre au Roi* forbad remarriage by the wife of a man with leprosy but the later *Livre des Assises de la Cour des Bourgeois* did allow just such a remarriage.[38] During the war of St Sabas in Acre between 1256 and 1261, the master of the Templars chose to shelter in the headquarters of the Order of St Lazarus rather than in one of the other Orders nearby,[39] so clearly he was not too concerned by contact with the disease. While there is only circumstantial evidence as to why this change may have taken place, it is possible that one contributing factor was that the successful reign of King Baldwin IV may have increased the tolerance of the population to people with the disease and demonstrated that those with leprosy could still make a useful contribution to society. Interestingly, Baldwin himself was not segregated from the rest of society in the way other members of the population would have been. This is despite the wishes of the royal court who, in the words of William of Tyre, hoped 'he could lead a tranquil life in retirement'. It is unfortunate that in the records there is little specific detail of the way he physically interacted with his court and it is not known if any coping mechanisms were employed to modify the degree of close contact he would have had with his courtiers.

---

[34] P.D. Mitchell, 'Tuberculosis in the crusades', in G. Palfi, O. Dutour, J. Deak and I. Hutas (eds.), *Tuberculosis: Past and Present* (Szeged, Hungary, 1999), pp. 43–9.

[35] F. Lee and J. Magilton, 'The cemetery of the hospital of St James and St Mary Magdalene, Chichester – a case study', *World Archaeology* 21 (1989), pp. 273–82.

[36] P.D. Mitchell, 'The evolution of social attitudes to the medical care of those with leprosy within the Crusader States', in B. Tabuteau (ed.), *Histoire et archéologie de la lèpre et des lépreux en Europe et en Méditerranée de l'Antiquité aux Temps Modernes* (Rouen, 2000).

[37] de Marsy.

[38] Shahar, 'Des lepreux pas comme les autres'.

[39] 'Chronique de Templier de Tyr', in G. Raynaud (ed.), *Les Gestes de Chiprois*, Publications de la Société de l'Orient Latin, sér. historique, 5 (Geneva, 1887), p. 153.

SUMMARY

Baldwin IV of Jerusalem was a twelfth-century king remembered by historians for contracting leprosy. This is probably the last thing he himself would have wanted, but is perhaps inevitable as this disease had such enormous social and religious implications in the medieval period. The earliest sign of the disease was as a child when he developed anaesthesia in his right hand and arm. It is most likely that at this point he had either the primary polyneuritic or border-line tuberculoid form of leprosy. Unfortunately for him, he was not able to overcome the infection, as many patients with these forms of leprosy do. Over time he downgraded to the lepromatous form and this may have been triggered by puberty. The ointments and other treatments tried by physicians such as Abū Sulaymān Dawūd were unable to cure him. By the time Baldwin was in his twenties he was blind, his face, hands and feet were deformed and covered in ulcers and he was carried about in a litter. Unlike other members of the Crusader States, he was not segregated into a leprosarium but continued to rule the kingdom. Baldwin died aged twenty-three, but there is insufficient detail in the chronicles to identify a specific cause of death.

Bibliography

PRIMARY SOURCES

Abel, F.M., 'Lettre d'un Templier trouvée récemment à Jérusalem', *Revue Biblique* 35 (1926), pp. 288–95.

Abu Shama, *The Book of the Two Gardens*, RHC Or. IV, pp. 3–522, V, pp. 3–206.

Aguado de Cordova, A.F., Aleman et Rosales, A.A. and Agurleta, I.L. (eds.), *Bullarium Equestris Ordinis S. Iacobi de Spatha* (Madrid, 1719).

Alberic of Trois-Fontaines, *Chronica a monacho novi monasterii Hoiensis interpolata*, ed. P. Scheffer-Boichorst, MGH SS XXIII (Hanover, 1874).

Alexander III, Pope, *Epistolae et Privilegia*, P.L. 200.

Alishan, L.M. (ed. and tr.), *Les Assises d'Antioche reproduites en français* (Venice, 1876).

Amari, M., *Biblioteca Arabo-Sicula*, Italian tr., 2 vols. (Turin and Rome, 1880–9).

I diplomi arabi del R. Archivio Fiorentino (Florence, 1863).

Ambroise, *Estoire de Guerre Sainte: Histoire en vers de la troisième croisade*, ed. G. Paris (Paris, 1897).

Anna Comnena, *Alexiad*, ed. with French tr. B. Leib, 3 vols. (Paris, 1937–45).

Annales Casinenses, ed. G.H. Pertz, MGH SS XIX (Hanover, 1866).

Annales Colonienses Maximi, ed. G.H. Pertz, MGH SS XVII (Hanover, 1861).

Anonymi Auctoris Chronicon ad Annum Christi 1234 pertinens [comprising *Historia Ecclesiastica* and *Historia Civilis*], ed. J.B. Chabot, CSCO, *Scriptores Syri*, 3rd ser., vols. XIV and XV (Paris, 1926), tr. A. Abouna, intro. J.M. Fiey, CSCO, *Scriptores Syri*, 3rd ser., 154 (Louvain, 1974).

Anonymi Laudunensis, *Chronicon universale*, ed. G. Waitz, MGH SS XXVI (Hanover, 1882).

Arnold of Lübeck, *Chronica Slavorum*, ed. I.M. Lappenberg, MGH SS XXI (Hanover, 1869).

Baha al-Din, *Anecdotes et beaux traits de la vie du Sultan Youssof*, RHC Or III, pp. 3–370.

The Life of Saladin, English translation: C.W. Wilson, revised from the

Arabic text by C.R. Conder, Beha ed-Din, *The Life of Saladin* (London, 1897).

Bar Hebraeus, *Chronicon Ecclesiasticum*, ed. with Latin tr. J.B. Abbeloos and T.J. Lamy, 2 vols. (Louvain, 1872–7).

The Chronography, ed. and tr. E.A. Wallis Budge, 2 vols. (Oxford, 1932).

Barthélemy, E. de, 'Obituaire de la commanderie du Temple de Reims', Collection des documents inédits sur l'histoire de France, *Mélanges historiques, choix de documents*, IV (Paris, 1882), pp. 301–36.

Benjamin of Tudela, *Itinerary*, ed. and tr. M.N. Adler (London, 1907): the English translation has been republished and annotated by M.A. Signer, *The Itinerary of Benjamin of Tudela* (Malibu, 1987).

Beroul, *The Romance of Tristan*, tr. A.S. Frederick (Harmondsworth, 1970).

Bongars, J. (ed.), *Gesta Dei per Francos* (Hanover, 1611).

Bresc-Bautier, G. (ed.), *Le Cartulaire du Chapître du Saint-Sépulcre de Jérusalem* (Paris, 1984).

Broë, Samuel de, seigneur de Citry et de la Guette, *Histoire de la conqueste du royaume de Jérusalem sur les chrestiens par Saladin* (Paris, 1679).

Broussillon, B. de, 'La charte d'André II de Vitré et le siège de Kérak en 1184', BHCTH (1899), pp. 47–53.

Campbell. E. and Cotton, J. (ed. and tr.), *The Surgery of Theodorich, ca. AD 1267*, 2 vols. (New York, 1955–60).

Cartellieri, A. (ed.), *Ein Donaueschinger Briefsteller. Lateinische Stilübungen des XII Jahrhunderts aus der orleanischen Schule* (Innsbruck, 1898).

Chronica Regia Colonienses, ed. G. Waitz, MGH Scriptorum rerum Germanicarum in usum scholarum (Hanover, 1880).

La Clef des Assises de la Haute Cour du royaume de Jérusalem et de Chypre, RHC Lois I, pp. 573–99.

Delaborde, H.-F. (ed.), *Chartes de la Terre Sainte provenant de l'abbaye de Notre-Dame de Josaphat*, BEFAR, 19 (Paris, 1880).

Delaville Le Roulx, J. (ed.), 'Chartes de Terre Sainte', ROL 11 (1905–8), pp. 181–91.

(ed.), *Cartulaire generale de l'Ordre des Hospitaliers de Saint Jean de Jérusalem (1100–1310)*, 4 vols. (Paris, 1894–1906).

(ed.), 'Inventaire de pièces de Terre Sainte de l'Ordre de l'Hôpital', ROL 3 (1895), pp. 36–106.

Desilve, J. (ed.), *Lettres d'Etienne de Tournai* (Valenciennes and Paris, 1893).

Documents relatifs à la successibilité au trône et à la régence (ed.), P.W. Edbury, 'The disputed regency in the Kingdom of Jerusalem 1264/6 and 1268', Camden Miscellany, 4th ser., 22 (1979), pp. 1–47.

Dölger, F. (ed.), *Regesten der Kaiserurkunden des östromischen Reiches*, 5 vols. (Munich and Berlin, 1924–65).

Edbury, P.W., 'The "Cartulaire de Manosque": a grant to the Templars in Latin Syria and a charter of King Hugh I of Cyprus', *Bulletin of the Institute of Historical Research* 51 (1978), pp. 174–81.

(ed. and tr.), *The Conquest of Jerusalem and the Third Crusade. Sources in Translation* (Aldershot, 1996).

L'Estoire d'Eracles empereur et la conqueste de la terre d'Outremer, ed. P. Paris, *Guillaume de Tyr et ses continuateurs,* 2 vols. (Paris, 1879–80).

L'Estoire d'Eracles empereur et la conqueste de la terre d'Outremer, RHC Occ I, II.

La Chronique d'Ernoul et de Bernard le Trésorier, ed. L. de Mas-Latrie (Paris, 1871).

Ernoul, 'Fragments relatifs à la Galilée', in H. Michelant and G. Raynaud (eds.), *Itinéraires à Jérusalem et descriptions de la Terre Sainte rédigés en français aux XIe, XIIe et XIIIe siècles,* Publications de la Société de l'Orient Latin, sér. géographique 3 (Paris, 1882), pp. 53–76.

Eustathius of Thessalonica, *The Capture of Thessaloniki,* Greek text with tr. by J.R. Melville Jones, Byzantina Australiensia 8 (Canberra, 1988).

Friedberg, E. (ed.), *Corpus Iuris Canonici,* 2 vols. (Leipzig, 1882).

Gabrieli, F., *Arab Historians of the Crusades,* tr. E.J. Costello (London, 1969).

Geoffrey Le Tort, *Livre,* RHC Lois, I, pp. 433–49.

Gerald of Wales, *Expugnatio Hibernica* and *Liber de Principis Instructione,* in *Giraldus Cambrensis, Opera,* eds. J.S. Brewer, J.F. Dimock and G.F. Warner, 8 vols., RS 21 (London 1861–91), vols. V and VIII.

Gervase of Canterbury, *Opera Historica,* ed. W. Stubbs, 2 vols., RS 73 (London, 1879–80).

Grumel, V., *Les Regestes des actes du Patriarcat de Constantinople, I. Les Actes des Patriarches, III. 1043–1206* (Paris, 1947).

Guiragos of Kantzag, *History of Armenia,* RHC Arm I, pp. 413–30.

Hiestand, R. (ed.), *Vorarbeiten zum Oriens Pontificius.*

   I. *Papsturkunden für Templar und Johanniter.*

   II. *Papsturkunden für Templar und Johanniter. Neue Folge.*

   III. *Papsturkunden für Kirchen im Heiligen Lande.* Abhandlungen der Akademie der Wissenschaften in Göttingen. Philologisch-historische Klasse. Dritte Folge, 77, 135 and 136 (Göttingen, 1972, 1984 and 1985).

Hildegard of Bingen, St, *Epistolae,* P.L. 197, cols. 145–382.

History of the Patriarchs of the Egyptian Church, tr. A. Khater and O.H.E. Khs-Burmester, Publications de la Société de l'archéologie Copte, Textes et Documents, 12, 4 vols. (Cairo, 1943–74).

Huillard-Bréholles, J.L.A. (ed.), *Historia Diplomatica Friderici Secundi,* 6 vols. in 12 (Paris, 1852–61).

Huygens, R.B.C. (ed.), *Peregrinationes Tres: Saewulf, Johannes Wirziburgensis, Theodoricus,* CCCM 139 (Turnholt, 1994).

Ibn al-Athir, *Kamil al-Tawarikh,* extract with French tr., RHC Or I, pp. 189–744.

Ibn Jubayr, *The Travels of Ibn Jubayr,* tr. R.J.C. Broadhurst (London, 1952).

Ibn al-Qalanisi, *The Damascus Chronicle of the Crusades,* tr. H.A.R. Gib (London, 1932).

Imad ad-Din al-Isfahani, *La conquête de la Syrie et de la Palestine par Saladin,* tr. H. Massé, DRHC 10 (Paris, 1972).

Imperiale di Sant'Angelo, C. (ed.), *Codice diplomatico della Repubblica di Genova*, 3 vols., Fonti per la storia d'Italia (Rome, 1936–42).
Itinerarium Peregrinorum et Gesta Regis Ricardi, ed. W. Stubbs, RS 38 (London, 1864).
Itinerarium Peregrinorum ed. H.-E. Mayer, *Das Itinerarium Peregrinorum. Ein zeitgenössische englische Chronik zum dritten Kreuzzug in ursprünglicher Gestalt*, MGH Schriften, 18 (Stuttgart, 1962).
Itinerarium Peregrinorum, H.J. Nicholson, *Chronicle of the Third Crusade. A Translation of the 'Itinerarium Peregrinorum et Gesta Regis Ricardi'* (Aldershot, 1997).
James of Ibelin, *Livre*, RHC Lois, I, pp. 451–67.
James of Vitry, *Lettres de Jacques de Vitry (1160/70–1240) évêque de Saint-Jean d'Acre*, ed. R.B.C. Huygens (Leiden, 1960).
 Libri duo, quorum prior Orientalis sive Hierosolimitana, alter Occidentalis Historiae nomine inscribuntur (Douai, 1597).
John Cinnamus, *Epitome rerum ab Iohanne et Alexio Comnenis gestarum*, ed. A. Meineke, CSHB (Bonn, 1836).
 The Deeds of John and Manuel Comnenus, tr. C.M. Brand (New York, 1976).
John of Ibelin, *Livre des Assises*, RHC Lois I, pp. 1–432.
 Livre des Assises, cc. 260–72, in P.W. Edbury (ed.), *John of Ibelin and the Kingdom of Jerusalem* (Woodbridge, 1997), pp. 110–26.
John of Joinville, *Histoire de Saint Louis*, ed. N. de Wailly (Paris, 1868).
 The Life of St. Louis, tr. R. Hague (London, 1955).
John Phocas, 'A general description of the settlements . . . and of the Holy Places in Palestine', tr. J. Wilkinson in *Jerusalem Pilgrimage 1099–1185*, Hakluyt Society, 2nd ser., 167 (London, 1988), pp. 315–36.
John of Würzburg, 'Description of the Holy Land', in J. Wilkinson (ed.), *Jerusalem Pilgrimage 1099–1185*, Hakluyt Society, 2nd ser., 167 (London, 1988), pp. 244–73; (also tr. A. Stewart, Palestine Pilgrims' Text Society 5 (London, 1896), pp. 1–72).
Jubb, M.A., *A Critical Edition of the 'Estoires d'Outremer et de la naissance Salehadin'*, Westfield Publications in Medieval Studies 4 (London, 1990).
Kamal ad-Din, *History of Aleppo*, French tr. by E. Blochet, ROL 3 (1895), pp. 509–65; 4 (1896), pp. 321–476; 5 (1897), pp. 37–108; 6 (1898), pp. 435–550.
Kohler, Ch. (ed.), 'Chartes de l'abbaye de Notre-Dame de la vallée de Josaphat en Terre Sainte (1108–1291). Analyses et extraits', ROL 7 (1900), pp. 108–222.
Libellus de expugnatione Terrae Sanctae per Saladinum, ed. J. Stevenson, RS 66 (London, 1875), pp. 209–62.
The Life of Leontios Patriarch of Jerusalem, ed. and tr. D. Tsougarakis (Leiden, 1993).
Les Lignages d'Outremer, RHC Lois, II, pp. 441–74.

Le Livre au roi, ed. M. Greilsammer, DRHC 17 (Paris, 1995).

Lucius III, Pope, *Epistolae et Diplomata*, P.L., 210.

Magnus of Reichersberg, *Chronica collecta a Magno presbytero – 1195*, ed. W. Wattenbach, MGH SS XVII (Hanover, 1861).

Mansi, G.D. (ed.), *Sacrorum Conciliorum nova et amplissima collectio*, 31 vols. (Florence and Venice, 1759–98).

al-Maqrizi, *A History of the Ayyubid Sultans of Egypt*, tr. R.J.C. Broadhurst (Boston, 1980).

    Histoire d'Egypte, tr. E. Blochet, ROL 6 (1898), pp. 435–89; 8 (1900–1), pp. 165–212 and 501–53; 9 (1902), pp. 6–163 and 466–530; 10 (1903–4), pp. 248–371; 11 (1905–8), pp. 192–239.

Marsy, A. de (ed.), 'Fragment d'un cartulaire de l'Ordre de Saint-Lazare en Terre Sainte', AOL IIB, pp. 121–57.

Martène E. and Durand, U. (eds.), *Thesaurus Novus Anecdotorum*, 5 vols. (Paris, 1717).

    (eds.), *Veterum Scriptorum et Monumentorum Amplissima Collectio*, 9 vols. (Paris, 1724–33).

Materials for the History of Thomas Becket, Archbishop of Canterbury, eds. J.C. Robertson and J.B. Sheppard, 7 vols., RS 67 (London, 1875–85).

Mayer, H.-E., 'Sankt Samuel auf dem Freudenberge und sein besitz nach ein unbekannten Diplom König Balduins V', QF, 44 (1964), pp. 35–71.

Michael the Syrian, *Chronicle*, ed. with French tr., J.B. Chabot, 4 vols. (Paris, 1899–1924).

    Chronicle for the years 1101–1205 A.D. in Armenian translation, ed. with a French tr., RHC Arm I, pp. 311–409.

Morgan M.R. (ed.), *La continuation de Guillaume de Tyr (1184–1197)*, DRHC 14 (Paris, 1982).

Müller, G. (ed.), *Documenti sulle relazioni delle città toscane coll'Oriente cristiano e coi Turchi fino all'anno 1531*, Documenti degli archivi Toscani, 3 (Florence, 1879).

Nerses of Lampron, St, *Reflections on the Institutions of the Church and Explanation of the Eucharistic Mystery*, extracts ed. with French tr., RHC Arm I, pp. 569–603.

Nicetas Choniates, *Historia*, ed. J.A. van Dieten, Corpus Fontium Historiae Byzantinae 11, 2 vols. (Berlin, 1975).

    O City of Byzantium, tr. J.H. Magoulias (Detroit, 1984).

Paoli, S. (ed.), *Codice diplomatico del sacro militare ordine gerosolimitano, oggi di Malta*, 2 vols. (Lucca, 1733–7).

Peter of Blois, *Passio Reginaldis Principis Antilocheni*, P.L., 207, cols. 957–76.

Pflugck-Harttung, J. von (ed.), *Acta Pontificum Romanorum Inedita*, 3 vols. (Tübingen and Stuttgart, 1881–6).

Philip of Novara, *Le Livre de forme de plait*, RHC Lois I, pp. 469–571.

Prologo, A. di G., *Le carte che se conservano nell'Archivio del Capitolo metropolitano della città di Trani, dal IX secolo fino all' anno 1266* (Barletta, 1877).

Ralph de Diceto, *Ymagines Historiarum*, ed. W. Stubbs, 2 vols., RS 68 (London, 1876).

Recueil des Historiens des Croisades
Documents Arméniens, 2 vols. (Paris, 1869 and 1906).
Historiens Grecs, 2 vols. (Paris, 1875–81).
Historiens Occidentaux, 5 vols. (Paris, 1844–95).
Historiens Orientaux, 5 vols. (Paris, 1872–1906).
Lois, 2 vols. (Paris, 1841–3).

La Règle du Temple, ed. H. de Curzon (Paris, 1886). Tr. J.M. Upton-Ward, *The Rule of the Templars* (Woodbridge, 1992).

Regni Iherosolymitani Brevis Historia, ed. L.T. Belgrano, *Annali Genovesi di Caffaro e de' suoi continuatori dal MXCIX al MCCXCIII*, Fonti per la storia d'Italia, 5 vols. (Genoa and Rome, 1890–1929), I, pp. 125–49.

Rigord, *Gesta Philippi Augusti*, ed. H.-F. Delaborde, *Oeuvres de Rigord et Guillaume le Breton*, 2 vols. (Paris, 1882–5).

Robert of Auxerre, *Chronicon*, ed. O. Holder-Egger, MGH SS XXVI (Hanover, 1872).

Robert of Torigni, *Chronicon*, ed. R. Howlett, RS 82(IV) (London, 1889).

Roger of Howden, *Chronica*, ed. W. Stubbs, 4 vols., RS 51 (London, 1868–71).
Gesta Regis Henrici Secundi, ed. W. Stubbs, 2 vols., RS 49 (London, 1867). [Published as the Chronicle of Benedict of Peterborough].

Roger of Wendover, *Flores Historiarum*, ed. H.G. Howlett, 2 vols., RS 84 (London, 1886).

Röhricht, R., *Regesta Regni Hierosolymitani (MXCVII–MCCXCI)*, 2 vols. (Innsbruck, 1893–1904).
(ed.), *Beiträge zur Geschichte der Kreuzzüge*, 2 vols. (Berlin, 1874–8).

Sandoli, S. de, *Itinera Hierosolymitana Crucesignatorum (saec. XII–XIII)*, 4 vols. (Jerusalem, 1978–84).
(ed.), *Corpus Inscriptionum Crucesignatorum Terrae Sanctae* (Jerusalem, 1974).

Sicard of Cremona, *Chronicon*, ed. O. Holder-Egger, MGH SS XXXI (Hanover, 1903).

Sigebert of Gembloux, *Chronographia*, ed. D.L.C. Bethmann, MGH SS VI (Hanover, 1844).

Smbat the Constable, *La Chronique attribuée au Connétable Smbat*, tr. G. Dédéyan, DRHC 13 (Paris, 1980).

Stern, S.M., *Fatimid Decrees. Original Documents from the Fatimid Chancery* (London, 1964).

Strehlke, E. (ed.), *Tabulae Ordinis Teutonici* (Berlin, 1869).

Tafel, G.L.F. and Thomas, G.M. (eds.), *Urkunden zur älteren Handels- und Staatsgeschichte der Republik Venedig mit besonderer Beziehung auf Byzanz und die Levante*, Fontes rerum Austriacarum, section III, 12–14 (Vienna, 1856–7).

Templar of Tyre, 'Chronique du Templier de Tyr', in G. Raynaud (ed.), *Les*

Gestes des Chiprois, Publications de la Société de l'Orient Latin, sér. historique, 5 (Geneva, 1887).

Theoderic, *Description of the Holy Places*, tr. A. Stewart, Palestine Pilgrims' Text Society 5 (London, 1896), pp. 1–86.

Tobler, T. and Molinier, A. (eds.), *Itinera Hierosolymitana*, Publications de la Société de l'Orient Latin, sér. géographique, 1 and 2 (Geneva, 1879–80).

Usama ibn Munqidh: *The Autobiography of Ousama*, tr. G.R. Potter (London, 1929).

Vahram of Edessa, *Chronique rimée des rois de la Petite-Arménie*, RHC Arm I, pp. 492–535.

Vartan the Great, *Universal History*, RHC Arm I, pp. 434–43.

Vincent of Beauvais, *Bibliotheca Mundi*, 4 vols. (Douai, 1624).

Walter the Chancellor, *Bella Antiochena*, ed. H. Hagenmeyer (Innsbruck, 1896).

Wilkinson, J., with Hill, J. and Ryan, W.F., *Jerusalem Pilgrimage, 1099–1185*, Hakluyt Society, 2nd ser., 167 (London, 1988).

William of Newburgh, *Historia Rerum Anglicarum*, ed. R. Howlett, RS 82(I) (London, 1884).

William of Tyre, *Chronicon*, ed. R.B.C. Huygens. Identification des dates par H-E. Mayer et G. Rösch, CCCM 63 and 63A (Turnholt, 1986).

A History of Deeds done beyond the Sea, tr. E.A. Babcock and A.C. Krey, 2 vols. (New York, 1943).

Die lateinische Forsetzung Wilhelms von Tyrus, ed. M. Salloch (Leipzig, 1934).

SECONDARY WORKS

Abraham, A., Kaur, S. and Sharma, V.K., 'Acid-fast bacilli in semen: correlation with bacterial index', *International Journal of Leprosy* 58 (1990), pp. 466–8.

Abu-Izzedin, N.M., *The Druzes. A New Study of their History, Faith and Society* (Leiden, 1984).

Abulafia, D., 'The Norman Kingdom of Africa and the Norman expedition to Majorca and the Muslim Mediterranean', *Anglo-Norman Studies* 7 (1984), pp. 26–49.

Adams, W.Y., *Nubia* (London, 1977).

Ahmad, M. Hilmy M., 'Some notes on Arabic historiography during the Zengid and Ayyubid periods (521/1127–648/1250)', in B. Lewis and P.M. Holt (eds.), *Historians of the Middle East* (London, 1962), pp. 79–97.

Ahrweiler, H., *Byzance et la Mer* (Paris, 1966).

Airaldi, G. and Kedar, B.Z. (eds.), *I comuni italiani nel regno crociato di Gerusalemme* (Genoa, 1986).

d'Albon, Marquis, 'La mort d'Odon de Saint-Amand, grand maître du Temple (1179)', ROL 12 (1911), pp. 279–82.

Andersen, J.G., 'Studies in the medieval diagnosis of leprosy in Denmark', *Danish Medical Bulletin* 16 (suppl.) (1969), pp. 1–142.

Angold, M., *The Byzantine Empire, 1025–1204. A Political History*, 2nd edn (London, 1997).

Archer, T.A. and Kingsford, C.L., *The Crusades. The Story of the Latin Kingdom of Jerusalem* (London, 1894).

Ashtor, E., 'Il regno dei crociati e il commercio di Levante', in G. Airaldi and B.Z. Kedar (eds.), *I comuni italiani nel regno crociato di Gerusalemme* (Genoa, 1986), pp. 15–56.

Aubé, P., *Baudouin IV de Jérusalem. Le roi lépreux* (Paris, 1981).

Avi-Yonah, M., 'The bath of the lepers at Scythopolis', *Israel Exploration Journal* 13 (1963), pp. 325–6.

Bahat, D., 'New discoveries in Jerusalem', *Bulletin of the Anglo-Israel Archaeological Society* (1984–5), pp. 50–3.

Baldwin, M.W., 'The decline and fall of Jerusalem, 1174–1189', in Setton, *Crusades*, I, pp. 590–621.

  Raymond III of Tripolis and the Fall of Jerusalem (1140–1187) (Princeton, 1936).

Balletto, L. (ed.), *Dai Feudi Monferrini e dal Piemonte ai nuovi mondi oltre gli oceani* (Alessandria, 1993).

Bar, M., *La formation du comté de Champagne* (Nancy, 1977).

Barber, M., 'Frontier warfare in the Latin Kingdom of Jerusalem: the campaign of Jacob's Ford, 1178–1179', in J. France and W.G. Zajac (eds.), *The Crusades and their Sources. Essays presented to Bernard Hamilton* (Aldershot, 1998), pp. 9–22.

  The New Knighthood. A History of the Order of the Temple (Cambridge, 1994).

  'The Order of Saint Lazarus and the Crusades', *Catholic Historical Review*, 80 (1994), pp. 439–56.

  (ed.), *The Military Orders*. I. *Fighting for the Faith and Caring for the Sick* (Aldershot, 1994).

Barthaux, J., 'Description d'une forteresse de Saladin découverte au Sinai', *Syria* 3 (1922), pp. 44–57.

Bates, M.L. and Metcalf, D.M., 'Crusader coinage with Arabic inscriptions', in Setton, *Crusades*, VI, pp. 421–82.

Bautier, R.-H. (ed.), *La France de Philippe Auguste* (Paris, 1982).

Benvenisti, M., *The Crusaders in the Holy Land* (Jerusalem, 1972).

Bériou, N. and Touati, F.-O., *Voluntate Dei Leprosus. Les lépreux entre conversion et exclusion au XIIème et XIIIème siècles*, Testi, Studi, Strumenti 4, Centro Italiano sull'alto Medioevo (Spoleto, 1991).

Boase, T.S.R. (ed.), *The Cilician Kingdom of Armenia* (Edinburgh, 1978).

Bosworth, C.E., 'The political and dynastic history of the Iranian world (A.D. 1000–1217)', in *The Cambridge History of Iran*, V, ed. J.A. Boyle, *The Saljuq and Mongol Periods* (Cambridge, 1968), pp. 1–202.

Bournoutian, A.A., 'Cilician Armenia', in G. Hovannisian (ed.), *The Armenian People from Ancient to Modern Times*, 2 vols. (London, 1997), I, pp. 273–91.

Brain, P., 'In defence of ancient bloodletting', *South African Medical Journal* 56 (1979), pp. 149–54.

Brand, C.M., 'The Byzantines and Saladin, 1185–92', *Speculum* 37 (1962), pp. 167–81.

Byzantium Confronts the West, 1180–1204 (Cambridge, Mass., 1968).

Bresc-Bautier, G., 'Les possessions des églises de Terre-Sainte en Italie du sud', in *Roberto il Guiscardo e il suo tempo* (Rome, 1975), pp. 13–34.

Brody, S.N., *The Disease of the Soul. Leprosy in Medieval Literature* (Ithaca, 1974).

Broussillon, B. de, *La Maison de Craon, 1050–1480*, 2 vols. (Paris, 1893).

Bulst-Thiele, M.L., *Sacrae Domus Militiae Templi Hierosolymitani Magistri. Untersuchungen zur Geschichte des Templerordens 1118/19–1314*, Abhandlungen der Akadamie der Wissenschaften in Göttingen Philologisch-Historische Klasse, Dritte Folge 86 (Göttingen, 1974).

Bur, M., 'Rôle et place de la Champagne dans le royaume de France au temps de Philippe Auguste, in R.-H. Bautier (ed.), *La France de Philippe Auguste* (Paris, 1982), pp. 237–54.

Cahen, C., 'Indigènes et croisés. Quelques mots à propos d'un medecin d'Amaury et de Saladin', *Syria* 15 (1934), pp. 351–60.

'Notes sur les seigneurs de Saône et de Zerdana', *Syria* 12 (1931), pp. 154–9.

Pre-Ottoman Turkey. A General Survey of the Material and Spiritual Culture and History c. 1071–1330, tr. J. Jones-Williams (London, 1968).

La Syrie du nord à l'époque des croisades et la principauté franque d'Antioche (Paris, 1940).

The Cambridge History of Iran, V. *The Saljuk and Mongol Periods*, ed. J.A. Boyle (Cambridge, 1968).

Cardini, F., Papi, M., Vannini, G., Marino, L. and Berretti, R., 'Ricognizione agli impiante fortificati di epoca crociata in Transgiordania. Prima relazione', *Castellum* 27–8 (1987), pp. 5–38.

Cartellieri, A., *Philipp II August, König von Frankreich*, 4 vols. (Leipzig, 1899–1922).

Clermont-Ganneau, C., 'La marche de Saladin du Caire à Damas avec démonstration sur Kérak', *Revue biblique internationale*, n.s., 3 (1906), pp. 464–71.

Recueil d'archéologie orientale, 8 vols. (Paris, 1888–1924).

Corbo, B.C., *Il Santo Sepolcro a Gerusalemme*, 3 vols. (Jerusalem, 1981–2).

Daftary, F., *The Isma'ilis: Their History and Doctrines* (Cambridge, 1990).

Dahan, Sami, 'The origin and development of the local histories of Syria', in B. Lewis and P.M. Holt (eds.), *Historians of the Middle East* (London, 1962), pp. 108–17.

Dauvillier, J., *Le mariage dans le droit classique de l'église depuis le Décret de Gratien (1140) jusqu'à la mort de Clément V (1314)* (Paris, 1933).

Day, G.W., *Genoa's Response to Byzantium, 1155–1204. Commercial Expansion and Factionalism in a Medieval City* (Urbana and Chicago, 1988).

Delaville Le Roulx, J., 'L'Ordre de Montjoye', ROL 1 (1893), pp. 42–57.

Dept, G.G., *Les influences anglaise et française dans le comté de Flandre au début du XIIIe siècle* (Ghent, 1928).

Der Nersessian, S., 'The Kingdom of Cilician Armenia', in Setton, *Crusades*, II, pp. 630–45.

Deschamps, P., 'Le Château de Saône et ses premiers seigneurs', *Syria* 16 (1935), pp. 73–88.

Les châteaux des croisés en Terre Sainte. I, *Le Crac des Chevaliers*. II, *La défense du royaume de Jérusalem*. III, *La défense du comté de Tripoli et de la principauté d'Antioche* (Paris, 1934, 1939 and 1973).

Dib, P., 'Maronites', *Dictionnaire de Théologie Catholique*, X(I), cols. 1–142.

Diehl, C., 'Les romanesques aventures d'Andronic Comnène', in his *Figures byzantines*, 5th edn (Paris, 1918), pp. 86–133.

Dols, M.W., 'Leprosy in medieval Arabic medicine', *Journal of the History of Medicine and Allied Sciences* 36 (1979), pp. 314–33.

Dondaine, A., 'Hugues Ethérien et Léon Toscan', *Archives d'histoire doctrinale et littéraire du Moyen Age* 19 (1952), pp. 67–134.

Ducange, C. du Fresne, *Les Familles d'Outremer*, ed. E.G. Rey (Paris, 1869).

Dunbabin, J., 'William of Tyre and Philip of Alsace, count of Flanders', *Academiae Analecta* 48 (1986), pp. 111–17.

Duncan, M.E., 'Leprosy and procreation – a historical review of social and clinical aspects', *Leprosy Review* 56 (1985), pp. 153–62.

Dzierzykray-Rogalski, T., 'Paleopathology of the Ptolemaic inhabitants in the Dakleh Oasis (Egypt)', *Journal of Human Evolution* 9 (1980), pp. 71–4.

Edbury, P.W., *John of Ibelin and the Kingdom of Jerusalem* (Woodbridge, 1997).

The Kingdom of Cyprus and the Crusades, 1191–1374 (Cambridge, 1991).

'The Lyons *Eracles* and the Old French Continuations of William of Tyre', in B.Z. Kedar, J. Riley-Smith and R. Hiestand (eds.), *Montjoie. Studies in Crusade History in Honour of Hans-Eberhard Mayer* (Aldershot, 1997), pp. 139–53.

'Propaganda and faction in the Kingdom of Jerusalem: the background to Hattin', in M. Shatzmiller (ed.), *Crusaders and Muslims in Twelfth-century Syria* (Leiden, 1993), pp. 173–89.

(ed.), *Crusade and Settlement* (Cardiff, 1985).

Edbury, P.W. and Rowe, J.G., *William of Tyre. Historian of the Latin East* (Cambridge, 1988).

'William of Tyre and the patriarchal election of 1180', EHR 93 (1978), pp. 1–25.

Edwards, R.W., *The Fortifications of Armenian Cilicia*, Dumbarton Oaks Studies 23 (Washington, D.C., 1987).

Ehrenkreutz, A.S., 'The place of Saladin in the naval history of the Mediterranean Sea', *Journal of the American Oriental Society* 75 (1955), pp. 100–16.

Saladin (Albany, N.Y., 1972).

Elisséeff, N., 'Les monuments de Nur ad-Din', *Bulletin d'études orientales de l'Institut français de Damas* 13 (1949–51), pp. 5–43.

Nur ad-Din, un grand prince musulman de Syrie au temps des croisades (511–569H/1118–1174), 3 vols. (Damascus, 1967).

Ellenblum, R., *Frankish Rural Settlement in the Latin Kingdom of Jerusalem* (Cambridge, 1998).

'Who built Qalat al-Subayba?', DOP 43 (1989), pp. 103–12.

Esmein, A., *Le mariage dans le droit canonique*, 2 vols. (Paris, 1891).

Eyton, R.W., *Court, Household and Itinerary of King Henry II* (London, 1878).

Farcinet, C., *L'ancienne famille de Lusignan*, 2nd edn (Vannes, 1899).

Favreau-Lilie, M.-L., *Die Italiener im Heiligen Land von ersten Kreuzzug bis zum Tode Heinrichs von Champagne (1098–1197)* (Amsterdam, 1988).

Folda, J., *The Art of the Crusaders in the Holy Land, 1098–1187* (Cambridge, 1995).

Crusader Manuscript Illumination at Saint-Jean d'Acre, 1275–1291 (Princeton, 1976).

'Manuscripts of the *History of Outremer* by William of Tyre: a handlist', *Scriptorium* 27 (1973), pp. 90–5.

The Nazareth Captials and the Crusader Shrine of the Annunciation (University Park, Pa. and London, 1986).

Forey, A., 'The Order of Mountjoy', *Speculum* 46 (1971), pp. 250–66.

France, J. and Zajac, W.G. (eds.), *The Crusades and their Sources. Essays Presented to Bernard Hamilton* (Aldershot, 1998).

Gabrieli, F., 'The Arabic historiography of the crusades', in B. Lewis and P.M. Holt (eds.), *Historians of the Middle East* (London, 1962), pp. 98–107.

Gibb, H.A.R., *The Life of Saladin from the Works of Imad ad-Din and Baha' ad-Din* (Oxford, 1973).

'The rise of Saladin 1169–1189', in Setton, *Crusades*, I, pp. 563–89.

Gillingham, J., *Richard the Lionheart* (London, 1978).

'Roger of Howden on crusade', in D.O. Morgan (ed.), *Medieval Historical Writing in the Christian and Islamic Worlds* (London, 1982), pp. 60–75.

Grandclaude, M., *Etude critique sur les Livres des Assises de Jérusalem* (Paris, 1923).

Gransden, A., *Historical Writing in England*, 2 vols. (London, 1974–82).

Grant, C.P., *The Syrian Desert. Caravans, Travel and Exploration* (London, 1937).

Grousset, R., *Histoire des croisades et du royaume franque de Jérusalem*, 3 vols. (Paris, 1934–6).

Haberstumpf, W., 'Guglielmo Lungaspada di Monferrato, conte di Ascalona e di Giaffa (1176–1177)', *Studi Piemontesi* 18 (1989), pp. 601–8.

Hamilton, B., 'Aimery of Limoges, patriarch of Antioch: ecumenist, scholar and patron of hermits', in E.R. Elder (ed.), *The Joy of Learning and the Love of God. Essays in Honour of Jean Leclercq* (Kalamazoo, Mich., 1995), pp. 269–90.

'The Armenian Church and the papacy at the time of the crusades', *Eastern Churches Review* 10 (1978), pp. 61–87.

'Baldwin the leper as war leader', in A.V. Murray (ed.), *From Clermont to Jerusalem. The Crusades and Crusader Society, 1095–1500* (Turnhout, 1998), pp. 119–30.

'The elephant of Christ: Reynald of Châtillon', SCH 15 (Oxford, 1978), pp. 97–108.

'Ideals of holiness: crusaders, contemplatives and mendicants', *International History Review* 17 (1995), pp. 693–712.

'The impact of Crusader Jerusalem on western Christendom', *Catholic Historical Review* 80 (1994), pp. 695–713.

'King consorts of Jerusalem and their entourages', in H.-E. Mayer (ed.), *Die Kreuzfahrerstaaten als multikulturelle Gesellschaft. Einwandere und Minderheiten im 12 un 13 Jahrhundert*, Schriften des Historischen Kollegs, Kolloquien 37 (Munich, 1997), pp. 13–24.

The Latin Church in the Crusader States. The Secular Church (London, 1980).

'Miles of Plancy and the fief of Beirut', in B.Z. Kedar (ed.), *The Horns of Hattin* (Jerusalem, 1992), pp. 136–46.

'Rebuilding Zion: the Holy Places of Jerusalem in the twelfth century', SCH 14 (1977), pp. 105–16.

'The titular nobility of the Latin East: the case of Agnes of Courtenay', in P.W. Edbury (ed.), *Crusade and Settlement* (Cardiff, 1985), pp. 197–203.

'Women in the Crusader States: the queens of Jerusalem, 1100–90', in D. Baker (ed.), *Medieval Women* (Oxford, 1978), pp. 143–74.

Hauzinski, J., 'On alleged attempts at converting the Assassins to Christianity', *Folia Orientalia* 15 (1974), pp. 229–46.

Hefèle, C.J. (ed. and tr.), H. Leclercq, *Histoire des Conciles d'après les documents originaux*, 11 vols. (Paris, 1907–52).

Hemptinne, T. de, 'Aspects des relations de Philippe Auguste avec la Flandre au temps de Philippe d'Alsace', in R.-H. Bautier (ed.), *La France de Philippe Auguste* (Paris, 1982), pp. 255–62.

Hiestand, R., 'Chronologisches zur Geschichte des Königreichs Jerusalem', *Deutsches Archiv* 35 (1979), pp. 542–55.

'Die Herren von Sidon und die Thronfolgekrise des Jahres 1163 im Königreich Jerusalem', in B.Z. Kedar, J. Riley-Smith and R. Hiestand (eds.), *Montjoie. Studies in Crusade History in Honour of Hans-Eberhard Mayer* (Aldershot, 1997), pp. 77–90.

'Die integration der Maroniten in der römische Kirche', *Orientalia Christiana Periodica* 54 (1988), pp. 119–52.

'Zum Leben und zur Laufbahn Wilhelms von Tyrus', *Deutsches Archiv* 34 (1978), pp. 345–80.

Hodgson, M.G.S., *The Order of Assassins. The Struggle of Early Nizari Isma'ilis against the Islamic World* (The Hague, 1955).

Holt, P.M., *The Age of the Crusades. The Near East from the Eleventh Century to 1517* (London and New York, 1986).

(ed.), *The Eastern Mediterranean Lands in the Period of the Crusades* (Warminster, 1977).

Hudson, E.H., 'Historical approach to the terminology of syphilis', *Archives of Dermatology* 84 (1961), pp. 545–62.

'Treponematosis and pilgrimage', *American Journal of Medical Sciences* 246 (1963), pp. 645–56.

Hulse, E.V., 'The nature of biblical "leprosy" and the use of alternative medical terms in modern translations of the Bible', *Palestine Exploration Quarterly* 107 (1975), pp. 87–105.

Huygens, R.B.C., 'Editing William of Tyre', *Sacris Erudiri* 27 (1984), pp. 461–73.

'Guillaume de Tyr étudiant. Un chapître (XIX, 12) de son *Histoire* retrouvé', *Latomus* 21 (1962), pp. 811–29.

'La tradition manuscrite de Guillaume de Tyr', *Studi Medievali* 5 (1964), pp. 281–373.

Isaacs, H.D., 'A medieval Arab medical certificate', *Medical History* 35 (1991), pp. 250–7.

Jacoby, D., 'Conrad Marquis of Montferrat and the Kingdom of Jerusalem (1187–92)', in L. Balletto (ed.), *Dai Feudi Monferrini e dal Piemonte ai nuovi mondi oltre gli oceani* (Alessandria, 1993), pp. 187–238.

Jacoby, Z., 'The tomb of Baldwin V, king of Jerusalem (1185–6) and the workshop of the Temple area', *Gesta* 18 (1979), pp. 3–14.

Ji, B. and Grosset, J., 'Leprosy', in P.D. Hoeprich, M.C. Jordan and A.R. Ronald (eds.), *Infectious Diseases. A Treatise of Infectious Processes*, 5th edn (Philadelphia, 1994), pp. 1008–17.

Johns, C.N., 'Medieval 'Ajlun', *Quarterly of the Department of Antiquities in Palestine* 1 (1931), pp. 21–33.

ed., D. Pringle, *Pilgrims' Castle ('Atlit), David's Tower (Jerusalem) and Qal'at ar-Rabad ('Ajlun). Three Middle Eastern Castles from the Time of the Crusades* (Aldershot, 1997).

Joranson, E., 'The Palestine Pilgrimage of Henry the Lion', in J.L. Cate and E.N. Anderson (eds.), *Medieval and Historiographical Essays in Honour of J.W. Thompson* (Chicago, 1938), pp. 146–225.

Jordan, K., tr. P.S. Falla, *Henry the Lion. A Biography* (Oxford, 1986).

Jotischky, A., 'Manuel Comnenus and the reunion of the Churches. The evidence of the Conciliar mosaics in the Church of the Nativity in Bethlehem', *Levant* 26 (1994), pp. 207–23.

Jubb, M., 'The *Estoires d'Outremer*: history or entertainment?', in G. Jondorf and D.W. Dumville (eds.), *France and the British Isles in the Middle Ages and the Renaissance. Essays by Members of Girton College, Cambridge, in Memory of Ruth Morgan* (Woodbridge, 1991), pp. 173–82.

Jurewicz, O., *Andronikos I Komnenos* (Amsterdam, 1970).

Kasting, N.W., 'A rationale for centuries of therapeutic bloodletting: antipyretic therapy for febrile diseases', *Perspectives in Biology and Medicine* 33 (1990), pp. 509–16.

Katzir, Y., 'The patriarch of Jerusalem, primate of the Latin Kingdom', in P.W. Edbury (ed.), *Crusade and Settlement* (Cardiff, 1985), pp. 169–75.

Kedar, B.Z., 'The battle of Hattin revisited', in *The Horns of Hattin* (Jerusalem, 1992), pp. 190–207.

'The general tax of 1183 in the crusading kingdom of Jerusalem: innovation of adaptation?', EHR 89 (1974), pp. 339–45.

'Genoa's golden inscription in the Church of the Holy Sepulchre: a case for the defence', in G. Airaldi and B.Z. Kedar (eds.), *I comuni italiani nel regno crociato di Gerusalemme* (Genoa, 1986), pp. 319–35.

'Gerard of Nazareth: a neglected twelfth-century writer in the Latin East. A contribution to the intellectual and monastic history of the Crusader States', DOP 37 (1983), pp. 55–77.

'The Patriarch Eraclius', in B.Z. Kedar, H.-E. Mayer and R.C. Smail (eds.), *Outremer. Studies in the History of the Crusading Kingdom of Jerusalem presented to Joshua Prawer* (Jerusalem, 1982), pp. 177–204.

'Some new sources on Palestinian Muslims before and during the Crusades', in H.-E. Mayer (ed.), *Die Kreuzfahrerstaaten als multikulturelle Gesellschaft. Einwandere und Minderheiten im 12 und 13 Jahrhundert*, Schriften des Historischen Kollegs, Kolloquien 37 (Munich, 1997), pp. 129–40.

'The subjected Muslims in the Frankish Levant', in J.M. Powell (ed.), *Muslims under Latin Rule, 1100–1300* (Princeton, N.J., 1990), pp. 135–74.

(ed.), *The Horns of Hattin* (Jerusalem, 1992).

Kedar, B.Z. and al-Hajjuj, M., 'Muslim villagers in the Frankish Kingdom of Jerusalem', *Res Orientales* 6, pp. 145–56.

Kedar, B.Z., Mayer, H.-E. and Smail, R.C. (eds.), *Outremer. Studies in the History of Crusading Kingdom of Jerusalem presented to Joshua Prawer* (Jerusalem, 1982).

Kedar, B.Z. and Pringle, D., 'La Fève: a crusader castle in the Jezreel valley', *Israel Exploration Journal* 35 (1985), pp. 164–79.

Kedar, B.Z., Riley-Smith, J. and Hiestand, R. (eds.), *Montjoie. Studies in Crusade History in Honour of Hans Eberhard Mayer* (Aldershot, 1997).

Kennedy, H., *Crusader Castles* (Cambridge, 1994).

Kohlberg, E. and Kedar, B.Z., 'A Melkite physician in Frankish Jerusalem and Ayyubid Damascus: Muwaffaq al-Din Ya'qub b. Siqlab', *Asian and African Studies*, Haifa: Gustav Heinemann Institute of Middle Eastern Studies 22 (1988), pp. 113–26.

Lamma, P., *Comneni e Staufer. Ricerche sui rapporti fra Bisanzio et l'Occidente nel secolo XII*, 2 vols. (Rome, 1955–7).

Lamonte, J.L., *Feudal Monarchy in the Latin Kingdom of Jerusalem, 1100–1291* (Cambridge, Mass., 1932).

'The houses of Lusignan and Châtellerault, 1150–1250', *Speculum* 30 (1955), pp. 374–84.

'The lords of Caesarea in the period of the Crusades', *Speculum* 22 (1947), pp. 145–61.

'The lords of Sidon in the twelfth and thirteenth centuries', *Byzantion* 17 (1944–5), pp. 183–211.

'To what extent was the Byzantine emperor the suzerain of the Latin Crusading States?', *Byzantion* 7 (1932), pp. 253–64.

Lawrence, A.W., 'The castle of Baghras', in T.S.R. Boase (ed.), *The Cilician Kingdom of Armenia* (Edinburgh, 1978), pp. 34–83.

Lay, S., 'A leper in purple: the coronation of Baldwin IV of Jerusalem', JMH 23 (1997), pp. 317–34.

Lee, F. and Magilton, J., 'The cemetery of the Hospital of St James and St Mary Magdalene, Chichester – a case study', *World Archaeology* 21 (1989), pp. 273–82.

Lewis, B., *The Assassins. A Radical Sect in Islam* (London, 1967).

'The Isma'ilites and the Assassins', in Setton, *Crusades*, I, pp. 99–132.

'Kamal ad-Din's biography of Rašid al-Din Sinan', *Arabica* 13 (1966), pp. 225–59.

'Saladin and the Assassins', *Bulletin of the School of Oriental and African Studies*, 15 (1953), pp. 239–45.

Lewis, B. and Holt, P.M. (eds.), *Historians of the Middle East* (London, 1962).

Ligato, G., 'Guglielmo Lungaspada di Monferrato e le istituzioni politiche dell'Oriente latino', in L. Balletto (ed.), *Dai Feudi Monferrini e dal Piemonte ai nuovi mondi oltre gli oceani* (Alessandria, 1993), pp. 153–85.

'Il *Magister* ospedaliero Ruggero des Moulins nella crisi finale del regno latino di Gerusalemme', *Antonianum* 71 (1996), pp. 495–522.

Lilie, R.-J. *Byzantium and the Crusader States, 1096–1204*, tr. J.C. Morris and J.E. Ridings (Oxford, 1993).

Lock, P.W., *The Franks in the Aegean, 1204–1500* (London, 1995).

Longnon, J., *Les compagnons de Villehardouin* (Paris, 1978).

Loud, G. A., 'The Assise sur la Ligèce and Ralph of Tiberias', in P.W. Edbury (ed.), *Crusade and Settlement* (Cardiff, 1985), pp. 404–12.

Luttrell, A., 'The Hospitallers' medical tradition: 1291–1530', in M. Barber (ed.), *The Military Orders*, I. *Fighting for the Faith and Caring for the Sick* (Aldershot, 1994), pp. 64–81.

Lyons, M.C. and Jackson D.E.P., *Saladin. The Politics of the Holy War* (Cambridge, 1982).

Magdalino, P., *The Empire of Manuel I Komnenos, 1143–1180* (Cambridge, 1994).

Markowski, M., 'Peter of Blois and the conception of the Third crusade', in B.Z. Kedar (ed.), *The Horns of Hattin* (Jerusalem, 1992) pp. 261–9.

Mas-Latrie, L. de, 'Le fief de la Chamberlaine et les Chambellans de Jérusalem', BEC 43 (1882), pp. 647–52.

Matthew, D., *The Norman Kingdom of Sicily* (Cambridge, 1992).

Maupilier, M., 'Les Lusignans du Bas-Poitou et l'Outremer', in P.J. Arrignon (ed.), *Les Lusignans d'Outremer* (Poitiers, 1995), pp. 190–200.

Mayer, H.-E. 'The beginnings of King Amalric of Jerusalem', in B.Z. Kedar (ed.), *The Horns of Hattin* (Jerusalem, 1992) pp. 121–35.

'Carving up crusaders: the early Ibelins and Ramlas', in B.Z. Kedar, H.-E. Mayer and R.C. Smail (eds.), *Outremer. Studies in the History of the Crusading Kingdom of Jerusalem presented to Joshua Prawer* (Jerusalem, 1982), pp. 101–18.

The Crusades, tr. J. Gillingham, 2nd edn (Oxford, 1988).

'Frederick of La Roche, bishop of Acre and archbishop of Tyre', *Tel-Aviver Jahrbuch für deutsche Geschichte* 22 (1993), pp. 59–72.

'Guillaume de Tyr à l'école', *Mémoires de l'Académie des sciences, arts et belles-lettres de Dijon* 127 (1988), pp. 257–65.

'Henry II of England and the Holy Land', EHR 97 (1982), pp. 721–39.

'Die Herrschaftsbildung in Hebron', ZDPV 101 (1985), pp. 64–81.

Die Kanzlei der lateinischen Könige von Jerusalem, 2 vols., MGH Schriften 40 (Hanover, 1996).

Die Kreuzfahrerherrschaft Montréal (Šobak). Jordanien im 12 Jahrhundert, Abhandlungen des deutschen Palästinavereins 14 (Wiesbaden, 1990).

'Die Legitimität Balduins IV von Jerusalem und das Testament der Agnes von Courtenay', *Historisches Jahrbuch* 108 (1988), pp. 63–89.

'Das Pontifikale von Tyrus und die Krönung der lateinischen Könige von Jerusalem. Zugleich ein Beitrag zur Forschung über Herrschaftszeichen und Staatssymbolik', DOP 21 (1967), pp. 141–232.

'Die Seigneurie de Joscelin und der Deutsche Orden', in J. Fleckenstein and M. Hellmann (eds.), *Die geistlichen Ritterorden Europas, Vorträge und Forschungen*, 26 (1980), pp. 171–216.

'Le service militaire des vassaux à l'étranger et le financement des campagnes en Syrie du nord et en Egypte au XIIe siècle', in *Mélanges sur l'histoire du royaume latin de Jérusalem*, Mémoires de l'Académie des Inscriptions et Belles-Lettres, n.s., 5 (Paris, 1984), pp. 93–161.

Das Siegelwesen in den Kreuzfahrerstaaten, Bayerische Akademie der Wissenschaften, Phil.-hist. Klasse, Abhandlungen, n.s. 83 (Munich, 1978).

'Studies in the history of Queen Melisende of Jerusalem', DOP 26 (1972), pp. 93–183.

'Zum Tode Wilhelm von Tyrus', *Archiv für Diplomatik* 5–6 (1959–60), pp. 182–201.

Mayer, H.-E. and Favreau-Lilie, M.-L., 'Das Diplom Balduins I für Genua and Genuas goldene Inschrift in der Grabeskirche', QF 55–6 (1976), pp. 22–95.

Mayer, H.-E. (ed.) and E. Müller-Luckner (assistant ed.), *Die Kreuzfahrerstaaten als multikulturelle Gesellschaft. Einwandere und Minderheiten im 12 und 13 Jahrhundert*, Schriften des Historischen Kollegs, Kolloquien 37 (Munich, 1997).

Metcalf, D.M., *Coinage of the Crusades and the Latin East in the Ashmolean Museum, Oxford* (London, 1983).

Miller, T.S., 'The Knights of St John and the Hospitals of the Latin West', *Speculum* 53 (1978), pp. 709–33.

Mitchell, P.D., 'The archaeological approach to the study of disease in the Crusader States as employed at *Le Petit Gerin*', in H. Nicholson (ed.), *The Military Orders*, II, *Welfare and Warfare* (Aldershot, 1998), pp. 43–50.

'The evolution of social attitudes to the medical care of those with leprosy within the Crusader States', in B. Tabuteau (ed.), *Histoire et archéologie de la lèpre et des lépreux en Europe et en Méditerranée de la Antiquité aux Temps Modernes* (Rouen, 2000).

'Further evidence of disease in the Crusader period population of *Le Petit Gerin* (Tel Jezreel, Israel)', *Tel Aviv* 24(1) (1997), pp. 169–79.

'Leprosy and the case of King Baldwin IV of Jerusalem: mycobacterial disease in the Crusader States of the 12th and 13th centuries', *International Journal of Leprosy and Other Mycobacterial Diseases* 61(2) (1993), pp. 283–91.

'Pathology in the crusader period: human skeletal remains from Tel Jezreel', *Levant* 26 (1994), pp. 67–71.

'Tuberculosis in the crusades', in G. Palfi, O. Dutour, J. Deak and I. Hutas (eds.), *Tuberculosis: Past and Present* (Szeged, Hungary, 1999), pp. 43–9.

Möhring, H., 'Eine Chronik aus der Zeit des dritten Kreuzzugs: das sogennante *Itinerarium Peregrinorum I*', Innsbrucker Historische Studien 5 (1982), pp. 149–67.

'Zu der Geschichte der orientalischen Herrscher des Wilhelm von Tyrus' *Mittellateinisches Jahrbuch* 19 (1984), pp. 170–83.

Morgan, D.O. (ed.), *Medieval Historical Writing in the Christian and Islamic Worlds* (London, 1982).

Morgan, M.R., *The Chronicle of Ernoul and the Continuations of William of Tyre* (Oxford, 1973).

Müller-Wiener, W., *Castles of the Crusaders* (London, 1966).

Munz, P., *Frederick Barbarossa* (London, 1969).

Nickerson, M., 'The seigneury of Beirut in the twelfth century and the Brisebarre family of Beirut-Blanchegarde', *Byzantion* 19 (1949), pp. 141–85.

Nicholson, H. (ed.), *The Military Orders*, II. *Welfare and Warfare* (Aldershot, 1998).

Nicholson, R.L., *Joscelin III of Edessa and the Fall of the Crusader States (1134–1199)* (Leiden, 1973).

Nicolle, D., 'Ain al-Habis. The "cave de Sueth"', *Archéologie mediévale* 18 (1988), pp. 113–40.

The Arms and Armour of the Crusading Era 1050–1350 2 vols. (New York, 1988).

Nowell, C., 'The Old Man of the Mountain', *Speculum* 22 (1947), pp. 497–519.

Ovadiah, A., 'A crusader church in the Jewish Quarter of the old city of Jerusalem', in Y. Tsafrir (ed.), *Ancient Churches Revealed*, (Jerusalem, 1993), pp. 136–9.

Pacaut, M., *Alexandre III. Etude sur la conception du pouvoir pontificale dans sa pensée et dans son œuvre* (Paris, 1956).

Frederick Barbarossa, tr. A.J. Pomerans (London, 1970).

Louis VII et son royaume (Paris, 1964).

Painter, S., 'The lords of Lusignan in the eleventh and twelfth centuries', *Speculum* 32 (1957), pp. 27–47.

'The Third Crusade: Richard the Lionhearted and Philip Augustus', in Setton, *Crusades*, II, pp. 45–85.

Pegg, M.G., 'Le corps et l'autorité: la lèpre de Baudouin IV', *Annales. Economies, Sociétés, Civilisations* 45(2) (1990), pp. 265–87.

Petit, E., *Histoire des ducs de Bourgogne de la race capétienne*, 9 vols. (Paris, 1885–1905).

Phillips, J., *Defenders of the Holy Land. Relations between the Latin East and the West, 1119–1187* (Oxford, 1996).

Plancher, U., *Histoire générale et particulière de Bourgogne*, 4 vols. (Dijon, 1739–81).

Porteous, J., 'Crusading coinage with Greek or Latin inscriptions', in Setton, *Crusades*, VI, pp. 354–420.

Powell, J.M., *Anatomy of a Crusade, 1213–1221* (Philadelphia, 1986).

Prawer, J., *Crusader Institutions* (Oxford, 1980).
Histoire du royaume latin de Jérusalem, tr. G. Nahon, 2 vols. (Paris, 1969).
The History of the Jews in the Latin Kingdom of Jerusalem (Oxford, 1988).
The Latin Kingdom of Jerusalem. European Colonialism in the Middle Ages (London, 1972).
The World of the Crusaders (Jerusalem, 1972).

Pringle, D., 'The castle and lordship of Mirabel', in B.Z. Kedar, J. Riley-Smith and R. Hiestand (eds.), *Montjoie. Studies in Crusade History in Honour of Hans-Eberhard Mayer* (Aldershot, 1997), pp. 91–112.
The Churches of the Crusader Kingdom of Jerusalem. A Corpus, 2 vols. (Cambridge, 1993 and 1998).
Secular Buildings in the Crusader Kingdom of Jerusalem. An Archaeological Gazetteer (Cambridge, 1997).
'Towers in Crusader Palestine', *Château Gaillard* 16 (1994), pp. 335–50.
'Town defences in the Crusader Kingdom of Jerusalem', in I. Corfis and M. Wolfe (eds.), *Medieval City under Siege* (Woodbridge, 1995).

Pryor, J.H., 'The *Eracles* and William of Tyre: an interim report', in B.Z. Kedar (ed.), *The Horns of Hattin* (Jerusalem, 1992) pp. 270–93.
Geography, Technology and War. Studies in the History of the Maritime Mediterranean, 649–1571 (Cambridge, 1988).

Rheinheimer, M., *Das Kreuzfahrerfürstentum Galiläa* (Frankfurt am Main, 1990).

Richard, J., 'Agricultural conditions in the Crusader States', in Setton, *Crusades*, V, pp. 251–94.
'Aux origines d'un grand lignage: des Palladii à Renaud de Châtillon', in *Media in Francia. Recueil de Mélanges offerts à Karl Ferdinand Werner* (Paris, 1989), pp. 409–18.
Le Comté de Tripoli sous la dynastie toulousaine (1102–87) (Paris, 1945).
Les ducs de Bourgogne et la formation du Duché du XIe au XIVe siècle, Publications de l'Université de Dijon, 12 (Paris, 1954).
Histoire des Croisades (Paris, 1996).
'Les listes des seigneuries dans le Livre de Jean d'Ibelin, recherches sur l'Assebebé et Mimars', RHDFE sér. 4, 32 (1954), pp. 565–72.
'Pairie d'Orient latin: les quatres baronnies des royaumes de Jérusalem et de Chypre', RHDFE, sér. 4, 28 (1950), pp. 67–88.

Le royaume latin de Jérusalem (Paris, 1953).

The Latin Kingdom of Jerusalem, tr. J. Shirley, 2 vols. (Amsterdam, 1979).

'Les turcopoles au service des royaumes de Jérusalem et de Chypre: musulmans convertis ou chrétiens orientaux?', *Revue des études islamiques* 54 (1986), pp. 259–70.

Richards, D.S., 'Imad al-Din al-Isfahani, administrator, litterateur and historian', in M. Schatzmiller (ed.), *Crusaders and Muslims in Twelfth-Century Syria* (Leiden, 1993), pp. 133–46.

Riley-Smith, J., *The Feudal Nobility and the Kingdom of Jerusalem, 1174–1277* (London, 1973).

'Government in Latin Syria and the commercial privileges of foreign merchants', in D. Baker (ed.), *Relations between East and West in the Middle Ages* (Edinburgh, 1973), pp. 109–32.

The Knights of St John in Jerusalem and Cyprus (1050–1310) (London, 1967).

'The Templars and the castle of Tortosa in Syria: an unknown document concerning the acquisition of the fortress', EHR 84 (1969), pp. 278–88.

'The Templars and the Teutonic Knights in Cilician Armenia', in T.S.R. Boase (ed.), *The Cilician Kingdom of Armenia* (Edinburgh, 1978), pp. 92–117.

(ed.), *The Atlas of the Crusades* (London, 1990).

Rogers, R., *Latin Siege Warfare in the Twelfth Century* (Oxford, 1992).

Rose, J.C., 'Crusader period disease in Jordan', in *Abstracts of the XIIth European Meeting of the Paleopathology Association, August 26–29, 1998 in Prague-Pilsen, Czech Republic* (Prague, 1998), p. 77.

Rose, R.B., 'The *Vita* of Saint Leontios and its account of his visit to Palestine during the Crusader period', *Proche-Orient Chrétien* 35 (1985), pp. 238–57.

Roserot, A., *Dictionnaire historique de la Champagne méridionale (Aube) des origines à 1790*, publié par J. Roserot de Melin, 4 vols. (Langres, 1945).

Rothenberg, B., *God's Wilderness. Discoveries in Sinai* (London, 1961).

Round, J.H., 'The counts of Boulogne as English lords', in *Studies in Peerage and Family History* (Westminster, 1901), pp. 147–80.

'Some English crusaders of Richard I', EHR 18 (1903), pp. 475–8.

Rowe, J.G. 'The papacy and the ecclesiastical province of Tyre', BJRL 43 (1960–1), pp. 160–89.

Rudt de Collenberg, W.H., 'Les Lusignans de Chypre', *Epeteris* 10 (1979–80).

'Les premiers Ibelins', *Le Moyen Age* 71 (1965), pp. 433–74.

Runciman, S., *A History of the Crusades*, 3 vols. (Cambridge, 1951–5).

'The visit of King Amalric I to Constantinople in 1171', in B.Z. Kedar, H.-E. Mayer and R.C. Smail (eds.), *Outremer. Studies in the History of the Crusading Kingdom of Jerusalem presented to Joshua Prawer* (Jerusalem, 1982), pp. 153–8.

Salibi, K.S., 'The Buhturids of the Gharb, medieval lords of Beirut and southern Lebanon', *Arabica* 8 (1961), pp. 74–89.

'The Maronite Church in the Middle Ages and its union with Rome', *Oriens Christianus* 42 (1958), pp. 92–104.

Maronite Historians of Mediaeval Lebanon (Beirut, 1959).

Schlumberger, G., *Campagnes du roi Amaury 1er en Egypte* (Paris, 1906).

Renaud de Châtillon, Prince d'Antioche, Seigneur de la terre d'Outre-Jourdain, 3rd edn (Paris, 1923).

Schlumberger, G., Chalandon, F. and Blanchet, A., *Sigillographie de l'Orient Latin* (Paris, 1943).

Shatzmiller, M. (ed.), *Crusaders and Muslims in Twelfth-Century Syria* (Leiden, 1993).

Siberry, E., *Criticism of Crusading 1095–1274* (Oxford, 1985).

Setton, K.M. (gen. ed.), *History of the Crusades*, 6 vols. (Philadelphia and Madison, 1958–91): I. ed. M.W. Baldwin, *The First Hundred Years* (Philadelphia, 1958); II. eds. R.L. Wolff and H.W. Hazard, *The Later Crusades, 1189–1311* (Philadelphia, 1962); V. eds. N.P. Zacour and H.W. Hazard, *The Impact of the Crusades on the Near East* (Madison, 1985); VI. eds. H.W. Hazard and N.P. Zacour, *The Impact of the Crusades on Europe* (Madison, 1989).

Shahar, S., 'Des lépreux pas comme les autres: l'Ordre de Saint-Lazare dans le royaume latin de Jérusalem', *Revue Historique* 267 (1982), pp. 19–41.

Singer, C., 'A thirteenth-century description of leprosy', *Journal of the History of Medicine and Allied Sciences* 4 (1949), pp. 237–9.

Sivan, E., *L'Islam et la Croisade* (Paris, 1968).

Smail, R.C., *The Crusaders in Syria and the Holy Land* (London, 1973).

Crusading Warfare, 1097–1193, 2nd edn, with a new bibliographical introduction by C. Marshall (Cambridge, 1995).

'The international status of the Latin Kingdom of Jerusalem', in P.M. Holt (ed.), *The Eastern Mediterranean Lands in the Period of the Crusades* (Warminster, 1977), pp. 23–43.

'Latin Syria and the West, 1149–1187', TRHS, 5th ser., 19 (1969), pp. 1–20.

'The predicaments of Guy of Lusignan, 1183–87', in B.Z. Kedar, H.-E. Mayer and R.C. Smail (eds.), *Outremer. Studies in the History of the Crusading Kingdom of Jerusalem presented to Joshua Prawer* (Jerusalem, 1982), pp. 159–76.

Smith, D.G. and Guinto, R.S., 'The association between the age of onset and mortality in lepromatous leprosy', *International Journal of Leprosy* 46 (1978), pp. 25–9.

Stenton, D.M., 'Roger of Howden and Benedict', EHR 68 (1953), pp. 574–82.

Stevenson, W.B., 'William of Tyre's Chronology', in *The Crusaders in the East* (Cambridge, 1907), pp. 361–71.

Tibble, S., *Monarchy and Lordships in the Latin Kingdom of Jerusalem 1099–1291* (Oxford, 1989).

Tournebize, F., *Histoire politique et religieuse de l'Arménie depuis les origines des Arméniens jusqu' à la mort de leur dernier roi à l'an 1393* (Paris, 1910).

Tyerman, C.J., *England and the Crusades 1095–1588* (Chicago and London 1988).

Urbansky, A.B., *Byzantium and the Danube Frontier. A Study of the Relations between Byzantium, Hungary and the Balkans during the period of the Comneni* (New York, 1968).

Usseglio, L., *I marchesi di Monferrato in Italia ed in Oriente durante i secoli XII et XIII*, 2 vols. (Turin, 1926).

Vogtherr, T., 'Die Regierungsdaten der lateinischen Könige von Jerusalem', ZDPV 110 (1994), pp. 51–81.

Vries, R.R.P. de, Eden, W. van and Rood, J.J. van, 'HLA-linked control of the course of *M. leprae* infections', *Leprosy Review* 52 (Suppl. 1) (1981), pp. 109–19.

Warlop, E., *The Flemish Nobility before 1300*, 4 vols. (Courtrai, 1975–6).

Warren, W.L., *Henry II* (London, 1973).

World Health Organisation, *Epidemiology of Leprosy in Relation to Control*, Technical Report Series no. 716 (Geneva, 1985).

Wilken, F., *Geschichte der Kreuzzüge*, 7 vols. (Leipzig, 1807–32).

Wilkinson, J., 'The Piacenza pilgrim', in *Jerusalem Pilgrims before the Crusades* (Warminster, 1977).

Zias, J., 'Leprosy and tuberculosis in the Byzantine monasteries of the Judean desert', in D.J. Ortner and A.C. Aufderheide (eds.), *Human Paleopathology: Current Syntheses and Future Options* (Washington, D.C., 1991), pp. 197–9.

Zias, J. and Mitchell, P.D., 'Psoriatic arthritis in a fifth-century Judean desert monastery', *American Journal of Physical Anthropology* 101 (1996), pp. 491–502.

Index